To Toronto: the Youngs lun... / with us at Club: shop. for B's bir... / in p.m: to Stfd. 7-10 & call on D... / Rae who is v. alarmed by crisis a... / approaching season & Floyd Chalmer... makes / him no better: F. Ch. v. vain but not / a really bad man but is so self-absorbed / he has no tact: we stay with the Bolls / & share double bed.

SATURDAY 10

To committee mtg. at / 9, & Board mtg. at 11-4: weary / & Ambridge of Abitibi paper v. / wearisome: a farcical tycoon: away / at 4 to Tor. & dine at ... Gtons. / Doubleday want WRD to write his / memoirs: talk with him till 9.30 / then to Stewarts till 1. B

1st Sunday after Epiphany SUNDAY 11*

Chat with WRD & Mgt. who is worried / abt illness of several elderly relatives: / to H-Lg's & chat with her & Sheila who / talks v-interestingly abt. Glen Gould: to / Ptro & to arena & see Ros. will dance- / pair trophy: proud of her: quiet ev. / & mitigated h.t.d. ... / most refreshing to b...

MEMORAN...

The Star col. already ... / made some slight str... / into a substantial thing if I / do it well: think abt. it a great / deal & hope to make it more / supple, but am still getting / the 'feel' of it.

B

Robertson Davies

A CELTIC TEMPERAMENT

ROBERTSON DAVIES
AS DIARIST

EDITED BY JENNIFER SURRIDGE AND RAMSAY DERRY

McCLELLAND & STEWART

McClelland & Stewart is a division of Random House of Canada Limited,
a Penguin Random House Company

Library and Archives Canada Cataloguing in Publication

Davies, Robertson, 1913-1995
[Diaries. Selections]
A Celtic temperament : Robertson Davies as diarist /
edited by Jennifer Surridge and Ramsay Derry.

Includes bibliographical references and index.
Issued in print and electronic formats.

ISBN 978-0-7710-2764-2 (bound).– ISBN 978-0-7710-2765-9 (html)

1. Davies, Robertson, 1913-1995 – Diaries. 2. Authors, Canadian
(English) – 20th century – Diaries. I. Surridge, Jennifer, editor
II. Derry, Ramsay, editor III. Title.

PS8507.A67Z45 2015 c813'.54 C2015-904373-5
 C2015-904374-3

All photographs are courtesy of Jennifer Surridge unless otherwise credited.
The photograph on page 6 in the second photo insert is courtesy of
York University Libraries, Clara Thomas Archives and Special Collections,
Toronto Telegram fonds, ASC07267.

Typeset in New Baskerville by M&S, Toronto

Printed and bound in the United States of America

McClelland & Stewart,
a division of Random House of Canada Limited,
a Penguin Random House Company
www.penguinrandomhouse.ca

1 2 3 4 5 19 18 17 16 15

For Brenda

CONTENTS

INTRODUCTION

—

ROBERTSON DAVIES WAS AN ASSIDUOUS DIARIST. He began keeping diary notes when he was a teenager and by the time he was eighteen it was an established practice, even though for many years it was sporadic rather than regular. But the total wordage is astonishing: over three million words. He was, from the beginning, skeptical and sometimes contemptuous of himself as a diarist. In 1934, when he was twenty, he wrote:

> I cannot imagine why I keep a Diary. It is, in spite of my best efforts, a thoroughly selective and dishonest document, a novel in which I am always the hero. I suspect that I hope someone will read it some day, and that I always write with an eye to effect. It is, however, a hard habit to break and I regard it rather superstitiously.

Fortunately he did not break the habit but, on the contrary, elaborated on it. Like many artists, literary and otherwise, he used his

diaries as *aides-mémoire* to store up experiences, emotions, perceptions, and ideas that he could recover at a later time. They were also a means of examining his own life, for he was a man who, throughout his lifetime, strove toward self-understanding and self-knowledge through his study of literature, drama, and art, and his extensive reading of Freud, Jung, and other major psychoanalytical authors. He recorded his states of mind, his dreams, and intimate details of his marriage. The diaries show a man who, despite frequent periods of frustration, illness, and depression, enjoyed life and believed it should be valued and taken seriously. He was deeply interested in the society he lived in and the people he encountered. More often than not, he found comedy in the world around him and delighted in recording it. As he established his reputation as a writer, he recognized that his diaries were part of his literary legacy and assumed that they would have future readers. This did not inhibit him from keeping them as honest and spontaneous responses to the day. They convey the immediacy of the experience, and what he described as his "celtic temperament"—his often mercurial changes of perception and judgment of events and people, and his swift changes of mood from dejection to exhilaration. And, like many great diarists, he recorded the interplay between the momentous and the banal, the descriptions of public activities and events in tight and often incongruous juxtaposition with totally personal experiences and feelings.

Davies also enjoyed the diary as a literary form. Among his first published successes were the semi-fictional diaries of Samuel Marchbanks, whom he had invented as an alter ego; these had first appeared in his early freelance newspaper columns, later became a regular feature in the *Peterborough Examiner,* were syndicated to other Canadian papers, and later still were published in book form, in 1947. The title of his weekly column for the *Toronto Star* was "A Writer's Diary," and he sometimes used the diary form for occasional pieces.

He took his diary-keeping seriously. In addition to his personal daily diary he kept what he called his "big" diary in which he periodically made longer, more considered entries. He kept a separate diary for major trips, and most years he kept a theatre-going diary. He loved all forms of live entertainment including circuses, magicians, and puppet shows, and he also went to the movies a lot, about thirty times a year. He enjoyed them primarily as relaxation and rarely wrote about them critically. His idea of a really wonderful movie experience was a horror double bill, although he usually had to go alone. After seeing one he wrote, "Have always had a taste for such things: they cheer me oddly." He kept a special diary covering the 1960 production of his play *Love and Libel,* and he began his separate diary about Massey College early in 1961, soon after he was offered the position of Master. This gradually became his regular diary over the twenty years he was at the College.

This selection of his diaries, the first to be published, is drawn from the years 1959 to 1963, a particularly busy time in his immensely productive career, a period that included what he considered his greatest failure, but from which he recovered swiftly with Vincent Massey's unexpected invitation. In 1959 Robertson Davies was forty-five. He was already known by this time as Canada's leading man of letters, a recognition that had not been his original ambition. Born in 1913, he had grown up in small-town Ontario, attended Upper Canada College in Toronto, Queen's University in Kingston, and Balliol College, Oxford (although formally graduating only from the last of these). He had hoped for a career in British theatre as an actor, director, and playwright, and in the late 1930s he worked in London in the famous Old Vic company founded by Lilian Baylis. By then the company was led by Tyrone Guthrie, the foremost theatrical director of his generation, who was to become one of Davies's closest friends. But shortly after war broke out in 1939, the company was forced to close, and Davies, who had recently

married Brenda Mathews, an Australian who worked at the Old Vic as a stage manager, was advised to return to Canada. Unfit for military service because of his poor eyesight, he began to establish himself as a literary journalist in Toronto, working for the weekly *Saturday Night* magazine. Then, in 1942, his father, Senator Rupert Davies, the proprietor of a small but by now very lucrative newspaper empire, pressured Rob, as he was known to his friends, to take over as editor of one of Rupert's papers, the daily *Peterborough Examiner*. Rob did not treat the job as a family sinecure but worked hard to make the *Examiner* the most admired small-city newspaper in the country, and he himself became a highly regarded editorial writer. However, by 1959 his work at the *Examiner* was mostly routine for him, and he rarely referred to it in much detail in his diaries.

Meanwhile, he and Brenda had thrown themselves into local amateur theatre, directing, acting, and, in his case, writing. By the mid-1950s Davies was the foremost Canadian playwright, with a dozen plays both published and frequently performed—although, to his frustration, not outside Canada. He also reviewed books and theatre for the Toronto papers and the national magazines. His first book for a general readership, *The Diary of Samuel Marchbanks*, and its successor, *The Table Talk of Samuel Marchbanks*, were followed by three novels, *Tempest-Tost*, *Leaven of Malice*, and *A Mixture of Frailties*, now known as the Salterton Trilogy. He had a broad interest in promoting Canadian culture, and he had made an influential submission to Vincent Massey's 1949–51 royal commission on Canadian arts, letters, and sciences. He had been involved in the founding of the Stratford Shakespearean Festival in 1953, was co-author of books about its first three seasons, and sat on its board of governors. But after nearly twenty years of living in Peterborough, both he and Brenda felt worn down by the obdurate ordinariness that overlay Canadian provincial life. They had a number of good friends in Peterborough, but they wanted to be more at the centre

of things. They longed for a change, for something that could take them at least to Toronto. So Rob welcomed the invitation to become a part-time guest lecturer in the English Department of Trinity College in the University of Toronto, starting in September 1960.

Davies was by now a prominent and easily recognized public figure. Tall, ample, and bearded, with a richly developed theatrical voice and with a wardrobe of grey flannels, unusual tweed jackets, three-piece suits in a slightly Edwardian style, a full-length greatcoat, and a swooping fedora, he had an imposing and distinctive appearance that made him seem older than he was, and that sometimes attracted the derisive attention of boys in the town. His rather magisterial presence hid well the mixture of ambition, anxieties, and insecurities, and often conflicting perceptions and emotions that all bubbled furiously within and that are recorded in the diaries.

Throughout the diaries, from the time of his marriage, his partnership with Brenda is a consistent theme. A letter Rob wrote to her in 1952, when she was making her first trip back to Australia since she had left at the age of eighteen, conveys something of their relationship.

> So let me say now how happy—deeply happy—I am that you have made this journey, for I feel it will be a turning point in our life together. It will, I hope, hitch you up again to a whole train of thoughts and feelings which our marriage seemed to cut you off from. Coming to live in Canada was a wrench and a nervous adventure, and I never forget or undervalue the great courage and trust in me which you brought to it. But from now on you will have, so to speak, all your luggage with you, and Australia, whatever it may mean to you, will never seem so far way again.

Brenda was his constant companion, his first reader, critic, and consultant. Widely read, but not "literary" by temperament or

education, she brought a direct, personal, and practical response not only to his work but to all the things they saw and did and read together. She was the family manager and also the family driver, for Rob did not drive, and she often drove him to and from his meetings and lectures in Toronto. She drove well and she enjoyed good cars. Brisk and athletic in bearing, stylish in appearance, Brenda spoke with an assurance that hid a shy and sometimes nervous temperament. Like Rob, she had grown up in a comparatively wealthy if idiosyncratic family, and they both assumed a certain level of social status. But together, they saw themselves rather as theatrical troupers, and their relationship is perhaps reflected in that of Sir John Tresize and Milady in Davies's 1975 novel, *World of Wonders,* or an earlier fictional couple, the Crummleses, in Dickens's *Nicholas Nickleby*: they were on their own in life together, they must move on from show to show, they must do the right thing, and they must always be prepared to put on a good face to the world. They were also devoted if demanding parents of three daughters, close in age, Miranda, Jennifer, and Rosamond.

A family member who appears only occasionally in the diaries but who was a powerful continuing presence for Rob was his father, referred to in the diaries as WRD. Senator W. Rupert Davies was loving and generous and was proud of his son's accomplishments, but he was also, from Rob's point of view, overbearing and judgmental, and to a surprising degree intruded into Rob's imaginative and creative life. Though he had formally retired in 1951, Rupert Davies continued to control the business he had founded, which came to include television stations as well as newspapers. The first two of his three sons were close in age. Fred, the eldest, had not been significantly active in the business, and had died in 1954. Arthur managed the *Kingston Whig-Standard,* the centrepiece of the family business. Rob was younger than Arthur by ten years. After the death of his first wife, Rupert Davies remarried, and Rob's stepmother,

Margaret, was approximately his own age. Rupert now lived in Toronto in a large house on Hawthorn Gardens and, in the summer, in a larger Gothic revival house, Leighton Hall, in Wales. Rupert had been born in Wales, had immigrated to Canada while a boy, and now enjoyed returning to Wales as a success, holding for a time the honorary title of Lord High Sheriff of Montgomeryshire.

At the beginning of 1933 Davies acquired a beautiful leather-bound book, about seven by ten inches, for what he called his "big diary," and he continued to use similar notebooks for many years. He wrote his theatre diaries and travel diaries in various note-books. For his daily personal diary he originally used a small commercial yearly diary and later small Smythson red leather-bound diaries. Until 1970 all of his diaries, including the Massey College diary, were handwritten in the distinctive italic script that he had taught himself in his twenties. But eventually he found that writer's cramp was literally cramping his literary style:

> FEBRUARY 16, 1970: Have decided to continue this Diary in typewritten form; my right arm is so stiff at the elbow and my hand in consequence so subject to jerks and unaccountable wriggles, that I cannot write decently. . . . But apart from the ugliness of my script, I am inhibited from saying what I really want to say because writing soon becomes difficult and painful with the consequence that the Diary becomes increasingly gnomic and confined to the stark narrative of my deeds. Whereas it was always my plan—was it Leland who said this?—"to be somewhat at large, and have orniture."

He was a fast two-finger typist from his days as a journalist and edi-torial writer, and once he began typing his diaries the entries became considerably fuller and have a great deal of "orniture."

Mainly for reasons of discretion, Robertson Davies had instructed that his diaries not be published or made available to the public until twenty years after his death, which was in December 1995, and with some minor exceptions this wish has been respected. He had always intended to do something with them himself and at one stage considered using them as the base for some form of autobiography. After her father's death, Jennifer Surridge, with the permission of Brenda Davies, his literary executor, began to type a literal transcription of nearly all the diaries, a project that took about fifteen years, and she invited Ramsay Derry, who had worked with Davies as an editor and was a long-time family friend, to review the typescripts. As the end of the twenty-year limitation approached, we began to consider possible publishing arrangements. Brenda had read all of the transcripts and took part in these discussions before her death in 2013 at the age of ninety-five.

The sheer size of the complete diaries, with their overlapping layers, presents a considerable editorial and publishing challenge. The layers are by no means watertight, and entries in one diary may often illuminate or coordinate with an entry in another. Accordingly, for this selection, in order to maintain an easily readable ongoing narrative, we have drawn on all the layers of the diaries and interleaved them without separate identification. Overall, our selection uses about 50 per cent of the original diaries for the years 1959 to 1963.

Because Davies published frequently in the diary form, we can project the editorial principles he might expect to be used in editing his diaries for publication. The diary style of the writing with incomplete sentences without a first person pronoun subject is generally maintained. However, in the interests of comfortable reading, we have expanded most of his contractions, frequently replaced the initials of people with their spelled-out names, reduced his use of capitalization, normalized his punctuation and corrected misspellings, and clarified inadvertent ambiguities.

A page of the 1959 daily personal diary.

Davies did not want the publication of his diaries to be gratu-
itously hurtful, and we have avoided a few passages that would in-
trude unfairly on private individuals, but otherwise the selections
are representative of the whole. We have resisted cleaning the dia-
ries up to meet current mores. It often amused Davies to interpret

people's characters and behaviour in terms of their appearance or their backgrounds, whether social, ethnic, religious, or geographic. These perspectives may now sometimes seem offensive. But by the standards of his generation he was not racist or prejudiced, and ultimately he judged people on their merits as he saw them. His snobbery was easily trumped by his appreciation of each person's genuine worth, talent, or achievement.

Robertson Davies himself frequently doubted the value or interest of his accumulating diaries, but when he was arranging to donate them to Library and Archives Canada in 1992 he wrote, "Brenda says my diaries are the stuff from which social history is made, and I cannot imagine that Canada has an embarrassment of such material." They were both right, but the diaries are more than social history, as we hope this introductory selection shows. In their variety, intimacy, and honesty, they present an extraordinarily rich portrait of the man and his times and an entertaining account of a life as it is being lived.

1959

—

AT THE END OF 1958, Robertson Davies was living at 361 Park Street in Peterborough, Ontario, with his wife, Brenda, and his three teenage daughters, Miranda, Jennifer, and Rosamond. Miranda and Jennifer were boarding at Bishop Strachan School in Toronto and Rosamond was at school in Peterborough. In addition to working and writing as publisher and editor of the *Peterborough Examiner*, a daily newspaper, Davies was just beginning to write a regular weekly literary column for the *Toronto Star* called "A Writer's Diary," and he was still contributing reviews to *Saturday Night* magazine. His most recent novel, *A Mixture of Frailties*, had been published in 1958, but his recently completed play about Casanova, called *General Confession*, had been declined by the Davis family, owners of the Crest Theatre in Toronto, for whom it had been written. He continued to serve on the board of governors of the Stratford Shakespearean Festival, where the artistic director was now Michael Langham. Meanwhile, he was being encouraged by his friend and theatrical mentor Tyrone Guthrie to adapt his novel *Leaven of Malice* into a play, which Guthrie

proposed to direct and which, through Guthrie's theatrical connections, was to be produced on Broadway.

In March 1958 Davies noted in his personal diary that he had received "a nice letter from A. Knopf about my reviews which has the effect of making me nervous of a decline." Alfred A. Knopf was a leading New York publisher. He had seen Davies's book reviews in *Saturday Night* magazine, been impressed by their breadth, sophistication, and enthusiasm, and in a subsequent letter proposed that Davies might write a book based on these reviews. Davies was thrilled by this invitation: "A dream come true: a conspectus of the modern literary situation. Can hardly believe this luck. Is the tide turning at last? A happy day." He met Knopf in New York on May 21 and quickly came to a publishing agreement. On June 2 he was "culling what may be of use of my *Saturday Night* pieces. Surprised by how bad some are. I never think anything I have written retains any value." On September 22 he wrote, "Began working on my sixteenth book. A beginning is always a nervous thing."

By January 1959 he was well into the new book. In fact, although it used material from the *Saturday Night* reviews, it was largely new writing, and rather than "a conspectus of the modern literary situation," it was turning into a series of explorations of books, many of them from the Victorian period, on subjects such as long forgotten bestsellers, drama, love, sex, pornography, and self-help. He was writing for a readership he called the "clerisy," intelligent, informed readers, encouraging them to be both more adventurous in their reading and more critical. For the Canadian and American markets the book was ultimately given the obscure title *A Voice from the Attic*, and for the British edition, more helpfully, *The Personal Art*. In his diaries Davies generally refers to it as "Knopfbook."

Rob and Brenda's close friends in Peterborough at this time were Ross and Ruth Thompson, Tommy and Sheila Currier, and Robert and Val Porter. Ross Thompson was an insurance broker

and Ruth a painter; Tommy Currier was a physician with an interest in psychiatry; and Bob Porter was the chief librarian in Peterborough. Ross Mathews was the Davies children's doctor, and Rob and Brenda saw Mathews and his wife socially on occasion. Other friends were the writer and sports reporter Scott Young and his wife (the parents of Neil Young), who lived in the country outside Peterborough.

During 1959 Davies kept his daily personal diary, made entries in what he called his "big diary," and wrote an extended travel diary in July, but he did not keep a separate theatre diary. Two entries from his 1958 diaries lead into 1959.

MONDAY, DECEMBER 8, 1958, NEW YORK: To Hugh MacCraig, astrologer, who appraised my character well: I am not as needful of people as many, and live much in my mind, and my health is bound up with my mental health; avoid doctors' drastic remedies and trust my intuitions about myself; am highly intuitive and should trust it; will be increasingly concerned with metaphysics; am entering on an important stage of my life which will mount for many years. My writing is especially successful when it relates the past to the present. The collaboration with Tony Guthrie will be difficult, but if I treat him with kid gloves his jealousy of me may be blunted (I do not believe this of Tony). The Casanova play will be a marked success. I am on an upward pathway. Will retain health and semblance of youth, and be increasingly with young people. Will live into my eighties, with good health. Brenda is an "Old Soul" and in many respects my teacher: respect her intuition. I should live southwest of my birthplace, and preferably on a hill with a view of water. Will in time move from where I now live and have already begun to meet the more interesting and influential people who will influence my life and thought. Will in later life be very much a sage and teacher.

WEDNESDAY, DECEMBER 31, 1958: H.t.d.—admirable—and spend the afternoon in bed with Brenda, naked, happy, and warm. In the evening to Tommy and Sheila Currier's for two hours, then to Bill and Gwen Brown's at 11:30 and see the New Year in. To bed at 2.

THURSDAY, JANUARY 1, 1959: Lay late, then to the Mathewses' bouillon party and as usual enjoyed it greatly. Worked on my *Star* article on Boswell and Johnson, then all of us to the movies to see *Damn Yankees*, very good, and admired Gwen Verdon, melting and very icy. Splendid dinner with Gevrey-Chambertin, and a quiet evening. Bed betimes. A happy day.

What did I achieve last year? *A Mixture of Frailties* came out in U.S.A., England, and Canada, and has had the best notices yet and is admitted by all to be my best work—but has not sold well. Yet I do not grieve, as once I would have done: my joy is to write and write well, and if fame and money do not follow I can do nothing about it. I finished the Casanova play *General Confession*, my best yet, and Michael Langham likes it much and says it has fifty times the content of the scripts sent him from New York. And now I am to do a book column for the *Star* for a high fee, and I am busy on the Knopfbook, which I greatly enjoy and of which I have high hopes, and the Theatre Guild wants me to collaborate with Tony Guthrie on a play from *Leaven of Malice*. Who says the world isn't my oyster? In addition the *Examiner* is doing better than ever.

In the home all is as well as I have any right to expect. Brenda said a few days ago that she liked her life and would not change it for any other, which greatly pleased me, for I sometimes feel guilt at keeping so talented a woman in Peterborough, which has so little use for her abilities. We both work faithfully at the Alexander Technique, which continues to help us and has made me more truly self-possessed than ever before. So all seems fair, and if I can continue to juggle all the bright balls which Fate has thrown me,

and drop none, it should be fairer still. I am a very lucky man and I must be sure to deserve my luck.

FRIDAY, JANUARY 2: As always on the first business day, much to do, and I pegged away unremittingly. In the afternoon wrote my *Saturday Night* book review column on some Canadiana books: hard work but came out better than I expected. Evening, slept a lot in my chair, and from 10 till 12 Brenda and I talked with Miranda and Jenny, who are dears but masses of temperament, especially Jenny, who weeps easily and drowns criticism.

SATURDAY, JANUARY 3: Enjoyed working on my next *Star* column. Hope my great pleasure in it continues. In the afternoon get the *Star* to see my first column and find it very flat and disappointing, but Brenda and Miranda say it is good. Did short notices for *Saturday Night*.

SUNDAY, JANUARY 4: This year I must organize my time more efficiently, for though I get a lot of work done, it is accompanied by much foolish fussing. If I could reclaim the fussing-time for leisure I should be rich indeed.

THURSDAY, JANUARY 8: Am making progress with Knopfbook but slowly: still, it will not need much rewriting. I have given the order that *Examiner* reporters must wear ties, an odd thing to have to do but they are obsessed by a dirty Bohemianism. In the evening read Brendan Behan and invited my soul,[1] which needs it.

FRIDAY, JANUARY 9: To Toronto: the Youngs lunch with us at the University Club. Shop for Brenda's birthday, then drive to Stratford

1 From Walt Whitman's "Song of Myself."

and call on Dave Rae, the president of the board of governors, who is very alarmed by the crisis about the approaching season, and Floyd Chalmers[2] makes him no better: Chalmers is very vain, not a really bad man but so self-absorbed he has no tact. We stay with Alf and Dama Bell[3] and share a double bed.[4]

SATURDAY, JANUARY 10, STRATFORD: To a committee meeting at 9, and the board meeting from 11 to 4; weary, and Doug Ambridge of Abitibi Paper very wearisome: a farcical tycoon. Away at 4 to Toronto and dine with WRD at Hawthorn Gardens. Doubleday wants him to write his memoirs.

SUNDAY, JANUARY 11, TORONTO: Chat with WRD and Margaret,[5] who are worried about illness of several elderly relatives. To Peterborough and to the skating arena and see Rosamond win dance-pair trophy: proud of her. Quiet evening and mitigated h.t.d. before the fire, most refreshing to both of us.

The *Star* column already seems to have made some slight stir: it could build into a substantial thing if I do it well. I think about it a great deal and hope to make it more supple, but am still getting the "feel" of it.

WEDNESDAY, JANUARY 14: Again very busy on Knopfbook: it goes better now. Wonderful letter from Hugh MacLennan about *A Mixture of Frailties*: praise from a pro is very sweet, for he knows what

2 Canadian publisher and philanthropist; at the time, president of Maclean-Hunter and Stratford board member.
3 First couple of Stratford Shakespearean Festival, who hosted the meeting between Tyrone Guthrie and the committee formed to start the festival. Dama Bell was on the board of governors for ten years, and Alf Bell served as its president from 1955 to 1957.
4 The Davieses avoided sleeping in a double bed as Rob was such an uneasy sleeper.
5 Margaret McAdoo, Rupert's second wife.

I have done as others cannot. Brenda rehearses[6] in the evening and I work.

FRIDAY, JANUARY 16: Hope now the muddle of Chapter 3 is over the Knopfbook will go more smoothly: Brenda says it is very compact and certainly I do not think it is padded; the trick is not to lose my theme and merely waffle in a bookish fashion.

MONDAY, JANUARY 19: Very busy day: wrote an editorial in the morning and a *Star* column in the afternoon and rewrote the end of Chapter 3 in evening. I can do this now, but ten years ago I could not without severe fatigue. Very heavy snowfall, the most since 1944, and I toil through it like a trapper.[7]

WEDNESDAY, JANUARY 21: Miss Rodney, our accountant, tells me we made $118,185.25 net at the *Examiner* in 1958: very good. Worked in the afternoon and evening at Chapter 4, which is amusing but material hard to control. I read and read and make notes and am a pedant and a drudge but happy. Rain and ice all day.

MONDAY, FEBRUARY 2: Our nineteenth anniversary and I thank God for the blessing my marriage has been to me. A very busy day but manage it all: Don Herbert, the partner with the Theatre Guild in New York, calls and schedules production of the *Leaven of Malice* play for January–February 1960. A meeting at the *Examiner* about advancing our press time: I *do* have varied interests! Quiet evening as we doze and read, rather old-folksy.

6 *Our Town*, by Thornton Wilder, with the Peterborough Little Theatre.
7 Many days Davies walked to and from the office, in the morning, at lunch, and in the evening.

THURSDAY, FEBRUARY 5: In the evening to Dr. Calvert's to discuss relations between local doctors and the *Examiner*: very genial, and doctors tell of a man at General Hospital here with lady's high-heeled shoe stuffed in his rectum, of monster bladder stones, of strange local rapes and prostitutions: a new light on Peterborough.

MONDAY, FEBRUARY 9: Jenny still ill and Miranda retires to bed: a positive lazar-house. Write a good deal for the *Examiner* and do a *Star* column on Mary Shelley's *Frankenstein*. In the evening chat with the girls and Brenda and read a little and groan about the winter: am panicking slightly about the work I have to complete this year.

WEDNESDAY, FEBRUARY 11: Ash Wednesday. I weigh 218, so embark on a Lenten no-second-helping diet. Miranda goes back to school, doctor says Jenny must stay home till Monday at least. Get good work done on book but wonder if it will be too dry for general reading. To the film *Gigi* with Brenda and enjoyed it greatly.

WEDNESDAY, FEBRUARY 18: Completed Chapter 4 and am excited about it: it may be criticism well above my usual level, but only revision will tell. In the evening I do make-up for *Our Town* dress rehearsal and it was really very good and I was moved—what a play!

SUNDAY, FEBRUARY 22: As always, February is a hard month but this year unusually so. I feel old and defeated and the long prospect of work this year gives me small pleasure: I try too hard and am losing the fight. But one turns on the wheel, like Ixion.[8]

8 In Greek mythology, for his sins against Zeus, Ixion was tied to a fiery wheel that rolled in all directions.

TUESDAY, FEBRUARY 24: Low and depressed: work on book but many visitors and a very frampold day. In the evening help Rosamond with her recorder, then read *Raising the Wind* by James Kenney, *Miss in Her Teens* by David Garrick, and *High Life below Stairs* by Rev. James Townley:[9] what good English they are in. But February has me in its clutch.

THURSDAY, FEBRUARY 26: Still much depressed: why? It is some time since I had such a fit. Laboured to write a review of Hugh MacLennan's book *The Watch That Ends the Night* and can praise it generously but do not want to knock the heroine, who is so obviously his wife. In the evening, worked on book but badly and was thoroughly unnerved.

FRIDAY, FEBRUARY 27: Depression the worst yet. The international situation[10] is especially gloomy. Brenda goes to Toronto and gets home on the late train; I read Jerrold and Sheridan Knowles and some Carl Jung,[11] most of which I do not understand, but his approach to mythology explains many popular theatre themes and thus is fruitful for me.

SUNDAY, MARCH 1: Lay late reading Jung. Confided my worry about international affairs to Brenda and felt much better. Analyzed my dread, which is of course personal, and think I hounded it almost to its lair, but some childhood memories still elude me. Introspection brought a lightening of mood and a kind of peace.

9 Eighteenth- and early nineteenth-century English writers.
10 The Tibetan rebellion had caused a Sino-Soviet rift.
11 Davies began to read Freud in 1938, but by the 1950s he had found Jung's thought and writing suited him much better. Jung saw religious and psychological matters in broad terms and had much to say about the second half of life. Many of Davies's novels introduced Jungian ideas.

FRIDAY, MARCH 6: Gloomy day. Felt like hell. In the evening to skating carnival: better than usual because quieter, but there are no more than six things that can be done on skates and all were done hundreds of times. Brenda says I am impossible about it. But I grow weary of boredom, always being kind, a good father, and all the rest of the bourgeois life.

SUNDAY, MARCH 8: My appearance on TV[12] was depressing because I appeared on it as such an oddity—a fat, woolly man, waving small fin-like hands, and cooing archly in a high, reedy voice—Brenda says this is not so, but one has one's unflattering view of oneself.

TUESDAY, MARCH 24: Busy: wrote editorials; talked to Miss Rodney about income tax which is heavy this year: I pay up to 48% on some money, which makes the *Star* column less gladsome than it seems. Later, wonder if my Casanova play is likely to creep upon me in autumn.

FRIDAY, MARCH 27, GOOD FRIDAY: A good day: worked morning and afternoon on Chapter 5 and finished it. In the evening saw T.S. Eliot's *Family Reunion* on TV, well done. I like Good Fridays as there is no obligation to make merry and one can do one's work in peace.

SATURDAY, MARCH 28: Very busy morning as Ralph Hancox[13] and Miss Whalon[14] not in: do lead editorial and *Star* column amid interruptions. In the afternoon revise Chapter 5; in the evening paint and fill Easter eggs with Brenda; then splendid h.t.d. on floor in bedroom: this improves with time though frequency inevitably less.

12 The program on CBC TV was called *Belief*. Davies was interviewed by the philosopher (and Massey cousin) George Grant.
13 Associate editor at the *Examiner*.
14 Moira Whalon, Davies's secretary from 1956 to 1995.

SUNDAY, MARCH 29, EASTER: To Communion[15] at 8; breakfast at 9 and unwisely ate a chocolate chicken, a gift of Mrs. Pedak.[16] Brenda reads fifth chapter and says it is stodgy: must open it up.

Thirty years this Easter since first I heard the *St. Matthew Passion* and now my daughters sing in it. Do I feel any older or wiser? A little, but not enough: the thought of the Theatre Guild job hangs over me like a sword of Damocles. Wish I were a less fearful creature.

FRIDAY, APRIL 3: Again very busy: worried by the Ireland visit this summer. CBC wants me to do commentary at Stratford when Queen will be there in July. Quiet and restful evening and finish Angus Wilson's *The Middle Age of Mrs. Eliot.* Some boys smash one of our windows with snowballs: Herod understood boys.[17] I am nervous and deeply apprehensive.

FRIDAY, APRIL 10: Up early and to Toronto. Dine at University Club and to Crest Theatre to *The Entertainer*, very well done but a hell of a play, the fashionable romanticism of despair.

SATURDAY, APRIL 11, TORONTO: Up early and take 8:10 train to Stratford for board meeting. Other board members Floyd Chalmers,

15 Davies was brought up as a Presbyterian and while at Oxford was confirmed in the Church of England. He had very strong religious beliefs but found that the church did not fulfill his needs. He felt that Christ had nothing to say to older people and they had to find their own way. This was one of the beliefs that led to his investigation of Jungian thought. He liked the pageantry and music of the Anglican church but was not a regular attender at services.
16 Anna Pedak was Estonian. She and her two daughters were interned during the Second World War in a camp in Germany. They came to Canada with the Displaced Persons Program. Her daughter Sylvia was with the Davieses in 1947 and 1948 as a mother's helper and went on to an accomplished career in early childhood education. Mrs. Pedak was with the Davieses as housekeeper from 1948 until 1968. She was a loyal and very moral person and a wonderful cook. With her idiosyncratic English, sense of romantic drama, and sweet singing voice, she became part of the family.
17 Matthew 2:16–18, Massacre of the Innocents.

Theodore Meighen,[18] and Erwin Schuller[19] on train. Long rather dull meeting and take 4:40 back with the same group. I enjoy Schuller's talk: a really literate man. Home on the 11:15—a very long day but pleasant.

SUNDAY, APRIL 12: As always my discontent with Peterborough mounts in spring, and talking with Schuller and Chalmers disturbs me: how hard I work compared with them. Of course they create nothing and my writing is my hardest work, but my life is so provincial!

TUESDAY, APRIL 21: Worked well on Chapter 6. Brenda home from Toronto for dinner and gives me a detailed account of Michel St. Denis's fine lecture and sharp criticism of the Method:[20] she found it refreshing and stimulating. We talked about possibility of undergoing a Jungian analysis and she advises me to investigate when we are in New York.

WEDNESDAY, APRIL 22: Wonderful day, but my allergy bothered me and made me heavy-headed; worked in afternoon on Knopfbook, not badly. Evening read Dr. Esther Harding[21] and have written to her for an appointment but will probably not get one. I could not manage analysis, if it meant leaving my job and living in New York.

18 Lawyer and philanthropist; eldest son of Prime Minister Arthur Meighen.
19 Austrian-born international banker. His marriage to the Canadian international administrator Mary McGeachy brought him into the Canadian arts world.
20 St. Denis, a friend from the Old Vic, was a leading theatrical director in Britain, France, and the United States. The Method is an acting technique derived from Stanislavski and developed in the United States by Lee Strasberg.
21 M. Esther Harding, prominent Jungian analyst then in her seventies. She wrote many works related to Jung, including *Journey into Self* (1956), the book Davies was reading at this time.

THURSDAY, APRIL 23: Another superb day: work well and in evening read Harding. Continue to toy with idea of analysis but practical difficulties are great: I could afford it, but it would mean both Brenda and me living in New York and what about the girls? And what would it do to my work?

SATURDAY, APRIL 25: Wrote *Star* column on Jung in the morning and then to the cottage,²² where it is very beautiful. In the evening we motor to Cobourg and see the Canadian National Ballet in the charming old Opera House. The governor general, Vincent Massey, was there and I spoke briefly to Lionel Massey,²³ who looks furrowed and harried. Ballet somewhat coarse—no elegance; home by 12:15.

SUNDAY, MAY 3: Lay late with deep sense of peace, for I have fought through a great amount of work since Christmas and especially the past two weeks, but it is done and well done. Feel that Knopfbook is well in hand and that the play may even be a pleasure. Till now I have thought of it only as a bugbear and certain failure, but even if it does not work on Broadway, it can be a very good piece of work.

In 1955 Davies had begun having trouble with his left leg. It was weak and he often lost feeling in it after long periods of sitting. He could get no useful medical advice, but a chance conversation with a friend led him to the Alexander Technique, a system of thinking about

22 The traditional summer cottage with outhouse and attendant domestic discomforts did not appeal to Rob or Brenda, but they had a cottage on a property called Bryn Camlas (Welsh for "hill on the canal") around the TV station on the Otonabee River outside Peterborough, which they used for day visits.

23 The governor general's son and secretary had become a friend of Davies's at Oxford.

movement for posture control and physical ease developed by F.M. Alexander at the end of the nineteenth century that had become popular particularly with actors and musicians. There was no Alexander teacher in Canada at the time, and in January 1956 Rob and Brenda went to New York for the first of many sessions with Lulie Westfeldt, who had studied with Alexander. Lulie Westfeldt and the Alexander Technique became important features in the lives of the Davieses. Most years they went to New York for lessons with her in May and again in December, and some years they met her in the summer as well.

TUESDAY, MAY 5: To Toronto, then fly to New York and to the Dorset Hotel. To supper with Brenda's friend from our Old Vic days, Jackie Davie, and meet Dr. and Mrs. Kingsbury, David King-Wood, two Jews and whatnot, and a jackass playwright named Herschel Williams who thinks the *Times* is dominated by Reds. A very jolly evening and fierce h.t.d.

WEDNESDAY, MAY 6, NEW YORK: Very good lesson with Lulie Westfeldt, who says I have made good progress. In the afternoon sleep, then h.t.d., then to film *Room at the Top*, excellent. Dinner at a downtown Longchamps and to *Mark Twain Tonight* with Hal Holbrook, who was excellent and held the audience spellbound. I was delighted with it.

THURSDAY, MAY 7, NEW YORK: Good lesson and marked changes in my lower back. Lunch with Willis Wing[24] at L'Argenteuil, then shop for shirts and books. In the evening to dine at David King-Wood's flat in Greenwich Village with Jackie Davie.

24 Willis Kingsley Wing, Davies's New York literary agent.

FRIDAY, MAY 8, NEW YORK: Brenda has a cold. A good lesson with Lulie, then to Dr. Esther Harding and get very good advice about a Jungian analysis. I am impressed by her. In the afternoon to the Museum of Modern Art to see Marlene Dietrich in von Sternberg's 1935 *The Devil Is a Woman,* amusingly dated. Brenda rests. In the evening to *Triple Play,* three one-acters by Hume Cronyn and Jessica Tandy: not quite a good evening. I was greatly pleased by Dr. Harding.

SATURDAY, MAY 9, NEW YORK: Very good lesson with Lulie and study "monkeying," then lunch with her at her club. In the afternoon to *J.B.* by Archibald MacLeish, which we liked very well in spite of having heard some bad comment. It is close to tragedy. Ideas begin to assert themselves for the *Leaven of Malice* play and I was vexed that some of these appeared in *J.B.*

SUNDAY, MAY 10, NEW YORK: Breakfast in bed, then excellent h.t.d., the effect of "monkeying." To the Metropolitan Museum and lunch there. In the evening to the musical *Once upon a Mattress,* which is very crude and uninventive but pleases a boob audience.

MONDAY, MAY 11, NEW YORK: To Lulie Westfeldt, then I call on Morton Levy and Don Herbert. Business arrangements with Tony Guthrie still vague. I take Alfred Knopf to lunch at the Stork Club and he complains cheerily of many things. Brenda to Hugh MacCraig the astrologer. In the evening, dinner at Jackie Davie's, very pleasant and we have a thoroughly good time.

TUESDAY, MAY 12, NEW YORK: Another good lesson, though changes consequent on Alexander Technique make me very tired. We shop for gifts for the girls. After lunch h.t.d., very good, then to the film *Doctor's Dilemma* directed by Anthony Asquith, excellent. We

dine at Stockholm, noisy, then to *Raisin in the Sun* for which we were supposed to have seats, but a muddle, and we end up at *Sunrise at Campobello* by Dore Schary, a mechanical piece.

WEDNESDAY, MAY 13: To Lulie Westfeldt for an excellent final lesson: we have made good progress. Lunch at the St. Moritz, then pack and away in some haste; roughish flight to Toronto; to the University Club and Margaret joins us for dinner. Toronto seems provincial and Victorian after New York. Drive home in rain, greet Rosamond, and in bed by 12.

SUNDAY, MAY 17: We have been bidden to dine with the Queen in Ottawa on July 1, representing Letters, a great honour and doubtless productive of some jealousy. Usual hubbub for women about what to wear.

FRIDAY, MAY 22: Finish rereading *Leaven of Malice* and my mind is a yeast of schemes to make a play of it. In the evening read some Jung: am I wise to tinker with this stuff, without going into it wholeheartedly? Yet it seems to be a kind of wisdom.

SATURDAY, MAY 23: Brenda to Toronto; I find Colin McDougall's *Execution* has the Governor General's Award, as I expected. In the evening, work on *Leaven of Malice* play and think I am on a good scent, more eager than I have been about a piece of writing in a long time.

SUNDAY, MAY 24: Am in high spirits about *Leaven of Malice* and think I have found a way to make a play of it: a great contrast to my former gloom. My great task will be to keep Tony Guthrie from destroying my ideas without replacing them with ideas which I think better.

SUNDAY, MAY 31: Lay late; to Bryn. Mosquitoes bad. We walked all over the property. Development is rapid out there but we do not want to sell though buyers nibble. We picnic, row boat.

TUESDAY, JUNE 2: Letter from Tony reassuring about terms and method of collaboration. In the evening, drive to Omemee in the new Jaguar, which is far the nicest car we have ever had and a relief from that vulgar beast of a Chrysler Imperial. Read all of Act 1 to Brenda, who makes some suggestions and thinks it good.

THURSDAY, JUNE 18: Letter from Tony about the *Leaven of Malice* contract. Very vague; I don't care but the lawyers do. Work hard and do a *Star* column on style. In the evening read Jung's *Answer to Job*. Brenda is undergoing some psychological changes and is nervous but eventually the outcome will be good, I am sure.

SUNDAY, JUNE 28: Tea at Bryn on hill, very beautiful, then home and fuss and pack. Am now, to all intents, on holiday, and very glad of it; have truly earned it. I am conscious of changes due to Jungian reading: should I go to a Jungian analyst? Am I not the kind who should go it alone?

MONDAY, JUNE 29: Drive to Stratford. Jenny drives much of the way. Very hot. Stratford governors' party a brawl, as always; *As You Like It* a delight but too much complicated by business extraneous to the play. Irene Worth[25] lovely as Rosalind, but a certain lack of unity in the production.

TUESDAY, JUNE 30, STRATFORD: Long committee meeting. Wilf Gregory's excellent luncheon; art show; cocktails at Dave Rae's.

25 The American stage star had also played in the first Stratford season.

Othello great: Douglas Campbell, Douglas Rain, Frances Hyland, and Kate Reid all first-rate. Have never responded to a tragedy so: shaken and fearful; and this is a production sans stars and with Canadian direction![26] To Toronto through the night.

WEDNESDAY, JULY 1: We fly to Ottawa at 12:00. Presentation of Colours at 4; tea with WRD, who is here as a senator. Government House at 7:45 for dinner with Her Majesty and the Prince: gathering of thirty-five Canadians from all walks of life. Had chats with Her Majesty about Stratford and Canadian literature and His Royal Highness about same. A wonderful affair very well done.

THURSDAY, JULY 2: Fly to Toronto at 9:15, then motor to Stratford. An awful dinner at the Country Club, then to the theatre. Broadcast on CBC TV on the Queen's arrival.[27] The director says brilliant but I was very scared. A good performance of *As You Like It* and Her Majesty and His Royal Highness remember Brenda and me, very kind. Parties at Raes' and Andersons', fireworks, fine h.t.d.

On July 6, Rob, Brenda, Jennifer, and Rosamond (Miranda was at a music camp) drove from Peterborough to New York City to put Rob on a plane for his working holiday with Tyrone Guthrie at Guthrie's house, Annagh-ma-Kerrig, in Northern Ireland, where he stayed until July 31. Davies began his travel diary and also wrote frequent letters home to Brenda, using a private nickname, Pink.

WEDNESDAY, JULY 8, NEW YORK: In the afternoon we go to the Swedish film which is so much talked of, *Wild Strawberries*, directed by Ingmar Bergman. Very good indeed and a use of symbolism

26 George McCowan and Jean Gascon.
27 Davies did the colour commentary for CBC TV and for the CBC Radio broadcast.

which was truly illuminating and not merely portentous. We have
dinner at L'Argenteuil, very good, and an excellent Puligny
Montrachet, then Brenda and the girls saw me away at the airline
terminal: I thought, as I looked at them from the 'bus window, what
a distinguished group they were in that blurred milieu. Hated leav-
ing. On arrival at Idlewild, to 'plane at once and we flew promptly
at 11. My seat-companion was a deaf Americo-Irish dizzard who left
the Old Sod in 1900, at fifteen, and was making his first return.
Stupid and a roarer, and unable to hold his tongue. As I was read-
ing *Little Dorrit* he favoured me with his literary history—"Used to
read all kinds—love stories and Westerns and them. Deepest book
I ever read was called *She* by a fella named Haggard. Ever read it?
Aw, that's *deep* stuff." The air thing by my seat was broken, and he
insisted on smoking his pipe—"You'll never notice: I use that mild
tobacca, rum and maple sugar cured." I slept quite well. Glad to
see Prestwick. Then a long 'bus ride to Glasgow, and another to
Renfrew, then a long wait, and very weary. But at last I take a small
'plane for Belfast, and Tony meets me in a tiny Morris, and we drive
about sixty miles to Newbliss and thence to Annagh-ma-Kerrig,
Tony and Judy's house. And to bed in a large room which is like
Bertram Rota's rare-books shop in London, for it is book-lined with
first editions (usually the only ones) of poets of the 'twenties.

FRIDAY, JULY 10, LETTER TO BRENDA
Dearest Pink and Darlings Jenny and Rosamond,

Here I am at the end of my first day at Annagh-ma-Kerrig, in a
comfortable and big bedroom, rather like a library, really, for it has
three walls all of books, a big, old bed with a terrible mattress and
seven wool blankets and an ancient eiderdown: also a hot bottle. A
dressing-room with a candle in it, but the bedroom has the elec-
tricity—a good Anglepoise lamp. A large white chummy which I
am bidden to use, but won't: would rather go down a long dark

passage to the w.c. A queer old house, this, somewhat ruinous and full of junk—part of the antlers of an Irish elk, two pianos in bad tune, endless chairs not quite safe. Big but rambling and inconvenient. A large lake in the park, icy cold, where Tony and Judy make themselves swim. A bouncy, yappy wee dog, and a marmalade cat. Plenty to eat, so far, but threats of having to eat fish from the lake. The fruit which isn't good enough to sell is kept for the house, and so wooden peaches turn up, and greenish raspberries. This sounds awful but is really very pleasant.

This morning Tony and I began work on the play. Read it all and he likes it very well but keeps saying "Wouldn't it make a good film." He has several good suggestions. That took all morning. Right after dinner I was put to work to pack raspberries, wild ones for the bottom of the baskets and tame ones on top. They fetch 1 shilling, 3 pence a pound, apparently. Then tea and right to work proof-reading Tony's book *A Life in the Theatre*. They seem to slave, and then stop and play patience. Judy's cough is, if anything, worse: I tremble for her. Tony looks a good deal older and has an arthritic elbow which gives him a good deal of pain. Not surprised, for it is terribly damp here. The countryside is pretty but rolling: no mountains. They are expecting a horde of guests and one came today— Tony's sister's adopted son, Joe Hone, who is very handsome in the Irish way—big eyes, high colour, and curly hair.

No doubt I shall settle down more as time goes on but at present I am restless. When we really get to work on the play I expect I shall feel better but just at present I find the atmosphere queer and disturbing. Hard to say why, for Tony and Judy are most hospitable, but the climate is odd—lovely sun today and roasting hot during the berry-picking—but damp and clammy at night, and though it is now dark it was light outside till 10:30. Tony says the climate is "very sluggish." But I am an awful old fusser and it isn't *clean*: it is disloyal to write this under my host's roof but it fidges me. When I

was in the w.c. today Tony peed in the face-basin! This sort of thing gives me the creeps, and I rather dread to wash. Call me North American if you will, but I don't like it.

Must climb under the seven blankets now. My love to you all and I wish you were here or I was there.

(Very special love to you, Pinkie dearest.)

Rob

SATURDAY, JULY 11: Worked on the play in the morning. Things begin to move, as Tony is getting notions for physical production and these spark off my mind for scenes and dialogue. This is what I had hoped for, and when he is working in this way he is very inspiring and it is all practical, for he knows to perfection what can be done and how. In the afternoon played the piano, they have fascinating heaps of old music, and thought about the play. Tony shows me family pictures, his great-grandfather Tyrone Power[28] the actor, and great-grandfather Guthrie, the Scots divine—Tony looks woundily like the latter.

SUNDAY, JULY 12, LETTER TO BRENDA

Dearest Pink and Cherished Poppets Jenny and Rosamond:

The people who said it could be cold and damp in Ireland were right: yesterday was a glorious day of sun and was quite bearable even when night had fallen, but it has rained all day today and tonight it is as cold as Greenland, and damp as a bog. I sit with a blanket around me, writing this by the light of the candles. Work on the play has begun and promises well: Tony has made some good suggestions and is working out a plan of production—how it will look and how we will get people on and off the stage, and all

28 Irish actor (1795–1841). The American movie actor Tyrone Power (1914–1958) was also a descendant.

that—which clarifies my ideas a good deal. He is much more extravagant than I and wants a good deal in the way of scenery and stuff, but I think his notions are imaginative and not merely representational. Anyhow, we are off to a start and I feel much better. How long it will take I can't say, but certainly no longer than the time I have allowed: so the chances are strong that I will come home with a finished script.

We work a good deal on the proofs for Tony's book: he reads them and laughs at his own jokes, I read them and make changes in style, and Joe Hone reads them for spelling and punctuation. I argue with Tony about the insulting stuff, but he wants it all kept. Now and then we take a rest and Tony sings in a very loud, trembling voice, and I play for him. Judy messes happily in the garden and boasts about the money she makes selling fruit. Tony is very fierce with her about the amount she smokes.

This evening at 6 p.m. a Mr. and Mrs. Rea (pronounced Ray) and a Mr. Zeisler from New York arrived: the Guthries had forgotten they were coming and were unflatteringly astonished to see them. They are theatricals of some sort and 5x2s, I expect, from sundry hooky beezers and florid manners. They brought some good wine, which Judy made the maids put under the hot tap!

I miss you all and it is like a little chat to write, even when I haven't much news. Now that things begin to move with the play I feel less lost but I am a family sort of creature. Good-night, my dears, and huge hugs and kisses to all (and especially to you, my darling Pinkie)

Rob

SUNDAY, JULY 12: Strange in this Irish country house to hear New York theatre gossip at breakfast, and the slick locutions of New York lingo—"This I believe . . . ," "The Bolshoi was fabulous technically, but lousy choreography-wise." After breakfast I take some

photographs and retire to my room to post this diary. In the after-
noon we all go for a walk around the lake; it pours with rain. Peter
Zeisler has no raincoat and is drenched. The Reas, like me, have coats
and are drenched. The Guthries have no coats and pay no heed to
the rain. They wade through brooks in their tennis shoes and squelch
through mud ankle-deep without seeming to notice. We pant up a
hill on the chance of a glimpse of Slieve Gullion, the highest point in
County Armagh. We fall into quite deep ditches which are full of
water. But no one is out of temper: one cannot be vexed with the
Guthries, though one has sometimes a sense of being over-ridden.

In the morning Tony is closeted with Rea and Zeisler,[29] who
want to found a company to do classics and plays of worth in the
U.S.A.—possibly in Cleveland. Their problems are familiar: they
want to be out of New York, but regard all else as "the sticks" and
cannot conceive of any good actors thinking otherwise. Idealists,
crippled by cynicism.

In the evening, at Tony's suggestion, I read the first two acts of
my Casanova play, *General Confession*, to them all: I think I read well
and Tony liked it greatly, though he suggests some small cuts, and
thinks Laurence Olivier the best cast for Casanova—as who would
not? Tony is doing *Hamlet* with Christopher Plummer in London
next winter, and there is general discussion about casting.

MONDAY, JULY 13: In the morning we all go to Monaghan to shop:
it is a glum, stony, rebarbative town, ugly as masonry can be made.
I am with Joe, a nice young man, proud to be Irish and anti–Free
State. We meet for a drink at a pub in the best room over a snug—a
hideous chamber, scabby-walled and furnished in damp, discour-
aged green velvet, with *three* broken radios and a piano deranged

29 Oliver Rea and Peter Zeisler, with Tyrone Guthrie, founded the Guthrie
Theatre in Minneapolis, which opened in 1963.

in its wits—anyhow it spoke in idiot tones. A town of poorly dressed, pinched-faced children: I saw one boy's toes peeping from under the upper of his boots. Saw two privileged insane, rather too many for the population, and a man with a horribly swollen face done up in a dirty rag—a toothache or a gathered ear. Betty Rea gave great scandal in the snug where, it appears, decent women do not go.

After lunch I did Tony's morocco scrap book with saddle soap, and tried to work on my play but was scant of ideas. The great event of the day was the return of Miss Bunty Worby, the late Mrs. Guthrie's nurse-companion, and her great friend Miss Davis: these two elderlies chatter and make more noise than schoolgirls. We men retired to Tony's room and read proofs for him: Joe is the great expert on punctuation, I on usage and style, Peter and Oliver forget themselves and read for pleasure, and laugh a lot. Under this regime the book undergoes some salutary changes and is going to be good, I think. Tonight I read Act 3 of my Casanova play and astonished them, I think. Tony thinks it wants minor cutting but is on the whole very good. Enjoyable reading it.

TUESDAY, JULY 14: This morning went over the last, and by far the best, chapter of Tony's book and was able to make a suggestion or two which he found useful, particularly the cutting of a final paragraph which was emptily rhetorical. Before tea walked to the post with Scamp, Bunty's dog: I think I see why lonely people like dogs, for they bounce about and are company. After tea to visit Lady Rossmore and her son, called by Tony "my young lord." They live in the dower house, Camlagh, for their hideous nineteenth-century castle is ruinous with dry rot. They have a fine library for which they care little, but are vaguely conscious that they could sell it for something: a wonderful collection of first quartos of John Dryden and Thomas Otway and their congeners, *Sir Martin Mar-All*, etc.; the first printed *Adam Bede*. Lady Rossmore has

mislaid a Shakespeare Fourth Folio and a first edition of *Pride and Prejudice*. Extraordinary people! Nice, but unconscious.

At dinner Betty and Peter wrangled about royalty, she for and he against. In the evening Tony read his last chapter aloud, then we had theatre gossip till 12:30, and chattered about MacLeish's *J.B.*

TUESDAY, JULY 14, LETTER TO BRENDA
Dearest Pink and Girls:

We are now nine in number: Tony and Judy, the Reas, Zeisler, Joe Hone, myself, and two old ladies, Miss Bunty Worby and Miss Meg Davis, who arrived on Monday. Miss Worby was Tony's mother's companion for many years and is now too old to be shifted. The nasty little dog, Scamp (who bit me in the leg yesterday), is hers, called "my wee man" rather unpleasantly. They are indefatigable pickers of the raspberries which Judy sells. Poor Mrs. Rea is a slave. "I think I'll go into Newbliss this morning," says she. "Oh, be a dear and pick five pounds of berries and leave them with Old Becky," says Judy. Five pounds is a lot of berries. But Judy is avid of gold. I don't think the petty sums thus realized mean much to her, but she is like a child playing shop, and presses everybody into service. It is rather amusing that the five men cluster around the sink and do the breakfast dishes, while the four women put on macs and rubber boots and rush out in the rain for 9 pennyworth of greenish raspberries.

On the *Leaven of Malice* play I am working virtually alone, because Tony will not settle down to it. He has finished his own book (and I have read all the proofs) and he cannot get at anything else. He talks about writing a "manifesto" for Rea and Zeisler, and has no stomach for the niggling work on *Leaven of Malice*. So I must do it and really I don't much mind, for it is his ideas rather than his actual writing which is valuable. So far the ideas have tended to be of the "That won't do: see if you can think of anything else" kind. But there are many worse things than that.

Yesterday we went in to Monaghan, a bleak ugly town with its share of madmen and dirt. The Reas are very good sports and do not shrink from the dirt, but their glances are eloquent. Here at Annagh-ma-Kerrig, of course, the towels and napkins are not changed, and the strain of nine people and the maids on the one gasping o'erparted w.c. is intense. I have been brought to using the chummy, and emptying it out of the window into the garden. In so damp a climate, it makes small difference.

Love to you all, from the bogs.

Rob

WEDNESDAY, JULY 15: At supper Tony and Judy were at their old tricks. Tony says, "Nobody who *is* anybody eats a peach with its skin on." Cries Old Meg, "Trash: nobody who is anybody cares if anybody thinks they're anybody or not!" She can daunt Tony. So can I. I Come the Scholarly and it quells them both; but I don't like doing it for it leads to pedantry, but it can be done. To my room at 10 to write to Brenda.

WEDNESDAY, JULY 15, LETTER TO BRENDA
Dearest Pink:

It is 10 o'clock and I have come upstairs because I wanted electric light: in the drawing-room (which boasts *one* globe) they have not yet put it on, and though I can neither read nor write, Tony and Meg Davis are playing patience. Meg is about seventy-five and an old friend from Belfast, and she and Tony bully one another unmercifully: she "knew the garden" in Tony's mother's time, and insists it has gone to ruin, and goads Tony to great feats of weeding and transplanting. I was sucked in after tea for some heavy weeding: they have the scutch-grass very badly. It is locally called "twitch" and is in the box-hedges, so when Meg says to Judy, "Ye've terrible twitch in your box," I know that no indecency is meant.

The Reas and Peter Zeisler left this morning. They were very nice and bid us look them up in New York. Tony and I did some good work on the play this morning. It is beginning to take shape: he wants more short scenes. Also the plan of production begins to emerge—many small trucks with wee bits of setting on them. This means a good deal of patching and tinkering, not as much work as I was prepared for but tinkering takes time. Fortunately I have a nice room to work in, and Tony's beast of a typewriter. So most of the day I peg away, and turn up for meals. Last night he read us all the last chapter of his book, which is very good. Then we talked about *J.B.*

Tony is a strange one. After the weeding yesterday I wanted a bath, to avoid stiffness. "Hurry up," he cried, "and I'll get into your water, so we won't run down the tank." And he did, and pushed in while I was having my bath and nakedly o'erhung me while I was in the tub. Then hopped in and swilled around in my suds, with a right good will.

My letters to you seem to be a long whimper about the dirtiness of the Guthries, which I do not mean, but it is worrisome. The dishwashing! But Old Meg will have none of it. "Put that back, Tony, it's DORTY!" she screams. I warm to her, I must say, and she to me, I think, for she offers me toffees from her personal store. Well, I am achieving what I came for, because the play goes ahead, and Tony's ideas are, on the whole, good. I remember Hugh MacCraig's advice, and handle him with kid gloves. But he intends to do it all right, and is truly interested in the collaboration. He has bushels of ideas, and thank Heaven he leaves it to me to carry them out.

Eleven o'clock now and quite dark outside. Goodnight, dearest Brenda: I miss you very much, and wish you were here to halve the discomfort and double the fun. Because there *is* a lot of fun, but the kind that would be twice as delightful if you were here to

share it. It was very stupid of me to come away without a picture of you.

Much love to the girls and unreckoned heaps of it to you—
Rob

THURSDAY, JULY 16: Worked with Tony this morning and then went on to try the suggestions he made. In the afternoon to Monaghan for his arthritis injection; Tony and Judy in front and Old Meg, Joe, and me in the back of the baby Morris—very squeezed. Then to Lady Rossmore's to a fête for the British Legion—a kind of raspberry social. Torrential rain, so it had to be indoors. Gave 10 shillings. Tony judged the hats, made by the ladies of bits of newspaper and paper ribbon. A dull affair. Returning, Tony sat in the back and I in the front as Old Meg insisted that I was bigger than he, but when she got him in beside her she found differently. In the evening Tony and I read aloud from *A Mixture of Frailties*, which reads very well, and brought many laughs, even from Miss Worby, who has read it twice. Then Tony and Joe and I sat up till 1, talking about J.B. Priestley,[30] and the miseries which can come from early success. The dirt here worries me: towels, napkins, all that sort of thing, never changed. Yet constant bathing. Strange.

FRIDAY, JULY 17: A wretched day when nothing seems to go right. Work all morning with a headache: work in the afternoon and Tony comes in, hears what I have done, and does not think any of it will do! He sees the play as a romantic comedy, I as fantastic farce. Walk to the post in pouring rain, with headache (sinus) and despair. The trouble is, Tony condemns what he has half heard and cannot have fully comprehended. But I must heed him, or he will want to write himself, and he can't. Hugh MacCraig warned me to handle him

30 Popular English novelist, playwright, and broadcaster.

with kid gloves, and I do, though longing to give him the rough side of my tongue. Tonight read more *Mixture of Frailties*; how it improves read aloud and how an audience multiplies its effect.

FRIDAY, JULY 17, LETTER TO BRENDA
Dearest Pink:

I am now working very hard, and get quite tired. Judy says I don't get out enough in the fresh air, which is nonsense, because the air in my bedroom is just as cold and wet as the air out-of-doors. The discomfort is of a special quality: the all-embracing damp cold is a big part of it; so is the oniony, very greasy food; so is the dirt—never a clean towel, and my napkin stinks and is grey. Judy grabs any fat off my plate that I don't eat and consumes it with relish. Their miserliness takes extreme forms: this morning Tony found that the proofs of his book had gone astray, but he wouldn't call the post office in Dublin, because the call might be a long one and could cost him £1! Yet in other ways they are so generous! It is just a thing about money. She makes £10 on the garden in a year but slaves £300 to get it.

So my days pass in work and lively evenings of talk and Irish whisky. Tony and I are reading *A Mixture of Frailties* aloud to the party and you'd be amazed how well it reads!

I miss you almost to bursting.

Much love to you and les girls

Rob

SATURDAY, JULY 18: Toil away all day to write the new opening for the play on the lines Tony wants. I am sure it rained five times today, and in between there would be perhaps half an hour of sunshine; in some of these intervals I took a few pictures. Tonight continued the reading of *Mixture of Frailties*, which gives pleasure and which Tony reads very well. Wonderful moonlight on the lake

and garden: done on a stage it would be monstrously sentimental, but Nature has none of these foolish qualms.

SUNDAY, JULY 19: In the morning Tony, Meg, and Joe to church and I talk with Bunty, who tells me Tony was very much his mother's son, and had a distant but not quarrelsome relationship with his father. When Tony returns I am conscripted to pull groundsel among the strawberries. After dinner Tony and I work all afternoon on the play: he likes my new opening, and we work on physical details of settings, and their management, and on this he is remarkable. Then we plan a new final scene and some contrapuntal passages. Very interesting and helpful and sets out my work for the week to come.

At dinner Tony asked those who had not read *A Mixture of Frailties* to guess what would happen: Old Meg predicted darkly that Monica would "come to no good and have to go home." Tonight we came to the scene where Monica loses her maidenhead in the bathroom at Neuadd Goch, and later asks Revelstoke to be her lover: Old Meg received it very sourly. As Joe says, to hear an author read such things from his own book seems to her an affront. Joe is in misery: an Irish film company has asked him to do a scenario from a book about a hideous dwarf in Galicia; he can make nothing of it, and we tease him with suggestions. Tony is particularly fecund of wheezes for giving the dwarf quality: he suggests a child of four on whom a huge head has been fixed. It continues to be chilly; they call it summer, but it is more like a bad November.

MONDAY, JULY 20: In the night I woke roaring because I dreamed Joe's dwarf was strangling me. Somehow I have taken a chill and feel miserable: sharp stabbings inside and a general weakness like 'flu. Keep to my room most of the day and sleep a lot: do not mention to the others that I am unwell, for fear of well-meant remedies.

Of course no work possible. Old Meg goes back to Belfast. She would not say goodbye to me: offended by my "dirty" book! To bed and have a poor night, with pain and sleeplessness. This is no house in which to be seedy: the general strenuosity, the greasy food, and the dirt are all against it. The methods of washing-up appall me: cigarette stubs and butter in the water, and the only dishes that are scraped are those the dog is given to lick. There is a bucket for the hens under the sink and so far as I can discern, the hens live on coffee-grounds, tea leaves, and empty cigarette boxes. I suppose I am ridiculous and faddy, but such things destroy my appetite. The bathroom hangs full of Isabella-coloured ladies' lingerie.

Tony has been going through a lot of family possessions, and his curious cast of mind is never better exemplified than with these. He has a fine enamel snuffbox given to Tyrone Power, for which a dealer has offered him £600 but he won't sell that; instead wants to sell a Victorian Power seal, a piece of trash worth perhaps 15 shillings. "Some American would buy it; they don't know anything." He wants money but wants it for trash, from Americans: he seems to have no sense that this is cheating.

I am aware that this diary seems very critical of the Guthries, whose guest I am: perhaps I should say that their conversation is plentifully packed with criticism of me, and I am astonished to be called "worldly," by which they mean ambitious and climbing. They are charmers, but loonies.

TUESDAY, JULY 21: Continue to be unwell: a restless and miserable night. Miss Worby takes me in hand and doses me with weak bicarbonate of soda solution every four hours, with good effect. Tony and Joe go to Dublin and it is quiet here all day, so I do a little work, read *Little Dorrit*, and doze in an armchair in my room, rather invalidish. Tony rouses me from a nap when he returns with his lifelong

friend Christopher Scaife[31] and Marc Blitzstein.[32] Both very charming. Later arrive Hubert and Peggy Butler and Peter Smithwick: Hubert is a landowner, Peggy is Tony's sister and rather like him, and young Smithwick is a son of the well-known brewers. So we are ten in number. After dinner we go for a walk and Blitzstein impresses me by the ease and charm of his address. I walk with Scaife and Smithwick: the former a genial and learned man, the latter a very polite, intelligent fellow of, I should have said, twenty but I believe he is twenty-three. Must get to work; my megrim has cost me two days.

WEDNESDAY, JULY 22: Feel better; the Butlers, Scaife, and Smithwick off on an antiquarian jaunt organized by the Georgian Society to Castle Coole and Florence Court. Work in the morning but not well. Tony comes in to say Marc has been playing *Juno* to him and he does not like it: shallow and mock-Irish. At lunch Marc talks about Schönberg, with whom he studied. He talks all the time, and well. In the afternoon he and I are set to picking raspberries by Judy. He said, "Will I cut my hands? They're my living." Tony said, "Rubbish." At dinner Tony was on one of his flights about the villainy of accents other than his own—Australian, Canadian, American. He is dogmatic in a schoolboy fashion. This evening he and Scaife sang: Scaife has great tenderness and musicianship and has had a sweet, charming voice. But Tony—boy again—wants everything very fast and ranting. It is sad to watch Judy when Tony is singing—she loves him so that she weeps unashamedly, but will not close her eyes for fear of losing sight of his face. I think this embarrasses him, for he will not heed her when she calls for her favourites. But Scaife is very sweet to her and sings *to* her. He sang Wood's

31 Professor of English literature, University of Lebanon.
32 American composer of musicals, including *Juno* (1959), from Sean O'Casey's *Juno and the Paycock*.

"Ethiopia Saluting the Colours" with fine feeling and Marc played it well. Then I was asked to read the Yarrows' party from *Leaven of Malice*, which I did, with good effect. A good evening, marred only when Bunty Worby's dog, Scamp, had too much music and had noisy hysterics.

WEDNESDAY, JULY 22, LETTER TO BRENDA
Dearest Pinkie:

I mention, just in passing, that it is beginning to arouse comment here how seldom I get letters from home. Actually I think it is their wretched postal system. But anyhow, stir up those lazy girls and save me from shame. I seem to have been away an age, though it is only two weeks today, and I miss you all—but you especially. The woe of parted lovers—wet dreams, which are *no* substitute, I can tell you, as well as being an infernal nuisance in a house as ill-plumbed and over-inhabited as this.

Tony and Blitzstein are banging the piano and rowing downstairs. Judy picking fruit like a demon. Me upstairs trying to rewrite the last scene and Tony bustling me. He doesn't seem to realize how long writing can take and wants everything in a hurry. So this must be brief—but I paused in work to write to you just to say that I love you to pieces.

Will let you know when I am going to London and my hotel, as soon as I know myself. It hangs on how long they stay here, as Tony wants me to leave with him—probably the 30th or 31st.

Much love to all, and especially to you, my dearest dear
Rob

THURSDAY, JULY 23: Hard work this morning and write a new finale to the play. In the afternoon the Butlers and Smithwick go and Blitzstein goes with them. After dinner Christopher Scaife read us some of his poems, which I liked, then Joe read us some of

his movie treatment of his dwarf theme; Tony is a tireless interrupter, but to good purpose. We talked about the dwarf till 1.

FRIDAY, JULY 24: Wretched sinus headache. Read my new stuff to Tony, who likes it and suggests some details of good change. We begin to approach a workable script. At 7 to Camlagh to dine with Lady Rossmore. A very good meal but she fidgets like any Peterborough hostess. Rather sad. Lovely old crested silver but coffee cups the cheapest quality. (At Camlagh the men's washroom is hung with eighteenth-century French erotic engravings, to Tony's puritanical disgust, but I thought them charming, as did Scaife.)

SATURDAY, JULY 25: The wonderful warm, bright weather continues. I work all morning on the play. After lunch a fascinating discussion about *Hamlet*, then to work again. But it is uphill work for it is so warm that it is a call to pleasure and I wish consumedly that Brenda were here. Go to the post, for the walk, and the others go across the lake and take their tea. I have tea with Bunty, who tells me Tony's father died of lung cancer. Work again, and my total day's writing is satisfactory. Play the piano for Tony to sing some Irish songs. After dinner he reads his libretto for a Nativity opera, which John Gardner has set. Good, but gloomy and hopeless in the last few pages. We then fall to a discussion of the nature of Christ, and am interested to discover how much Tony's ideas chime with mine, though he thinks Christ was a proletarian, I, an aristocrat. While here have read Chayefsky's *The Dybbuk from Woodhaven*, which Tony will direct in New York this autumn: a good play but leans very heavily on Jewish ritual and also on Ansky's Jewish classic, *The Dybbuk*, in my opinion, though Tony says not. Exciting, rich mixture.

SATURDAY, JULY 25, LETTER TO BRENDA
Dearest Pink:

Now: I go to London next Friday, July 31, as that is when Tony goes to Edinburgh. He wants me to fly with him. We leave here at 6 a.m., motor to Belfast, and fly at 8:30. I shall be glad to get to London, because it will be a rest. I really work very hard here, and Tony, who does not know how long writing takes, hounds me. But I hope that before I leave I shall have a script of which he approves. It is maddening to read to him—continual interruptions, often about things which come in the next three words. But I find he often comes back to my notions, the next day. He is in no sense a *private* person: he can live and work in hubbub, and doesn't know why I can't. He wants to *help* me by reading my script to me as I type it on his horrid, bucking wee portable: such help would drive me out of my mind. But the collaboration is working well and I think the final script will be a great improvement on what you have seen. Of course Tony knows how he can make it work on the stage, which is a huge advantage.

Will let you know my London address as soon as I have a confirmation from the hotel. I too find this parting long, and look forward eagerly to getting back—though not back to work. This has been fun, but very taxing. I hope London may be a few days of holiday—but one never knows. Will write again soon but must get on the treadmill now.

Hugs and kisses to all, and special intimate sorts to you, my dearest,

Rob

SUNDAY, JULY 26: After tea began reading my *Leaven of Malice* play, but Mrs. Tyner came and the Guthries had forgotten they had asked her, which was a little awkward. But she stayed for supper and Tony and I finished reading the play. It went very well, and Scaife

was most complimentary about it. Judy coughed maddeningly: curious how unsympathetic one can be toward such an obvious affliction, but she roars on and on at odds with one's efforts to amuse. Discussion afterward, much of it valuable, and particularly grateful for Scaife's sympathetic criticism.

MONDAY, JULY 27: Work on reshaping the first part of the play. The work goes surprisingly easily. In the afternoon with Judy to Newbliss, taking Old Becky, Tony's partly paralysed nurse, who lives with her daughters in an outlying wing of this odd rookery. God knows how many hangers-on there are. Before dinner James Forsyth,[33] the playwright, arrives with his young son Richard. Judy very strange: tonight in reply to some very simple question I asked her (why she held some opinion, or something) she replied, "Because I'm high-born, and not common and vulgar and sex-obsessed like you"—and then kissed me. Whether this is her notion of pleasantry, or a real belief, I don't know, probably both, but sometimes I am uncomfortably conscious that Judy could topple over into madness very easily: sometimes she looks very oddly, and I have always thought it fatigue. This attitude is not to me alone: Scaife is "a dirty Levantine." At lunch both Guthries carried on with childish spleen about the vulgarity of American pronunciations—yet Tony pronounces "minute" as "minyit"—which is bog-Irish.

TUESDAY, JULY 28, LETTER TO BRENDA
Dearest Pinkie:

As you requested I am trying to get some Irish linen napkins to replace our threadbare fishnets at 361 Park. Like a fool I asked Judy to tell me of a good shop. At once the Guthrie parsimony was

33 Forsyth later wrote Guthrie's biography: *Tyrone Guthrie* (1976).

evoked: I mustn't *dream* of it, for they would cost the *earth*! (In actual fact they would cost 75 shillings a dozen for the best quality, 22 inches square, which I do not call a lot.) But no, she will get a friend of hers to ask a friend of *hers* to get me seconds at the factory for *next to nothing.* I cannot make it clear without being nasty that I do not want fucking *seconds*—I want the *best* and am ready to pay the shop price. The upshot will probably be that I shall get them in London and have them sent, and when the duty is paid they will cost plenty but we'll *have* them and they'll be *good* and last forever.

Today, Tuesday, I went to Dublin where I hadn't expected to get, with Tony, Joe Hone, and Christopher Scaife. Lovely drive and Dublin is a charming city, but smaller than I had foreseen. The Liffey is a dirty creek. Tony went off on business and Joe took Christopher and me to Trinity College Library, a superb building, where we saw the Book of Kells, one of the greatest of all illuminated manuscripts—a thrill. Then we went to the National Gallery, which was not very good—too many pictures of not very famous Irishmen by nobodies. Then to a very good bookshop. Then to a famous bar, immortalized in *Ulysses*—Davy Byrnes—a dump. Then I took the lot to a very good restaurant for lunch and crammed them, and tanked them up with Canadian whiskey, and washed them all over in wine, while they exclaimed at my princely extravagance. Total bill £4, 15s, which I do not call a lot for a first-rate lunch and wizard booze-up for four!

We dropped Joe, and rushed Christopher to the airport; then Tony and I drove home and he talked casting for my play. He thinks a Canadian cast, with a few of name, would have class. Tony will be in New York in late September and thinks we ought to see the Theatre Guild together. Could we drive down then? or go by 'plane? You *must* come; can't do any more on this play without you. It is practically done now, and much changed for the better: as you will see, Mrs. Bridgetower is in as a principal character and a good one.

Tony has made me see it as a *play* and formerly I could not get rid of the idea of the novel. But what hard work it has been: I have really toiled, and I look forward eagerly to London for a rest and change.

Good night, my dearest: in two weeks exactly I shall be home. Huge hugs and kisses

Rob

WEDNESDAY, JULY 29: Worked all morning and most of the afternoon with Tony on the play, cutting, tidying, and I hope improving. He wants one more sequence, a series of dreams which I suggested, and I must do it tomorrow. In the morning there arrived Dr. and Mrs. Steele and their young sons Jonathan and Charles, who the Guthries thought were not coming until tomorrow. Steele is a dull, slow fellow, an anesthetist, given to ponderous, nit-witted generalization. They are friends of Bunty and the boys are her godsons; the wife, Meriel, is the more intelligent but a worthy dullard. A wasp has stung Steele in the groin and he is in some pain, and vulgar shame at the location of his wound. Their boys are beautiful, and one wonders if they will become grey and spiritless like Dad and Mum. English children are amazing: "non Anglos sed Angles,"[34] but they say something dim whenever they open their lips. Later, Dr. Steele, a keen gardener, confesses that the secret of his success with dahlias and tomatoes is that he brings home from the hospital an occasional bucket of placentas, which he thriftily retrieves from the delivery rooms and which make, he says, a plant food unrivalled. All this told without a speck of astonishment at himself, or a crumb of humour, or even the suggestion that a placenta-fed tomato is a mite anthropophagous for the queasy.

When the others have gone to bed, Forsyth and I sit up with Tony

34 *Non angli sed angeli* ("Not Angles, but angels"), attributed to the sixth-century pope Gregory the Great.

and talk about morality, art, and poetry, arising from the fact that Tony has accepted £125 payable to a charity to endorse Albany cigarettes: Forsyth and I say this is immoral and he makes a wildly erratic defence. I question the breeding of such an action and ask him why he makes such a fetish of it. He makes a good joke of it, but I do not believe anyone becomes so exacerbated about something which is no more than a joke to them. Speaking of Scaife yesterday, Tony made as near an admission of his homosexuality as I have heard. Said he admired Christopher because "he had made life serve him," had gone east where he could live as he pleased. Tony, I fear, does *not* live as he pleases.

THURSDAY, JULY 30: At breakfast Tony hears from his publisher, McGraw-Hill, that his first sixty galleys have not arrived and to hasten with his spare copies thereof. Reason: Joe Hone posted them in the old envelope in which they came and seeing "Return postage guaranteed" on the label, popped them in without stamps. He and Tony crowed about this as £1 saved in postage. But of course it went to the dead letter office. So we had to set to work at 9:30 and with a lunch interval slaved till 7, getting the work done all over again! I insisted Tony pay some tribute to Fagan[35] and he said, "Oh, you do it!"—so I did. He owed much to Fagan. I was glad to be of help, but thought it the wages of penny-pinching. About 6:30 a transatlantic call and I feared some calamity: but it was Brenda calling to be cheerful. I was inhibited by having to shout, and troops of people rushing about and obviously listening, so could not say much. But a great thrill and comfort to hear her.[36] Tonight

35 James Bernard Fagan, Irish-born actor, producer and playwright, and mentor of Guthrie.
36 Davies was not good on the telephone at any time and was worse if he was surprised. It would take a little time to get him ready to have a reasonable conversation, and if it was with one of his children, he would often pass the telephone to Brenda and hear the news from her.

pack to leave Annagh-ma-Kerrig and not sorry, for while I have enjoyed it here I have worked very hard, and look forward to some pleasure in London, and a few days when I am not either working on the play, or put to weeding or berry-picking.

FRIDAY, JULY 31: Up at 4:30, breakfast in kitchen (the one warm and dry place in the house), and away to Belfast in Dr. Steele's big Citröen, a nice car, but he is an enthusiast, so Tony and Judy took against it: it has front-wheel drive and goes round curves very fast.

Fly to London at 8:30. Tony and I share a taxi to Drury Lane, then I to the Norfolk Hotel, Surrey Street, which proves quite different from what I expected, and remembered that the one I had in mind was the Howard, in Norfolk Street. My room is a dingy kennel. Depressed, and reflect that I have twelve days of this room, this hotel, and loneliness before me, because I have come to London a few days before I expected.[37] Have lunch at the Café Royal, and rejoice in mixed grill, a banana and a pear, and a half carafe of a good red wine and real coffee: best food in three weeks! Then buy some theatre tickets and to Mr. Franklin's,[38] which is lucky for he closes today for a fortnight. Looked at a lot of things and dawdled over an Elizabethan pendant, a relief portrait of Elizabeth Regina in gold knot, and several dingy, old-cut diamonds. But it was curious rather than beautiful. At last bought a pair of seventeenth-century Spanish earrings, gold and enamel, and a silver gilt box, 1800, of curious interest and beautifully made. Tramped till I was footsore and dined at the Norfolk, bad. Then to the Wyndham and saw *The Hostage* by Brendan Behan, much praised but to me a mish-mash of jokes, songs, and Irish

37 Davies would rarely change an arrangement once it was made, nor would he complain about bad service. It was unusual that he changed his flight to Canada, and it showed how much he wanted to get home.
38 Dealer in antique jewellery, which Brenda collected.

whimpering and growling about the Troubles. And this charade is hailed as a masterpiece!

FRIDAY, JULY 31, LETTER TO BRENDA

Norfolk Hotel: Surrey St.
London W.C.2.

Dearest Pinkie:

Hope my cable about the phone call got to you in good time and was reassuring. I know I sounded idiotic on the phone, but I could hardly hear you, and a horde of people were milling about, excited by a call from Canada, and I could not say anything but grumpy nonsense. But I was thrilled to bits to hear your voice, and thank you for calling.

I am at the Norfolk, which is a mistake because I thought it was the Howard. It is smaller and dumpier, but what the hell, Archy,[39] it is very *clean*. Will write again soon, so great big hugs and lewd massagings. I count the hours till we are together again—
Rob

SATURDAY, AUGUST 1, LONDON: Changed my flight from Aug 11 to Aug 8, which gives me a week in London, which is all I want alone; family life and travel with Brenda has ruined me for lonely pleasures; I want people with me—the right people. After a dreadful lunch to the Coliseum and saw the Sadler's Wells people do Lehar's *Land of Smiles*: very poor house in that vast, ugly place. The operetta, written in 1929, is in the style of 1910 and they had taken it seriously—realistic scenery, follow-spots for the leads and all.

39 From Archy and Mehitabel, by Don Marquis, a newspaper column beginning in 1916.

Theme: renunciation, this time a Chinese nobleman giving up his Viennese bride because of East being East and West, West. (Specifically, she minded him having four other wives.) Full of ambassadors, heel-clicking, Oriental splendour, and loud, tuneful music. Sat among old ladies, who adored it. "She's goin' back to England, dear," screamed one to a deaf beldam, though the heroine had just said she was going back to Austria. This is identification indeed: the heroine had golden hair and was In the Right: ergo, she was English.

To make up for my terrible lunch dined at the Café Royal and then to the Royal Court to Noël Coward's *Look after Lulu*, adapted from Feydeau. Not good Coward. Of Lulu when she is in bed with her lover in the next room: "Afraid she can't see you; she's on the telephone." Comic Old Man: "Ah, I hope she's making a good connection." The kind of thing Tony tried in *Haste to the Wedding*, better done. Vivien Leigh is very beautiful and very funny; Tony Quayle funny, but falls on his behind rather too often; Max Adrian not quite up to scratch, in a rather bad part. But one rarely sees a good dirty farce.

SUNDAY, AUGUST 2, LONDON: To Matins at Southwark Cathedral and took Communion; very high, but not fancy-dress. Quite good sermon by the precentor about the Transfiguration. Then looked at the cathedral, which is handsome, but essentially a fake. It claims acquaintance with St. Swithin, St. Olav, Chaucer, Gower, Shakespeare, Jonson, Fletcher, Massinger, Goldsmith, Bunyan, etc. but the nave dates from 1890 and most of these are "associations": i.e., they *believe* these men worshipped here. There is a bad Shakespeare window and below it a big stone Shakespeare looking as if he had been knocked down by a 'bus. But it is a fine church, even if it makes worldly claims that ill become it. Gave 5 shillings; should have been £5; it is a poet's church.

Tea at Royal Festival Hall, nasty; then to a Russian film of Tchaikovsky's *Eugene Onegin*, very well done, with actors acting and singers singing, as in *Tosca*. But I do not like it so well as on the stage; filmed opera is so restless; the camera must be bobbing about and the pace established by the music is disturbed. It set my own works going, and on return to the Nasty Norfolk wrote the whole dream sequence of the play at a sitting.

SUNDAY, AUGUST 2, LETTER TO BRENDA

Dearest Pink:

I have lopped three days off my intended stay here as I am not keen to spend two weekends in London and anyhow I want to get home. The play needs quite a bit of tinkering before it can be typed and I can't do it here—too much to see and do. Also, I want to get back to you, as I miss you all the time, at plays, and sights and meals and in bed and everywhere. The fun of everything is cut in two. Only a week and we shall be together! I can hardly wait. My love to Jenny and the others when you write (I send them postcards) and huge hugs and kisses to you my darling from

Rob

MONDAY, AUGUST 3, LONDON: Worked from 10 till 1:15 revising my dream sequence and copying it to send to Tony. I like it and if he does not I shall be disappointed, but what is probable is that he will want some changes. Lunched at Café Royal (mixed grill and a pear washed down with lager, and a Martini of a type unknown to me), then to National Gallery, which was very crowded and smelly; took time and looked only at my favourites—Veronese *Darius and Alexander*, some Titians, some Dutch, and my never-failing delight, the Bronzino *Allegory* of Venus, Cupid, Folly and Time,[40] which I

40 The painting is referred to in *What's Bred in the Bone* (1985).

examined at leisure and in detail; had not before noticed that Venus has her tongue thrust into Cupid's mouth, or that the Sphinx is so oddly drawn. Then to St. Martin's for rest and quiet for half hour and to the Mermaid Theatre, which is behind the dilapidated rookery which houses the mighty *Times*. The Mermaid is an attractive theatre, but *Lock Up Your Daughters* was not good. Those who have compared it to *The Beggar's Opera* at the Lyric in the 'twenties are claiming too much. There are good performances by Harry Locke as Justice Squeezum and Stephanie Voss as Hilaret, but the rest were coarse and loutish and it often sank to college dramatics. The open stage is good but they do not use it well: one does not want to see the electrician and the red-legged stage manager at their necessary but undramatic tasks. This jolly amateurism extends everywhere: the ushers are enthusiastic girls, the bar has no ice and no gin, the shop which sells records has no wrapping-paper. And as for the play, these indecencies must be done with style, not raucous romping. Had dinner at Maxim's and as it was still only 9 walked Regent Street and saw condoms in a window as "The Working Man's Friend, extra strong English make."

TUESDAY, AUGUST 4, LETTER TO BRENDA
Dearest Pink:

No use writing anymore after this, as I shall be home on Saturday and the letter would follow me. Certainly I shall be glad to be back: London is wonderful, but not alone. Curious the feeling you mention in your letter that I might be so taken with the joys of solitude that I would not come home: nothing could be less likely. I am a domestic creature, quite apart from love for you, and the children. I quite like travel, but don't really know how to do it. I can't *joy* in travel when my heart is elsewhere. And my heart is where you are. In future we must avoid these partings whenever we can—it may not always be possible but we must try. But as you say, your

childhood did not dispose you to think of husbands as home-loving creatures. Maybe home wasn't as happy for them as mine is for me.

Got a handsome present for WRD—a pair of William IV wine coolers, designed like our salts, beautiful melon bottoms, and a nice simplicity. Wish they were for us? Should we bag them and give him something else? They would look marvellous on our sideboard and just the thing for flowers. What do you say? Got them in the Silver Vaults: what awful trash most of the stuff down there is! Victorian junk. But these have the real look. I'll ponder the matter, but we've liked those salts so much that I know we would like these too. And they would be a nice reminder of my journey—I MUST stop selling myself those coolers! When I began to write to you there was no such notion in my head—honest!

How would it be if, when I get home, I get the play all corrected and ready for Miss Whalon, and then read it to you and Jenny? It will take a few days, but not too long. I like it very much in its present form.

Great hugs and kisses and I shall be watching out at Malton:[41] if I'm long in Customs don't worry—no exemption and I'll have to declare one or two things.

Rob

WEDNESDAY, AUGUST 5, LONDON: Woke at 6 and could not sleep again, which was a nuisance: have slept badly the whole of this trip. To Kensington Church Street to look for silver but the shops there have gone down, and except for two or three good antique furniture places they deal in trash jewellery or wretched china figurines. Did see an original Augustus John drawing—Dorelia in her usual dress and turban—at £70. But would WRD think it was anything? No. Nor was it a particularly interesting example of his work. At last

41 Now called Toronto Pearson International Airport.

found, in Victor Crichton's in the High Street, a pretty pair of Sheffield sauce-boats—little charmers—and bought them. Shall ask Brenda to choose which of the possibilities we shall keep for ourselves. Then to Zwemmers, and bought two Ardizzone lithographs. Lunched at the Café Royal, then to Alec Clunes's shop[42] in Cecil Court and chatted with George Hart, but must return. To a French film, *Mon Oncle*, in which Jacques Tati is very funny. At 8 to the Cambridge Theatre in Seven Dials and saw Lonsdale's *Let Them Eat Cake*, vintage of 1913: a trivial piece, but very well made in a manner no longer fashionable, but not without value. Michael Denison and his wife, Dulcie Gray, played the leads: Michael is not a good actor, but he is handsome and has great charm. But he seems to have learned nothing since he played Orlando for the Oxford University Dramatic Society. Miss Gray is better but shows the distressing leading lady's tendency to laugh archly, and play tricks. Got some dinner at Maxim's. Was hailed in the street by some woman who knew who I was: English, not Canadian; also stopped by an intensely embarrassed youth who thought I was Edward Hyams.[43]

THURSDAY, AUGUST 6, LONDON: One of the oddities of the London streets is the beatniks—dirty boys in jeans, with Elvis hair arrangements, accompanied by girls with long unbound hair, loose bags, and bare feet, which they defiantly plant in the dog-dung, puke, effluent from the fish-shop, or whatever. They strive for Bohemianism but look simple and their mouths tend to hang open.

To a matinée, as I thought it would be nice to sit down: *Roots* by Arnold Wesker with Joan Plowright as star. Good play well acted; good theme, and three or four good parts. Glad I went. Then to

42 Rare-book shop dealing in theatre material.
43 Prominent English writer; unlike Davies, left-wing, pacifist, and a keen gardener.

Clunes's and saw and bought a rarity—a run of fourteen consecutive Edmund Kean playbills, of the performances preceding his visit to America in 1820: all his famous roles—Richard III, Shylock, Othello—and some rarities—Jaffeir from *Venice Preserv'd* and Richard II. Very pleased to get them and as I took all, Hart gave me 10% off, making it £23 for the lot. Have now some very nice Kean things.

To *The Complaisant Lover* by Graham Greene, which is the mighty thing talked of in theatre circles. Good, but weak conclusion. Sir Ralph Richardson is a bag of tricks but in this as in *Flowering Cherry* he managed two or three fine moments: wept so that tears fell diamond-like to the floorcloth. But a gloomy piece: love *cannot* last, marriage *must* be dull, men *are* fools and women sneaks. Wonder how it will go in the U.S., for the most-used joke is the English snob one that there is something inescapably common and funny about being a dentist. Americans do not feel this: the dream of every third Jew is to get out of old iron and into old ivory.

FRIDAY, AUGUST 7, LONDON: The great news is that the Queen is pregnant, thus explaining her fatigue in Canada—that, and the continued meetings with John Diefenbaker. This leads to strange messages on the paper stands: "The Queen: A Baby Official" is the one I liked best.

A hot night and the Criterion, where I went to see *A Taste of Honey*, was stuffy and the audience sweaty. The play was formless and had nothing much to say except perhaps that frowsy living and frowsy thinking sometimes gets you into messes, and that it is better to be loved than not. But it had dramatic impact, began in high gear and kept it up until, suddenly and arbitrarily, it ended on a note of false pathos.

Over too early to go to bed, so I walked down Regent Street and Cumberland Steps, thence to Trafalgar Square and admired the

dramatic lighting of Nelson. But if I had my way I would light Charles I, certainly one of the finest statues in London. Thence back to that ill-run, understaffed dump, the Norfolk, and after fifteen minutes' diplomatic negotiation for a lager got a lukewarm Double Diamond, English beer at its most insipid. Shall be glad to be quit of the Norfolk.

SATURDAY, AUGUST 8, LONDON: Wake very early, which has been my plague all through this trip, and in due time get away from the Norfolk with a light heart. To the terminus in Buckingham Palace Road: a long wait; then a 'bus ride to the London airport; another long wait, for the caterer had not arrived to provision the 'plane. At 1 p.m. away by jet; from then for nine and a half hours it was whizz, fizz, and rumble, with a procession of people plying me with sweets, Madeira and biscuits, gin and tonic, champagne, tea, coffee, and anything else that could be forced down the human gullet. A brief stop at Gander. Then to New York, where the car compass in my briefcase set off an electric eye, and alarmed Customs. Lurked in the chapel till flight time (for the quiet), then to Toronto.

SUNDAY, AUGUST 9: Unpack. H.t.d. in p.m. Immense satisfaction to be home again.

MONDAY, AUGUST 10: Return to office and find plenty of work. Am tired and cannot do anything on play. Sleep after lunch and dinner. Evening to *Escapade* by Roger MacDougall, badly done by the Peterborough Summer Theatre company—a strange contrast to last week's play-going in London. Peterborough the same old dump, but weather and countryside lovely.

FRIDAY, AUGUST 14: Much better: I sleep well and am regaining my energy. Work all afternoon on the play to good purpose and have

one or two good notions. In the evening slept again, read Peter De Vries, and talked to Brenda about Dr. Harding, whom she reads with mounting delight. Admirable h.t.d. in the window seat.

THURSDAY, AUGUST 27: To Toronto on 7 a.m. train: very hot and crowded. Stratford planning committee meeting in Maclean-Hunter board room at 12, mercifully air-conditioned. It goes on till 4, then to University Club and meet Miranda. On the train home she tells of her splendid summer at music camp. Glad to get home and take off clothes.

FRIDAY, AUGUST 28: My birthday. I am forty-six: Miranda gives me a record of Australian songs, Jenny a jar of honey, Rosamond a knee-robe, and Brenda a very handsome set of evening studs. Work hard and am troubled by sinus and nausea. Even wondered about polio, which rather darkened my day.

WEDNESDAY, SEPTEMBER 2: In the evening I had an anguished call from Don Herbert in New York: Tony Guthrie's agent has withdrawn him from the play and the Guild won't have my play without him.[44] I'm sure this is just agent's power politics but worrisome and the part of this thing I really hate, and of course I shall get no sense out of Tony if it were to cost him a cable.

THURSDAY, SEPTEMBER 3: Low and despairing all day: I have no energy and my hopes seem to be crumbling beneath me; nevertheless work, work, work, the joyless industry of the damned: write *Star* column about Irving Layton. In the evening review *Edith Sitwell's Anthology*.

44 This problem was quickly resolved.

FRIDAY, SEPTEMBER 4: In the evening, a special dinner for my birthday. The great news is that Miranda has been accepted for Trinity College at the University of Toronto, so much talk of clothes, of which she has no notion, to Brenda's despair. Read poetry: much moved by Walter de la Mare.

THURSDAY, SEPTEMBER 10, STRATFORD: Board meeting 9:30 till 12:30, then to the Country Club for lunch for the governor general, Vincent Massey. We gave him a costume sketch and orb from *Richard III*. Then to the costume and book exhibition. We dine at the Victorian Inn and then to *As You Like It*, somewhat disordered since the first performance in June. Afterward to a party given by actors, very jolly: talk to Douglas Rain and Irene Worth. Bed at 3.

FRIDAY, SEPTEMBER 11, STRATFORD: Unwell at waking: hangover? Only three whiskies last night. Took sinus pill and hot bath and felt very much worse. Don Herbert phones from New York and calls my play "a true high comedy": very heartening. Dine at the Bells'. We see *Othello* but it is now much diminished though Rain has improved. This should not happen. Excellent h.t.d.

SATURDAY, SEPTEMBER 12: To Toronto: meet Jenny at the Royal York, where we have a suite, and Rosamond comes in from Peterborough on the Dayliner. To film *North by Northwest*, Hitchcock thriller, very good. Early to bed at hotel.

SUNDAY, SEPTEMBER 13, TORONTO: Maygames on waking. Breakfast in our suite, to Rosamond's great satisfaction. Matins and Eucharist at St. Mary Magdalene, very fine. Then rest and to Hawthorn Gardens for WRD's eightieth birthday: Percy, Mary,

Arthur, Kit,[45] and all grandchildren. Welsh boasting, weeping, and singing, and a lot of champagne. Strange to think of WRD as eighty. He is hale and vigorous mentally, though garrulous, but then he always was so. Interesting to observe grandchildren, family resemblances, though all very different and on the whole a good lot.

MONDAY, SEPTEMBER 14: Bad day at office: men resign, men drunk, Wilson Craw[46] sorely tried. Spend much time trying to resolve chaos. Shrimpton going—he finds Peterborough dull! God, and what do I find it after eighteen years? Evening, read and work on Knopfbook. Rosamond has cold and Brenda is unwell. Mrs. Pedak has lumbago.

SUNDAY, SEPTEMBER 27: A week of worry about the final chapter of Knopfbook, which obsesses me. It is as though I had never written a line before. I'm scared to death of it: am I really a writer, or simply an impostor, a hack with a writing neurosis?

FRIDAY, OCTOBER 2: The continued work on the book is wearing me down and today I got into a rage about the usual street jeers which greet me from the anthropoid youth of this squalid town.

FRIDAY, OCTOBER 23: Gordon Roper[47] called to sound me out about being a guest professor at Trinity next year, to do a course or two and talk to students: should like it immensely and it would get me among new people.

45 Percy Davies, Rupert's brother; Mary Bonyun, Rupert's sister; Arthur, Rupert's second son; Kit, the widow of Rupert's son Fred.
46 Managing editor of the *Examiner*.
47 A close friend Davies met in Peterborough during the Second World War; by this time a professor of English at Trinity College, University of Toronto.

SATURDAY, OCTOBER 24: *Star* column in morning on old music; *Star* column in the afternoon on witchcraft; Brenda in Cobourg rehearsing.[48]

SUNDAY, OCTOBER 25: Lay late. In the afternoon work with Brenda to clean tool-house at the end of the garage thoroughly, a dirty job but satisfactory when done. This has been a refreshing week but has also served to emphasize how weary and empty I am. When all this is done, I must refill my well of inspiration, read and think. Don Herbert's production of Robert Bolt's *Flowering Cherry* seems to have done well in New York.

MONDAY, OCTOBER 26: No: *Flowering Cherry* came off Saturday night: how chilling! But I thought it poor in London. I hope failure of *Flowering Cherry* does not put Herbert in a nervous and carping mood. Brenda in Cobourg for rehearsals and returns tired and pale.

TUESDAY, OCTOBER 27: Uneasy day: fidgeted and fussed with revisions of Knopfbook but made no progress—wrote a page and tore it up. My bowels are a basket of eels, I cannot hear what people say to me, I eat to quell my mounting dismay and sense of failure, yet beneath all this I am calm and resolute: the work will be done.

SUNDAY, NOVEMBER 1: Completion of the book leaves me very nervous and disorganized but this will pass. Wish I had it all to rewrite, however. I'm sure I could do it better: it seems formless to me, but not to Brenda.

TUESDAY, NOVEMBER 3: My disintegration proceeds apace. Wrangle on the phone with a man who says his daughter was nearly raped.

48 Directing and playing in *Arms and the Man,* by G.B. Shaw.

Have begun Proust and do not know how far I shall go, but am more engrossed than when I tried in 1938.

WEDNESDAY, NOVEMBER 4: Collapse in full tide: muddled through the day and did quite a bit of work. In evening read Proust and tend to find him a brilliant bore: so good, but who gives a damn? Brenda returns from Cobourg shredded by the ineptitude of her cast. These are dull days in our sordid home.

FRIDAY, NOVEMBER 6: To Toronto and chat with Gordon Roper and Provost Owen of Trinity College. It is now settled that I shall be visiting professor in 1960–61: am well pleased. Lunch at Trinity very bad.

MONDAY, NOVEMBER 9: Don Herbert phones and weeps about the terms my agent Willis Wing is asking. I sympathized but won't interfere. He also said Tony Guthrie plans to rehearse the *Leaven of Malice* play in Stratford next August, which is good news. In the evening to Cobourg with Brenda to her rehearsal of *Arms and the Man*—a very amateur group with no concentration and she has done well for them, but a silk purse–sow's ear impasse.

TUESDAY, NOVEMBER 10: Am beginning to come out of exhaustion: worked on Knopfbook revision; can never master the grammatical nicety of "that" and "which." H.t.d. in sunroom, best in many months.

FRIDAY, NOVEMBER 13: Ralph Hancox unwell, so write lead editorial for Saturday paper. Letter from Honderich[49] via Willis Wing saying he likes my *Star* columns. After lunch h.t.d., unforeseen and delightful. See Vincent Massey on TV and he speaks of me!

49 Beland Honderich, editor-in-chief of the *Toronto Star*.

SATURDAY, NOVEMBER 14: Lunch with Jenny and her friends: odd girls, boy-crazy and firmly resistant to any sort of education. Revised end of the final chapter. In the evening chatted with Brenda and read. Unforeseen h.t.d. at bedtime.

SUNDAY, NOVEMBER 15: In the morning read Proust, and Brenda cut my hair. Afternoon to Bryn and was annoyed by boys prowling with a gun: to shoot water birds?

Release from pressure of book has released my sexual powers from an icy grip: Brenda says it is always so. Called Judy Guthrie in New York on Saturday evening. Of course Tony has forgotten we were to meet in Toronto and is off to San Francisco; he has eye trouble (retina).

WEDNESDAY, NOVEMBER 25: Very busy day and Miss Whalon almost completes Knopf book manuscript. To bed early and just in process of h.t.d. when Judy calls, proposes to change our Toronto appointment with them to Friday: we decide we cannot do so and call her back. After all this business h.t.d. resumed with added gusto and quite wonderful.

SATURDAY, NOVEMBER 28: To the high school at 6:30 for the drama competition performance of Brenda's Cobourg theatre group's *Arms and the Man*. They win the cup—all delighted: besides directing, Brenda was very good as Catherine. About thirty-five people in after for food and beer. Bed 1:30.

SUNDAY, NOVEMBER 29: Go over my manuscript: Miss Whalon has made 5 errors in 427 pages! H.t.d. in p.m. Evening to Thompsons': other guests drank too much, cocktails, champagne, Irish coffee, and beer; long, good talk, bed 1:30.

Busy week and tiring but our New York holiday approaches. We

have both had considerable success of late but bought with hard work, and some sort of break is very desirable.

WEDNESDAY, DECEMBER 2: Fly at 3:20 to New York and at Dorset Hotel by 6; dine at Le Gourmet on 55th, then buy some theatre tickets. Brenda has a cold and is frail but hope holiday will help.

THURSDAY, DECEMBER 3, NEW YORK: To Lulie Westfeldt at 9:30: we have made progress. Lunch with Willis Wing at Camillo's, having given him the Knopfbook manuscript. I sign the Theatre Guild contract. We shop for the girls' Christmas presents, rest, dine, and to Shaw's *Heartbreak House*, brilliant but never moving. H.t.d. with delight: both free and off the chain after our autumn's work.

FRIDAY, DECEMBER 4, NEW YORK: Lesson at 9:30 with fine result; dine at Luchow's; to Ingmar Bergman's film *The Magician*, finely acted with powerful, Jungian plot: see it through twice and much excited by it. It had what *Heartbreak House* so notably lacked—poetry.

SATURDAY, DECEMBER 5, NEW YORK: Excellent lesson. Afternoon h.t.d. most eloquently. To *Wild Strawberries*, as good as on July 8, and enjoyed it and doubly admired Ingmar Bergman. We shop in the Village for clothes for girls very successfully. In the evening to *Lysistrata* at the Phoenix, good but rather loud.

SUNDAY, DECEMBER 6, NEW YORK: Lay late, then by train to White Plains to lunch with Alfred and Blanche[50] Knopf. Alfred and Blanche quarrelled sans intermission and it was a heavy and somewhat embarrassing occasion. Back to New York with Blanche in full

50 Alfred Knopf's wife, Blanche, was a co-founder of Alfred A. Knopf Inc. and a
 prominent editor.

cry at 4:50 and were quit of her by 6. To Eisenstein's *Ivan the Terrible, Part 2*. Crude but very powerful. A strange and revelatory day. Why revelatory? As showing the hellish home life of a very successful and able man; as showing our own compatibility in contrast; as showing how dark life can be where there is no love. We have seen the movies at their most subtle and also at their most powerful in three days.

MONDAY, DECEMBER 7, NEW YORK: Good lesson, then shop and buy a purse, $90, and a watch, $140, for Brenda and get things for girls. Evening dinner at Jackie Davie's: altogether charming.

TUESDAY, DECEMBER 8, NEW YORK: Remarkable lesson with Lulie Westfeldt, then shop, lunch, and shop again. To *La Plume de Ma Tante*, very good fun in the French manner, somewhat too much pee-fun and peeping up girls' skirts but very clever panto. We both feel great changes as result of Alexander Technique and we are both delighted.

WEDNESDAY, DECEMBER 9, NEW YORK: Another good lesson, then to Knopf's and see Lemay, the publicity man, and Alfred Knopf, who thinks the theatre section of the book is too long but says I am the only man in North America who could have written this book! To matinée of Chayefsky's *Tenth Man*, finely acted, and directed by Tony; Chinese dinner and then to *At the Drop of a Hat*, with Flanders and Swann. Brilliant.

THURSDAY, DECEMBER 10, NEW YORK: Very fine h.t.d. on waking: the Alexander changes the pattern here, too. Pack and to Lulie Westfeldt for final lesson, then we take her to lunch. Much bustle and frustration to get to air terminal, but a good flight to Toronto, then on home and find the house decorated for Christmas by Rosamond, and much mail.

WEDNESDAY, DECEMBER 16: Again very busy, a horde of details plague me. In the evening address Xmas cards. I dream I am deserting a derelict old taxi-driver for much better one: an old pattern rejected for new?

THURSDAY, DECEMBER 17: Pressure continues: Brenda to Toronto, returns with Miranda and Jenny, both very lively and both now sing very nicely and we have carols, but Rosamond has a streaming cold.

FRIDAY, DECEMBER 18: No let-up in work. Finish Christmas cards. Hear that Massey Foundation gives $1,500,000 to found a graduate school at University of Toronto. Would do something like that if rich. Nice letter from Alfred Knopf.

SUNDAY, DECEMBER 27: Have enjoyed past week, though humiliated to learn from Knopf's editor Strauss that I have misused the word "comprise" for forty-six years: just when I begin to think well of myself, some new abyss of ignorance opens at my feet.

THURSDAY, DECEMBER 31: Worked in the morning, and in the afternoon at Brenda's insistence went tobogganing in Jackson Park, which was toilsome as the snow heavy. Brenda is unwell with intestinal 'flu and could not go so I was goat.

H.t.d. 79 times in '59, being absent one month.

This has been a year of hard and unremitting work for me, and I enter the New Year depleted and exhausted. The Knopf book, now called *A Voice from the Attic*, was demanding, though a kind of agonizing pleasure went with it. Alfred likes it. Wrote the dramatization of *Leaven of Malice*, took it to Ireland, and revised it with Tony. This was pleasant, but not easy. And I wrote fifty-two columns for the *Star*—"A Writer's Diary"—which are syndicated and have had

favourable reception. A year of slogging hard work. Kind friends assure me that getting a play on in New York will be a desperate experience, but I refuse to be panicked: Tony says we shall resist nonsense together, and I believe him. But this may be a fateful year, with the book and the play. May it be propitious! If I am ever to make a name it must be soon. The *Examiner* goes well, in spite of staff difficulties, and makes money, so we live comfortably.

In the home all is well. Brenda has established herself as a professional director of plays, and does well, not merely getting a show on but helping the actors to find something of themselves and to act *truly*, so far as in them lies. Miranda is an undergraduate at Trinity. Jenny is at BSS and finds school work hard going. Rosamond will go to BSS in September.

My resolve for 1960 and the future is to be more true to myself, more insistent on my critical standards, less compliant and yielding toward what I think unworthy. The day for *encouraging* anything and everything in Canada has gone and the younger men know it: I must not fall behind them. I am now on the committee for the Governor General's Awards, and must try to promote high standards, and this cannot be done without hurting some feelings. The other members, D.V. LePan[51] and Northrop Frye,[52] are good company. And in the autumn I go to Trinity as a visiting professor, a welcome taste of academic life. Otherwise, the notable event of the year was the Dominion Day dinner at Government House with Her Majesty the Queen and Prince Philip, a taste of high life which greatly appealed to us both. Had the satisfaction of making the Queen laugh with a mild joke about the modest rewards of literature in Canada. She is beautiful, but when she laughs she is also delightful.

51 Douglas LePan, diplomat, poet, novelist, and professor of literature, University College, University of Toronto. He and Davies met on their way to Oxford in 1935.
52 Canadian literary critic and literary theorist, Victoria College, University of Toronto.

1960

—

THROUGH 1960 ROB AND BRENDA were spending more time in Toronto, particularly in the autumn, as Rob started lecturing at Trinity College, University of Toronto, and rehearsals began for the *Leaven of Malice* play, which eventually came to be titled *Love and Libel*. They often saw and sometimes stayed with their closest Toronto friends, Clair and Amy Stewart and George and Norah Harris. Rob had become friends with Clair Stewart in 1941, while both were working at *Saturday Night*, and Clair was now one of Canada's most distinguished graphic designers; Amy was a daughter of J.S. McLean, the president of Canada Packers and a well-known art collector. George Harris was a member of a long-established and sporadically wealthy London, Ontario, family; Norah was the daughter of John M. Lyle, a leading Canadian architect whose buildings included the Royal Alexandra Theatre in Toronto. Both couples were dedicated patrons of the arts, particularly supporting the Stratford Shakespearean Festival and the Crest Theatre in Toronto. Two other friends Rob and Brenda often saw were Herbert Whittaker and Helen Ignatieff.

Whittaker was the long-time theatre critic for the *Globe and Mail*; Helen Ignatieff, his frequent social companion, was a curator at the Royal Ontario Museum; she was the widow of Nicholas Ignatieff, who had been warden of Hart House at the University of Toronto. His brother George was a prominent Canadian diplomat and the father of Michael, later an author and politician.

Another close friend was the artist Grant Macdonald, whom Rob had met on an Atlantic crossing in 1935. A great lover of the theatre, Macdonald was a portraitist of London and New York actors in his early career, and he was commissioned to do a series of portraits of actors in the first seasons of the Stratford festival. He illustrated two of the three books Davies co-wrote about the festival and made several portraits of Brenda and Rob. By 1960 he was living in Kingston, teaching at Queen's University.

During 1960 Davies continued running the *Peterborough Examiner* and writing his weekly column for the *Toronto Star*. He maintained his personal and "big" diaries, and in March he began a separate diary focusing on the production of his *Leaven of Malice* play. Selections here are drawn from all these.

SUNDAY, JANUARY 3: Lay late; entered my "big diary" for 1959 and did tidying for our party. At 6:30 the Thompsons, Curriers, Mathewses, and Porters arrive, twenty-one in all for supper, drinks, games, and a puppet show written and given by our girls, Tim Thompson, and Tim Currier. It was excellent and I was delighted with them. Party over at 12:30.

Everybody we meet seems to have had quite enough of the festive season and to be lumpish and sagged, but our party went well and was gentle but not dull. I have gained three pounds without seeming to eat inordinately.

MONDAY, JANUARY 4: A letter from George Chamberlain:[1] Tony Guthrie is critically ill and must have a long rest, but he will do *Leaven of Malice* as a play if possible. I refuse to be panicked by this news but it could be very serious. I write George and also a letter of cheer to Judy Guthrie. In the evening, long talk with Jenny about her schoolwork, which is a bugbear to her. I assure her that it is not the only reason for living.

FRIDAY, JANUARY 8: To Toronto; a long lunch at Winston's[2] with Herbert Whittaker. Then to Hawthorn Gardens and talk with WRD and dine, then to Hart House to adjudicate inter-college drama festival. I carried through my New Year's resolve to be more forthright in asserting my artistic opinions.

SUNDAY, JANUARY 10: To lunch at Batterwood with Vincent Massey.[3] Afterward he talks to me for two hours in his study. The Queen wants to give him the Order of the Garter,[4] and the prime minister won't have it and wants Mr. Massey to tell him to tell the Queen to desist. I agree to do what I can. I am fascinated by Vincent Massey's position about the Garter. He ought to have it, he wants it and deserves it, but Diefenbaker is a real small-town Western Baptist. Canada is a hard land in which to get one's deserts.

MONDAY, JANUARY 11: In the evening heard recordings of Douglas Rain reading from *Merchant of Venice*, which he did well, poignantly

1 Stage director at the Old Vic Theatre, London.
2 Restaurant on King Street named after Winston Churchill, which catered to entertainers and the business establishment.
3 Massey had retired as governor general the previous September. Batterwood was his house near Port Hope.
4 The Order of the Garter is the highest order of British chivalry conferred by the monarch and is accompanied by a knighthood.

reminding me of its lack of success, which I try not to think of.[5] Wonderful h.t.d. with both of us laughing uproariously.

TUESDAY, JANUARY 12: In the evening heard all of Mussorgsky's *Boris Godunov* and was thrilled—it is my kind of opera.

WEDNESDAY, JANUARY 13: A very busy day and as so often, I write well under stress, but I quickly weary of newspaper concerns now. In the evening frowsted by the fire and read. Then to bed and dreamed I was accused of fathering an illegitimate child, and I must revise for the Theatre Guild a play not mine, which they said was.

SUNDAY, JANUARY 17: I walk in the afternoon and in the evening read Dostoyevsky's *The Possessed*, great stuff; then chat with Brenda till bedtime. My fatigue seems boundless and the fate of Tony Guthrie is a counsel to rest. The more I rest the more new areas of fatigue reveal themselves; but I make progress, which means doing as little as possible.

WEDNESDAY, JANUARY 20: Brenda groggy with 'flu in the evening and takes to her bed. I sit up and read *The Devils*, as the translator, David Magarshack, calls *The Possessed* and am greatly caught up in its slow, python-like coils.

SUNDAY, JANUARY 24: Dyed beard, scrubbed, washed hair. On our afternoon drive the Jaguar conks out on a country road. I read *Hedda Gabler* and am once more lost in amazement at Ibsen's *insight*, astonished anew by his genius and the appropriateness of his

5 The 1955 Stratford Shakespearean Festival production of *The Merchant of Venice* aroused a great deal of criticism about the play's perceived anti-Semitism.

plays to so much of Canada today. But I have made some of these points in my own work and they have passed unnoticed. A strangely obtuse country.

FRIDAY, JANUARY 29: Quiet day; read and thought. Great news by the afternoon mail: the *Saturday Evening Post* wants Chapter 1 of *A Voice from the Attic* for Adventures of the Mind, at $2,500! I'm happy to be in a series with Aldous Huxley, Bertrand Russell, etc. and making an entry into a big popular magazine. A quiet evening and read *The Old Curiosity Shop* to Rosamond. Early to bed and h.t.d.

SATURDAY, JANUARY 30: To Cobourg at 12 and then for ten and a half hours I live in the devitalized, self-castrating world of a little-theatre "workshop." The adjudicator was Alan Nunn, who has nothing to say and says it at great length. The production of my *At the Gates of the Righteous* went well. The other play performed was *The Boor* by Chekhov. Bad dinner with ninety others.

TUESDAY, FEBRUARY 2: Our twentieth wedding anniversary. To Toronto and see Herbert Irvine, the interior decorator at Eaton's, about redecorating our house, which is a real anniversary present. What a chatterbox Irvine is! But life enhancing: an Agreeable Rattle.[6] We gave a dinner at the University Club for the Harrises, the Stewarts, Walter and Liz Gordon,[7] Helen Ignatieff, and Scott Young: turtle soup, lamb chops, asparagus hollandaise, endive salad, and water ice with kirsch-peach sauce. Châteauneuf du Pape. To the Stewarts' afterward, a delightful evening and a real celebration.

6 *She Stoops to Conquer*, Act 3.
7 Walter Gordon, eminent Canadian accountant, businessman, politician, and writer.

SUNDAY, FEBRUARY 7: Spend much of the day reading Richler's *The Apprenticeship of Duddy Kravitz* for the Governor General's Literary Award. Much talent but a derivative and ill-planned work. Brenda and I rearrange furniture in the living-room with excellent effect and banish the gold sofa. Result, room much unified.

A good deal of loafing this week goes far to restore my calm of mind: I *must* be idle at times or my activity loses all meaning and becomes mechanical. This is the last quiet weekend for at least five to come.

FRIDAY, FEBRUARY 12: To Toronto to a meeting of the Press Freedom Committee. A good meeting and I am put on an even smaller committee. I shop and meet Brenda, who has a massage, then we sup at the University Club and drive home. Very cold. Hear the Franck symphony which I bought, long a favourite of mine; Rosamond home from skating carnival at Lakefield. Very jolly h.t.d.

SATURDAY, FEBRUARY 13: Write a *Star* column about Ronald Knox.[8] Herbert Whittaker and Helen Ignatieff with her nephew Michael Ignatieff come for the weekend. We begin conversation which continues sans break—gossip and good cheer. Michael Ignatieff is a nice boy of twelve. Herbert tells me of being interviewed for the *New York Times* position as drama critic. He does not expect to get it. He looks unwell but Helen is flourishing.

SATURDAY, FEBRUARY 20: To Toronto by train at seven a.m. Collision with the Ottawa train at Claremont, and I am thrown on floor. There is a delay and we reach Toronto at 12. Cocktails with the Fleurys.[9] We get Jenny and Miranda from Bishop Strachan

8 English writer, broadcaster, and priest.
9 Bill Fleury was an architect who had been at Upper Canada College with Davies. He later designed Rob and Brenda's country house, Windhover.

School and spend a quiet afternoon at our Royal York suite. In the evening I address the Ontario Association of Architects and do it well, Brenda says. My speech for the architects was very carefully composed and rehearsed and I *acted* it.[10] It is the best method for me. But all such affairs too long—it is murderous to put a man up at 10:30 when everybody else in the place has fatigued the audience and they long for release.

SUNDAY, FEBRUARY 21: We leave our grand suite and are home by 11:30. In the afternoon a country walk and hear some music. To dinner at the Porters' with Ruth Thompson and the Curriers. Very pleasant and lots of jolly talk about profanity, black mass, and music. Home about 12:30.

MONDAY, FEBRUARY 22: To Toronto at 4 p.m. and to the Park Plaza[11] to dine with the Harrises, Helen Ignatieff, and Grant Macdonald; and then to the Crest Theatre where Dame Edith Evans reads poetry. She was sad, mannered and empty, no intelligence, and she wearied before the end and was pathetically nervous and shaky. Afterward to the Harrises' for chat and we all were very sorry about Dame Edith, but she is an actress, not a verse-speaker.

TUESDAY, FEBRUARY 23: Home and I find a letter from Tony about casting which I find very depressing for no good reason. I felt low all afternoon and in the dumps all evening; a long time since I had such a fit. To bed but woke with *proctalgia fugax*[12] in midst of the night. I seem to fight and reject my success, in the depths of my spirit. Why?

10 "How to Design a Haunted House," in *One Half of Robertson Davies* (1977).
11 Now the Park Hyatt Toronto.
12 A deep pain in the rectum that feels like a severe muscle cramp.

MONDAY, FEBRUARY 29: Busy day: wrote three editorials and did much incidental work. In the evening worked on Governor General's Awards books, a dreary lot, and wonder if awards should be made. I am out of love with Canada these days, a country of stupid, ill-educated, timid, narrow-gutted pseudo-Scotchmen.

TUESDAY, MARCH 1: Yousuf Karsh, the photographer, comes to lunch with an assistant, Monty Everett, and they photograph me from 2 until 5. It was interesting but exhausting. In the evening we saw on TV *The Importance of Being Earnest* with Dame Edith Evans, the 1952 film directed by Anthony Asquith. The box and the Ford ads ill became it but she is still great.

THURSDAY, MARCH 3: Wrote a lead editorial, wrote a *Star* column, worked on the Governor General books, a full day. In the evening worked on the books again and a damned dull lot they are, in the main. Yearned for just one *alive* writer. H.t.d. in midst of night, surprising and good.

FRIDAY, MARCH 4: Short morning at the office and then take the train to Ottawa at 11:30. Read *Joseph Vance* by William De Morgan.[13] Usual wait at Smiths Falls, that mudhole. To the Château Laurier, a quiet dinner, and to the film *Spartacus*, surely world's worst, and *Room at the Top* again, admirable. A restful, happy day.

SATURDAY, MARCH 5, OTTAWA: Governor General's Award committee meeting with Northrop Frye in the morning. Lunch at La Touraine with Norrie Frye and Douglas LePan. Full committee from 2 to 5. LePan makes difficulties by wanting to withdraw on

13 English potter, designer, and writer. His novel *Joseph Vance* (1906) was an immediate but not enduring success.

conscientious scruples! He had not read some of the books! Drinks at Dr. Trueman's,[14] then dine at the Château with Norrie Frye, Duncan Grant, and LePan. A long chat about pornography and we drink till 12. Very genial, these professors, excellent company. Guy Sylvestre, on our committee, asks, Why are English Canadian writers all connected with universities? Why indeed? Frye and LePan and Duncan Grant nice chaps but all *scholars* rather than creators. Me too? Dire and inadmissible thought!

SUNDAY, MARCH 6: Breakfast at 10; 'bus at 12:30; home 4:30. I sustain such journeys and such meetings better than I did.

MONDAY, MARCH 7: Felt dull and took the day in a restful spirit. Lunatic letters from a woman in Philadelphia: am I especially attractive to madwomen? A father-figure, Ralph Hancox says, laughing.

TUESDAY, MARCH 8: Continue to feel dull. Miranda comes home in the evening for a short rest. Brenda is unwell, as if 'flu. We are all fagged from winter; but I do a good deal of work all the same.

THURSDAY, MARCH 10: Weariness lifts. In the evening played duets with Miranda: Mendelssohn, Mozart, and Handel, then hear Franck and Elizabethan songs: restorative.

SATURDAY, MARCH 12: In the morning tinkered with a *Star* column. Afternoon, to bed with Brenda to sleep and h.t.d., most restorative and delightful. In the evening read in *Heart of Jade* by Salvador de Madariaga and began Mann's *Magic Mountain* and at once am drawn to it. Brenda to a skating party at 10, and I hear music till she and Rosamond return, big with carnival gossip.

14 Albert Trueman, first director of the Canada Council.

SUNDAY, MARCH 13: Lie late. We drive to Toronto in the afternoon and dine with Claude and Christine Bissell[15] in their handsome president's residence to meet Jacques Barzun,[16] Provost Derwyn Owen of Trinity College and Mrs. Owen, Dean and Mrs. Rogers (a battleaxe), and others. Very pleasant and rather grand—two manservants. How restorative to meet some people with *minds*. Chats with Barzun and Bissell were not remarkable for what was said but for all the good sense and knowledge that lay behind it. Barzun said to me, "The theatre will kill you." No it won't, but such assertions are depressing, coupled with Derwyn Owen's that "Canadian things seem ill-fated on Broadway."

MONDAY, MARCH 21: Felt tired and unwell. Carpenters and electricians invade the house in the first blast of redecoration. At the office much work and temperament. I do some work against the grain, and in the evening work on the play. An excellent and restorative h.t.d., but wake in night terrified by dream in which Mother appears as a baby guarded by ghosts.

TUESDAY, MARCH 22: Felt much better and worked well—a *Star* column on De Morgan in the morning and two editorials in the afternoon, and many letters and decisions. In the evening worked on *Leaven of Malice* and heard from Tony. Also, began a diary of the production of *Leaven of Malice*, and hope I have the heart to keep it up, but refuse to despair. If the play does not do well it is not the end of the world.

LEAVEN OF MALICE: MARCH 23, 1960 TO JANUARY 1, 1961

In 1959, William Gibson published an account of the writing

15 Claude Bissell had become president of the University of Toronto in November 1958.
16 Famed historian at Columbia University.

and production of his very successful play, *Two for the Seesaw*, called *The Seesaw Log*. He found the procedure extremely painful, disappointing, and disenchanting. I hope to record here the facts and some of the experience of dramatizing, and seeing through production, the stage version of my novel *Leaven of Malice*, published in 1954.

FIRST: Joseph Hayman wanted a dramatization, with *one* setting and the love story prominent. He tried several dramatists, and I tried, but he was not satisfied. This was 1956–7–8.

SECOND: Manuel D. (Don) Herbert took an option on the book. I first saw him December 4, 1958, and met his partner Philip Langner. They get Tyrone Guthrie's assurance that he will direct the play.

THIRD: I go to Eire July 8–9, 1959, taking a draft dramatization, and work revising it with Guthrie July 10–30.

Tomorrow, March 23, 1960, I go to Toronto to work with Tony Guthrie on casting and here, I suppose, the fun may be said to begin.

The Theatre Guild was a theatrical society founded in New York City in 1918 by Lawrence Langner and three colleagues. Langner's wife, Armina Marshall, also served as a co-director. Its original purpose was to produce non-commercial works by American and foreign playwrights, and its productions included plays by George Bernard Shaw and Eugene O'Neill. It differed from other theatre groups as its board of directors shared in the choosing of plays, management, and production. At the time of the *Love and Libel* production the Theatre Guild consisted of Lawrence Langner, Armina Marshall

Langner, their son Philip Langner, and Warren Caro. The play was produced by Theatre Guild Productions Inc. and Don Herbert by arrangement with the Canadian Theatre Exchange, whose members were Tom Patterson, Robert Whitehead, Ernest Rawley, Jane Massie, and Ted Jolliffe.

Davies's novel *Leaven of Malice* is a social comedy set in the early 1950s in the town of Salterton, which has many similarities to Davies's hometown, Kingston, Ontario, with its university, Anglican cathedral, and local newspaper. The plot follows the complications, revelations, and consequences that result from a false engagement notice that appears in the Salterton daily newspaper. The unwilling young couple, Pearl Vambrace and Solly Bridgetower, are quite un-interested in each other and deeply embarrassed by the announce-ment. But they are both frustrated by their lives and trapped by over-loving and overbearing parents: Pearl's father, the self-important Professor Vambrace, and Solly's mother, the smothering and per-petually demanding Mrs. Bridgetower. Several other characters find themselves, willingly or otherwise, involved in the hoax: Gloster Ridley, the much-put-upon editor of the newspaper; Swithin Shillito, a hopelessly old-fashioned journalist; the officious Dean Knapp of the cathedral; and a dubious newcomer to the town, Bevill Higgin. Three other couples demonstrate different versions of more-or-less happy married love: Humphrey Cobbler, the exuberant, pleasure-loving organist at the cathedral, and his wife, Molly; Norm and Duchy Yarrow, relentlessly optimistic social scientists; and the hearty vulgarians George and Kitten Morphew. The play, as it evolved, re-tained the plot and most of the characters of the novel but ultimately was structured quite differently.

The play was revised by Davies for production at Hart House in 1973 and again for the Shaw Festival in 1975. It was published under the title *Leaven of Malice (A Play)* in 1982 and 2008.

[1960]

WEDNESDAY, MARCH 23, TORONTO: Meet Tony at the Royal York
Hotel and discuss casting. Esme Church has turned down Mrs.
Bridgetower as the part repels her, which does not astonish me. She
is elderly, Roman Catholic, and rather indisposed to like my work,
but Tony advises further persuasion and we write a joint letter. His
phone rings every ten minutes but he handles it all with ease. He
has lined up some actors to be seen.

THURSDAY, MARCH 24, TORONTO: H.t.d. on waking, which dispels
fatigue. Work with Tony. We agree to circumvent, so far as may be,
the nerve-wracking part of taking a play to New York, by working
amicably together. He thinks the contracts are too long delayed. We
have made advances to Amelia Hall (for Edith), Tony van Bridge
(for Shillito), Leo Leyden (for Higgin), and Robert Christie[17] (for
Ridley) as well as John Milligan (for Solly).[18] Tony always explains
to the actors that the play is a dramatization of a novel, and they
charmingly indicate that it is the *one* recent Canadian novel that—
doubtless owing to the agency of an ill-natured fairy[19]—has not
come their way. Of course actors seldom read anything. But this
has become a joke between us.

In the evening we go to a Crest performance of *Honour Thy
Father* (very bad) to see Charmion King (for Kitten). Tony thinks
Charmion too well-bred and beautiful, in which I suppose he is
right, but I still think she could do it well. He suggests a freer
treatment of the public opinion theme and comes around to the
notion of a chorus, which is what I wanted last summer. I am to
work on this and we will continue with it in June. I see also Marie
Day, who is to design the costumes, but as these are surely quite

17 Christie, a Canadian actor and director, had met Davies at the Old Vic. He
 was married to Grania Mortimer and was the father of actress Dinah Christie.
18 Davies and Guthrie wanted to cast major Canadian actors wherever possible.
19 From Gilbert and Sullivan, *The Pirates of Penzance.*

commonplace, it should be interesting to see what comes of this. Bought a bottle of Irish whiskey for Tony, who dislikes our Canadian "liquor lounges," very properly. He tells me Alec Guinness[20] is a bastard, but knows who his father is, and has a rather disgraceful, boozy old mum. Guinness is embarrassed by elderly wives who approach him to say: "Used to be a drinking-companion of your mother's"—very hurtingly. Is this why Guinness became a Papist, searching for some certainty, some unfailing distinction or patrician note, in his personal life? Marie Day came all in black, with dead-white face and kohl round her eyes, and Tony thought her a slut and seductress, but I thought her just a girl trying to put her best foot foremost.

FRIDAY, MARCH 25, TORONTO: Last night Tony and I supped in the coffee shop of the hotel here where many little ladies from a congress of the Order of the Eastern Star were, and amused ourselves casting Kitten from among them. Tony never reads the papers and did not know Leonard Warren[21] was dead. Tony says Rudolf Bing, the general manager of the Metropolitan Opera Company, hated Warren, who was not so fine an artist as his publicity asserted and was hard to work with. Tony thinks the O'Keefe Centre[22] is a great mistake and refused to sign an approving comment on it prepared for him by Mary Jolliffe, the publicity agent. Herbert Whittaker says Mary Jolliffe hated doing it, and I can well believe it.

This evening Brenda, Tony, and I dined with Clair and Amy

20 Alec Guinness played the title role in *Richard III*, directed by Guthrie, the first play produced at the Stratford Shakespearean Festival, in July 1954.
21 Warren, a prominent American dramatic baritone, had died at age forty-eight on March 1 onstage at the Met, having just sung the aria "Morir, tremenda cosa."
22 The O'Keefe Centre (now the Sony Centre for the Performing Arts) was funded by E.P. Taylor of the O'Keefe Brewing Company and was to open on October 1, 1960. With a capacity of 3,200, it was designed for touring musicals and other large-scale theatrical productions.

Stewart to discuss the Crest: Tony thinks it can come to no good in its present theatre, which chimes with Clair's eagerness for a new house. We went with the Stewarts to Tony's touring production of Friedrich Schiller's *Maria Stuart* with Eva Le Gallienne and Signe Hasso. It was bad and dull, racked to pieces on tour. But it is a *bad* play. Have the Germans any real drama?

SATURDAY, MARCH 26, TORONTO: Wake ill—'flu. Take Tony and the girls to lunch at the Lord Simcoe Hotel, then drive home. I shiver and chatter and whisk into bed with hot-bottles and aspirin and sleep heavily: first cold in years and I think fatigue and excitement and the awful hot dryness of the Royal York brought it on— and sinus.

SUNDAY, APRIL 3: Lay late; feel dull and achey. A dreary week; have not been so ill in years. Felt middle-aged and grey and unsuccessful and declining.

SUNDAY, APRIL 17: Feeling much better and spring gives me new heart; but I dawdle over getting to work on the play. My chief weakness as an author is my hatred of revision.

THURSDAY, MAY 5: Today I sent copies of all the revisions of the play to Willis Kingsley Wing, incorporating all Tony's suggestions and also all those of Don Herbert. Can a playwright be more obliging, I ask? Have cut the Morphews substantially. Don Herbert phones to say that Dennis King[23] is interested in playing Bevill Higgin, and he would be a strength, perhaps that great desideratum, a *Name*. Tony saw Maud Whitmore as a possible

23 English-born actor and singer. King had starred in Broadway musicals through the 1930s and into the 1950s. He was now sixty-two. Ultimately he was to play the role of Humphrey Cobbler.

Mrs. Bridgetower and put her in a tizzy, but I fear he never seriously considered her. She has written me a letter, sad because courageous and not very hopeful, asking when she will know. I must write her and do not like to do it, for she is a good woman if not a good actress.

SATURDAY, MAY 7: To Stratford. Governors' meeting, very busy, then a cast reception at 5 where I see Tanya Moiseiwitsch,[24] Christopher Plummer, etc. Drive to Toronto in rain and fog and have a bad dinner at Guelph. Lie with the Harrises, and chat pleasantly 'til 1.

At Stratford learned from John Hayes that the Guild is moving: a scenery construction firm in Toronto has been approached, and Bruce Swerdfager has had a letter about playing George Morphew. So something is doing. A certain cordiality among the actors (those seaweed barometers of one's theatre fortunes) also marks me as a man with a play and perhaps parts to give.

N.B. A title? Of course *Leaven of Malice* won't do, chiefly I think because it exists, is good, and can be had without any trouble, but they say that "Leaven" is a hard word and people won't understand it.

People insist that having a play done must be a Gethsemanic ordeal. At dinner at the Bissells' on March 13 Jacques Barzun kept repeating, "It will kill you; it will kill you." Today Julie Harris's husband, Manning Gurian, whom I met at Stratford, said, "Your hair can't get any whiter but you can still lose it." What do they mean? Of course everyone knows this sort of thing is a nervous strain. But why this hysteria, this assumption that horror is inevitable? Even failure in its most complete form can be borne with some dignity.

24 Distinguished theatre designer, brought to Canada by Guthrie to design the original Stratford stage. She returned to Stratford frequently, designing costumes for several productions.

SUNDAY, MAY 8: Up at 9:30. Leave Harrises at 11:30 after splendid breakfast. Collect another load of Miranda's junk at St. Hilda's and home by 2. Slept in afternoon and wrote account of *Leaven of Malice* in my theatre diary. Brenda depressed by demands of approaching summer.

SUNDAY, MAY 15: Up at 9 and do books in the guest-room and put records back in cabinet. In the afternoon we drive to Toronto and meet Mrs. Newbold[25] at Malton airport. She is well and full of high spirits. At home we talk with her till 11.

SUNDAY, MAY 22: H.t.d. on waking; rainy day and projected picnic impossible. Mrs. Newbold much freer-spirited now her mother[26] is dead, but talks very confidently of what she has rearranged in her memory: truly, the world is her idea and her grip on fact joyously frail.

FRIDAY, JUNE 3: Write a *Star* column. In the afternoon to a reception for L.B. Pearson.[27] Politics fascinates me but what odd people compose local committees! There is a theatre strike in New York. If it goes on long this will certainly affect my production date. Redecoration and the fuss of proof-reading the book and writing the play make this a bad time to think or read. I live in the shadows of the spirit.

TUESDAY, JUNE 7: To Kingston at 11:45, taking Mrs. Newbold: a superb day. We see some sights and dine with Grant Macdonald. Very good but rich. A Governor General's Awards committee

25 Muriel Newbold, Brenda's widowed mother, now in her sixties, who had come from her home in Australia for a three-month visit.
26 Ethel Larking, Brenda's grandmother, died in 1952.
27 Then leader of the federal Liberal opposition.

meeting. A good meeting and I suggest leather-bound books as prizes. Back to Grant Macdonald's for chat and listen to records, and then to the motel: unwell in night; rich food.

WEDNESDAY, JUNE 8: Return to Peterborough for lunch. A beautiful day and lovely drive. The painter has finished the bedroom which looks fine. But this roving, disturbed life and the constant visitors are hard on work. Corrected and returned last Knopf book proofs.

THURSDAY, JUNE 9: To dentist in the morning—political talk as usual. In the afternoon wrote two editorials and a *Star* column on the Pre-Raphaelite artist John Collier. The *Star* syndicate advertises me as "the bearded bard"—cheap stuff. In the evening much chat with Brenda, Mrs. Newbold, and Miranda. Slept very poorly. Six at every meal makes for jollity, but is also rather wearing. As a family we are so *excitable* and waste so much energy in mere talk and word-play: but it is life-enhancing.

FRIDAY, JULY 1: The New York theatre strike in June somewhat delayed progress, but I have just returned from Stratford, where I saw Tony and he says all goes well. Rehearsals to begin October 10, open Toronto November 2, and in New York mid-December. Tony likes the revisions, and I have, I think, persuaded him that the piece is more than just funny. He likes the dreams and says they must emerge as the reality, the waking-life as the unreality—which is what I wanted. The last scene is to be revised to build up Cobbler and Mrs. Bridgetower, which should be easy.

MONDAY, JULY 4: All day I collogue with Wilson Craw, managing editor, and Bill Garner, general manager, about appointing Ralph Hancox as assistant managing editor. Craw's Scotchness and

jealousy very apparent. Oh, Temperament! What a concealed nuisance in business! Consequently very tired by evening.

THURSDAY, JULY 7: At 9:15 Brenda, Mrs. Newbold, Jenny, and Rosamond all left for New York to see Jenny off on a school tour to Europe. Jenny greatly excited. Hard work at the *Examiner* as Ralph Hancox is in Stratford. Home is dull and silent. In the evening I played Gilbert and Sullivan's *The Sorcerer* and thought the recording dreadful and the voices bad: D'Oyly Carte at its lowest ebb.[28]

FRIDAY, JULY 8: Busy day: wrote two leads and a *Star* column about Sullivan. Mrs. Pedak offers very good meals and not her usual stingy quantity. In the evening to the Summer Theatre's production of *The Glass Menagerie*, well done and more poetic than I had remembered. Hot weather.

THURSDAY, JULY 14: Another crowded day but Brenda, Rosamond, and Mrs. Newbold return and the house comes alive again. They had a good time in New York and Mrs. Newbold was thrilled. Admirable h.t.d.

FRIDAY, JULY 15: An hour and a half in the morning with Craw and Bill Garner about office problems. After Craw leaves, Bill says, "There's your problem." I will have to be firm; a busy afternoon and write three editorials. Gay h.t.d.

TUESDAY, JULY 26: To the *Examiner* and find the quarrel between Craw and Hancox worse and have to work on it. Do much work to small purpose and feel wretched—aches and sore throat.

28 The D'Oyly Carte Opera Company staged the original productions of all the Gilbert and Sullivan operas, starting in 1875 and continuing until 1982, and for many years controlled the copyrights.

WEDNESDAY, JULY 27: Busy day at the *Examiner*: get Craw and Hancox in my office and make peace—I hope. Had an important dream, in colour: the *Examiner* was being restored at the front door corner (Hunter and Water Streets) and when the builders took down the modern building, they found walls and ornament of a Victorian one in red and gold—a naked-breasted caryatid, cartouches of nymphs and satyrs, and gold and scarlet walls and moulding. I remembered the *Examiner* building was once a hotel, but not, of course, like that. A girl in a raincoat appeared briefly, but only so that I could show her the discovery. Outside it was raining; inside, warm and handsome and exciting.

SUNDAY, JULY 31: Wonderful day of rest. I sit in the garden and read Jung, putter with flowers and invite my soul. In the evening, play Glenn Gould records and chat. A day like this takes the ache out of weeks of fidget. I am at the time of life when, as Jung says, I must meet my "opposites" but I must not be superficial in identifying them, if I am to do this alone.

SATURDAY, AUGUST 13: Only to note that David Hays is to be the designer, and I have sent him two colour slides of the Kingston skyline. The title is now *Love and Libel*, which I do not like, but the Guild and Tony like it greatly.

Rob and Brenda went for a holiday in Arlington, Vermont, as Lulie Westfeldt, their Alexander teacher, was at her country home near there and had invited them for a week of lessons.

SUNDAY, AUGUST 14: Away at 10 and drive to Ivy Lea Bridge at 1. Wonderful drive through the Adirondacks, renew knowledge of the dinginess of Tupper Lake, stop at Saranac, and have a good dinner at a German restaurant. First holiday in some time, for last

year's was demanding work, though delightful. I do not like vaca-
tions *alone*: hope for real rest this week before the autumn change
of gears.

MONDAY, AUGUST 15: Away by 9, in rain, wonderful mountain
scenery. See Fort Ticonderoga, a good reconstruction, and to
Arlington about 3; rest, and to Lulie at 4:30 for a good lesson. We
both respond at once to her ministrations. Staying at the Candle-
light Motel.

THURSDAY, AUGUST 18, ARLINGTON: Lesson in a.m.; dizziness im-
proves. Picnic again, read, and walk. In the evening to drive-in
movie theatre at Bennington, my first, and see two good films, but
four and a half hours long! It is Arthur's fifty-seventh birthday and
I wire him from a Western Union branch in a funeral home!

SUNDAY, AUGUST 21, ARLINGTON: H.t.d. on waking. Leave at 10
and drive through mountains, picnic lunch, cross Ivy Lea Bridge,
and home in heavy rain at 6:15. Many messages and news await us.
First true holiday in some time and greatly refreshing, marred only
by dizziness which I think is sun. An admirable week's work with
Lulie Westfeldt and my spirit and body are really refreshed; now—
to hold on to some of that!

WEDNESDAY, AUGUST 24: Alexander Technique makes me less
mealy-mouthed: yesterday I clouted a boy in the street who jeered
at me; today I blew up a Moral Re-Armament pest. Gordon Roper
comes to dinner and outlines my Trinity work, which sounds fasci-
nating: look forward to being a don.

SUNDAY, AUGUST 28: I am forty-seven. I was given a handsome at-
taché case from Brenda, and an Edwin Booth playbill; a nightshirt

from Mrs. Newbold and bottle of rum from Miranda and Rosamond. We had a fine picnic at the cottage, a special dinner in the evening, and then to the film *Oliver Twist.* A happy day. Nearing fifty and not a bad record, but *Love and Libel* is a break into a larger world and I hope *Voice* may gain some reputation. I am no genius, but I think I am better than I have yet been esteemed.

TUESDAY, SEPTEMBER 6: Tom Patterson writes that Canadian Theatre Exchange Ltd. are co-producing *Love and Libel.* This seems to mean they are trying to raise some of the money. May he approach WRD? I say no.

SUNDAY, SEPTEMBER 11: I dream (in colour) that I return to Oxford. It is all very delightful, and I can smell it. But a fine set of rooms has been assigned to me, and then taken from me by the porter, and I have to arrange to have all my things taken to an inferior set, and no one will help me. I am having oppressive, apprehensive dreams of late. Am also melancholy at the end of summer, and the girls going away. The gnawing beast of Angst is never appeased: hope this fit will soon pass.

MONDAY, SEPTEMBER 19: To Toronto to see Tony, who has cast *Love and Libel,* all but Pearl and Molly. He hopes Charmion King may change from Kitten to the latter. We see Corinne Conley for the former, at a coffee shop on College Street, where she and Tony become matey over coffee and toasted Danish. I think she would do very well. Also saw designs for the front-curtain and the drop, both much to my taste, and very stylish and up-to-the-minute. Tony's description of his plan of production is exciting—the sort of complexity within simplicity in which he excels. He suggests some further touching up of the script to which I agree; I am getting a strong taste for tinkering: it will bring up the theme of *provincialism.*

By this time the play had been cast.

Corinne Conley	*Pearl Vambrace*
John Milligan	*Solomon Bridgetower*
Laurence Hardy	*Professor Vambrace*
Madeleine Christie	*Mrs. Louisa Hansen Bridgetower*
Robert Christie	*Gloster Ridley*
Dennis King	*Humphrey Cobbler*
Charmion King	*Molly Cobbler*
Gene Saks	*Norman Yarrow*
Roberta Kinnon	*Dutchy Yarrow*
James Edmond	*Dean Jevon Knapp*
Amelia Hall	*Edith Little*
Barbara Hamilton	*Kitten Morphew*
Leo Leyden	*Bevill Higgin*
Bruce Swerdfager	*George Morphew*
Tony van Bridge	*Swithin Shillito*
Grania Mortimer	*Townspeople of Salterton*
Edward K. Holmes	
Cynthia Bebout	
Kay Hawtrey	
Ken Pauli	
Paul Robin	
David Hays	*Scenic and Lighting Design*
Grania Mortimer	*Prompter, Production Assistant*
John Cook	*Musical Advisor*
Marie Day	*Costume Design*
Jack Hutt	*Stage Manager*
Nat Dorfman	*General Press Representative*
Irvin Dorfman	*Press Representative*
Lee Martinec	*Business Manager*
Jack Merigold	*Assistant to Tyrone Guthrie*

THURSDAY, SEPTEMBER 22: Revised a love-scene, wrote a new scene for Cobbler and Mrs. Bridgetower, and revamped the last scene. A full day and kept me at it till 9:30. Brenda is unwell, and missing Rosamond. I heard Rossini's *The Turk in Italy*. Did all this and had plenty of energy: Alexander Technique, diet, or both?

SATURDAY TO MONDAY, SEPTEMBER 24–26: The Guthries spend the weekend with us. Tony is pleased with my new scene in the cathedral, which enlarges Cobbler's part, and my tightened and heightened last act. We read the play Saturday night and I read Mrs. Bridgetower rather well, and was amazed how good the Yarrow-Vambrace scene is. (In the night I dream my mother comes to strangle me—what of that?) Corinne Conley is not in the bag— haggling about money: she wants $500, the Guild came up from $200 to $300. Tony says the Guild are very mean about paying the actors. He also warns me of the distress of the pre–New York tour, but is realistic and says the tinkering not always the author's, but the director's. On Monday the Guild's notion of a poster comes—a winking Cupid bearing a newspaper clipping, done in whorehouse pink. We agree that I shall return it with a polite but firm refusal to allow it, and this I do in the afternoon. I have a fit of revulsion against the title and suggest *Ill Wind*, which Tony likes, but later I have cold feet: it sounds unlucky, and Willis Wing says it doesn't sound like a play people go easily to see. Miranda now accepted for next season at Stratford.[29]

TUESDAY AND WEDNESDAY, SEPTEMBER 27–28: Willis Wing says there is "great pride of authorship" at the Guild about the name *Love and Libel*. How people love the names they concoct! Tony

29 Miranda was accepted as an acting apprentice for the 1961 season. The apprentices were to help in all departments while taking acting, fencing, and voice lessons and walking on and dancing in the plays.

phones to suggest *Social and Personal, The Engagement Is Announced, Joking Apart, Sweet Bells Jangled, Tangled Web, Kettle of Fish, Solly and Pearl,* or *The Organ Voluntary, A Biter Bit,* or *She Who Laughs Last*—all of which fill me with dismay. When, in turn, I suggest *Love Is Libel* he is cold toward it, and is right, I now think.

On September 28, Davies began his classes at Trinity College with one on the nature of tragedy. He continued to lecture twice a week until the production of *Love and Libel* left Toronto for Detroit. This in addition to his *Star* column, the *Examiner*, and the continual revising of the play.

THURSDAY, SEPTEMBER 29: John Cook phones to ask me where to find the music used in the play, which I would have thought he would have known. Am astonished at the amount of music very able musicians do *not* know.

FRIDAY, SEPTEMBER 30: Busy day but enjoyable: write editorials in the morning and in the afternoon a *Star* column on *The Sot-Weed Factor* by John Barth. In the evening read *La Belle Bête* by Marie-Claire Blais and think it extraordinary to make such a fuss about it. Then read Shaw's *Man and Superman*. It is read, read, all the time, but a pleasant change.

SATURDAY, OCTOBER 1: Brenda and I motored to Toronto for the great opening of the O'Keefe Centre with the Loewe and Lerner musical *Camelot*. An audience of thirty-two hundred, of whom not more than fifty on the ground floor were not in evening dress. The lieutenant governor was there, so we had six bars of "The Queen" and the whole of "The Star-Spangled Banner," that pompous, windy tune. Moss Hart, the director, appeared to warn us that it would be long, and it was—8:40 to 12:25. The piece is said to be

founded on T.H. White's *The Once and Future King,* but all his wit, fantasy, knowledge of chivalry, and love of Malory were missing. Instead, American "manlydom," mockery of Lancelot (Robert Goulet) for his purity, and a prissy Guenevere (Julie Andrews) and an Arthur who is an idealistic cuckold (Richard Burton). Tons of handsome, rather too garish scenery by Oliver Smith, and costumes which, rich as they were, did not suggest anything. Everything heavy, slow-moving, and repetitious; Hart's production uninventive. Music commonplace: not one tune remains. Must see this in New York to see what changes have been made. But where is Malory? Where is White? Is the Arthurian legend impossible on stage? Shakespeare would have given us an *Othello* on this theme— Arthur's love for Lancelot at war with his love for Guenevere. This could still be done, by a master. As it was, we got Arthur being shy with Guenevere and left at the end with a small boy—Tom Malory. Unintentional but symptomatic of what was wrong with this costly, vulgar, wrong-headed piece.

SUNDAY, OCTOBER 2: We drove home to Peterborough after the show finished at 12:25, which was a mistake, and we arrived very weary. Woke at 11:30 feeling rotten and with swollen gum; lay about all day, wrote a notice of *Camelot* for the *Examiner,*[30] read some Malory to sweeten my imagination, and listened to music. Have not been so low in a long time.

SUNDAY, OCTOBER 9: To Toronto on the 8 a.m. 'bus and take up flat at 88 Charles Street.[31] Thus begins a new phase in my life: truly

30 Davies's review of *Camelot* in the *Examiner* was considerably more generous than his actual opinion of the play.
31 Rob and Brenda rented a furnished apartment for rehearsals and the Toronto run of *Love and Libel.*

professional theatre writing. Whatever the upshot it is exciting now and immensely educative.

Tony has already put a shape on Act I, but thinks the play should be in three acts instead of two. What interests me is the way in which a good actor can convey two or three lines of text with a look, making a cut possible. Not cutting amusing or characteristic lines, but simply those which *say* what is better *acted*. Dennis King as Cobbler resists cuts, the others not. Too early to say who is good and who is not, but Charmion King as Molly Cobbler is disappointing—edgy and small.

After rehearsal Tony and I returned to his flat and made some cuts; I am not at all difficult about this, and indeed I see their great value; my good lines are closer together when the unwanted ones are taken out.

Tony rates me for my notice in the *Examiner* of *Camelot*. It was useless to say that the *Examiner* is not the paper in which to launch crusades against New York theatre customs.

MONDAY, OCTOBER 10, TORONTO, THANKSGIVING DAY: Rehearse at 10. Tony has now covered the whole play except for Yarrow's scenes, a remarkable feat of drive. Dennis King fussed and sulked because he has so little in the last scene and Tony was very firm with him. King gave me a great tale about what would be expected of him in New York, and asked for five good jokes, but I shall do nothing without Tony's express command. The rest of the cast behave in exemplary fashion and some of them—Laurence Hardy, Leo Leyden, Barbara Hamilton—begin to give a taste of their quality. I like Laurence Hardy, a fellow enthusiast for the Italic hand. We do some cutting and I am delighted with the way the company seem to like the play and abandon themselves to its spirit. A business manager, Lee Martinec, arrives from New York.

TUESDAY, OCTOBER 11, TORONTO: Rehearse at 10 a.m. Tony has so quickly laid out the play in rough that already we reach that dull stage where the actors are trying to do without their books, which means that for my carefully composed lines they substitute vulgarities and illiteracies of their own, especially John Milligan and Corinne Conley, who think their native wood-notes[32] the normal speech of educated Canadians. Grania Mortimer, who is on the book, is a first-rate prompter and checks this sharply, so I have hopes of a decent text in the end. Dennis King in a much more accommodating mood today.

Lunch at the Club and to Trinity and give a lecture on Dryden and Restoration tragedy. I did well, I think. Then to the flat and work on lectures for Wednesday and Thursday, then sleep. We dine at La Chaumière restaurant and go to a silly film, *School for Scoundrels*.

WEDNESDAY, OCTOBER 12, TORONTO: Several of the actors want to tinker their parts—not seriously, only what Tony calls "tucks" and "tuckettes," and in general the effect is good. But Dennis King hounds me for new material, a speech to the young people at the end, all to enhance the wonderful character *I* have created: insists he is quite selfless in this. I weary of him. He cannot sing "The Light of the Moon," as I thought might be the case, but I think "The Magpie's Nest" may serve. Tony Guthrie at the dentist's this afternoon, and I had to cope with Ernest Rawley,[33] Irvin Dorfman, the Guild's publicity man, and a reporter and photographer from the *Star*—the latter seeking that dreary jejune shot, me "looking over" the script. How barren of fancy most journalists are! More bustle and nervous excitement today than before.

32 From *Pygmalion* by G.B. Shaw.
33 As well as being a partner in the Canadian Theatre Exchange, Rawley was manager of the Royal Alexandra Theatre.

THURSDAY, OCTOBER 13, TORONTO: Morning rehearsal compli-
cated by photographers and Irvin Dorfman, who wants me to go
on the air with Nathan Cohen.[34] At first I refuse, then agree, as it
is foolish to harbour so much animosity against a critic, fat, preten-
tious cad though he be. Dennis King nags on about the finale, and
Brenda says this is pitiful, but I do not pity him; such naked egotism
repels me. This is what the stage can do to a man if he lets it. We
brought Madeleine Christie and Laurence Hardy home to the flat
in our car, and they were laughing at Dennis King's foolishness.
Tonight worked on rewriting, fattening King's part and (more fun)
fattening Tony van Bridge's part as Shillito. The Guthries came in
to see what I had done, and liked it. Tony says he thinks the verse
chorus must go, and I agree, for though good in itself, it is some-
what *outside* the play. The worry is that Charmion King is not good,
and I ask Tony, very seriously, to have a talk with her, as I am sure
she can do better. Rob Christie as Gloster Ridley is very nervous
and Tony bullies him.

FRIDAY, OCTOBER 14, TORONTO: Equity says if we have a choirboy
record nine bars of "Hear My Prayer" the boy must become an
Equity member, and must have two and a half weeks' salary for re-
cording, and $10 a week for the run—about $500 altogether. So it
looks as if Madeleine Christie would tape it, faking the voice. Cast
paid today; I get nothing but of course when the run begins I get
royalties and $30 *per diem* living costs on tour, and transporta-
tion. We do a lot of cutting as Tony wants fifteen minutes out of
the script, and I write a folk song lyric of a mildly scurrilous sort
for the first cathedral scene. The actors like the play, or it may be
they merely like Tony's direction, but in any case rehearsals go

34 *Toronto Star* theatre critic, notorious for his acerbic and hypercritical reviews.

spankingly. I am impressed by the way in which some slow starters, like Leo Leyden and John Milligan, show worth now.

SATURDAY, OCTOBER 15, TORONTO: Arrive at rehearsal to be greeted by Tony with the news that he had had "great weeps" from Dennis King about his part, and he wants the finale rewritten to give him an "entrance." This makes me angry, but he *is* a good comic, and the star (though not so noticeably as he probably thinks), so I shall do it, though I pretty well dislike him as a person, dyed hair and all. John Cook comes and rehearses the music, making splendid difference to the singing. Further (a triumph for me), he introduces the jive element into it I had wanted and Tony shrank from, and now Tony loves it. I must busy myself on Sunday reshaping the finale. The interview with me in the *Star* contains much, in direct quotation marks, that I have never said or written, and says my library is forty thousand books![35] I know why people hate newspapers. Made an estimate of the running-time: 131 minutes plus two intervals = 151 minutes—as Tony says, "square on the pig's back," the result of early cutting.

SUNDAY, OCTOBER 16, TORONTO: Work from 3 p.m. to 11, with an hour for tea, completely reshaping finale, with an "entrance" for Dennis King, and some rather good stuff for the others. But I resent this, for I sense Tony will want to mess it about, and King will not be satisfied unless everything centres upon him. Why can't I have *my* way? The answer is plain: Tony has "the weight" and King shameless sulks: but I shall dig in my heels tomorrow.

MONDAY, OCTOBER 17, TORONTO: Gene Saks arrives this morning to play Yarrow, which he will obviously do very well. A witty, subtle

35 Davies's library at its greatest held ten thousand books.

actor and he makes Yarrow's folly most engaging. In the after-
noon, we rehearse and tape music at St. Paul's. John Cook again
shows great command, but Dennis King cannot do quite simple
things, though he worked for years on the musical stage. It emerg-
es that Lee Martinec worked to be an orchestral conductor and
enjoyed the music greatly; he talks enthusiastically of the effect of
the organ music in a theatre. Madeleine Christie records the
choirboy sequences very well, for which she is to have an extra $10
weekly. Then Tony returns to our flat and we discuss the new
finale. As I foresaw, he cut two of my best jokes, but liked it on the
whole, and says Dennis King must accept this or quit, and we
agree that in the latter event Rob Christie could make a good fist
of Cobbler. Says also that we shall have a good notion after the
first night whether the piece is likely to do in New York or not—a
fearsome thought.

TUESDAY, OCTOBER 18, TORONTO: Tony had a bad night with his
teeth. Today some signs of *acting together* began to appear, which is
very helpful to such as Charmion King and Jim Edmond, whose
parts do not stand alone. The love-scenes—at which Tony works
very hard, to my surprise—are coming nicely. He says he does not
much like Dennis King—thinks him a nuisance and no "draw"—
but he likes King's rather Old Actor effects. Some of these began
to show today through the snorting, harrumphing, gobbling, and
snarling at the prompter. I am sticky about one or two minor chang-
es Tony wants, which I do not think good for the play, but work this
evening on a new end for the first Morphew scene, which now con-
cludes Act 1.

WEDNESDAY, OCTOBER 19, TORONTO: I lecture at Trinity on
Oedipus at 12, very well, and Miranda says masterly. Gordon Roper
says Trinity thinks of asking me to join the staff next year—a great

compliment. At rehearsal, Tony was suffering with teeth and very under par. He departs, leaving me to give some cuts in the Cobbler bedroom scene, no easy task. But Dennis King very decent and it goes well. I get the feeling that if I have the name I must have the game, so I direct a bit and please old King by giving him some comic business. Also revise the design of Molly's costume. The rehearsal with recorded music goes very badly. At 5 I record a TV conversation with Nathan Cohen, which he manages skilfully, and does not try to put me on the spot, and we part on very friendly terms. But he will slate the play when it appears, mark my words.

THURSDAY, OCTOBER 20, TORONTO: Rehearsals now enter Tony's "interesting stage" when character is developed and fine points worked over. The taped organ music is unsatisfactory and something has to be done about it—I know not what. Late this afternoon I returned from my Trinity lecture and found them at work on the new finale, and it goes well and everyone is much better displayed. Tony wants a few extra lines here and there. This evening went to see the Canadian Opera's *Otello*, and after working all day with a master of stage movement and grouping, I found the director Geiger-Torel's dull tableaux looked very unsophisticated, false, and undramatic.

FRIDAY, OCTOBER 21, TORONTO: This afternoon a run-through of almost all the play and I was pleasantly surprised by the speed, variety, and texture of it—a good meaty play. Decided to put the flashback of Higgin and Solly into the scene in Mrs. Bridgetower's bedroom, removing it from the Cobbler bedroom. Several developments show up in the run-through, such as the note of pathos in the play. This evening, Laurie Hardy and Madeleine Christie come to dinner with us, and they tell me that the copies of *Love and Libel* they received had a shaming blurb in the front about how Tyrone Guthrie

would turn the script into another *Tenth Man*;[36] obviously prepared for the Guild to send to possible investors. I hope their faith in their magician is justified. I think the play contains much that is good, and true, lively, witty, and funny: even Tyrone Guthrie cannot succeed with a worthless play, and sometimes not with a good one.

SATURDAY, OCTOBER 22, TORONTO: Greeted by Tony this morning with the news that King is still not content with what he has in the finale, and wants more. I sense that Tony is bowing to whatever seems to be the strongest wind, and thinks I am weaker than Dennis King: therefore I blow very chill indeed and make rather a fuss. Tony looks poorly: the white of his eye is a phlegmy blue, and he droops. But yesterday he and Dennis King lunched together, had a lot of drinks, and I suppose he gave in to cajolery, thinking I could be bullied. But what can I do? What King wants is all straight from the novel, so I cannot say it is not good. Tony says "we"—I suppose he means I—must bow to Dennis King's vanity, that he has been forty years on the stage, etc. I ask when he is going to begin to work on his part. So far he has read, mumbled, and played the baby at rehearsals. Tony, like many another, talks a lot about what he will say and do to difficult people, but he dominates those who will be dominated, gives in to the bullies, and is thoroughly Irish all round. This evening, at home, I reworked the scene, which is now less tight than it was, and I do not for an instant think this is the last. King already gags[37] a good deal and he will probably go mad before an audience.

The girls lunch with us, then Brenda and I bring Rosamond back to Peterborough. To the *Examiner* and do a few jobs, do some revision in the evening and hope for a day of peace tomorrow.

36 Guthrie's immensely successful production of Paddy Chayefsky's *The Tenth Man* was still running on Broadway.
37 Improvising rather than following the script.

SUNDAY, OCTOBER 23: Delightful day. Work on Trinity lectures in circumstances of real convenience, quiet, and comfort. In the afternoon hear music. Return to Toronto after tea, take Rosamond to school, and to the Harrises' to chat. A splendid restful change.

MONDAY, OCTOBER 24, TORONTO: My alterations in the finale seem to be satisfactory, at least for the present. Dennis King is now at work getting back lines which have been cut. The play seems to have taken a decided step forward today. John Cook came this afternoon and sorted out the music, but nothing is going to make it really good, I fear; the actors coarsen the tone as soon as they move about. Tidied Acts 1 and 2 this afternoon. I discovered that Marie Day had procured the cheapest kind of Roman Catholic cassock for Dean Knapp and checked that. Why do designers not consider such significant points? Are they all infidels, or Anabaptists? Write some new stuff for Ridley's second soliloquy. A number of props and some furniture have arrived and there is a sense of progress. Tony was in good form and did some excellent things. He says tomorrow some managers are coming to look at a run-through, to see if they want us in their theatres in New York. Wish we had assurance of a theatre; not my affair, but wish that matter were settled. I want to be home at Christmas.

TUESDAY, OCTOBER 25, TORONTO: This morning Tony worked hard on the Vambrace-Yarrow scene and lectured Gene Saks, who is a Method actor and cannot stick to a plan of moves or cadences. Rather like a very good amateur. Quite impossible for that excellent actor Laurence Hardy to work with. This afternoon a visitation from New York—Lawrence Langner, Billy Rose,[38] Ben Hecht,[39]

38 Impresario and lyricist.
39 Screenwriter, director, and playwright.

Don Herbert, and Dick Horner[40]—who saw a run-through (not the finale) and spoke well of the piece. Unless they were being quite needlessly tactful, they really liked it, and our chances of getting a theatre seem good. Then Tony comes back with us to our flat for tea and rum, and declared himself to be my father in the theatre, as Lewis Casson is his.[41] He says we do not understand King, who came from a bicycle shop in Birmingham, was a great star before he was thirty, and now sees everything as a threat, has trouble with his lines, and complains of the Canadian actors "they're all so good." Tony scolded me again for being easy about *Camelot*; I reply that *Love and Libel* is what I can do for the Canadian theatre, not criticism, and he admits the justice of that. Lawrence Langner had good criticism and a good idea—that the young people are excluded from the dreams. So tonight I work up a dream for Pearl.

WEDNESDAY, OCTOBER 26, TORONTO: Very heavy day. Rehearse at 10, Trinity at 12 (Greek and Elizabethan tragedy compared), rehearse at 2. Gene Saks is still in search of his part: if he were not such a nice fellow and so obviously a good actor, I would say this was a pompous and unprofessional bore. This afternoon Tony was at his dentist's, and when Dennis King found this out he declared himself tired and refused to rehearse. I took the others through most of it and fiddled with some lines. Tony is very bad about *words* and lets them get away with meaningless intonations. Most of Saks's trouble is that he does not trust the words. We put in Pearl's dream, which was very funny as Corinne dashed through it like the Fairy Bob-about. Back to the university at 5; to Hart House and talked to representatives of the college drama societies, with some effect,

40 Producer, stage manager, and theatre owner.
41 Guthrie (born 1900) was thirteen years older than Davies. Sir Lewis Casson
 (born 1875) was a leading British actor and director and the husband of
 Dame Sybil Thorndike.

I think. In the evening do a *Star* column on Thomas Mann and reshape Molly Cobbler's dream to include Shillito; hope it works. Poor Charmion as Molly simply cannot do it alone. She has no overflow, no *give*. Hope we move forward tomorrow. I count this a day almost lost.

THURSDAY, OCTOBER 27, TORONTO: This morning Tony was in his best form and did fine things with the dream sequence. I have done a dream for Pearl which threads through the others, and Molly's dream is much better with Tony van Bridge, who brings to it much of the tenderness she lacks. "This is what the theatre is about," Tony whispered, when it was going smoothly, and I agree. This is that theatre magic which cannot be created in quite the same way by any other means. When I returned from Trinity at 4, a rehearsal in costume was in progress. Many of the outfits look cheap and dreadful, and Marie Day has the oddest indifference to accuracy: the choirboy's medal worn by Higgin in his dream is the most hideous stage jewel! But it is unfair to criticize yet. However, some very trashy stuff appears among the props. Mrs. Bridgetower's mirror was an 87-cent thing (the price was still on it) framed in pink plastic. I complained, and a suitable silver one has replaced it. Amateurs would not be content with such rubbish. The Guild is notoriously mean, but the production should not look downright shabby.

FRIDAY, OCTOBER 28, TORONTO: Tony called this morning to say he had a letter from Lawrence Langner, advising certain revisions. I feared these might be drastic but when we met they proved to be: (1) Delay completion of Solly-Pearl romance. (2) Introduce dreams more carefully. (3) Heighten quarrel of Solly and his mother. (4) Let Cobbler draw the lovers together at the end. All quite easy. Tony says he thinks (4) was inspired by Dennis King, but not a bad

idea anyhow. Then we taped a radio interview with a man named Lillico. Tony was rather gruff with him and wanted to be paid if there was any pay going, and then referred to Ben Hecht as "a scruffy old Jew," and said his opinion was of no account. One of his Bad Boy performances. Watched the afternoon rehearsal and made some changes on the spot. This evening did the others fast and neatly. Tony writes in the *New York Times* that authors will do anything if threatened, for fear their work may be dropped. He despises authors, but also envies them, I think, for he writes well as an amateur but is short-winded and uncritical.

SATURDAY, OCTOBER 29, TORONTO: Typed the new material and took it to rehearsal. Quite a fuss with Tony because a Mrs. R.H. Lorimer Massie has asked the whole company to a party after the first night; he protests he will not go, that vulgar "backers" will be there, etc. Then it is proved Mrs. Massie is herself the big noise in the Theatre Exchange, our Canadian producers, and the party is a private one for the company alone. So Tony's wrath is assuaged. We now have bits of scenery and these complicate rehearsal. Tony goes at 4:45 to his dentist, and at 5 my new finale comes from the typist. I distribute it, and it is read once, and immediately Dennis King expresses disappointment and dissatisfaction; he wanted *far* more, and funny stuff. Also Corinne Conley and John Milligan put in their oars, wanting things for themselves. This after Rob Christie and even, God help me, Ed Holmes[42] have been giving me advice about how to improve the play! I am disgusted and furious and feel ill. Call Tony and say I think further changes inadvisable, and to my surprise he agrees, and says he will back me up. We shall see. But I am sick of being pushed around by actors.

42 He played one of the Townspeople of Salterton.

SUNDAY, OCTOBER 30, TORONTO: Worked on my *Lear* lecture in the morning and then to rehearsal about 12 and we tried the new finale. Hopeless: no life or reason in it. Before this I had quite a wrangle with Dennis King and frightened him, I think, for he became apologetic and compliant. But the new material was 100% no good. So I buckled down and reshaped it and in quite good measure rewrote the finale: love interest up, tension better maintained, and a better deal for old Dennis. Took it down at 5, just as they broke, and Tony was well pleased but thought the end indecisive. What about a couplet, said I for a joke. Nothing better, said he: so a couplet it is. We then tried to find a public stenographer, but none on Sunday, so to the Royal Alexandra Theatre where David Hays was hanging the scenery, and very exciting it looked. Stood on the stage and admired the handsome old house. Before dinner worked three-quarters of an hour on the two couplets, and after much brain-wracking produced something and read it down the phone to Tony—who was so kind as to call them brilliant. But we shall see.

No more rewriting before opening, I judge. Nervousness begins but at least one has something sizable to be nervous about: and rationalize as I may, I *do* cherish hopes of something better than failure.

MONDAY, OCTOBER 31, TORONTO: Rehearse new finale at 11, and again at the theatre (in the circle foyer) at 7 p.m. It works well. Then the technical rehearsal; an unnerving experience as the stage seemed to be filled with garish and distracting rubbish, and all the shifting of scenes and furniture is done visibly by the actors. Under all these antics the play suddenly disappeared. Tony drank a lot, became uproarious, kicked Rob Christie (his usual whipping-boy), and was rather above himself, though wholly in control of the situation. Not so King, whose feeble grasp on his words was further relaxed by drink. I kept out of the way and said nothing, and

suffered a good deal, but not so much as if these antics were utterly unknown to me. This went on from 8 until 2 a.m. and Act 1 had been technically rehearsed. Acts 2 and 3 tomorrow at 7; no dress rehearsal till Wednesday, the day of opening. What I dread is that my play may be scuppered by these *avant-garde* ornaments and a production too ingenious. The theatre reports poor booking—less than 50%—and says this is the case with most Canadian ventures, which I can well believe.

TUESDAY, NOVEMBER 1, TORONTO: Rehearse finale in circle foyer at 4:30, and Martinec interrupts with new drama: the musicians' union won't let us use our taped organ music because it is "hot"— i.e., John Cook, a London union man, recorded it in Toronto without informing the Toronto local. So an organist and a Hammond organ must be used. I undertake to find the organist and at last secure Miranda's friend at Trinity, Cecilia Anderson, who will be glad of the money. Technical rehearsal of Acts 2 and 3 at 7 p.m. and much less wearing than last night. Tony has accepted some of my suggestions and many staring colours have been greyed down. King is still very bad in his words and is ratty about it and explains a lot. Rob Christie muddled his dream speech badly; he is much disordered, I fear. Ernie Rawley took Brenda and me to his office and drank to the play and recalled when my *Fortune, My Foe* appeared at the Alex, in 1949, I believe. Kind of him. Now we stand on the brink of the first performance. Ernie Rawley says the advance booking $12,000: not the $18,000 he hoped for, but the Guild is very pleased. Of course good notices would bring some more into the house but I fear they will be guarded, and Cohen's a panning.

WEDNESDAY, NOVEMBER 2, TORONTO: To theatre at 10:30 and work with Cecilia Anderson, who is to fill in the music on a Hammond

organ. Then to Trinity to lecture on *Lear.* Dress rehearsal at 2:30—
long and full of accidents.

FIRST NIGHT: full house and the play well received. First act
slow; second goes very well; third plays to great laughs. Best scenes
as received by the audience: the Yarrow-Vambrace, and Solly and
his mother in her bedroom, and Higgin seducing Edith. Biggest
laugh: finale, Mrs. Bridgetower about "four bare legs in a blanket."
Many curtain calls and I am called for twice, and am rattled and
do not make a speech. Great enthusiasm and many backstage visi-
tors. I liked seeing the girls best: they seemed so real after all the
nervous nonsense of the production. Langner and Herbert very
well pleased, and Rawley also. But Tony was nervous and scratchy,
and Judy wanted to blame the play for whatever had gone wrong,
and I had to be rather firm when we drove them home. Tony, to my
astonishment, called the play "a realistic social comedy"! Mrs.
Lorimer Massie, a wealthy backer, entertained us all at Winston's
after the play. I hated it. How dismal such things can be! But as
such things are judged, the first night was promising.

THURSDAY, NOVEMBER 3, TORONTO: Lay late and felt very tired.
Notices not very helpful. Whittaker's friendly but guarded, presum-
ably for fear New York might reverse any firm decision for or
against. *Telegram* liked the production and thought the actors
splendid, but the play trivial. Cohen in the *Star* most sensible of all,
but expressed in his accustomed sneering style. Both evening
papers say I am imitating Thornton Wilder badly, and this irks me.
But the word-of-mouth is good and the house tonight not at all bad,
and Martinec says the worst we shall have. Lecture at Trinity on
Synge's *Playboy of the Western World* and walk both ways, very refresh-
ing. Worked with Tony on changes, and write a new dream for
Pearl, and one for Vambrace, under the stage in the orchestra
room, on an old envelope. Dine with Brenda at University Club and

to the theatre. Watched the dreams, which are better, and the Yarrow-Vambrace scene, which was very rocky. Tony says if we watch too much every night we shall lose our ability to discriminate.

FRIDAY, NOVEMBER 4, TORONTO: To the theatre and saw the new dreams and improved production of the party scene: all improvements. Talked with Corinne about her part. She was distressed that Charmion scooped the notices, but Corinne's is the part upon which the audience can project its dreams. Corinne can improve her performance by playing against her lines, by being more courageous.

SATURDAY, NOVEMBER 5, TORONTO: At 11 a.m. to St. Paul's to re-record the music to fit union demands; Dr. Charles Peaker[43] to play. He understands the situation perfectly and means to turn over part of his fee to Cook, who is to be "disciplined," i.e., bilked of $500 by the union. Charley plays far better than Cook, makes a fine tape, then regales us with rye in his snuggery, full of books and the console of the old St. Paul's Casavant organ. Have a jolly time, Cook, Charley, Tony, Lee Martinec, Madeleine Christie, and me. During the afternoon I revise the finale, and shift the Yarrow party a page or two onward. An excellent performance in the evening with eight curtain calls. Good party at the Stewarts' and of course everybody full of advice, about one third of it good.

A strenuous week and life-enhancing. Failure or success, I have had a jolly good time in Toronto. But what will the U.S. response be to this very Canadian play?

SUNDAY, NOVEMBER 6: Train call to Detroit at 8 a.m. and we all assemble in Union Station looking like nothing so much as a

43 Organist at St. Paul's Anglican Church.

company of touring theatricals. The crew are smart in Tyrolean hats and sunglasses, and hard to recognize. Leo Leyden comes as *Le Juif Polonais*[44] in a fur cap and a coat with a fur collar; Rob Christie very actory in a raglan coat and a broad-brimmed hat; Lewin Goff (an "observer" from Kansas University, on a grant to watch Tyrone Guthrie at work) has a brown derby, not worn as a joke but in good sadness;[45] Charmion King wears a honey-coloured coat with a very big collar, which has the effect of making her look short-legged, and a Eugénie hat of fur felt,[46] and is a modern Miss Snevellicci, the young actress in *Nicholas Nickleby*. We have a parlour car to ourselves and everybody sleeps, eats, frets about immigration; and Ed Holmes emerges as a great cut-up, as does Gene Saks, who does a turn as a presidential candidate, and makes a speech from the back of the train. To Detroit at 2:30 and there is an immigration holdup; the manifest has not come. Grania Mortimer worried because she is pregnant and the U.S. authorities fear (with some cause, I suppose) that gravid women invade their land to gain for their young the dubious boon of American citizenship. At last all is well and we get to the Fort Shelby Hotel and change our $9.50 room for a $12 one.

MONDAY, NOVEMBER 7, DETROIT: The Cass Theatre is big and old and smells. We rehearse in the foyer. I have my troubles with people who want to give advice and who want to lecture me on what my characters are, and how they would speak and act. I display a patience I did not know I had. At night there is one of those depressing "U.S.–Canada Cultural Exchange" gimmicks. The house is good but mostly paper;[47] we have "Star-Spangled," "Queen," and "O Canada"

44 *Le Juif Polonais* (1900), an opera by Camille Erlanger.
45 Act 5, Scene 2, *The Taming of the Shrew*.
46 Named for Empress Eugénie, wife of Napoleon III, a hat tilted over one eye with a brim folded up on both sides.
47 Non-paying invited guests.

vilely played. And the play goes like lead. The invitees cough and cough and cough, and laugh intermittently and reluctantly. But I am told Detroit is a dull theatre town. Afterward to a meeting in Lawrence Langner's hotel room with Armina Langner, Philip Langner and his wife, Don Herbert, and Tony. Long talk about the play, much of it very sensible, and at last these things emerge:

(a) The story line is confusing and a greater use of narration is suggested.

(b) The van Gogh backdrop is confusing and oppressive and must be replaced.

(c) Rob Christie is the only failure in the cast and they want him replaced.

(d) The moral about malice should be more strongly brought out.

Langner regrets that the title was changed; I do too, and wish they had had sense enough to see it beforehand.

Before the Langner meeting Don Herbert warned me that it might be tough: after eighteen years editing a paper it was child's play.

TUESDAY, NOVEMBER 8, DETROIT: Worked all day on revision; hired a typewriter. Became weary and disgusted by 3 and had to sleep. Tony came at 5 and I showed him the new Pearl-Higgin bit and my plan for revision. We decided that this would cope with (a) above, agreed on (b), agreed (c) could not be entertained for humanity's sake, and agreed (d) could be managed. Not a bad house tonight, though the presidential election was today and as I write, John F. Kennedy is a little ahead. I saw the dreams and wonder mightily if I should not be ruthless, cut them out, and use the time for a new Cobbler scene in Act 1. The play would then be straight comedy and not a trivial one; but the dreams are not really good except for Mrs. Bridgetower's, and their shallow pretentiousness shows nakedly. News at last of a New York theatre, the Martin Beck, which we could have after Boston.

WEDNESDAY, NOVEMBER 9, DETROIT: Wrote continuity and a new Cobbler scene this morning and went to rehearsal of new Pearl-Higgin scene. Lunched with Tony and Judy and we talked very cheerfully about the play and the theatre altogether. Brenda and I went to the show of medieval Flemish art, which was a great rest after so much writing. Both Lawrence and Philip Langner have written, recapitulating what was said on Monday, and most of what they suggest is already in progress. All suggestions sensible. I work to strengthen and clarify the story line—Tony agreed to abandon the dreams and was good enough to say he thought my reason for urging it showed true humility. But I know that these dreams were not written but manufactured, and they lack artistic integrity, which the rest of the play has.

THURSDAY, NOVEMBER 10, DETROIT: Worked on revision but my hired typewriter stuck, which put me off unreasonably. To rehearsal of new things at 11:30 and was depressed because King was scornful of his new scene, which I thought good; but the ass had not seen the possibilities in it and when he did he began to warm to it. I am an idiot to be so influenced by what actors think. A curious thing is that the line "Bugger little Earl," which was such a big laugh in Toronto, is nothing here, because it appears that to Americans the word is merely a synonym for "fellow." Terrible reaction today; I am sterile, gloomy, weak, and ill. But tonight we took the Guthries to hear the Detroit Symphony and Robert Casadesus play the Brahms Piano Concerto No. 2—superb! Most refreshing and noble, put me right back on my feet.

FRIDAY, NOVEMBER 11, DETROIT: Wrote a new scene for Ridley-Vambrace-Pearl in the morning and think it helps plot and character, though Brenda feels it lacks flash. Showed it to Tony and he havered a bit about how it was to be got on the stage. I have a

disquieting feeling that he is now rather tired of the production and hates the endless fussing with it. But tonight I saw the play through, and the changes in Act 1 strengthen it greatly, as the response of the audience showed. I think I have strengthened Act 2 and cutting the dreams will strengthen it more. Now Act 3, especially the finale, wants strengthening; I am tired but by no means at the end of my tether and am determined to conquer all the faults in the play that I can see. Tonight Brenda and I had drinks in the Tiger Bar here with Lee Martinec, and he chattered for an hour about the play and how *he* would rewrite it. As so often with these amateur playwrights, there were some grains of sense in his chaff. But the outcome of taking advice is so often a muddle. Martinec proves to be an interior decorator as well and calls plants "growies." Brenda has a good idea to strengthen the finale and I am going to work on it.

SATURDAY TO MONDAY, NOVEMBER 12–14, ANN ARBOR AND DE-TROIT: Horace Davenport[48] takes us to Ann Arbor at 2 p.m. on Saturday; he is professor of physiology there and much respected. Glad to get away from the theatre atmosphere and let the play sink below consciousness. This was easy, as the university people think of nothing but their own concerns.

We are put up at the university union, and on Sunday Davenport shows us his department and I am rather sickened by some monkeys immobilized in chairs, with electric wires embedded in their brains for some kind of neo-phrenological experiment. However, Horace is one of my oldest friends and I was happy to see him so successful and in such a good way of life, and I was impressed by the Davenports' devotion to their clever, nice children.

48 Davenport was one of Davies's closest friends at Oxford. He named his first son Robertson Davies Davenport.

Returned Monday, and at once revised the end of the finale, along lines suggested by Brenda. In the afternoon, wrote a new third act Solly-Pearl scene including Yarrow, which Tony likes, and we shall try it in rehearsal. He thinks the new Cobbler-Shillito scene does not work: I think King will not work on it. Hope the heavy revision is now over. Everything the management wants has been done—even a moral has been included.

TUESDAY, NOVEMBER 15, DETROIT: Rehearsal in the morning of the new Vambrace-Pearl-Ridley scene, and it is embarrassing as Guthrie hounds Christie without mercy—and unquestionably he is maddening. In the afternoon, prepared the new ending to the finale for use tonight, and Dennis King was sulky and said he had nothing to do. When I went to see him in his dressing-room, at Tony's behest, he huffed and puffed and threatened to leave the play—most unconvincingly, poor old goat. Then Corinne had a fit of telling me I did not know Pearl, and Tony dressed down the electrician, and all was dark and drear in the fun-shop. This evening, I saw the whole play through, and it is much improved by the cuts and new pieces. Lawrence and Phil Langner and Don Herbert were present and we had a pow-wow afterward in the Richelieu. They are well pleased with all that has been done. We have an unbosoming about King, who appears to be a famous nuisance, and finally agree to give him a new piece, a soliloquy. Altogether a good meeting, and their confidence was cheering in this deadly waste, Detroit, where nobody seems to laugh.

WEDNESDAY, NOVEMBER 16, DETROIT: All morning I work on revision and write a good soliloquy for Dennis King in the romantic vein prescribed by Tony. But Tony does not think the soliloquy for King will do: it does not advance the play. The naked truth is that his role has all it is entitled to in the play; he chose to play Cobbler,

rather than Vambrace or Higgin, either of which would have been simpler to build into a star part. No dramatic logic suggests that he should have more; even violent wrenching won't do it. But he is indignant, and a shameless pouter and an egotistical bully. I am near the end of my tether and cannot go on forever working up new stuff. Tony says he likes King because he loves a mountebank; so do I, but not at close quarters.

THURSDAY, NOVEMBER 17, DETROIT: Extraordinary that, under necessity, the mind *will* produce something which seems impossible. This morning I woke early, with a solution for the problem of Dennis King, rooted in a suggestion made by Brenda, casually, last night. I showed it to Tony at lunch and he thought well of it, and indeed was complimentary. He told me that Thornton Wilder rewrote the first act of *The Matchmaker* at least ten times, and that the rewriting on *Love and Libel* was perhaps less than is usual. So now, I hope, the bones of the play are set.

Tonight, Alf and Dama Bell of Stratford dined with us and the Guthries. Tony, rather tight, was being his usual haughty and dismissive self and spoke of Lawrence Freiman, who is on the board of governors at Stratford, and is owner of a chain of department stores in Ottawa, as "that little shopkeeper from Ottawa." "He's a shopkeeper in the sense that you are a Punch and Judy man," said I, sharply, for I had had enough. Then the fat was in the fire, and poor old Judy called me "a little person who printed a paper in Peterborough," etc., which made me laugh. But it grieves me that they cannot stop playing the haughty aristocrats, though they have no noble lineage, and this suggests some gnawing sense of insecurity, for God alone knows what reason. They also made a great fuss over what everything on the menu cost, and Judy wanted an ice that "belonged" to Alf Bell's dinner, and which he did not want. Then they paid for us all, which made us feel that we had cost them

money that was dearer than ordinary coin. All their friends know of this penurious trait and laugh at it, but it is painful to see them at it. They inveigh against Americans for worshipping money, but they make of it not a god, but a cruel master.

I saw the whole play and am pleased with the changes: the Solly-Molly bit after Act 2, Scene 4 does the work of the dreams without the cumbrous machinery.

FRIDAY, NOVEMBER 18, DETROIT: At last get the conclusion of the finale to my satisfaction. Tony devises a fancy music and dance conclusion, very difficult, and then departs for Stratford. He is very casual about such things, and I think since his illness is more slap-dash in direction. Anyhow, the performance tonight was rough and uncertain. King gagged a lot, and to no purpose, and I think Tony should have stayed on the spot. Lee Martinec annoys me by muttering about the first act, which does not please him. What a lot of insignificant people who are never really pleased there seem to be in the theatre world.

SATURDAY, NOVEMBER 19, DETROIT: Tonight the performance was shaky and uneven and King gagged remorselessly, to my dismay, and when beginning the finale music he gave the singers one note and began on another himself, and it was disgraceful. Later Swerdfager, van Bridge, and Saks complained to me that King is sapping the morale of the company, and that he calls some cast members to his dressing-room for notes! They asked me to speak to Tony and offered to come with me if I wished. Then, of course, I heard a mixture of flattery and venom from Martinec, who loves intrigue, but makes a kind of sense. He says that if this play were a success it would bring me a quarter of a million. I cannot think of such a thing and do not believe it. But it would bring me reputation.

SUNDAY, NOVEMBER 20, DETROIT: H.t.d. on waking; lay late reading. Dined very well at Stockholm, a Swedish restaurant; pack and fly to Boston. I detested Detroit and its awful car-making people, their provincialism and stupidity: Toronto is by comparison an Athens. The company was certainly tried in the fire in its two weeks in the auto capital.

In Boston Brenda and I stop at the Statler Hilton. I talk to Tony about the disaffection among the actors, and Dennis King's bad behaviour, and work out a plan: no drastic action, but careful re-rehearsing of the whole play, and a showdown if necessary. But, of course, the two bad scenes must be worked on tomorrow.

MONDAY, NOVEMBER 21, BOSTON: To the Wilbur Theatre at 10, and it proves to be a charming house built in the eighteenth-century manner, and decorated in fawn, gold, and garnet. Talk again with Tony and Jack Merigold about Dennis King. Brenda and I take the Guthries to lunch, then we see some Boston churches including a hideous Baptist emporium near the Parker House. Dinner with Leonid Kipnis[49] and his cousin Alexander, the former opera basso, and then to the play. It goes pretty well after the first act, but in his new scene—which we had rehearsed from 5 to 6 in the afternoon— Dennis King dried disastrously, forgot his Zoo song utterly, and left the stage, leaving Tony van Bridge to clear up the mess as best he could. Tony Guthrie found King in tears in his dressing-room. The audience took the play better than we had dared to hope, for both Tony and I were very nervous. Afterward we went to the Ritz to see the Langners and Don Herbert: they are pleased on the whole but want a lot of fiddles, and the first two

49 American producer of the film of Guthrie's production of *Oedipus Rex* at
 Stratford, 1957.

acts made into one, which suits me. I walk home with Tony across Boston Common.

TUESDAY, NOVEMBER 22, BOSTON: Boston notices are said to be important and ours verged from fair to splendid, the best being that of Elliot Norton of the *Record*, considered one of the most influential critics outside New York, and Boston's best. The cream of it is that his review is mostly praise of the play! But I must keep my hopes and ambitions in control. Martinec says we are virtually sold out for the fortnight, except for second-balcony seats. I talk to Miss Elinor Hughes of the *Herald* at lunch: a sensible woman but hates the Morphew scenes. The Langners call on us briefly in our room, in the afternoon, to recapitulate their remarks of last night. Then Tony and I work to shape the new Act 1. At 6:45 p.m. Tony and Dennis King appear on Elliot Norton's TV program to discuss *Love and Libel*, and to my astonishment Norton keeps the emphasis on the play, and I am likened to Chaucer, to Dickens, to Goldsmith! Balm after the thorns of Detroit. Wish I dared think New York would take the play in this spirit. This evening to work on the new stuff.

WEDNESDAY, NOVEMBER 23, BOSTON: Work on revisions and join a confab of Tony and the stage management in his room. Problem: if we throw Acts 1 and 2 together, our first act runs eighty-eight minutes; how to get it down to seventy-five? There are reasons, both artistic and technical, against moving any scene into the second act. Tony and I did some cutting, but nothing like the necessary time. I see no way out; perhaps tomorrow's rehearsal will reveal one. Matinée to a full house.

THURSDAY, NOVEMBER 24, BOSTON: American Thanksgiving. We rehearse for cuts in the morning in the echoing, noisy marble

foyer. Much labour and little time saved. Then lunch with the Guthries at Pieroni's with Mrs. Rona Mavor (James Bridie's[50] widow), Arthur Cantor, the impresario, Jack Merigold, Madeleine Christie, and Laurence Hardy. Very merry from 1:30 to 4. Hardy tells a good story of Basil Dean[51] rehearsing Baliol Holloway and nagging at him about the proper way to open, go through, and close a door which, as the stage was bare, was wholly imaginary. When at last he had done this to Dean's satisfaction, Holloway paused, mimed writing something, then stooped and shoved it under the imaginary door. "What's that?" called Dean. "My resignation," said Holloway.

I wrote an article (750 words) for the *New York Herald Tribune* about *Love and Libel*. Not easy, as I may not praise it or give away the plot. Very tired today: this unremitting work begins to tell. But a full house tonight, and sold out for next week, and Elliot Norton has given us another column of praise!

FRIDAY, NOVEMBER 25, BOSTON: Rehearsal of new material, cuts, and making one act of 1 and 2. Try all this in the evening. We sit in the last row of the second balcony, and I am glad I lured Tony up there, as he finds much inaudible and sees things he had not seen before. The new first act takes an hour and twenty-five minutes, which I think too long, but the audience takes it well and is lively. Meet Philip Langner and Don Herbert after at the Statler, and Mrs. Philip Langner is tiresome about reconstruction, and talks a lot about what she called the "great" scenes—meaning the funny ones—and cannot understand that not every scene can be funny, or none will be funny. A decent creature, but drunk with being a producer's wife. I reason with her, and am not, I hope, uncivil.

50 James Bridie was the stage name of Osborne Henry Mavor, Scottish
 playwright.
51 English actor, writer, film and theatrical producer and director.

Brenda points out, gently, that the play is not so simple a comedy as Mrs. Langner seems to think.

SATURDAY, NOVEMBER 26, BOSTON: Deeply fatigued and when I try to work on some new bits, so many keys on the hotel typewriter stick that I abandon the struggle. But I sort notes made last night and take them to Tony. Philip Langner comes and we decide to try a three-act form again, with a new distribution of scenes. This evening we sold out completely, for the first time. Both Herbert and Langner think the play will be a hit; I dare not allow myself an opinion.

SUNDAY, NOVEMBER 27, BOSTON: This afternoon to the Old North Church and heard the Collegium Musicum sing some Bach, Buxtehude, and J.H. Schein, in the candlelit dusk. Splendidly restoring. Tonight did several revisions for rehearsal tomorrow. Elinor Hughes's piece about me appeared in today's *Herald*: she reported me as saying what in fact *she* said—the common vice of journalist-critics.

MONDAY, NOVEMBER 28, BOSTON: Rehearsals at 11 and 2. Discussed what lay behind the park scene with Johnny Milligan and Corinne, and later Tony said he thought such discussion fruitless: an odd and I think rather shallow view, but perhaps not. Tonight some fuss at the theatre as the Langners *père* and *fils* and Herbert were there but no Tony. Word came he was ill—stomach. But I think he now saves himself, perhaps fearing for his heart. The upshot was that I took the full force of the Langners' displeasure afterward because the play, in three acts, is ten minutes longer than in two—i.e., the length of an interval. Lawrence Langner was, as always, full of notions about cutting, and has borne away a script to do some! God knows what he will suggest. What disgusts me is that at the second

interval Philip Langner was like a courtier, urging me to write a new play and let him have it at once, and afterward he was barely civil. Is it any wonder people say hard things about Jews? I now know that we shall know no peace until after our opening December 7, and that if its decision is negative, the Theatre Guild will know my name no more.

TUESDAY, NOVEMBER 29, BOSTON: Last night hyssop and gall; this morning dove's milk. The Guild people met Tony and me in the downstairs foyer, amid the stink of disinfectant from the lavatories, and bullied sweetly about cuts. I was desperately depressed for the first time since all this began. For twenty years I have been a writer, and never before have I been in a milieu where every consideration came before literary considerations, and the opinion of anybody—the humblest actor, money counter or baggage man—weighed equally or heavier than that of the author. My disgust is like a cap of fire bearing down on my head. Why would an author of any pride submit to the impertinences of theatre people?

WEDNESDAY, NOVEMBER 30, BOSTON: Rehearse this morning some fairly extensive cuts: learn this evening that they take a scant three minutes off our playing time: let the Guild take note. This afternoon our company was asked to be the guests of *Do Re Mi*, Garson Kanin's musical starring Phil Silvers at the Colonial. One ought not to see plays when one has a play in production. I could not abandon myself to enjoy it, for they have flash-backs: we have flash-backs. They have some newspaper montage: so have we. They have a couple in bed: we also. The resemblances are not great but enough to make me glad we go to New York first. I thought the piece full of clever things, but not a unity, and Silvers has not enough variety to carry a show. I cannot bear all that Jewish sentimentality about failure; it *cringes* so.

THURSDAY, DECEMBER 1, BOSTON: A cold impends: psychosomatic, I suppose. To the art museum and the Isabella Gardner Museum where music and pictures soothed me. This evening to the play and sat at the back of the top balcony with Brenda and Tony and made notes. King has been compelled to drop some of his enormities but he still gives a vain, selfish performance. I am not reconciled to it—only quiescent. Tomorrow we do final touches and arrange a new curtain call.

FRIDAY, DECEMBER 2, BOSTON: Rehearsal at 12:15 where Tony gives notes and arranges a fancy call: what lesser folk delight to call "sealing" or "freezing" the production, though he scorns such terms. In the afternoon George and Norah Harris's daughter Adrienne shows Brenda and me the new Loeb theatre at Harvard—a costly toy for amateurs: she says the engineers take great delight in it, but the work is poor. Later we go to cocktails aboard the visiting HMCS *Bonaventure*, courtesy of Captain O'Brien. Lee Martinec corners me and says if we do not have rave reviews in New York, we are through, because "we have nothing to sell"; if we get the reviews we are still in trouble as Dennis King is not a draw, and Tyrone Guthrie is thought "arty." So, with the best possible luck, we need a gigantic publicity campaign. *All the Way Home*[52] opened Wednesday and closes tomorrow, and we can do the same. (*Later note*: No, the producer Arthur Cantor saved it by a brilliant defiance of the critics and a direct appeal to the public.) All this depresses me, though I know Martinec loves drama and with him as with so many people, drama means gloom. I judge the play's chances to be about 1,000 to 1, or roughly none at all. But if it fails I may hope for something short of *All the Way Home*'s débâcle. Have a very bad case of cold feet, not improved by news that the Harrises, Stewarts, and Gordons are

52 By Tad Mosel, from the James Agee novel *A Death in the Family*.

coming to New York for the opening. *Post scriptum*: Slept wretch-
edly, dreaming I was being chased through slum alleys full of bar-
riers and barbed wire by fat dwarfs dressed in black, long overcoats
(the Theatre Guild uniform). I am in a bad way.

SATURDAY, DECEMBER 3, BOSTON: See the play through tonight
with Tony. It goes well. Elliot Norton comes for the third time! Johnny
Milligan cannot consolidate his effects. Dennis King cannot or will
not shake off his gags and enormities. Tony says he is a fine talent but
he has no industry or taste. Whatever happens in New York, Boston
has used us well. This morning I revised and strengthened Cobbler's
last speech in the bedroom scene and gave it to Dennis King. Hope
he can manage it by the dress rehearsal in New York.

SUNDAY, DECEMBER 4: Train call at 9:30. Roberta Kinnon loses her
ticket and has sent all her money ahead in her trunk; Judy says this is
an attention-getter and she may be right. Pleasant journey to New
York: Tony shows us plans of the theatre in Minneapolis which is to be
named after him; very splendid inside and ugly outside. Madeleine
Christie, Jim Edmond, and Tony van Bridge get drunk in the restau-
rant car, with Madeleine singing drunk. On the journey I had a long
talk with Gene Saks about the Method, which makes excellent sense
as he describes it, as a search for truth and a rejection of cliché. My
name appears thrice in the *New York Times*. We stay at the Dorset Hotel
as usual. Tonight at dinner at the Russian Tea Room, Brenda scolded
me for my gloom about the play and says that if it fails the world has
not ended: no, but twenty-five years' work and hope have been re-
buffed, and I grow no younger or more eager for the struggle.

MONDAY, DECEMBER 5, NEW YORK: A *dies non* respecting *Love and
Libel*. To Lulie Westfeldt, whose teaching did much to allay my anxi-
ety. At Argosy, the rare-books store, we bought for Tony a playbill

of his great-grandfather, Tyrone Power. Tonight Brenda and I went to Anouilh's *Becket* at the St. James, and admired Laurence Olivier in the title role, but was not really interested in the play, a homosexual nonesuch. Then to the Algonquin for drinks with Barbara Hamilton and Charmion King, very pleasant. This morning we surveyed the Martin Beck, a Moorish theatre, like a large Turkish bath and rather too big for our play, in my view. Tonight Brenda said that, from what she hears and judges, the play will do pretty well and not be a shaming muddle and flop. This is comforting. This morning as we passed the door of Hugh MacCraig, the astrologer, I thought of asking him, but rejected the notion as futile. We shall know soon enough. I should report that Willis Wing says the talk around Broadway that he hears is good, and much of it comes from movie people.

TUESDAY, DECEMBER 6, NEW YORK: At 12 noon I went to the Guild offices having been summoned by Don Herbert, and find him with Philip Langner, who gives me a great rigmarole which summarizes thus: (1) They have spent all the money collected for the play. (2) If we get anything short of rave notices we must close Saturday, or carry on for two weeks with a fund of $20,000, and will I put up $10,000 of it? All this muddled with such bypaths as (a) Langner and Herbert are not sleeping from worry; (b) Lawrence Langner won't put up any more money as he is providing for his old age; (c) playwrights have sometimes made more from plays than the producers, which is, of course, contrary to God's will, and they ought to take some of the financial risk. I heard all this with an impassive countenance and said I would think about it. Talked to Brenda who said Nothing Doing, and to Willis Wing who said the same. They must think me a gull. Among other Langner proposals is that I take no royalties for a while: that might make some sense.

We rehearse at 4 and I meet Stuart Little of the *Herald Tribune* at

6 for a brief interview, then to a press cocktail party at the Canadian consulate. A preview at 8:30 to an audience chiefly of secretaries. The play goes encouragingly well and is well received by the odd, inchoate house. If we fare so well tomorrow night our chances are good, I should say.

WEDNESDAY, DECEMBER 7, NEW YORK: Rehearse at 12 for a few notes, then a splendid lunch and excellent talk with Tony and Judy at the Famous Kitchen next door to the Martin Beck. We also dined with them at Café de France and then to our first night. The audience laughed in all the Boston places, but less heartily; some scenes, notably the Act 2 bed scenes and the Oedipus scene, went admirably, but on the whole my impression was of an audience unwilling to commit itself. Afterward we went on to Philip Langner's apartment at 135 Central Park West to wait for the notices: an excellent party, but no notices. Reason: it appears that a strike of newspaper distributors impends and we may get no notices at all—a frustration nobody had foreseen.

THURSDAY, DECEMBER 8, NEW YORK: Slept poorly, anticipating bad news, or perhaps no news of any kind because of the strike. However, it delayed the papers but did not quash them. Willis Wing called about 10: Taubman in the *Times* did not like the piece. Irvin Dorfman called a few minutes ago: *Times* and *Herald Tribune* bad; *News* and *Mirror* good and quotable. I am to lunch with Willis Wing and will learn more. But I do not feel so downcast as I well might: relieved rather than otherwise. All the reviews, though not bad, were heavily qualified and all faulted the play.

We dined with the Harrises at the Baroque, then to theatre. The Notice is up for Saturday: no time lost there. Thankful for friends. We took leave of Judy and Tony, who says it's time to "get on to the next thing."

FRIDAY, DECEMBER 9, NEW YORK: We dine with Jackie Davie and others, then go to the theatre and take farewell of actors, who are delightful.

Davies posted this letter at the theatre after "the Notice" went up:

December 9, 1960

My dear friends

It is too bad that our venture should be so soon over, but—never explain, never apologise. It has been a great pleasure to work with you all and I hope that I may do so again—soon, and under more favourable stars. Brenda and I wish you all the happiness you so plainly deserve.

Robertson Davies

SATURDAY, DECEMBER 10, NEW YORK: To Lulie Westfeldt at 9:30 a.m. for an excellent lesson. Then pack and away on the 2:45 flight. At Toronto we find there is no 6:30 train so we get the 6 p.m. 'bus and are home by 8:30. Everything looks very good and welcoming and Mrs. Pedak has lots of food. We revel in the space and the cleanliness!

SUNDAY, DECEMBER 11: Lay late and finished Trollope's *The Three Clerks.* In the afternoon, read *Bracebridge Hall* by Washington Irving for a *Star* column. At 8:45 p.m. the Thompsons come to the house—they had been to the train to meet us! But a day late. We went home with them for drinks and gossip and are pleased to be so kindly treated.

This is failure. But so many people have been so kind it is almost better than success; and *A Voice from the Attic* has done well, and a writer to the *Globe* says my novels approach genius, so life is not really black and I begin to recover.

Some later notes: After the débâcle, Lee Martinec informed whoever

would listen that the moment he set foot on Broadway, he had a premonition that *Love and Libel* would never do. *All the Way Home* fought bad notices courageously, and won. *Do Re Mi* has been acclaimed as a golden musical by Taubman, who found my fun dusty and professional. After the failure Hume Cronyn and Irene Worth went out of their way to be very kind, and said the Guild was a bad management. Tony Guthrie said, "Well, this settles it; none of us will ever work for the Guild again." But how, then, have they been in business, and good business, since 1920? By failing in courage? By asking authors for $10,000 the day before opening? People behaving very characteristically, as when Dennis King gave an interview to the *Herald Tribune*, in which he said that if he had not been wasted, the play might not have come to grief. As WRD, asserting that if he had known $10,000 was wanted, he would gladly have furnished it. As when Brenda and I took farewell of the actors on Friday night, and they showed the greatest courage, kindness, and humour; a much-abused and decent profession. As when we returned to Peterborough, and found that Ruth and Ross Thompson met us, to show friendship and bid us to a meal, lest we should feel unwelcomed. Everything considered, everyone has behaved well.

For some months, the Guild talked with enthusiasm of trying the play in London, but the plans fell through. They were pressing Tony too hard and on April 26 he wrote me, saying he had withdrawn from the whole affair. What irks me is that he writes: "If it had meant that you and your wife and Little Ones would otherwise have starved, *of course* I'd have been proud to bow the knee to Mr. Herbert, but as you're nicely fixed as the Biggest Fraud in the Academic Racket, I feel I can consult my own wishes. I hope, nay feel confident, dear Meliboeus, that thou wilt not chide." I do not like to have it put on this level—"you have a job, so I don't have to provide for you." Tony has never understood why I want a theatre reputation—or perhaps he does, and seeks thus to tramp on my

ambition. The truth is, he hates redoing a show, and I fully understand why. Nor do I think it wholly desirable that he should do *Love and Libel* again. But why phrase it as he has done?

MONDAY, DECEMBER 12: Return to the *Examiner* and am happy to find it in excellent condition, and I am greeted by many friendly and sympathetic words. I grapple with accumulated mail, talk to department heads, write a *Star* column on Washington Irving, and in the evening work on a lecture on *As You Like It*. Home is very clean, convenient, and delightful.

WEDNESDAY, DECEMBER 14: To Toronto and lecture at Trinity on *As You Like It* at 12 and then farewell to those fatheads. In the afternoon shop very hard, then have dinner with Brenda and Miranda and we go to *The Seventh Seal*, another fine Bergman, then to Hawthorn Gardens and chat with Margaret till 11:30. Admirable h.t.d.

THURSDAY, DECEMBER 15, TORONTO: To Trinity for lunch and talk about next term's work, and lecture from 2 to 4: Gordon Roper declared this a great success. To the Bishop Strachan School Nativity. Jenny sang Second King. We dine with the Stewarts, very jolly but I drank too much.

FRIDAY, DECEMBER 16: Bad night and hangover. To Peterborough on train with Kit for our *Examiner* directors' meeting and year-end business. Very weary. Brenda, Jenny, and Rosamond home about 7, very jolly, and we have an uproarious dinner. I then read and plan what must be done in the next few days, which is plenty, and I must take care not to rush and destroy myself.

SUNDAY, DECEMBER 25: Up at 9; breakfast and the tree take 'til 12 with many handsome gifts. In the afternoon we walk in the woods

near Chemong Lake, very fine. Christmas dinner, then Miranda reads a "consequences" story to which we have all contributed. We read aloud, then to bed at 10:45.

I took Xmas more lightly this year than usual, with good effect. Did not strain to enjoy, nor agonize over gifts, yet all has gone well. So much of my life has been darkened by anxiety and the wish to excel!

MONDAY, DECEMBER 26: Write a *Star* column on Beerbohm in the morning. Then in the afternoon, Vincent Massey calls, very mysterious, wants to see me on Saturday. Is this anything to do with the university? We go to parties at Curriers', Mort and June Knox, and Thompsons', and then dine and play games till 1. To bed but cannot sleep: could Vincent Massey's call signal escape from Peterborough? The thought unsettles me.

TUESDAY, DECEMBER 27: Took the afternoon off and slept. Brenda has read my mind about Vincent Massey and we discuss the matter, but I have not one crumb of reason to hope or believe in such an appointment. Nonetheless, I am much stirred and cannot control my fancy. I did a little work on lectures but am out of sorts.

WEDNESDAY, DECEMBER 28: To Toronto at 8:45 for radio and TV meetings,[53] and then WRD and Arthur lunch with Brenda, Jenny, and me at the Club; we are home by 7. I work on lectures and the others skate. WRD is getting discursive but looks very well; I continue to stew unwarrantably about Vincent Massey's call.

53 At this time Rupert Davies, in partnership with Roy Thomson (later Lord Thomson of Fleet), owned the Frontenac Broadcasting and Kawartha Broadcasting radio and TV stations.

THURSDAY, DECEMBER 29: Work hard and make headway with first lecture:[54] what hard work! In the evening the girls give a party and sleigh ride for ten. Brenda and I lurk in the study, and they go home about 1:30 and seemed to have a good time. I still stew about Vincent Massey. Foolish.

FRIDAY, DECEMBER 30: Complete first lecture and Brenda says it is good, and funny, which had not occurred to me. In the evening WRD calls to say Tyrone Guthrie has been knighted—he heard it on radio. This is recognition long deferred and greatly merited.

SATURDAY, DECEMBER 31: Work at the *Examiner* till 11:30; wrote an editorial about Tony. Vincent Massey's chauffeur collects me at 11:45 and I drive to Batterwood with a heavy heart. It cannot be. But it is! He and Claude Bissell want me to be the first Master of Massey College and have no other they want. We discuss this from 12:45 to 5:45 and are at one on many of the things, great and small, which would shape such a venture. I return home elated and tell Brenda. The family drinks 1961 in with champagne.

What a year! I am really too fagged to rehearse it. The appearance of *A Voice from the Attic* meant a quantity of proof-reading, indexing, and fussing beyond my previous experience, and from May on the play was always with me. A failure at last, but I do not count it lost, nor shall I give up hope of the theatre. But such a blow is bound to depress and affect my health. Curious: in Detroit I went to the Episcopal cathedral and prayed that I might be given grace to take success or failure with courage and decency of behaviour. And I was! First time, to my recollection, that a prayer of mine has been answered. Then—yesterday, before going to Batterwood to

54 Davies was preparing a series of three public lectures drawn from *A Voice from the Attic*, to be given at Trinity College in January 1961.

see Vincent Massey, I consulted the *sortes virgilianae*[55] with Mencken's *Dictionary of Quotations* and hit upon *Veni, sancte spiritus.*[56] Now, does this mean that religion, with which I have so long struggled, is at last asserting itself more directly in my life? But then I went to Vincent Massey who asked me to be first Master of Massey College! This means escape from Peterborough, from newspaper life, of which I have had enough, and a new beginning in that academic world which has so long attracted me—entering it at the top! My life becomes, more clearly, a strange, phantasmagorical external-izing of my dreams! But a dream that comes true, as I know from experience, is always the matter, or substance of one's dream, re-worked so that it takes some penetration to recognize it for what it is. Our decision is made, but I expect details will take some time to work out, and being head of a new college cannot be beer and skittles; but it should undoubtedly be interesting.

My resolve for 1961 must be to fit myself for my new work. I think I have done pretty well with my 1960 resolve, which was sharply tested by the *Love and Libel* adventure: I tried to be a reed, bending but not breaking. If I am to be master of a college my sense of hospitality must be improved: if I cannot really delight in people, I can at least learn to be civil, and let them talk, which I believe is the great secret.

55 A form of divination in which advice or predictions of the future are sought by randomly selecting a passage from Virgil's *Aeneid*. It was most widely practised in the later Roman Empire and in medieval times.
56 "Come, Holy Spirit."

1961

—

SEVERAL MEMBERS OF THE MASSEY family who were Davies's col-
leagues, patrons, and sometimes protagonists in the establishment
of Massey College now appear frequently in the diaries. At this time
Vincent Massey was the most distinguished man in Canada. He was
the head of his generation of a family that had made a fortune in farm
machinery, and his career had been marked by a succession of diplo-
matic and government appointments culminating in the office of
governor general from 1952 to 1959. Widowed since 1950, he was
somewhat lonely and, at the age of seventy-three, had by no means lost
interest in the possibility of remarriage. He lived at Batterwood, a
large English-style country house north of Port Hope, Ontario, that
he and his late wife had developed in the 1920s. While he was gover-
nor general, he had relied on his elder son, Lionel, as secretary and
Lionel's wife, Lilias, as hostess. To some extent these three were still
decompressing from their vice-regal lives. Lionel now lived in Toronto
and had a senior if uncertain position at the Royal Ontario Museum
as director of administration.

Vincent's grandfather, Hart Massey, who had made the family fortune, had also established a family tradition of philanthropy, which Vincent inherited. While he was still an undergraduate at the University of Toronto in 1910, he had persuaded his father and other family members who were executors of Hart Massey's estate to make a major gift to the University of Toronto, the great student centre Hart House. Now, fifty years later, he had decided he wanted the Massey Foundation to make one final gift to the university of a post-graduate residential college. Vincent was inspired in large part by his own undergraduate experience at Balliol College, Oxford, although the new college would function more like Oxford's post-graduate college, All Souls. Like Hart House, Massey College was originally intended for men only.

In 1961, Vincent Massey was chair of the Foundation and its senior member. Other members of his family who sat as trustees were Lionel, now forty-four; Hart, Vincent's younger son, forty-two, a noticeably short man, an architect, considerably more independent from his father than Lionel; Raymond Massey, Vincent's taller, nine-years-younger brother, an actor, famous as a London, New York, and Hollywood star, with a breezy, extroverted American manner quite different from Vincent's more formal British style; and Raymond's eldest son, Geoffrey, thirty-six, who had inherited his father's height and good looks and was now an architect in Vancouver. The disagreements among these family members as well as their various changes of mind in the course of establishing and financing Massey College were to be a major source of vexation to Robertson Davies, and of entertainment in these diaries.

Despite their shared theatrical interests, Davies had never met Raymond Massey, but he had met Vincent a number of times. Though they worked closely and mostly happily together in the first years of the College, Rob continued for some time to address the older man as Mr. Massey. Rob had overlapped with Lionel at Upper Canada

College and with Lionel and Hart at Oxford. Both Lionel and Hart had been seriously injured in the war, and Lionel had been a prisoner-of-war.

The Masseys were represented, to some extent, by Wilmot H. Broughall, a lawyer and trust officer at the National Trust Company, which looked after the Massey money, both for the Foundation and for the Masseys individually. In this role Bill Broughall carried out the Masseys' wishes, and sometimes instructed them on what their wishes were. He and Rob were exact contemporaries and swiftly became allies, and he became a key figure in the creation of the College.

At the University of Toronto, the leading figure in the establishment of the new college was Claude Bissell, at forty-two the comparatively young and recently installed president. Like Davies, he had grown up in small-town Ontario, in his case Meaford. An English literature scholar by academic discipline, he had been president of Carleton University before his Toronto appointment. From its inception he understood the purpose of Massey College, supported it consistently, and never shared in the suspicion and obfuscation that marked the attitude of some of his academic colleagues toward Davies and Massey College. At a much later time he wrote the biography of Vincent Massey.

Rob and Brenda continued living in Peterborough in 1961 but were spending increasing amounts of time in Toronto, where Rob lectured at Trinity two days a week. At various times they rented a furnished apartment or stayed in hotels, with friends, or at the Hawthorn Gardens house of Rob's father.

A month after Davies was invited by the Masseys to accept the job of Master, he realized that the establishment of the new college would be an important development, not only for himself but also for the university and the country. Accordingly he decided to start a separate diary devoted to the College, backdating it to his December 31, 1960, meeting with Vincent Massey. The early entries have a somewhat stiff

and formal quality, in the nature of minutes of meetings, but they swiftly degenerate into a compelling, ongoing, indiscreet dramatic narrative. Davies continued to keep his personal diary, though the entries become more cryptic, as well as his occasional travel and theatre diaries. Selections from all these diaries are interleaved here.

SATURDAY, DECEMBER 31, 1960: I visited the Right Honourable Vincent Massey at his country home, Batterwood, near Port Hope, and he asked me to be the first Master of Massey College. I was not wholly unprepared, as he had made the appointment for me to come the previous Monday, Boxing Day, and I had an intuition it was about the College, and probably the Mastership. Had not Hugh MacCraig, the astrologer, said that I should spend the latter part of my life among young people, and be something of a sage and prophet? So, though of course I gave no sign, I was not taken by surprise, and promised to consider the proposal most carefully, and spoke with enthusiasm of the project. How often does one receive such an offer? How often is one asked to take part, from the beginning, in a really exciting project? How often is one given the opportunity to shape something which is of significance to large numbers of other people? That is why I have determined to keep this record of the history of the beginnings and growth of the College from the time I became involved with it. I want to make it an honest chronicle, perhaps of interest and use to the College itself in some time to come. But it had better be secret; I have no disposition to be scandalous but I want to be candid, and my tendency toward what is satirical and possibly *farouche* unfits me to write a flat-footed record.

SUNDAY, JANUARY 1: Lay late; up at 12 and write my yearly diary and theatre notes; in the afternoon we walk in Jackson Park. In the evening New Year's dinner and we tell the girls of the Massey

College offer, enjoining them to secrecy; they are delighted and full of questions. The *Love and Libel* disappointment is so soon salved! The offer bears out Hugh MacCraig's comment that I have a very protected horoscope and seems to point the direction I should go. Hope this is not mystical nonsense.

WEDNESDAY, JANUARY 4: With Brenda to Toronto by train and to our rented flat at the Waldorf-Astoria, and then to Trinity to my new office, a plaster box. This afternoon a long talk with Claude Bissell in his office in Simcoe Hall which dispels my misgiving about Massey College. The university is strongly behind it and will not see it sink under a deficit. We got down to figures: the Master is to have a college head's stipend, between $15,000 and $20,000; in addition I would have a university professorship, whatever it is worth—something like $8,000 to $10,000, I believe. (*Later note*: Misunderstanding: $15,000 altogether, which is what I get from the *Examiner.*) So it would not be a backward step financially, with a house as well. We looked at the model—a handsome building. Bissell and I agreed that some of Vincent Massey's ideas about the number of Senior Fellows[1] would not work in a Canadian university, if they were expected to maintain rooms. Also, that the College would more probably be ready in 1963 than in '62, as such a structure should not be rushed or scamped. But the whole thing is now much clearer. Bissell sees the university as the "angel" of the College. He wants all financial control (which would extend, in time, to everything of importance) in the university's hands. I know Vincent Massey does not want this, and asks for an independent corporation. But there can be no independence without money, and College revenue will be small. This

1 The College was to consist of Junior Fellows, who were post-graduate students in the School of Graduate Studies, and Senior Fellows, who were leading university professors and other men of particular distinction.

is the basic dilemma and the one which must be solved before I can agree to taking the mastership. I made it clear to Bissell that I am not a financier and cannot and will not beg up and down Bay Street for funds. He assures me nothing of the sort will be required. But—ah!—I must have something more solid than any assurance either side has offered. Nonetheless, very reassuring. This clinches it. We dine with Arnold and Letty Edinborough,[2] very jolly.

FRIDAY, JANUARY 6, EPIPHANY: Wrote Vincent Massey assuring him that if details can be worked out (meaning College finance) I will take the post.

SUNDAY, JANUARY 8: Lay late. In the afternoon, walked in Burnham Wood.[3] Did some work on the second Trinity lecture. In the evening heard *Tales of Hoffmann* on the gramophone with increased admiration, while browsing among my books—something I rarely have time to do.

I am becoming somewhat more accustomed to the Massey College idea which overset me for a while, as being so extraordinary and beyond all foreseeing and perhaps not quite real; but it is real enough, and looks better all the time.

WEDNESDAY, JANUARY 11: To Toronto and when I arrive at Trinity College, a letter from Claude Bissell awaits me, with an offer of the mastership and an academic appointment—probably a special lectureship—at a total of $15,000 *per annum*. Precisely what I get for editing the *Examiner*, but a heated, lit, tax-free, and maintained house goes with the post, so it is worth decidedly more. Bissell and

2 Arnold Edinborough was editor of *Saturday Night* magazine.
3 A wooded area near Peterborough.

I are agreed I must have an academic post as Master, as without it I shall always be under the reproach of being a mere lodging-house keeper, or another warden of Hart House. Meanwhile I have sought the advice of Gordon Roper as I would like my academic appointment to be to Trinity, where I am now a visiting professor. He will speak to Derwyn Owen, the provost.

At tea I told my father of the Massey proposal and asked his advice. He was immediately and strongly for it. One of his comments was Victorian and characteristic of his concern with putting the family in a good way of life: "It will lift you right above commerce," said he. Delightful, and out of key with the attitude of so many businessmen who despise academic life. My brother Arthur also expressed strong approbation and is confident we can make good provision to run the *Examiner.*

SATURDAY, JANUARY 14: Busy morning. Meant to work on lecture in the afternoon but slept, then h.t.d., vastly more humanizing. Walked with Brenda before dinner. In the evening, heard Tchaikovsky's *Eugene Onegin* with the score and enjoyed it greatly. Talked with Brenda about the Massey College move: it will not all be fun, but it is a chance to do something new, which is rare at my age, and I do not see why I cannot write, too.

SUNDAY, JANUARY 15: Once again ambition burns in me to have a D.Litt. from Oxford[4] but on what basis? *Voice from the Attic?* Not an original contribution to learning. Or is it? But for my professional work and status as Master it would be helpful: shall I look into this? Write the secretary of faculties.

4 Davies achieved a B.Litt. from Oxford in 1938 with his thesis, *Shakespeare's Boy Actors.* He did not succeed in getting a D.Litt at this time but was given an honorary D.Litt. from Oxford in June 1991.

WEDNESDAY, JANUARY 18: To Toronto and see the Reverend D.R.G. Owen, provost of Trinity College, who has been talking to Vincent Massey at a dinner party. Owen gloomy and not very pleasant; he has got the notion somewhere that Trinity is being asked to pay some of the stipend of the Master of Massey College. He utters gypsy warnings about college finance. I feared this: the jealousy and obstructionism of other colleges will be one of the hazards of this project. They will not mean to be discouraging and disagreeable—at least, not markedly so—but they will have to be more than human to avoid it. And I, as a non-academic person becoming head of a graduate college, will not be to their taste. All the more reason to insist that the College have enough money to have some measure of independence.

THURSDAY, JANUARY 19, TORONTO: I see Bissell again, at 3. He is reassuring, but it is clear the university wants control. As their vice-president in charge of finance, Frank Stone, puts it, if they "pick up the tab" they must virtually dictate policy. Bissell and I agree that the trustees of the Massey Foundation are not being very realistic about money. But Bissell thinks they will see the light. I hope so. The present state of affairs worries me and I am not sleeping well. Already, psychologically, I have allied myself with this venture more perhaps than is wise, and so has Brenda. We have discussed some of the things we could do, as a pair, to make the College a success.

SATURDAY, JANUARY 21: Some work on the third lecture in the morning; in the afternoon rest, then work and finish the lecture, and Brenda says it is good. Very tired, and sub-zero weather does not help matters. But I am glad the lectures are composed: delivery is not so wearing; ninety-seven pages altogether and close-packed stuff, most of it. Brenda is in low spirits: the children are away and she feels she has nothing to do and is worried about a lump in her

breast. We discuss holidays. In Toronto she will have much to do. She says it is the ennui of middle age.

MONDAY, JANUARY 23: Felt unwell and took aspirin and a lot of water: 'flu symptoms. Rehearsed my no. 1 public lecture, which seems trivial and disgusts me. Why can I do nothing really well?

TUESDAY, JANUARY 24: In the afternoon to Toronto, a very cold drive as the Jag is not for sub-zero weather. In the evening give the first public lecture at Trinity and it is a success. A good audience, and they were pleased. I was nervous and suffered from the hot, dry hall. Afterward a party at the Harrises'—the Stewarts, Helen Ignatieff, Marion Walker, and Basil Coleman.[5] Pleased it went so well.

WEDNESDAY, JANUARY 25, TORONTO: To Lionel Massey's house and see the plans and drawings of the College.[6] Like all such drawings, they make everything look much bigger than it can possibly be. Some parts look handsome—chiefly the facades of the Quadrangle and the appearance from Hoskin Avenue, but within much looks heavy and dowdily old-fashioned—a suggestion of Art Nouveau which is odd in a new building. The Hall and stairway leading to it are especially hideous. Library small, too small, and a foolish chapel, a mere doll's chapel in Square Modern. The plan of the Master's house seems good, though the kitchen is very small, but it is open to discussion. I say little, as the time is not propitious.

5 Actor and opera, drama, and film director who directed many productions for Benjamin Britten at the Aldeburgh Festival; he came to Canada in 1954 and worked at the CBC in Toronto. He was a student with Brenda at the Old Vic and remained close to all the family until his death in 2013.

6 Ron Thom, the architect of the College, had won the competition to design the building and begun work before Davies was appointed Master.

THURSDAY, JANUARY 26, TORONTO: At 4:30 to the National Trust offices to meet the only non-Massey trustee of the Massey Foundation, Wilmot H. Broughall, a trust lawyer. He is about my own age, a dark, wild-eyed man in whom the temperament of a lawyer wars with something vastly more wild and romantic. He is exasperated and fascinated by the Masseys and tells me more about them than is lawyer-like (but I find lawyers are great gossips). They know nothing of money, says he, and cannot grasp that talk of an independent college without some financial resources is mere gas. Vincent Massey never touches money: the National Trust pays even his household bills. Lionel has no independence: the Royal Ontario Museum pays his salary to the National Trust, which pays his bills and gives him an allowance. (No wonder he likes to chatter about being poor.) Talk of spending money alarms all Masseys, says Broughall, because they don't understand it and think the world is trying to get it away from them by subtle means. (He says all rich people fear this, but my father does not—not to a serious degree.) He wants the trustees to make all the Foundation's funds available to the College, which would take the place of an endowment. We discuss many matters of principle and detail and I like him. "I love all the Masseys dearly," he says, "but they drive me crazy. And they all have a fabulous ability to create schemes and dream dreams, and turn them over to somebody else to make into realities." According to Broughall, Vincent Massey is the brains and imagination of the Foundation; his brother Raymond a romantic, not really involved, nor Raymond's son Geoffrey; Hart intelligent but detached; Lionel not intelligent (but a very sweet nature devoted to his father and consumed by him). So when Vincent Massey dies, who runs the Foundation? Broughall's solution—let the Foundation exist to maintain the College. Can this be brought about? I promise to write him a letter restating some of the points we agreed on today.

FRIDAY, JANUARY 27: Get my letter to Broughall off today. My points: something in the nature of an endowment is absolutely necessary or the College cannot exist save as the university dictates; non-resident Junior Fellows very necessary, and a library for their use commensurate with College aims; an examination room for *viva voce* examinations of graduate students as the centre of the College and the focus of most of the Graduate School; a thorough understanding that learning and scholarship must be the foundations of the College (for the Masseys waffle a little about grand dinners in Hall, wine cellars, and kindred Oxonian pomps which are the ornaments and not the necessaries of what they want). I pitch it strong. If they don't like it, I can't go. I want to go, but I won't be a slave to the university, or the doll on top of a wedding-cake college.

TUESDAY, JANUARY 31: Lumbago very bad. To Toronto in rugs and hot-water bottles. Give second lecture at 8:15—a decided success and much better than last week.

WEDNESDAY, FEBRUARY 1, TORONTO: At 2 p.m. meet Vincent and Lionel Massey and W.H. Broughall in VM's offices in the Shell Building on University Avenue. Quite simply, Bill Broughall has won the day and all my points are agreed to. The Foundation undertakes to give the College money each year, the sum not specified and probably variable so as to keep the university guessing. The Library to be made much more important and to include some of that space under the Common Room now marked for television viewing and ping-pong. The examination room to be given prominence. The chapel to go: I had advised this as there can be no chaplain and no regular services, and the Junior Fellows may be United Churchers, Jews, nullifidians, and infidels of all sorts, so the chapel would be a toy, for an occasional

christening. The Masseys have just built a chapel at Upper Canada College which has cost them $45,000. So the chapel is out, and I hope that will make more space for the Library. In any case, I am to see the architect at the end of February, to talk to him about changes and possibilities. When these things had been discussed, vm wanted a final consent from me to accept the mastership and whether I gave it or not I do not quite know, but I think I did. We are to exchange letters at some future time, to make all secure. But if the finance of the College is secured, and I am to have a very free hand in so much that pertains to it, why would I demur? As Broughall says, the Masseys (or, one had better say, Vincent Massey) have fine, romantic dreams and this is why I admire him and am willing to work with him, though my temperament is contrary to co-operation, and I have been my own master for so long. But rich men and dreamers must have others to body forth their dreams, and I am no trivial dreamer myself. Indeed, is not this prospect and so much it includes part of a daydream I have cherished for years, and never seriously thought would come to realization? Such an out-of-the way dream, too, and so unlike Canada. But perhaps some changes can be made in some aspects of Canada, or rather, some aspects of Canada revealed of which Canada is not yet conscious.

After this meeting an odd struggle for power took place. vm wanted to see Claude Bissell on Friday, so Broughall made the appointment by phone. Result, Bissell is to visit vm at *his* office though vm had been fully prepared to go to Bissell. What fancy jockeying for prestige! I must beware in university circles. But I have my own techniques of establishing an easy or a difficult atmosphere, and I have learned to trust them.

Dinner at the University Club for our anniversary (tomorrow): Stewarts, Edinboroughs, Basil Coleman, Helen Ignatieff. To our flat afterward for drinks.

THURSDAY, FEBRUARY 2, TORONTO: Our twenty-first wedding an-
niversary, *LAUS DEO*! Lecture on Ben Jonson and humours. Lunch
with Brenda and to Birks to buy pearls, very pretty, and to film *Never
on Sunday*, Greek and naïve. Dine at La Chaumière and are en-
tranced by the seduction conversation at the next table. Brenda to
St. Hilda's College for a drama workshop, and I begin work on my
Massey College record, and we get home at 1:15.

FRIDAY, FEBRUARY 3: W.H. Broughall (H. = Haggerty, an old
Canadian family, one a chief justice) phones at about 4 p.m. to say
that Vincent Massey and Claude Bissell are drafting a joint state-
ment about my appointment, from which I assume matters are
going well between them. Bill was asked to find out what my de-
grees were. "Never mind about your matric," said he, genially, from
which I assume he knows what I have never thought it necessary to
conceal—that I never passed that hateful examination,[7] failing dis-
mally in algebra, geometry, and, if I remember correctly, Latin
composition. But if they had wanted a jewel from the diadem of
Ontario conventional scholarship, I assume they would have chosen
one. However, I wonder if Broughall is a man who makes a hobby
of knowing something discreditable about everyone. He has said
enough to me about the Masseys, on short acquaintance, to put me
on my guard, and he has his knife into Frank Stone, the university's
money man, because he did not finish his course at Trinity. One
must be careful with such a man, and though I am inclined to like
and trust him, he has that strain of jealousy which can make a man
a dangerous friend and a bad enemy. He tells me that VM is inordi-
nately afraid of death. Bill is the son of a former bishop of Niagara
and it amuses him that an Anglican should dread death. Of course

7 The Ontario Grade 13 Senior Matriculation Exams at the time were essential
 for admission to an Ontario university.

the Masseys were originally Methodists and their churchmanship, like mine, is by choice rather than birth. Does one ever escape a cradle faith? My Presbyterianism often asserts itself.

I do not go to Ottawa for the Governor General's Awards meeting because of lumbago: madness to sit four and a half hours in a 'bus in the cold. Wire Sylvestre and Frye my choices: Callaghan and Underhill and no prize for poetry. In the afternoon work on my Massey College record, and Bill Broughall calls to say things go well between Vincent Massey and Claude Bissell. In the evening, read several books and invite my soul: h.t.d. by fireside; most refreshing.

SATURDAY, FEBRUARY 4: Bill Broughall phones in the morning to say he has run into further difficulties with the university solicitors; they are afraid of the word "covenant" as applied to the university's agreement to pay the deficits of Massey College. This is lawyer's stuff and does not concern me. But Broughall says he and I are to meet the university's legal people in Claude Bissell's office on Thursday next at 3 p.m. and we shall try to reach some final agreement which can then be taken to the Legislature. I look forward to this. Meanwhile I have begun work on my Proposal and shall try to get it under three heads: academic, housekeeping, and character. I wonder if the meals and cleaning could be done by contract, thereby keeping college staff to a minimum. Great advantages in farming out as many of the trouble-making departments as possible.

MONDAY, FEBRUARY 6: A good day's work: arranged the Hart House speech,[8] and lecture on Jonson, and rehearsed public lecture no. 3 for Trinity. In the evening, worked up lecture on Shakespeare

8 Speech for a Hart House Debate on February 9, on the resolution "Canadian Culture Is a Mixture of Frailties." It was reported in the *Globe and Mail*, the *Peterborough Examiner*, and the *Varsity*.

comedy. Like a beaver, I chew through these tasks but long for time to think more and do them better; the weekend has greatly rested me.

Must take care of my health: poor sleep, lumbago, and *lichen planus*,[9] all signs of overstrain. Brenda suggests a holiday in England this spring and I am attracted, though I dislike 'plane travel; but much pleasanter than a rushed week in New York.

TUESDAY, FEBRUARY 7: To Toronto at 2:30. Flat tire at Bayview, third in 29,000 miles. Give third public lecture at Trinity at 8:15. A success but Derwyn Owen, the provost, made a dismal speech of thanks. The university atmosphere is curious and as Brenda points out, jealous as anywhere if not more so. Dull reception in the Trinity Buttery and then to the Stewarts for an excellent party.

THURSDAY, FEBRUARY 9, TORONTO: Bill Broughall lunched with me at the University Club. He tells me Vincent Massey says "a gentleman never takes soup with luncheon at his club" because Lord Curzon said it. I fear I shall run into many things a gentleman does not do, and which are unknown to me; but I am a writer, and therefore a bit of a bounder. We talked of the organization of the College and he thinks my idea that *all* members of the Foundation should be Fellows is a good solution to a difficult problem. And why not? It is their money; let them see what is being done with it. The Oxford principle of "founders' kin" comes to my aid here. Also I want Broughall as our money advisor; who better? And the Massey family will be encouraged to maintain their interest and enthusiasm, and make the College the chief charge on the Foundation money. He explained one or two things in the agreement which

9 Non-contagious skin condition producing bumps that are shiny, firm, and reddish purple. Davies's seemed to get worse when he was nervous.

had puzzled me. At 3:30 we went to Claude Bissell's office. With him are Frank Stone (who looks inoffensive but I am assured he is dangerous) and Laddie Cassels, the university's solicitor, whom I liked on sight. We toiled through the document, agreed that it satisfied us all, and sent it to Vincent Massey in Barbados for his signature. Then, a public bill in the Legislature and the College is legally in existence.[10] Claude Bissell said to me at parting that when the Master's appointment is announced on February 24, he will meet with me and Gordon Roper and the formidable Dr. Woodhouse[11] at University College to discuss my professional appointment.[12] I must be a full professor in order to sit on the board which directs graduate studies.

I met the university's publicity man, Ken Edey, yesterday at 2, and under his direction was photographed on the College site by his man. I am warmed by the enthusiasm of such people as Cassels and Edey for the College and my appointment. I am so engrossed with details that the general outline escapes me. But it is gratifying that some people think my appointment will give lustre to the project. There will be detraction as well. Miranda tells me Dr. Arthur Barker of Trinity, just before taking off for an academic appointment in the U.S., declared it would be "just for a few Oxford snobs." No, it won't.

SUNDAY, FEBRUARY 12: I think my public lectures went well but have had no repercussions. I must get used to lack of response in the university. It is part of their intellectual deadness and failure to get over to the young. But I did them as well as I could, and that is what matters.

10 Bill 115, incorporating Massey College, was given royal assent on March 29, 1961.
11 A.S.P. Woodhouse, long-time and eminent chair of the University College English Department and Milton scholar.
12 Davies was to teach a fourth-year undergraduate course at University College.

WEDNESDAY, FEBRUARY 22: To Toronto, lecture and lunch with English dons, then with Brenda to the museum and look at fine things in the Lord Lee of Fareham collection. To the Royal York for a rest, then to the J.K. Thomases'[13] to dine with Morley Callaghan and Rosamund Merivale.[14] Good talk.

THURSDAY, FEBRUARY 23, TORONTO: H.t.d. on waking. Lecture on *The Alchemist* at 11. We lunch with Basil Coleman at his flat. He is returning to England. To Broughall at 4 to discuss Massey College. Dinner at the club with Brenda. Work in office, meet her at St. Hilda's, leave at 10:15 and home by 12:30.

FRIDAY, FEBRUARY 24: My appointment as Master Designate is ratified and made public today. Luckily I am able to send out my Proposals for organization today, as well. They have meant a great deal of work, for I want to make them as complete and workable as possible; and if I am to have the job of organizing I must have the main voice in it. I called on Broughall yesterday at the National Trust; he is full of anxieties which I have already dealt with in my Proposals. He is as full of gossip as ever, and anxious that Vincent Massey be bound to the College with hoops of steel, for he fears caprice, and it appears VM is in love—with the widow of Major Edward Dudley ("Fruity") Metcalfe,[15] who was Lady Alexandra Curzon, youngest daughter of the great proconsul who never took soup at lunch at his club. Ah, to be Curzon's son-in-law, even posthumously, even at *seventy-four*! But the lady is unkind, Bill says. He also tells me that the Foundation has about $4 million; if the College costs $2.5 million, we have an endowment of $1.5, less

13 Thomas was a leading Toronto psychiatrist.
14 Actress and daughter of British actors Philip Merivale and Vita Birkett, and stepdaughter of Gladys Cooper.
15 Metcalfe was equerry and a close friend of Edward VIII. In fact, Metcalfe and Lady Alexandra had divorced.

some obligations, and he thinks we might get $35,000 to $40,000 yearly, which would be handsome. Raymond Massey, he says, is all in favour of the Foundation devoting all its funds to the College. I am glad my appointment is now official and public, so that I can act more freely. The *Toronto Star* has given it a good deal of notice, identifying me as one of their writers, and I suspect in consequence the *Globe* has carried no mention of it whatever, which is small of it—but the Toronto newspaper world is a petty one. I shall have to be careful in dealing with the Toronto press, or I shall get the College, and myself, into hot water.

On Wednesday, I was in the Royal Ontario Museum, looking at the Lord Lee of Fareham collection, and saw it contains about ten handsome illuminated books. Now, this collection belongs to the Massey Foundation and is on loan to the Royal Ontario Museum, so I suggested to Bill that these books would make a fine beginning to the treasures of the College Library. Rather to my surprise, he was immediately taken with the idea, and will see what can be done. The ROM complains of the insurance the collection carries, and on pretext of lowering the premium, we might get the books! But I shall believe this when it happens. Bill also suggests that the duties of College secretary and bursar might be combined in one capable woman; I wonder if my present secretary, Moira Whalon, would be up to it. The Thompsons and Porters to dinner and to see Canadian Players in *Saint Joan* and to a party at the Cherneys'. Bed at 2 a.m.

SATURDAY, FEBRUARY 25: Nothing in the *Globe and Mail* about my appointment because I write for the *Star*: what small behaviour! Write a *Star* column in the morning and a critique of *Saint Joan*. In the afternoon, loaf and read Jung; Rosamond comes for the weekend, very lively; in the evening go through Browning's "Andrea del Sarto" with her and read Rabelais.

MONDAY, FEBRUARY 27: Now that the news is out, and the world has received it with exemplary calm, and my Proposals are out of my hands, I feel a deep depression, a regression of the libido, what might be called the Hump. What have I let myself in for? What am I, a mere magpie of learning, and certainly no scholar, doing with a learned appointment in that collection of medieval schoolmen and learned but vulgar thrusters, the University of Toronto? My one desire now is to crawl into a hole and work on the novel which has been in my mind since before *A Mixture of Frailties*.

THURSDAY, MARCH 2, TORONTO: I meet Ron Thom, the College architect, a withdrawn, very likable bachelor[16] from Vancouver: he lunches at the University Club with Lionel and me, and at 4 p.m. Brenda and I collect him at the Park Plaza Hotel and drive to Peterborough; we talk all the way, and as he sits in the back and speaks very low and inward it is not an easy journey. But after dinner we get down to serious business, and he explains the plans, materials, and above all his conception of the building, which is a fine one. We discuss the Master's house, which will be "modern" but not too much or too modishly so, and now that he sees the creatures who will inhabit it, his ideas will be influenced, for this is the sort of man he is. We discussed the Examination Room very thoroughly and I suggest a circular room, with perhaps twenty desks surrounding it on a dais, and a place for the examinee in the middle—impressive but not inhuman. He likes it.

FRIDAY, MARCH 3, PETERBOROUGH: We worked in the afternoon and at last produced a workable scheme for the Library—working quarters and stacks under the Common Room and a Reading Room and treasure room upstairs by the Common Room. Ron Thom says

16 A misapprehension, soon corrected.

it will take six months to produce working drawings and more than a year to build, so Vincent Massey's notion of beginning in autumn 1962 is impracticable. But haste could only harm the building and if we could get in by January '63, we could make preparation for our first group of Junior Fellows.

Meanwhile I have a very generous letter from Claude Bissell about my appointment, which seems to have pleased the governors. Bissell also thanks me for smoothing the way with Vincent Massey, which I am not conscious of having done: he seems to me eminently reasonable, and when his imagination is aroused, truly a patron; but I suppose the university's money men ruffled him. Both Lionel and Bill Broughall have said very kind things about my Proposals. Next tasks: to agree on the plan and the price and then try to arrive at some notion of Fellows and budget.

WEDNESDAY, MARCH 8, TORONTO: Lunch at the York Club with Dr. Andrew Robertson Gordon, dean of the School of Graduate Studies. Explain the College idea to him as he knows little about it. Am surprised how many people who are vital to this plan are not kept abreast of developments. Bill Broughall tells me Raymond Massey is in the dark, and I have written to him. But Dr. Gordon likes all my ideas and is especially enthusiastic about the Examination Room. After lunch he took me to the present dingy quarters of the Graduate School, and their examination room is a squalid attic. From him I learn a good deal about how the Graduate School works and wish we could include more of its doings in Massey College, but I fear the effect of that would be to make it a university departmental building, and I would be, in effect, dean of residence.

THURSDAY, MARCH 9, TORONTO: Lunch at the York Club with Claude Bissell, who is entertaining for Harold Clurman.[17] Bissell welcomes me very graciously to the academic community. I get a taste of university spite when Norman Endicott[18] tries to draw me about Massey College. Is it true, he asks, that it is to be called St. Vincent de Souls? A very good joke, but there will be a lot of them and I must not seem to enjoy them, nor yet to be huffy. Would Endicott make a good Senior Fellow? I am sounding out Gordon Roper as senior librarian and he is much attracted; the thought of building a collection, particularly of manuscripts, works on him like *aqua vitae*.

FRIDAY, MARCH 10: We were to have met at the National Trust, but as Vincent Massey is unwell (a return of his prostate trouble), I drive to Batterwood in a grand hired Cadillac limousine with Lionel and Bill Broughall. In the study, VM in dressing gown and corduroy trousers, Hart, Geoffrey (who is like his father, Raymond, but handsomer), and Ron Thom, as low-spoken as ever. We discuss the plans and, without much difficulty, approve them in the form Ron Thom and I had reached. It is also clear that midsummer 1963 will be the time of opening, a long time to wait but not so long to me as to VM, I judge. He has hopes of getting a bell for the tower from England, the very one which rang the alarum in the Citadel at Quebec when Wolfe attacked; the English looted it, and it is now in a London church. My guess is that they will stick to it on the principle of "What we've stolen, we hold." Hart raises curious objections: though no believer, he does not like the abandonment of the chapel; will the kitchen be able to produce a *good* sole meunière? These people have the most unworldly notions of

17 American theatre director and drama critic.
18 Long-time member of the English Department at University College.

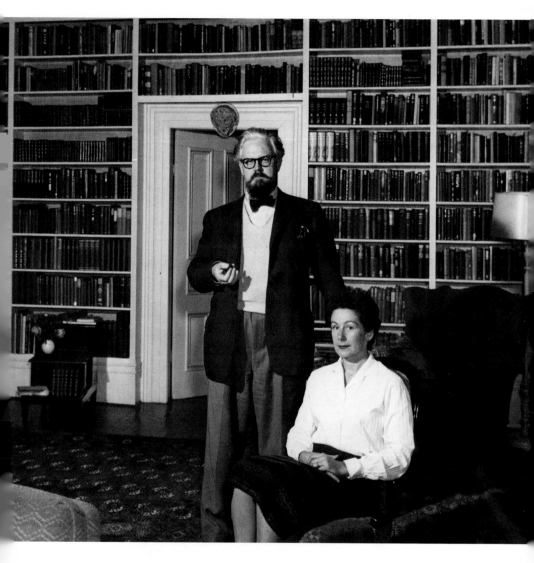

Rob and Brenda Davies, in the sitting room at 361 Park Street, 1957.

Anna Pedak, who was with the
Davies family from 1948 until 1968.

Muriel Newbold, Brenda Davies's mother,
on a visit to Canada.

Jennifer, Miranda, and Rosamond, October
1959.

Brenda's is a Shetland name
 And used to mean a Viking;
But now it means a golden heart
 Enclosed in beauty striking:
So if our girls are handsome, gay
 Have gentle hearts, I tender
Unstinted praise where most it's due —
 To pretty, witty Brenda.

A valentine for Brenda by Davies.

Senator W. Rupert Davies, Robertson Davies's father.

Leighton Hall.

Grant Macdonald's portrait of Brenda Davies as Katherina in *The Taming of the Shrew*, 1949.

There was an old man, & he lived in the West & his trade it was cutting of broom green broom, he had but one son & his name it was John

MEETING

of the

BOARD OF GOVERNORS

of the

STRATFORD SHAKESPEAREAN FESTIVAL

FOUNDATION OF CANADA

Thursday, September 10, 1959 in the Festival Theatre

at 9:30 A.M.

Committee meetings from 9:30 A.M. to 10:30 A.M.

Board meeting at 10:30 A.M.

Luncheon at 1:00 P.M.

A G E N D A

1. Minutes
2. Report of Artistic Director Michael Langham
(a) Drama - 1959, 1960
(b) Music - 1959, 1960
3. Planning Committee Report Mr. Floyd Chalmers
4. Financial Report Mr. V.C. Polley
5. Box Office Report Mr. V.C. Polley
6. Property Committee Report Mr. Hans Buscher
7. Publicity and Promotion
8. Festival Singers
9. Other Business

- - - - - - - - - - -

COMMITTEE LOCATIONS
Programme and Planning Committee - V.I.P. Room
Budget and Finance Committee - Mr. V.C. Polley's office
Public Relations and Promotion - Press Room (below foyer)
Property Committee - Green Room

Davies's copy of the agenda of the Board of Governors meeting of
the Stratford Festival on September 10, 1959.

Mrs. Muriel Newbold takes tea with the Inspiration of the Canadian Stratford Festival.

Judy and Tony Guthrie from Davies's sketchbook.

Brenda and Rob with Tony and Judy Guthrie, at Miranda and Jennifer's christening, 1945.

ROYAL ALEXANDRA THEATRE
ERNEST M. RAWLEY, Manager EDWIN DeROCHER, Associate Manager

NOVEMBER 2 - 3 - 4 - 5, 1960

EVENINGS AT 8:30
MATINEE SATURDAY AT 2 P.M.

FIRE NOTICE—Look around now and choose the nearest Exit to your seat. In case of fire, walk (not run) to that Exit. It is prohibited by law to light matches in this theatre. NO SMOKING. For the safety of all, this law must be obeyed.

LADIES ARE REQUESTED TO REMOVE THEIR HATS

Under the Sponsorship of
CANADIAN THEATRE EXCHANGE, LTD.

THE THEATRE GUILD

in association with

DON HERBERT

presents

DENNIS KING

in

"LOVE AND LIBEL"

a new comedy by
ROBERTSON DAVIES

with

TONY VAN BRIDGE MADELEINE CHRISTIE ROBERT CHRISTIE
CORINNE CONLEY JAMES EDMOND AMELIA HALL
BARBARA HAMILTON LAURENCE HARDY CHARMION KING
ROBERTA KINNON LEO LEYDEN JOHN MILLIGAN
GENE SAKS BRUCE SWERDFAGER

Settings and Lighting by
DAVID HAYS

Costumes by
MARIE DAY

Incidental Music arranged and played by
JOHN COOK

Production Staged by
TYRONE GUTHRIE

Love and Libel opened in Toronto on November 2 and toured to Detroit, Boston, and New York.

(Walter Curtin/Library and Archives Canada/PA-137078)

Davies at a rehearsal of *Love and Libel* in 1960.

Portrait of a Canadian author joyfully contemplating his first assault on Broadway, after years of modest provinciality.

From Davies's sketchbook for Muriel Newbold in 1960.

what young Canadians with their careers to make want to eat and drink. VM read a letter from Raymond, who makes some minor objections to my Proposals (though on the whole is very favourable) and, like Hart, wants to play the True Believer. The Massey arms could well be adapted to the College; their motto *Dum terar prosum*[19] I am not so keen on—nineteenth-century pretentiousness, I should judge.

Brenda and Jenny came for me about 5:30. VM very friendly to Brenda, though he had not long before been inveighing against women as post-graduate students, a strange crotchet but not impossible to understand.

Home, h.t.d. after dinner. Caught cold, I fear, and slept ill.

SATURDAY, MARCH 11: Wrote a *Star* column on Montaigne. I feel ropey, sore throat. In the afternoon to bed and read a detective story and slept. In the evening with Brenda and Jenny to *The Marriage-Go-Round*, a bad film. Why am I ill? Not exhaustion: excitement, I should say, and psychological disturbance and meeting people.

Now I know that the College will not be ready till 1963 I can organize some of my own work: first, find what I have to do at the university and prepare to do it well.

FRIDAY, MARCH 17: Received a friendly letter from Sir David Lindsay Keir, master of Balliol, on my appointment, saying how pleased he is that the Founder and first master are Balliol men. This is rain on thirsty ground to me, for I have regretted losing touch with Balliol, owing to Roy Ridley's[20] being turfed out, and my lack of rapport with A.D. Lindsay.[21] Must try to visit Keir when I am in England in May.

19 "Though I am trodden down, I am of service."
20 Davies's tutor at Oxford.
21 Master of Balliol College while Davies was there.

SUNDAY, MARCH 19: My voice utterly gone: keep to the house all day and take steam and read *Sinister Street* by Compton Mackenzie and enjoy it greatly. The misery of this 'flu is dizziness: to bed early and more steam; wrote to Guthries in the afternoon.

MONDAY, MARCH 20: I am wobbly and my voice still gone: do a fair day's work and write to the master of Balliol. In the evening work on *The Duchess of Malfi*. The worst of this 'flu is the vertigo; but end of term approaches and spring can be sniffed in the chill air.

I am ill almost every March. Exhaustion? Winter? This combination of *Love and Libel*, Trinity, Massey College, and the *Examiner* has made this the hardest winter I have ever known. God! Alas!

WEDNESDAY, MARCH 22: To Toronto at 8:30 and lecture on *The Tempest*. To see Claude Bissell at 3. My suggestion that I give a post-graduate course in drama has been received with unexpected enthusiasm by Prof. A.S.P. Woodhouse, so I am to continue with undergraduates at Trinity in 1961–2 and begin such a graduate course in autumn '62, and drop the undergraduate work. They think I may have several theses a year to oversee and this is considered taxing work. About the College, I inform CB of our progress and he assures me of all co-operation on budget and business matters from his staff. He thoroughly understands the Masseys' attitude, and was so frank as to tell me that he resents Frank Stone, who is Eric Phillips's[22] man and apt to assume authority and by-pass CB. With Bissell's help I feel certain all that is necessary can be done; as always when I have seen him I feel refreshed and have a renewed sense of the dignity and importance of the work I am undertaking. My natural gloom is rebuked. CB assures me that the university governors would not mind a yearly

22 Chairman of the board of governors of the university since 1945.

deficit of $25,000 on Massey College. He says also that the one governor who disliked the idea of the College was Irene Clarke[23] of Clarke, Irwin, who was bitter because women could not be included in it. Her son Garrick has left the publishing house and is studying for the ministry. Religion has always been the brandy of the Clarkes and the Irwins.

MONDAY, MARCH 27: In 1960 my income was $55,741 and my tax $16,192.16. I am surprised by how much I earn, for I always feel very modest with men who probably do not earn half what I do. It is something ingrained in me. In the evening we see the film *Great Expectations* on TV. Excellent.

SUNDAY, APRIL 2, EASTER SUNDAY: To Communion at 8 and home by 9:30; breakfast, then heard Berlioz's *Damnation de Faust* with girls and liked it. In the afternoon go for a walk in a snowstorm and the car goes crook—brakes fail. Notable dinner and Miranda goes to Toronto by train; read Evelyn Waugh 'til midnight.

Lectures done, articles done, only *Star* columns left to do: how weary I am! What a fool's life to work so hard, earn so much, and be weary! I am always at odds with myself and I think *this* is the mainspring of my character. (H.t.d. 18 to date.)

MONDAY, APRIL 3: Am obsessed by sense of failure and despair; work hard all day: *Star* column on Compton Mackenzie's *Sinister Street* in the afternoon. In the evening, read C.S. Lewis on words; Brenda to bed early and burns herself with the sun-lamp; Jenny to a dance and finds it a bore. Oh! woe, woe! When will the weight lift?

23 Clarke, Irwin had been Davies's publisher for nearly all his books until 1958, but he had found the firm, which was run by Irene Clarke after the death of her husband, W.H. Clarke, increasingly unsympathetic. The Clarke and Irwin families were Methodist and teetotal.

FRIDAY, APRIL 7: H.t.d. on waking; wrote a *Star* column on C.S. Lewis in the afternoon; evening with Brenda to *Tunes of Glory,* good Alec Guinness film; *lichen planus* very troublesome: am I really as low as this suggests? It always asserts itself when I am nervously exhausted and has been getting worse since Christmas.

SUNDAY, APRIL 9: The cloud begins to lift and I think of Portugal with pleasure: our first visit to a southern land. Will Massey College make great travellers of us? I am incorrigibly provincial and want to know the world—but painlessly.

Rob and Brenda travelled to Portugal and England from April 14 until May 24. They were tireless tourists, as these selections of the travel diary show. This was a holiday, but Massey College was much on their minds, particularly when they visited the old city of Coimbra with its university founded in 1290, the oldest in Portugal and one of the oldest in the world.

MONDAY, APRIL 24, ÓBIDOS: A very good lunch at Leiria and bought some sugared almonds. Then made a by-jaunt to Milagres to see the great church built to celebrate the miracle of Manuel Francisco Maio. Well worth the trouble. A boy let us in and some charming children followed us; at parting, 2 escudos to the boy and a solemn distribution of sugar-plums. Thus on through Coimbra to Bussaco to the Palace Hotel, a former royal hunting palace built in late nineteenth century; tasteless Victorian Manueline, showing what this style may become when vulgarized. Ghastly, huge *azulejos*[24] with naked women on them in the opera-singer taste of the time. Richly comic relief after the splendours of the day. Excellent dinner and we finished with glasses

24 Painted, tin-glazed ceramic tilework.

of Madeira from the Leacock firm, a reminder of Stephen's ancestral business.

TUESDAY, APRIL 25, BUSSACO: In Coimbra, ask two girls the way to the university and they prove to be English-speaking students who take us in tow most charmingly and show us the library, superb, and the examination room, splendidly dignified and the same general plan as I devised for Massey College, and the veranda, which gives a splendid view over the city. One of the girls explains to us that the black suits and capes are the student uniform of the university; the Prince Albert coats give a very solemn look to the young men, but love-making is as much in evidence as in Toronto.

THURSDAY, APRIL 27, LISBON: After dinner to the Teatro da Trindade to see *A Casa dos Vivos*—Graham Greene's *The Living Room*. Direful direction and acting ranging from mediocre to actionable. Afterward we asked directions of a student, who told us that the company was amateur—decidedly not skilled amateur. He walked back with us to our hotel, which was courteous, if a little embarrassing. How charming these European theatres are! How built for pleasure! But Graham Greene's Papist humbug ill survives a stark and heavy-handed attack by people for whom Catholicism is the very air they breathe. It demands a certain Protestant resistance in the audience; here there was none, of course. The worst acting was that of a girl who played Tia Teresa; she seemed about nineteen and had got herself up to look like a poorly preserved ninety-five, and trembled, shuffled, and quavered with the vigour of hearty youth. Her great "collapse" was right out of an acting book; she looked into the flies, clasped her brow, gave at the knees, turned her body a little, and fell smack on her bottom, with such force that her feet flew into the air and came down like a couple of

auctioneer's hammers. And there she lay, dead as an amateur actress can be.

In London Rob and Brenda's days were filled with visits to old haunts and to old friends and they did some enthusiastic shopping.

TUESDAY, MAY 2, LONDON: Collected our theatre tickets and went to the Folio Society gallery and saw some old Italian drawings, but none we wanted. To Liberty's where I bought two madder handkerchiefs, a reversible jumper, and a silk dressing gown, at huge cost. Lunched at the Café Royal. Then to Mr. Franklin's and bought a memorial ring, and a ring with a fine cut peridot, and a handsome eighteenth-century pendant of swans, and a George Washington memorial brooch for Jackie Davie at a cost of about £200, and three fine Stuart brooches. Mr. Franklin also presented me with a handsome ivory-handled paper-knife, as he insists I paid him £10 too much in 1959. Great good will shown on both sides; he grows old, and I thought we might not see him again. Then I went alone in search of Clunes, who is gone from Cecil Court; heavy rain came on, and the demon of diarrhea seized me, and I had to go to the public lavatory at the end of Tottenham Court Road, a disagreeable experience, for in the booths a notice in red warns against VD and on the walls are scrawled the obscenities of homosexuals—their wishes, their complaisance, their personal measurements all crudely phrased. Then to Foyles[25] and got the Caldecott illustrated *Bracebridge Hall*; a German girl on the staff irritated me by her barbarous method of dusting the books—clapping them vigorously and noisily together. Tonight to the Old Vic to see the much talked-of *Romeo and Juliet* directed by Franco Zeffirelli. I did not like it:

25 W. & G. Foyle Ltd., bookstore.

severely and maimingly cut; vulgarly spoken; no pace, but alternations of pause and frenzy; coarse insistence on physical sex, denoted by panting and gobbling kisses; too much of Romeo's bum—yet it was more expressive than his face; everything sacrificed to an ingenious and beautiful set and lighting—"Old Master" effects. We felt that the Old Vic we had known under Miss Baylis[26] and Tony Guthrie was quite gone. But we do not repine, for were we not there when some great things were being done? We were too out of sorts for grand food and went to a small Italian place on the Waterloo Road and were served by a girl with three large port-wine marks on her face—a lifelong misery, I suppose, and she had developed a somewhat haughty manner to make up for it.

In Oxford Davies followed up on his exchange of letters with the master of Balliol College, Sir David Lindsay Keir.

FRIDAY, MAY 5: From Paddington to Oxford in glorious sunshine. A good lunch at the Mitre and looked at All Souls, Queen's, Magdalen, and Trinity, all fresh and beautiful. At 4:30 to Balliol to tea with the master and Lady Keir; very pleasant and Keir probing me in a very Balliol way, but did not catch me in any stupidities so far as I know. I would like to enlist his good will for Massey College. Lady Keir a great change from Lady Lindsay—a *mondaine*, humorous person. Left at 5:45 and took the 6:20 to London.

TUESDAY, MAY 9, LONDON: This afternoon visited St. Paul's Covent Garden and saw the tablets to many actors, including Macklin and Ellen Terry. I was most touched by that of May Whitty and Ben

26 Lilian Baylis, a major figure in British theatre, managed the Old Vic from 1912 until her death in 1937.

Webster; I shall not forget how good he was to me at the Vic when I was a beginner, and how he kept his dignity when Tony Guthrie humiliated and nagged him for his lapses of memory. How long kindness lingers in the mind! This evening to *The Lady from the Sea* at the Queen's; the best acting we have seen in London. A perfect cast with Margaret Leighton and Andrew Cruickshank at the head of it, but Vanessa Redgrave, Michael Gwynn, John Neville, et al. to back them up. Deeply touching and moving to both mind and heart. Astonishing what a *Jungian* play *Lady from the Sea* is! Must look at Ibsen again with this in mind. Excellent supper at the Café Royal.

THURSDAY, MAY 11, LONDON: Drive to Blenheim and eat our picnic in the grounds, then go through the palace, which is very crowded with visitors, mostly English. A magnificent place, but dead, and the guides have the refined, regretful accents, and the air of keeping up their spirits under difficulties, proper to undertakers. The grounds, too, are not really well kept up. So on, and get to Broadway, to the Lygon Arms, about 4:45. A rest, then to Stratford and see *Much Ado about Nothing*, which is mediocre, except for Christopher Plummer; a complex, fussy set, and too much movement and music; the result, supposedly, of Michael Langham being ill during much of the rehearsal time. Afterward I went to see Plummer, who was naked except for a kind of dancer's corset-drawers; he gives off energy as a stove does heat. He was somewhat depressed by Stratford England and nervous about opening in *Richard III*. He told me of Langham's illness, which worried him greatly. I think he was really pleased to see me. Lonely.

SATURDAY, MAY 13: Up betimes and leave the Lygon Arms about 10 and motor at leisurely speeds to Henley and to Fawley Bottom

Farmhouse to visit John and Myfanwy Piper.[27] A pleasant place: met two of their daughters; the younger played some Beethoven for me, not well. They live very much as artists are supposed to do, in comfortable mess. A very good lunch off a clean but bare table, no napkins. Mrs. Piper looks overdriven; he is youthful of face though white-headed. Also at lunch was the man who does his stained glass. He showed us the model for his great window at Coventry Cathedral. Piper says he likes working for the Church: "It is always worthwhile." A delightful person. We looked at a lot of his pictures, including the original studies for the *A Midsummer's Night's Dream* sets and some of his stained glass sketches, and roof-bosses. But decided on two of his watercolours of Stowe, romantic and evocative—the Congreve monument in one. Got them for £60 and I call this a bargain.

They returned on the *Empress of Canada*, sailing from Liverpool to Montreal.

TUESDAY, MAY 16: We find we are at table 39 with the Parsonses, an English couple in their sixties, and the Bolgianos, Americans from Maryland, and with all the bumptious inquisitiveness, lodge rings, Rotary buttons, opinionativeness, and guileless good will of their race. Must study to get our meals at different times from the Bolgianos, who waken all the curmudgeon in me. Today I finished Boswell's *Tour of the Hebrides*.

FRIDAY, MAY 19: The Parsonses gave us cocktails and at dinner we stood the table to a couple of bottles of Moët & Chandon, which loosened tongues and made Parsons more a Tory, and Bolgiano

27 John Piper was an artist, known for watercolours, theatre sets, and stained glass. His wife, Myfanwy, was an art critic and opera librettist.

more a man of some intelligence and independence of thought. Then talked with David Walker[28] over drinks. He says Nicholas Monsarrat[29] is a very unhappy man, which I can well believe, but Brenda thinks David Walker is at some kind of crisis, too, perhaps about his wife. But he has the writer's bad habit of not really thinking that anyone else has insight or sensitivity; therefore he does not really hear what is said to him—though in this he is by no means so bad as many I have known. Brenda talked some excellent Jungian sense to him about women, and he seemed rather surprised to hear it. A charming fellow, very tense, thin-skinned, and just now very worried.

SATURDAY, MAY 20: Brenda competes in table-tennis finals and comes second—very good as she has not played for some time. Mrs. Bolgie was absent from dinner—over-eaten, presumably: she and Bolgie eat vastly, for tiny people. Brenda in a tape-cutting game; then we had drinks with David Walker who continues to reveal his mind, as romantic and feeling, rather than thinking, and doubtless a very good way for a novelist's mind to be, and I would be better if more inclined that way.

SUNDAY, MAY 21: Spoke to David Walker about Massey College, which he regards as a good idea, and broached the notion to him that he might be a Senior Fellow; he jumped at the notion. A personal friend of Lionel, and of Vincent Massey, a writer, a soldier, and a traveller, I think he is the sort of man we want. He is somewhat gloomy about Vincent Massey's health, which strikes chill upon my heart.

28 Scottish-born Canadian writer. His most popular novel was *Geordie* (1950).
29 English author of *The Cruel Sea* (1951), who had been living in Canada.

TUESDAY, MAY 23: Disembarked Montreal. Fly to Toronto. See Jenny and Rosamond at BSS. Stay at Hawthorn Gardens.

WEDNESDAY, MAY 24: Home by 6. The house is splendidly clean; travelling, even in good places, one forgets this sort of fresh cleanliness. Thus ends our Portuguese journey, which has been a brilliant success—quite the best holiday I have ever had.

THURSDAY, JUNE 1: On returning, I found a letter from Bill Broughall warning me that feeling between Vincent and Raymond is still uneasy and that Raymond is still set on a chapel, but it is hoped he may be pacified with a sort of praying-closet, housing what Broughall calls "the artifacts of our sect." This difficulty, he says, antedates my appearance on the scene, and stems from Raymond's pique that Geoffrey was not asked to design the College. There are also the problems that the university would like us to use their solicitor and perhaps their bank. Also awaiting me are more detailed plans from Ron Thom of the Examination Room with places for sixteen Senior Fellows; no one of course has told him that there are to be eighteen, and he says no more can be accommodated. This is what comes of designing a college first and trying to make the organization fit it. We are all to meet on September 16 for a full-dress discussion, and probably the first meeting of the Master and Fellows.

Miss Whalon tells me she hears some discussion in Peterborough as to why I bother with a small Toronto college and do not "put in" for the presidency of the proposed Trent college here. Of course they never thought of me until I was asked elsewhere.

Abroad got a Ben Jonson Folio, a fine *Mabinogion*, and two Beerbohm manuscripts which will look well in my office in the new college and establish me in a better range as a collector.

Massey College has already had an applicant (Nikola Stanacev), which cheers me, and *Maclean's* has carried a friendly piece about

my appointment. Also the summer issue of the *Graduate* has appeared with my article in it, which reads well and I hope will answer some questions. It is modest in tone but not creepy. Question: will my appointment to the university staff come through on July 1 as proposed? If it is to do so I ought to have some sort of formal proposal from them shortly.

TUESDAY, JUNE 6: To Montreal to receive the Lorne Pierce Medal from the Royal Society. What is this Lorne Pierce Medal?[30] What a lot of medals there are that carry no real distinction with them. I am gracefully presented by Frank Scott; otherwise the affair is Canada at its most gauche, a provincial gallimaufry.

THURSDAY, JUNE 8, TORONTO: With Bill Broughall at his office this afternoon from 3:30 to 5:30: like many lawyers he is very slow to get things said. The pattern with him is business laced with gossip. The business is that he wants to have the statutes which establish and govern the corporation drawn as soon as possible so that we can go smartly to work on September 16. He is especially anxious to assure the College of its endowment, which means it must have the funds of the Foundation made over to it from time to time, and this must be tactfully dealt with, for Vincent Massey gets $7,500 yearly as head of the Foundation and he may be loath to relinquish it, as he is so convinced of his poverty—though Bill says he pays tax up to 65%. Broughall's gossip is that Hart Massey is pressing for a chapel because his wife, Melodie, who has run through Christian Science, Moral Re-Armament, and Anglo-Catholicism, is now an Orthodox convert; I should welcome an Orthodox chapel. I must try to arrange some system whereby the Senior Fellows have

30 Lorne Pierce was the long-time editor of the Ryerson Press. The medal was first awarded in 1926 and recognizes "an achievement of special significance and conspicuous merit in imaginative or critical literature."

committees—Financial, Housekeeping, Library, etc.—in order to get the best out of them.

MONDAY, JUNE 19, STRATFORD: Visit Miranda during the day. In the evening picnic very grandly with Harrises in the motel; *Coriolanus* at 8 p.m. but curtain delayed by half an hour because of heavy rain. A splendid performance. Very warmly greeted and see many friends. Party at Len Webster's.

TUESDAY, JUNE 20, STRATFORD: Judy Finch's party at 12. Gregorys'³¹ lunch at 1: chat with Judy Guthrie. Raes' garden party. With the Arnold Edinboroughs for bad dinner at the Steak House. *Henry VIII* rather tasteless but good bits: Miranda is beautiful as court lady.

WEDNESDAY, JUNE 21, STRATFORD: Lunch at Miranda's flat. Opening of the exhibition; opening of Meighen Gardens;³² Beth Hall's party—meet Tuzo Wilson³³ and James Coyne.³⁴ Dine at the Bells'; *Love's Labour's Lost* delightful. Party for the company. Hospitality is very intense.

THURSDAY, JUNE 22: Leave Stratford at 11 and to Brantford, then long drive to Peterborough to a fusty house, accumulated mail, and empty cupboards. Splendid h.t.d. Enjoyed the social part of Stratford very much: am I growing to like people? Or am I better at coping with them? Do not talk so foolishly as I did: speak my true mind more.

31 Wilf Gregory was president of the board of governors.
32 The Arthur Meighen Gardens in front of the Festival Theatre were named for Canada's ninth prime minister and funded, in large part, by the Meighen family foundation.
33 Internationally renowned geophysicist at the University of Toronto.
34 Governor of the Bank of Canada.

FRIDAY, JUNE 30: Busy with detail as Ralph Hancox goes on holiday. In the evening hear music, Handel and Brahms *Liebeslieder.* Am uneasy and inward-looking and wonder what I should be writing.

The to-do about the College chapel continues. This evening Hart Massey called me; he is on his way to Vancouver: what about the chapel? I repeat my stand: yes, if it can be dignified, not too expensive, and confined to prayer only. I suggest an ikon as the devotional object about which the plan should gather. Hart wants a crypt-chapel under the Examination Room—not a *cellar,* oh, no, no! but a crypt. I asked him to urge Ron Thom to answer my letters. What difficult chaps architects can be!

WEDNESDAY, JULY 12: Brenda away to Toronto at 7. Work well and read some Jung in the afternoon. Brenda returns at 6:15 with the new Sunbeam Alpine sports car. In the evening we all go for an enjoyable country ride, Jenny driving. Summer at last; I feel well and enjoy life.

TUESDAY, JULY 18: Brenda drives me to Batterwood; arrive on the stroke of 10. We spend all day on the right-hand side of the terrace—Vincent Massey, Lionel, Hart, Bill Broughall, and I— discussing Ron Thom's revised plans. Some things must go; the circular desks in the Examination Room to my regret, for though I agree movable tables will give more flexibility, the other arrangement had a certain inquisitorial air I liked. They seem to want more than eighteen Senior Fellows; I suggest twenty-four: some bad candidates and some good ones were named. The kitchens come up again: Thom has neglected my letters about them, but Hart says he is breaking up with his wife, and is *distrait.* Vincent Massey has the grant of arms: the Massey arms, with a gold hart on the chevron, a castle on its back and its forefoot on a scroll. But Raymond will not have my motto, *Dilige, et quod vis*

fac,[35] and VM seems greatly to regret this. Says Raymond "lives by his emotions" and cries him and Geoffrey down very much. Indeed I have never known him so free-spoken: he said Mrs. W.H. Clarke was "quite the most charmless woman I have ever known—in fact, a pain in the neck." Bill Broughall won a major victory for common sense; he persuaded the Masseys to have a cost-accountant make a dummy budget to see what we shall *really* need. So far we have been ridiculously vague about money; suppose we find we cannot finance the College on what the rents, the Foundation, and the university can produce? Bill thinks we shall need a yearly income of $100,000 or $150,000—that shows how vague we are. Left when Brenda called for me after 6 p.m.

I puzzled much about a new motto. At last hit on *Tamquam scintillae in harundineto*[36] from Wisdom of Solomon 3:7. Hope the Masseys will like it. I do not want some milk-and-water tag of nineteenth-century provenance. I wish passionately that the details of this College could be fixed and money security assured and all the castle-in-the-air atmosphere dispelled. Since July 1 I have been a professor in the university but I am Master of Cloud-Cuckoo College and I am sick of that position. We talk of Fellows and wine cellars, but we do not know if we can support them.

THURSDAY, JULY 20: Very hot; extremely busy in the afternoon. Write *Star* column on Logan Pearsall Smith and in the evening read Jung and chat with Brenda. Rosamond unwell; Jenny is coming out of her shell and tonight played tennis 'til 11. Found an excellent Massey College motto in the Apocrypha.

35 "Love God, and you may do as you please."
36 "As sparks in the reed bed."

FRIDAY, JULY 21: H.t.d. on waking; a very hot, miserable day. The *Manchester Guardian* says there are no Canadian authors: ah, that wonderful Mancunian certainty. Ron Thom sends plans of Master's house: it is smaller than I foresaw.

SATURDAY, JULY 22: Again very hot. Write to the *Manchester Guardian*, moderately but firmly. In the afternoon, sleep and read: am good for nothing. Oh! that depression would lift! It is some time since I had one of my fits of depression: despair that my work has not found a public, that I grow old but not wise, that I have missed the boat. I breathe slowly and can hardly drag my body. This is the Blue Devils indeed!

SUNDAY, JULY 23: In the afternoon to Bryn and row and sunbathe and picnic. Very pleasant; return about 7 and show the College plans to Rosamond and Jenny. My depression lifts and I feel immeasurably better.

MONDAY, JULY 24: The Masseys do not like my motto from the Apocrypha: afraid it will be interpreted as claiming special merit for the Junior Fellows. Does no one else see the good of having a proud motto and having to fight to uphold it? Apparently not. How timid, how creepy-crawly! So I suggest the first verse of Psalm 42: "Like as the hart panteth for the water-brooks so longeth my soul for thee, O God"—*Quemadmodum cervus desiderat*. Provide a heraldic pun. I bet they will take it. It has just the Creeping Jesus quality of most college mottos.

THURSDAY, JULY 27: To Toronto and meet Young and Gwillim of Commercial Caterers at the Board of Trade Building on Adelaide Street. They have drawn blueprints of the kitchens and seem to understand everything and want our business. I see a kitchen, one

of their buffets, and some of their food, and am impressed. They can take care of the College at $2 a day per head, including uniforms, laundry, and insurance. I was encouraged by their attitude. Then to the York Club where Brenda and I lunch with Robert Dale-Harris and Richard Butterfield, who are to do the financial investigation for us. Dale-Harris is externally a caricature silly-ass Englishman: in reality a Canadian and a shrewd man of business. Butterfield takes on the actual work, and as it is not really very complex thinks it can be done by September 16. I want to get the Masseys down to realities about money as soon as possible. But they have gone too far to draw back now. Let the College cost what it may, they must find the money somewhere. In reality I have small doubt that it will be forthcoming, but I should like to know what the facts are.

On July 30, Rob and Brenda again drove to Arlington, Vermont, for a series of Alexander lessons with Lulie Westfeldt.

MONDAY, JULY 31: To Arlington in heavy rain, arriving about 3:30 to the Candlelight Motel. To Lulie Westfeldt, who does wonders for us both, then treats us to Scotch and chat. She asks us to call her Lulie. A quiet dinner and early to bed, drunk with mountain air.

SUNDAY, AUGUST 6: Home by 6: total journey 1,163 miles. The Alexander Technique is very disturbing and sometimes makes me out of sorts when big changes occur as this time. Takes a form of dissatisfaction with my literary work: I wish I thought I might someday achieve some real recognition in that realm.

MONDAY, AUGUST 7: Breakfast in bed; write long letter to Miranda.

WEDNESDAY, AUGUST 9: A significant dream: on the night of August 7 I felt myself violently shaken—opened my eyes to find my mother, her face filled with fury, hovering in the air above my bed, dressed in a white robe, shaking me! Terror! I scream! Brenda calls to me (she says next day she never woke) and the phantom vanishes. I get to the bathroom and turn on the light, much shaken. Is this because I wrote frankly about Mother to Miranda?

THURSDAY, AUGUST 17: To Toronto and from 2:30 to 5:00 in the offices of McDonald, Currie at 100 University Avenue with Butterfield, and McClellan and Whalley of his staff. Work our way through a fourteen-page draft of their findings which grows more dismal at every page. The upshot is that at a rough guess it may cost $135,000 *per annum* to run the College and our income is esti-mated at $54,600; with $25,000 from the university, that leaves $56,000 deficit. Has the Foundation that kind of money? I don't know. But we are all in too deep to draw back. Butterfield thinks we shall need a bursar to be business director of the College, as Tom Symons[37] says my secretary will have her hands full doing that job. I should be happy to have the actual day-by-day management off my neck but did not think we could afford it. But Butterfield thinks if I undertake that, I shall have no time for any academic work—which is what I am hired for. But now we are coming to grips with facts and one of them seems to be that we should have done all this investigation long ago. But there is no point in fretting about that now. Butterfield promises the report for the 10th and I think it will be a bombshell. The most careful reckoning I can do

37 T.H.B. Symons, dean of Devonshire House, a University of Toronto residence for engineering students across the street from the land on which the College was built.

with the figures I have gives a deficit of $38,015, which is not bad, and takes no account of rentals to Senior Fellows.

FRIDAY, AUGUST 18: My trouble is that I do not really know anything about anything thoroughly, and am ignorant, superstitious, spiteful, and third-rate. Arthur is fifty-eight: I phoned him and he was merry. Worked very hard on a *Star* column and a piece for *Holiday* magazine.[38]

SATURDAY, AUGUST 19: In the afternoon I work from 2:30 to 5:45 on the speech for organists[39] and enjoy it; finish notes in evening but fear the subject too specialized. Great changes at work within me and I think I am altering radically. Worried about Berlin.[40]

SUNDAY, AUGUST 20: Lay late reading *Final Curtain* by Ngaio Marsh. Dye my beard too dark—must look into this. Loafed all day never stirring from the place and found this very refreshing: my condition of mind asks for inactivity; worked on my speech.

I am indeed changing: trying to purge my writing of ornament and mere eccentricity and my thinking of bile, emotionalism, and vulgarity. Oh! that I may make some progress in these things!

MONDAY, AUGUST 21: Ralph Hancox at Stratford. I write some editorials, a relief to be free of the demands of his personality, good chap though he is. In the evening, read Jung on the Mother archetype, then talk with Brenda about my own mother; have *proctalgia fugax* in the night: a consequence?

38 "Party of One: Book Collecting," *Holiday*, May 1962.
39 Given on August 31 at the convention of the Royal Canadian College of
 Organists in St. Catharines, Ontario.
40 On August 13 East Germany had started building the Berlin Wall.

TUESDAY, AUGUST 22: Busy about *Examiner* affairs and at 6:30 to Toronto with Brenda and stay at Hawthorn Gardens. To *The Magician* by Ingmar Bergman for the third time and like it greatly except that bad American voices have been dubbed in with coarsening effect. Admirable h.t.d.

WEDNESDAY, AUGUST 23: To Stratford. In the afternoon saw *The Canvas Barricade* by Donald Lamont Jack, the Canadian play which won the *Globe and Mail* contest. Bad play though with witty interludes and lively production. It was about a painter who sacrifices everything to his art and fights Canadian materialism: mode— farce. But no attitude contrary to materialism was ever put forward, and the materialist world was flat and foolish. No character developed or experienced anything; some moments of poetry were approached and hastily shied off from. Characters came and went who were sheer waste. One, an old farmer, seemed pinched from my *Overlaid*. The play contained many good things but was not as a whole a Good Thing. Sad it should be the first Canadian work on that stage. George McCowan had produced with obvious contempt for the play. Miranda tells me the actors hate it, and why not? It gives them nothing to work on but caricatures. The critics have abused it—even Herbert Whittaker, who had so great a part in bringing it into being. All very bad for Canadian playwriting. In the evening, *Henry VIII*, duller than before. A good visit with Miranda. Drive to Toronto from 12:45 to 3 a.m. in heavy mist, demanding and alarming.

THURSDAY, AUGUST 24, TORONTO: At 2:15 to see James Gow of Blake, Cassels & Graydon in the Bank of Commerce Building. A short, dumpy man with a potato nose, agreeable in a lawyer-like way. He reads and explains the statutes which set the College in motion; the Act of the Legislature merely declares that it exists.

They seem clear and he seems very capable; I had the satisfaction of explaining to him what a "Visitor"[41] was; he had supposed the office to be merely honorary, or ornamental. One of his partners is Cassels, the university's solicitor, and we discussed the mistrust of the university among the Masseys; he sees its cause, but believes as I do that tact and decency can check any officiousness from the university's financiers. To my astonishment he showed me the deed of gift of the Lee Collection to the Massey Foundation; Bill had already given me a copy: how *confidential* these lawyers are! He says the Masseys are vague about money, but suggested the endowment of the College would be about a million, which will not be a penny too much.

Meanwhile I debate a personal problem: should I give up writing for the *Toronto Star*? I want to be rid of the book articles but they do not want to lose me and I have hinted that I might revive Marchbanks's Diary. But the pros and cons of that are, so far as I can determine, thus: *PRO*: (1) Keeps me associated with journalism, which has grown to be an addiction. (2) Gives me an alter ego for the clownish, anarchic, Rabelaisian side of my nature. (3) Brings me $6,500 per annum. (4) Leacock was both professor and humorist and it kept him human. *CONTRA*: (1) Is Marchbanks a dignified creation for an academic, and will this diminish me in the eyes of the College? (2) Marchbanks will not be the same creature: is this resurrection a backward step? (3) Would Marchbanks take creative ability which should be used in more important work or can I, like Dickens, spend freely? *DECISION*: I drop it: but not for the CONTRA reasons above. I simply have no time for it if I am to do any writing in addition to the College work which impends. (*Later*

41 Traditionally a Visitor has a right or duty of supervision over a university or college. The description of the office at Massey College reads, "The Visitor is the College Ombudsman and fulfils important constitutional and ceremonial functions."

note: Under persuasion, I continued it. But did resign and the last column appeared June 16, 1962.)

MONDAY, AUGUST 28: I am forty-eight: was given a magnificent camera, slide viewer, records, scissors. Arnold Edinborough calls— would I write for *Saturday Night* after year's end? Excellent dinner and with Brenda and Jenny (Rosamond ill) to *Gone with the Wind*, very good after twenty years. How lucky I am in my family, how fortunate in my life, for which God be thanked.

WEDNESDAY, SEPTEMBER 6: On Saturday, September 2, Vincent Massey called me, very anxious that on our meeting of September 16 we should elect J. Tuzo Wilson (geophysics), James Eayrs (political economy), Caesar Wright (dean of law), and Gordon Roper (English at Trinity) to senior fellowships; he wanted me to defer approaching them till he had discussed them with Claude Bissell. But Bissell is in Calgary for Canada Council meetings. This was impossible as these men must have explanations and time in which to approach their college heads. On Tuesday, September 5, I met Lionel and Bill at the Toronto Club at 12:25; they asked me to phone VM at once. He was insistent and hurt: said it would not take *him* long to decide to accept such an honour. But we discussed this matter and many others until 5 p.m. and Lionel undertook to persuade VM to wait. Impatience now could wreck us. We also discussed finance: will the university give us anything so long as any Foundation money is to be had? We have a verbal agreement from Bissell but would the university businessmen honour it? Lionel tells me that Raymond never wanted a college, is jealous of Vincent, and that awful family rows break out when Raymond accuses Vincent of using Foundation money for his own aggrandizement. (VM gets $7,500 p.a. for bossing the Foundation.) Raymond has had an operation for double hernia and cannot be present on September 16,

God be praised! Lionel makes more sense about money than any of the Masseys. We cleared the air usefully and I think we may defer furnishing the chapel for a while. Meanwhile I think I have a plan to circumvent the university accountants: let the Library be a separate entity under the College to which the Foundation makes gifts; the Library can transfer funds to the College *for specific improvements* but these may not include current financing. Can the lawyers make this work?

Bill tells me a curious bit of gossip relating to VM's detestation of women in universities and indeed in any but a social capacity. Charity Grant,[42] VM's wife's niece, when drunk, lays it to his resentment, perhaps unconscious, of his wife Alice, the late Mrs. Massey, Charity's "Aunt Lal." Charity says VM was no great shakes when they married and Aunt Lal, as Sir George Parkin's daughter, was much in demand among the nobility and gentry. Aunt Lal introduced VM into the best English society and in this sense "made" him—which he does not care to remember and thus discounts women in men's affairs. But this sounds to me like family jealousy, and a too-glib bit of psychologizing. I think it more likely to be rooted in his Edwardian view of life, and of women, if "ladies," doing their work by boudoir-government.

I disagree with Bill Broughall about the character of the meeting on September 16. I want it to be formal, to wear my gown and to read the statutes in full, all according to Cocker[43]; he thinks the statutes could be taken as read. But I think formality and perfect propriety are better: let us begin as we mean to go on.

Lionel is anxious that all business be arranged so that VM shall not be fatigued; apparently two hours is about the extent of his endurance without a rest.

42 Dean of women at the Whitney Hall residence, University of Toronto.
43 "According to Cocker" means absolutely correctly (from Edward Cocker, seventeenth-century author of a math textbook).

Lionel asks if I am on the payroll of the university; I answer that I am nominally but that I have had no tangible evidence of it yet. I am working on this College so far unpaid, but I do not really care so long as the end is achieved.

SUNDAY, SEPTEMBER 10: Lay late, then to Bryn with Brenda for lunch, long intimate chat, and a glorious afternoon in the sun. We discuss happiness and we are agreed it is not lack of cares but a touchstone deep within to which one can appeal at any time with confidence of being upheld. It is self-preservative, a serenity below the power of outward disturbances. We go for row later. In the evening Jenny returns from Stratford full of gossip.

MONDAY, SEPTEMBER 11: On Saturday last Vincent Massey called Bill and gave him a long scalding about the statutes: he resents references to "the head office of the corporation," thinks "assistant master" should be "vice-master," etc. All trivialities but these things dominate his mind. Then he called me; I had had two teeth drawn in the morning and was muddle-headed, but calmed him. Today he called again, fussing about who should be secretary at the meeting on Saturday next, and stewing that I should see Ron Thom about the kitchens, as if that were not in hand. What a Meddlesome Massey he is! During the day Bill called twice: he had Lionel to lunch and pushed him to the point of facing *money*, which the Masseys hate. Bill wants $50,000 for College extras right away, and $20,000 a year for the Library right away. But will he get it? We shall see. Called Ron Thom in Vancouver. It seems that on Saturday I must make some things clear which the Masseys cannot see: that this College is not as yet of interest to more than a few people, and that it must be presented to the public as an institution of higher learning of the most serious kind, and never as a museum of bygone customs. This will demand some tact.

Note on Bill Broughall. He is fond of violent language: VM "shits all over Lionel"; difficult Foundation meetings are "shit-sessions"; Massey parsimony over trifles is "skinning the turd." I take this to be the safety valve of a very high-strung, emotional man encased in the shell of a lawyer. He says VM's haemorrhoids and prostate bother him very much and the relict of Fruity Metcalfe is unkind and will not write. Poor old man! Bill says VM is pleased by my suggestion that his papers come to the College.

FRIDAY, SEPTEMBER 15: To Toronto and see Ron Thom at the Park Plaza and lunch with him and Geoffrey Massey. I saw the revised plans for the Master's house and also some bad drawings of the drawing-room and study, filled with vulgar furniture—some draughtsman's notion of the academic life. I liked the plans. At 3:30 to the Shell Building and meet with Ron, Hart and Vincent Massey, and Geoffrey 'til 7, a long session in which we canvass and approve all the plans, and it looks as if we may break ground in mid-November. VM pernickety about nomenclature—perhaps wisely so—and so we speak of "Hall," "the Common Room," and "the Round Room."

SATURDAY, SEPTEMBER 16, TORONTO: I meet the Foundation at the Toronto Club at 2:30 and we go carefully through McDonald, Currie's long, windy, twaddling, but useful and enlightening report, and much of the basis of College organization becomes clear. They had met in the morning and voted $100,000 for the beginning of College investment, and $50,000 for current funds, but have not decided on a Library sum. This was because Bill brought them up to the mark at last, after months of work. Also, they are going to take advantage of new trust laws to invest more profitably, and do not seem dismayed by the large deficit McDonald, Currie foretell. I am hugely relieved. At 7 p.m. we assemble again, with Claude Bissell and the dean of graduate studies, A.R. Gordon,

and have an excellent dinner at which VM proposes my health, and I propose the College's. Then our first meeting; I put on my gown, read the first statute. We vote in Lionel, Hart, Geoffrey, and Bill Broughall, and I speak seriously; we then vote Vincent Massey as Visitor, and propose Tuzo Wilson, James Eayrs, Gordon Roper, and Caesar Wright as Senior Fellows. A.R. Gordon won't have Tuzo, as he is never at home and is a "glamour-boy of science"—some jealousy there? So put in Haines the biologist, and Robert Finch,[44] French literature. An excellent meeting and everyone seemed well satisfied; I think I chaired it well without being *too* efficient, and it was dignified but not stuffy. Much has been done this weekend to bring the College out of dreamland. I am much happier about the whole project.

SUNDAY, SEPTEMBER 17: Lay late and h.t.d., my fatigue having disappeared. In the afternoon finish *Franny and Zooey* by Salinger and walk in the garden preparing my lectures for Thursday. In the evening chat with Brenda. Colder today and I welcome it.

I am greatly relieved that the College is launched and money worries pretty well taken care of: the past two days the culmination of weeks of fuss and confabulation. I feel better about it than I have in months.

MONDAY, SEPTEMBER 18: Very busy, wrote the five candidates for Senior Fellows, and wrote a *Star* column on Frederick Rolfe.[45] In the evening to the film *Raisin in the Sun* with Brenda and Jenny, excellently acted. H.t.d., admirable.

44 Robert Finch was a long-time professor of French at the University of Toronto, and also an artist, musician and Governor General's Award-winning poet. He was a resident Senior Fellow at Massey College for many years, living in the suite of rooms above the main gate.
45 Also known as Baron Corvo, English writer, artist, photographer, and eccentric.

WEDNESDAY, SEPTEMBER 20: To Toronto and Trinity and discuss his senior fellowship with Gordon Roper, who wants it and looks with pleasure on the task of forming a library. Derwyn Owen, the provost, is against it on grounds that it will take time that Trinity is paying for—could Massey College pay Trinity the hire of a lecturer to make up to them what they lose on Roper? This meanness from a college which has just inherited $7,000,000 from Gerald Larkin! Am very annoyed with Owen. At 3:45 to the president's address to the freshmen: all heads and deans in full academic fig, and we process with the mace. Claude Bissell makes a very friendly reference to the College and also, when he talked of choice, said some students would have to choose between calculus and burlesque, adding, "Though the Master of Massey College reminds me that 'Euclid alone has looked on beauty bare'"[46]—a chance remark I made on Saturday evening. I saw him afterward and his beautiful and charming wife, Christine, and mentioned Owen's strange attitude to Gordon Roper's senior fellowship. He said Owen sulks a lot, and has to be talked out of it, and is neurotically afraid somebody will get some money out of Trinity unjustly. (Amusing, as Trinity has got its wires crossed and is paying me $1,500 for my services, and I shall have to set them right: I am a university appointee and will, I presume, be paid by University College.) Then to UC and chatted with Prof. A.S.P. Woodhouse, who is sympathetically interested in Massey College. He was delighted that only men working for "serious"—i.e., humanities or science—degrees[47] would be admitted and quoted very wittily from *Lycidas*:

46 Edna St. Vincent Millay, 1923.
47 The act incorporating the College said that all Junior Fellows should be men registered in the School of Graduate Studies. However, in 1963, three of the new residents were in the University of Toronto Law School, which was not part of the School of Graduate Studies. At first they were known as sizars, but in 1964 they were accepted as Junior Fellows.

Two massy keys he bore of metals twain,

The golden opes, the iron shuts amain.

The iron key of exclusion, said he, was the secret of quality.

Saw *The Threepenny Opera* by Bertolt Brecht at the Royal Alex and found it old-fashioned: music much of the mode of 1929 and the play construction the same—studious avoidance of climaxes, with the resulting sag at the end of every scene, and devices once new but now over-worn. Gypsy Rose Lee was starred, and played Jenny, but could not sing or act and was too plainly on hand because her name might draw some who would expect her to strip. But she has wonderful bodily ease and charm. The singing was all bad, and the production wanted pulling together; deathly pauses, and final curtain at 11:20.

THURSDAY, SEPTEMBER 28, TORONTO: Bill lunched with me and we discussed College finance and investments, or rather he did and I pretended to understand. The law which demands that charitable trusts spend 90% of their income each year is the sticker, but I do not fully understand the complexities of the affair. He tells me also of his talk on the 25th with Derwyn Owen about Roper: Owen simply did not listen, he said, but decried Roper's abilities—"What do you want him for, a dull fellow"—astonishing toward a member of his own staff. He admitted he disliked the notion of doing anything which might oblige the Masseys; said the College might be of use to graduate students not already attached to a college. His parting words: "It'll be interesting to see if you ever get it off the launching-pad." Bill was shocked at such pettiness in a clergyman. I had a higher opinion of Owen. But if he chooses to be small, nothing can be done except to beware of him in future and to see that so long as he is provost, Trinity men are not asked to be Senior Fellows. Meanwhile poor Roper looks miserable.

FRIDAY, OCTOBER 6: Vincent Massey calls about the College motto: Bill Broughall has suggested it be the Massey motto—*Dum terar prosum*—nineteenth-century strenuosity as opposed to scholarship. I do not like it but it is tactless to protest more than I do: damn Raymond, stupid ham! Miranda and Rosamond come home, Rosamond with the 'flu.

SUNDAY, OCTOBER 8: Lay late, then dyed my beard. A very pleasant day, we all do as we please: I read and garden a little, Brenda plays tennis; the girls go to the Waddells'[48] cottage and poor Rosamond lies abed; an excellent Thanksgiving dinner. Now the girls are adults how much simpler these holiday weekends are: no need to plan and whip up enthusiasm for projects.

MONDAY, OCTOBER 9: I garden in the morning. In the afternoon read, and to film *Fanny* with Jenny: quite good. Vincent Massey calls: *still* fussing about motto! I spend all evening seeking one and grow weary of the project, but I must not settle for a poor one. The plain fact seems to be Vincent Massey dreads a row with Raymond. I propose Horace: *Sapere aude*[49] (*Epistles* 1.2.40). VM likes this very much, but instead of putting it up to Raymond as he was supposed to do, he wants me to bring it up at the next meeting and get it passed by vote. If Raymond objects then I think I shall have to make difficulties myself and be firm, for this havering has gone on long enough and we need our grant of arms.

THURSDAY, OCTOBER 12: To Toronto. Feel unusually well and do an excellent day's work—two good lectures, two good interviews. I lunched with R.H. Blackburn, the university librarian, who offers

48 Hugh and Mary Waddell. Their daughters, Sara and Ann, were friends of Jennifer and Rosamond.
49 "Dare to be wise."

help in purchasing and cataloguing our books, and also their reference catalogue as a preliminary list and guide: this in return for duplicates of our cards and some assurance that our special collection will be reasonably available to all legitimate students, which seems fair enough. I spoke to him of a possible drama library and he was pleased with the idea. See WRD and Margaret. Both very well. Home by 7.

FRIDAY, OCTOBER 13: Feel ill. Rise, but cannot eat. Back to bed with 'flu and am miserable all day with temperature and exhaustion. Doze most of the time and read some of *Martin Chuzzlewit*. Very sudden and astonishing how well I was yesterday.

Roper phoned—the provost has relented, he speaks of the need for the older colleges to help the new, etc.—somebody has been at him and I presume Bissell—but I mistrust this devious Welshman and shall watch him carefully. Now we have all our Senior Fellows except Haines, who lingers, excellent reasons of scruple, fearing he is too old and too busy to be able to help us.

TUESDAY, OCTOBER 17: To Toronto. A fine day: I talk with Gordon Roper about the Library, about which he is enthusiastic. We take Miranda to dinner and to the Crest: Beckett's *Krapp's Last Tape* and Albee's *The Zoo Story*. Brenda hated *Krapp*, I liked both. Then to Jane Mallett's with Bruno Gerussi and Bill Needles for drinks and chat. Stay at the Benvenuto.[50]

WEDNESDAY, OCTOBER 18, TORONTO: 9 to 11, Ph.D. exam. I speak to the Osgoode Hall Legal and Literary Society at lunch at the King Edward Hotel. I had prepared a careful speech and it went

50 Now a condominium, it was a hotel at the time.

well. To the Art Gallery with Brenda, tea with WRD, evening to *A Taste of Honey* at Royal Alex, then to chat with the Harrises.

THURSDAY, OCTOBER 19, TORONTO: A very busy morning: graduate students demanding, very egotistical. The car is mended at last and we get away about 4 and arrive home very tired. Noble Brenda insists on driving me in again tomorrow for more Ph.D. examinations!

SUNDAY, OCTOBER 22: This past week I have had my first experience as an examiner of graduate students and have sat on three Ph.D. preliminaries. They are fascinating and enlightening. There was no very good examinee, unfortunately, and I am amazed at the sloppy thinking and limited vocabulary they display—and these fellows hope to earn their bread as scholars! One, whom I examined on Shakespeare, could not even remember who Malvolio was! Another, who wanted to do a thesis on Wilde, was mulish about the pronunciation of Pinero. But the examiners are the really interesting ones: those who assert powerfully what proves, when I check later, to be at best half-true; the learned and gentle, like Philip Child; the punitive, like Priestley; the "I-pity-your-ignorance-and-despise-you," like Foakes; the businesslike and crystal-clear like Gordon Roper. Prof. Woodhouse says I am a good examiner, to my delight. I try to give the candidate a chance to show what he knows, but will not let him chatter.

I saw Roper on Tuesday. He is very pleased that Owen relented. He has several schemes for enhancing the Library, including a collection of Canadian fiction: the real collector's flair—using knowledge before money. Bill tells me Vincent Massey is very cheerful these days and keen on the College. On Thursday VM calls and asks me and Brenda for the weekend of the 28th. On Friday I met Father Shook of St. Michael's College at a Ph.D. exam: he expresses warm interest and approval of the College.

Every time I look at the site I am annoyed that nothing is being done: I would like to see demolition and some signs of action. We have gone as far as we usefully can without something physical happening. Get the building under way and new zeal will be generated.

THURSDAY, OCTOBER 26: To Toronto at 7; lunch with Brenda and Tom Symons and discuss Trent University till 3:30. We visit WRD and ask him about life in Thamesville.[51] Robert Finch dines with us and is very interested in the housekeeping of the College. To Ward-Price for the Larkin sale and buy a tapestry for $1,000,[52] some plates, and a chair; home at 2 very weary.

SATURDAY, OCTOBER 28: Brenda, Jenny, and I to Batterwood by 4. The other guest was Vincent Massey's goddaughter Sarah Butler from McGill (daughter of Rab Butler), about Jenny's age. Brenda and I walk with VM, who seems weary and old. But excellent dinner and conversation cheers him. Early to bed and h.t.d. twice, very jolly.

SUNDAY, OCTOBER 29, BATTERWOOD: To church and Father Fairweather of Trinity preaches well. In the afternoon a sleep, then solid talk from tea till 9 when we leave. Vincent asks Brenda and me to call him Vincent. We are charmed by VM as a host, and complimented by the freedom with which he speaks of his experiences in public life, especially with Mackenzie King. For the first time we feel real affection for him, as distinguished from admiration. We spoke often of the College but do not talk shop. A delightful experience of hospitality on a high level.

51 Rupert Davies and his family lived in Thamesville, Ontario, from 1907 to 1919, and Robertson Davies was born there in 1913. The village is the model for Deptford in Davies's Deptford Trilogy.
52 It hung in the sitting room of the Master's Lodgings from 1963 to 1981.

THURSDAY, NOVEMBER 9, TORONTO: At 4:30 I meet Bill Broughall at Osgoode Hall, where we have an appointment with Judge Wilson, who thinks the Woodrow Wilson National Fellowship Foundation might do something for us. (When investigated this proved not to be so.) He showed us the hall, a fine old building with a handsome law library. A portrait of Broughall's great-grandfather as, I believe, chief justice—"an unforgiving eye, and a damned disinheriting countenance."[53]

FRIDAY, NOVEMBER 10: Very busy: marked first-year English essays on *Richard II*: illiterate donkeys who patronize Shakespeare because they are too stupid to understand him. O Canada, thou arsehole of middle-class complacency! In the evening work until Brenda returns from badminton; excellent h.t.d.

MONDAY, NOVEMBER 13: Worked on *Saturday Night* piece "Pleasures of Love."[54] In the evening looked over old MSS of novels and plays and reread diary of *Love and Libel* a year since: still painful, and it *might* have succeeded: useless to repine.

FRIDAY, NOVEMBER 24, TORONTO: The second meeting of the Master and Fellows, in the Senate Room in Simcoe Hall, at 3:10. I am not as prompt as I had hoped and meet all the Masseys on the stairs, moving at a snail's pace, the snail being Vincent. He *acts* the old man, I think: Raymond, whom I met for the first time, is nine years his junior and moves with the light step and high head of an actor. He was very pleasant. Eayrs, Finch, Roper, and Wright are with us for the first time and I change the agenda to vote them in at once, as I think we should be above the Masonic nonsense of

53 Sheridan, *The School for Scandal*, Act 4, Scene 1.
54 *Saturday Night*, December 23, 1961.

keeping men hanging about in the hall while we vote on them. I was apprehensive, but VM gave us splendid news: seven tenders on the building, *all* below Ron Thom's estimate, but all close, and they have given the job to Eastern Construction Co., who will begin as soon as they can. This takes a great load off all our minds. So $25,000 has been voted for the Library, about which Gordon Roper spoke well and carried his point about the Canadian collection. The discussion about our arms and motto was amicable, and Raymond likes *Sapere aude* so that is fixed at last, thank God! Finally I brought up the question of the academic status of the College; we must not be a mere residence. But both Bissell and Gordon are sure our non-resident Senior Fellows' rooms will be much in demand for tutorial work, and the Round Room and small dining-room will also be available for small groups. I am eager that the place be a teaching college in its own fashion.

From Thursday, November 30, to Monday, December 4, Rob and Brenda were in New York for Alexander lessons, shopping, and theatre.

SATURDAY, DECEMBER 2, NEW YORK: Good lesson, then to Zolotnitskys and buy three fine ikons, and are well pleased.[55] To the matinée of *Daughter of Silence* by Morris West, bad, old-fashioned, and Emlyn Williams wasted. Dine at the Astor and to the Metropolitan Opera: *Lucia di Lammermoor* with Joan Sutherland. Superb and a really great reception: thrilling to be at something on this scale. Rarely does one experience something splendid in its kind like Sutherland in *Lucia*: unmistakably first-rate, and when it happens, what exaltation!

55 The gallery was called A la Vieille Russie. The icons hung in the sitting room of the Lodgings from 1963 to 1981.

MONDAY, DECEMBER 4: Fly back from New York, arriving at Malton at 7 p.m. in heavy rain. Drive to the Park Plaza by 8 and spend three hours with Ron Thom and Bill going over the final plans. They are exciting and beautiful. Vincent wants me to see them in case there is anything unworkable. We agree that the Upper Library should be returned to its former proportions and a music room built on top of the Round Room. Also some arrangements for filing space, a lavatory for the secretaries, and a safe for the bursar. To Hawthorn Gardens and sleep ill.

WEDNESDAY, DECEMBER 6: Busy at the *Examiner* but happy to be home and among all my handsome conveniences. Wrote VM about changes in the College. Arnold Edinborough wants me to do a monthly piece for *Saturday Night*. Chat with Brenda in the evening and unusually fine h.t.d. and early to sleep.

THURSDAY, DECEMBER 7: To Toronto in the Alpine. Graduate students at 11. Lecture on *The Way of the World* at 12. Lunch with Lionel Massey. VM calls me at University College very testy: he and Hart veto the music room as being too expensive. I do not argue, but am not pleased: why waste my time if my opinion is not wanted? See the museum with Lionel. Home through snow. Brenda has a painful left leg. Look at plans.

FRIDAY, DECEMBER 8: Two calls from Bill, very angry. He feels his time is being wasted. He calls Vincent and, I gather, is angry with him. Result, VM calls me and is all compliance: the College must be as I wish it, but he and Hart thought, etc. So after some palaver this results: the Upper Library to be large and have a dais or pulpit, or something for lectures; no music room (which I do not regret, for the Junior Fellows can listen to music in their own rooms if they wish, and won't miss what they've never had); and the chapel is to

be completed. I am pleased, for Thom's chapel design looks interesting and if we do not have to relinquish anything else to get it, I am for it.

Hart may be a nuisance: he has been an obstructionist and a Doubting Thomas all along, concerned only for sole meunière, the wine cellar, and a "gentleman's library." None of the Masseys appear to have any real notion of scholarship. At 4:45 to Toronto with Brenda and Jenny to the UCC Prep[56] to see *A Masque of Aesop* well done. Train was slow and home at 2:30.

SUNDAY, DECEMBER 17: Lay late, then bathed and dyed my beard. In the afternoon we shift furniture for the party next Wednesday, then for a walk in the dusk, very beautiful. In the evening heard some of *Boris Godunov*.

A very full week and needed rest. I have promised the UCC Prep a new play; cannot undertake *Saturday Night* work as next year is sure to bring many duties and great detail.

On Thursday evening Hugh MacLennan called to say my "Pleasures of Love" in *Saturday Night* was the finest essay he had read in many years: such praise revives my shaken faith in my ability to write.

MONDAY, DECEMBER 18: A pleasant day and work not heavy: get away more Christmas cards to Massey College Senior Fellows and revise a *Star* column. In the evening read *The Tempest*. Relief of term end very pleasant.

TUESDAY, DECEMBER 19: To Toronto in soft weather. Final fourth-year class at University College. Leave Toronto at 3: car breaks

56 The junior school of Upper Canada College. Davies wrote the play for the school's jubilee year in 1952.

down, limp to Oshawa, two hours' repair and home in bad storm. Brenda wonderful. Music.

WEDNESDAY, DECEMBER 20: Quiet day: make a timetable for next term and write a *Star* column. In the evening Miranda's twenty-first-birthday party: many guests from Toronto and great merry-making. Brenda and I to bed at 2 and uproar continues 'til 3:30. A success, but parties overwhelm me.

THURSDAY, DECEMBER 21: I write Vincent Massey about the "honourable augmentation" of his arms;[57] in the evening see the film *The Holly and the Ivy* on TV, admirable. Then Cecilia Anderson and Miranda play and sing lieder and some English songs. Cecilia plays the first movement of the great posthumous Schubert sonata.

MONDAY, DECEMBER 25: H.t.d. on waking. The tree, and everyone very happy about gifts. In the afternoon hear records, then a walk and a nap, an admirable dinner, and hear Ruth Draper and Hal Holbrook as Mark Twain. A delightful family day, and am very grateful therefor.

SATURDAY, DECEMBER 30: Quiet morning at the *Examiner.* In the afternoon to bed and h.t.d. In the evening, look at the College plans and try to form a notion of its appearance and workings. I feel the benefit of rest: ideas for my novel and the servant book[58] crowd in upon me.

57 The Masseys wanted to use their coat of arms over the gate of the College but sought an augmentation to the arms in acknowledgement of Vincent Massey's service to the Queen as governor general.
58 Davies never developed the "servant's memoir," but, as pointed out by Judith Skelton Grant in *Robertson Davies: Man of Myth,* he used some of this material in his 1991 novel, *Murther and Walking Spirits.*

SUNDAY, DECEMBER 31: Up betimes for Sunday and dye my beard and bathe; in the afternoon look at old photographs and walk at Chemong Lake. In the evening, to the Curriers' till 11:30, then home for champagne with the girls, then all on to the Porters' and sing rounds and make merry till 2, very pleasant.

This year I have made some progress with my metamorphosis from an editor to a professor, and remain obstinately a writer. I am doing quite a lot of undergraduate teaching, both honours and pass, and a couple of graduates. Next September it will be all graduate work on courses covering English drama from 1660 to 1925 or so, a splendid "field." But I must swot for it, because my knowledge though varied and curious is not "scholarly." Nor is it likely to be, if scholarship means the barren pedantry some of my new colleagues evince. But I feel release and enlargement, getting shut of the *Examiner*, grateful to it though I am.

Work on the College building is now begun. Prince Philip is to lay the cornerstone in May: by this time next year we should see much of it completed. There is criticism and opposition, of course, but less than I had thought.

My personal work has meant some concern about my *Star* column, "A Writer's Diary": I was so discouraged and out of temper with it I considered dropping it, but was persuaded not to do so. The novel 5B[59] continues to shape itself in my mind, and also the servant's memoir suggested by Warburg.[60] And I have promised the Upper Canada College Prep a new play about Punch.

All goes well domestically, though as the girls grow older, new and inevitable problems arise. I think the change in our prospects has meant much to Brenda and we are very happy though we scrap

59 *Fifth Business* (1970).
60 Fredric John Warburg of Secker & Warburg, which published *The Personal Art* in the U.K. in 1961.

more than we did. We can afford to do so: our relationship will bear it and we are both more determined and opinionative than we were.

Financially we have never been so well off: we have upward of $70,000 in savings, apart from this house and my holding in the *Examiner.* Can afford luxuries, and bought $4,500 worth of paintings in December, and I have been acquiring some really fine books.

In health the Alexander Technique serves us well, and I have lost about ten pounds since returning from Portugal, and hope to do as much or better in the year to come. We are both clearly middle-aged and our sexual life is not so active as it was—74 times in 1961—but I think we take a deeper pleasure in it than ever. Have been rummaging through this book and I am struck by the repetitive pattern of these yearly entries: I suppose one's life does have a pattern and that character is destiny. But I want to *reform* myself, at whatever age!

1962

—

ROB AND BRENDA CONTINUED TO live in Peterborough, and he remained editor and publisher of the *Peterborough Examiner*. But they spent more and more time in Toronto as Rob became increasingly involved in the planning of Massey College, continued to lecture to undergraduates, and began teaching graduates at the University of Toronto. From January to March they rented a furnished apartment on Charles Street, then stayed variously at the Lord Simcoe, Royal York, and Park Plaza hotels or at Hawthorn Gardens. They frequently lunched and dined at the University Club on University Avenue. Miranda was at Trinity College, University of Toronto; Jennifer was working at the *Examiner* and living at home; and Rosamond was at Bishop Strachan School in Toronto.

During this year Davies kept his personal, Massey, and theatre diaries and made entries in his "big diary."

MONDAY, JANUARY 1: To the Mathewses' bouillon party as usual, but this time with all of us as a family. In the afternoon walk with

Brenda in the raw cold. Miranda went to a friend's wedding so our New Year's dinner was without her. I hate to see the family holiday come to an end.

TUESDAY, JANUARY 2: Had my familiar bad dream of teaching ignorantly and inadequately. A busy day at the *Examiner*. Discuss salaries with Wilson Craw and increase some. In the evening read Angus Wilson's *Old Men at the Zoo*, which I like: literate, if raw-nerved and thin.

FRIDAY, JANUARY 5: Busy day at the *Examiner*, and talk with Bill Garner about business affairs. Write a *Star* column. In the evening made notes on George Meredith to assist Miranda with an essay, and read for my lectures and for pleasure. This ease and command of work is delightful but can it last? If only I could be on top of my job all the time!

SUNDAY, JANUARY 7: Severe storm and rain, lie late. In the afternoon go through papers, make notes, timetables, and fuss, then a walk in the storm with Brenda. In the evening hear our new records of Weber's *Der Freischütz* and am very pleased with its romantic scene in Wolf Gulch, or whatever it is called. The dismal part of winter comes early this year and already I feel depleted and gloomy—but this will not—must not—last. This year is the worst, because of the quantity and variety of undergraduate teaching.

WEDNESDAY, JANUARY 10, TORONTO: A busy day and lectures go well. The fact that I have no B.A. comes up, as I knew it would.[1] Vincent Massey is steamed up about College furnishings. In the

1 Because Davies failed to complete his Ontario Senior Matriculation, he attended Queen's University as a special student, so he could not take a B.A. degree.

evening Miranda dines with us and we go to Hart House Theatre to see the Victoria College Drama Society do *Cymbeline*. It was appalling, unimaginative and vulgar.

FRIDAY, JANUARY 12: Busy on College matters. Call Vincent Massey and also Ron Thom about changes in plans and decoration. Write a *Star* column on John Cowper Powys. In the evening hear a recording of *Macbeth* in preparation for my Stratford season lecture and am greatly stirred by it.

SUNDAY, JANUARY 14: Brenda says I am greatly changed and will write in a new way. I think the change is owing to the Alexander Technique to a great degree. Certainly I am not so subject to nervous exhaustion and am able to do university and College work without becoming emotionally involved in a destructive way.

WEDNESDAY, JANUARY 17, TORONTO: Brenda is forty-five. I have a slight hangover. Give good lectures, then I am joined by Brenda and we order her some letter paper. To the flat and h.t.d. Dinner at the Lord Simcoe and to the Royal Alex to see Gratien Gélinas and La Comédie-Canadienne in his play *Bousille et les Justes*. Old-fashioned in form: all the characters are second-rate except honest, lovable little Bousille; all the actors shout and overdo except the star, who murmurs and plays very modestly. The crude appeal to sentimentalism reminded me of plays I used to see as a boy. This was worse in the light of Gélinas's lecture at the university yesterday in which he went on about the need for *real* Canadian plays that truly reflect the Canadian people. Does he mean this—several nasty hypocrites harrying one half-witted saint?

FRIDAY, JANUARY 19: Pack after lunch and away at 4:45 to Toronto alone. Dine at the Club and then to the flat to read, dye my beard,

bathe, and try to rest for what will be a long day tomorrow: how I dislike all this jaunting!

SATURDAY, JANUARY 20, TORONTO: Heavy snow but drive to Stratford with John Lockwood[2] and George Harris. A good board meeting. Michael Langham explains the new stage.[3] I talk with Lionel Massey at lunch about the College. Drive back to Toronto by 5:30 to catch the 6:30 train with Jenny, Sara Waddell, and Miranda to Peterborough.

SUNDAY, JANUARY 21: In the evening Brenda tells Miranda about her family and childhood and shows her photographs. I think much of the importance of keeping a family record and urge this upon Brenda and have got her a book for the purpose.[4]

TUESDAY, JANUARY 23, TORONTO: I begin to lose my voice. Do a lot of College business, then to the ROM at 3:15 and talk with Dr. Vic Mean of Mineralogy till 5.

Dinner at the flat and then to the Crest Theatre to see *Caesar and Cleopatra* very well done. Mavor Moore as Caesar and Toby Robins as Cleopatra, both good, though Moore somewhat lacks greatness—but he makes excellent sense. Direction by Leon Major skilled and subdued to the play. All of Act 3 cut and not much missed: result, we were out at 11 instead of emerging beaten at 11:40. I last saw this play in 1951 when Laurence Olivier did it with *Antony and Cleopatra.* Toby Robins was better than Vivien Leigh. (I should like to see her in my Casanova play with Major directing.)

2 Toronto businessman and Stratford governor.
3 The new stage was the first reconstruction of the original Festival Theatre stage designed by Tanya Moiseiwitsch in 1953.
4 Brenda wrote her privately published autobiography, *Beads in a String,* in 2001.

WEDNESDAY, JANUARY 24, TORONTO: Voice gone but enough to give two lectures. To a Hart House "Library Night" with Ron Thom to discuss Massey College with any interested undergraduates. The audience, counting the warden of Hart House, Joe McCulley, and his assistant, numbers thirteen—so much for "interest"; but these affairs are futile anyhow. What really interests me is the notion Joe McCulley seems to have that Hart House and Massey College are twin institutions. And the curiosity of undergraduates as to what sort of "student government" we shall have! Some questions sharp and a few impudent, but nothing really difficult. Hart and Geoffrey Massey drop in afterward and Thom and I go to the Park Plaza with them for drinks. All Ron says makes the building sound exciting and beautiful.

THURSDAY, JANUARY 25, TORONTO: My voice worse so cancel my lecture but go to Lionel Massey's house to meet Vincent Massey, Hart, Lionel, and Ron Thom to discuss furnishings. My suggestion that Eaton's be our buying agent and advisor has been approved. They want to get a typographer on the job to design our stationery, lettering, and, immediately, the cornerstone, which HRH Prince Philip will lay on May 25th. VM wants more Senior Fellows as soon as possible; I would prefer not to have them till we have something for them to do. But it is exciting that we are now going ahead full steam. The governor general has written the Queen about the "augmentation" and I hope she will move quickly, as we need that coat of arms. I must see Claude Bissell and talk to him about the academic work of the College and especially my own, as I am determined this must always be the foundation of all we do.

Brenda very kindly drives up; we lunch at the Club and drive home in splendid sunshine. It is my old trouble—exhaustion. To bed with remedies.

SATURDAY, JANUARY 27: In bed till noon; Jenny to Toronto at 1. Write two *Star* columns, both good, and hear recordings of *The Winter's Tale*. My nose purging and cough going full blast—the full hell of a bad cold. Brenda and Jenny return at 8:15. I am restless and want something special to read and can't find it.

SUNDAY, JANUARY 28: Rose at noon: eyes swollen, nose runs like a faucet. Am I mad to think of work—university work—next week? Read William Gaunt's *Aesthetic Adventure* and E.H. Shepard's two books.[5] What about my cold? It is the rise and fall that surprises; periods of improvement followed by abysmal slumps, pain, and depression.

MONDAY, JANUARY 29: Really ill: Dr. Dobson comes and prescribes. I abandon all thought of work this week. Read *The Rack* by A.E. Ellis—a novel about TB. Very ill-chosen. Take a sedative and antihistamine.

TUESDAY, JANUARY 30: Deaf, tasteless, and sans scent. Finish *The Rack* and begin Angela Thirkell's *The Headmistress* but can't bear its ill-organized waffle. I have a libidinous fantasy, as usual with a cold—why?

WEDNESDAY, JANUARY 31: Brenda to Toronto. I spend all day in bed. Read *A Victorian Poacher* and some of Dr. Harding's Jungian exposition. Brenda returns at 8:30.

THURSDAY, FEBRUARY 1: H.t.d. on waking, a great renewal of humanity. Feel better but cold is still heavy. Read *Relief of Lucknow*

5 E.H. Shepard, the illustrator for *The Wind in the Willows*, wrote two books of
 memoirs of English country life.

and began Waugh's *Unconditional Surrender.* We discuss Brenda's visit to Australia in April.

FRIDAY, FEBRUARY 2: Our twenty-second wedding anniversary. I give Brenda spring flowers; she gives me whisky. I am up in the afternoon and dictate many letters to Miss Whalon. We have an excellent dinner—steak, soufflé, and champagne—and read and hear music. Splendid h.t.d.

TUESDAY, FEBRUARY 6: To Toronto by train. Teaching goes well. Gordon Roper says the new dean of the Graduate School is one Ernest Sirluck,[6] who is dubious about Massey College. I must work on this. To the ROM at 3:30 and a boring talk with Heinrich.[7] With Brenda to *El Cid*, very good melodrama and refreshing.

WEDNESDAY, FEBRUARY 7, TORONTO: Saw Claude Bissell at 3:15 and discussed College affairs. I asked him directly if he wanted Eric Phillips as a Senior Fellow. He said he had not thought of it. Vincent Massey says Bissell has hinted about this to him, but VM is very prone to see hints and portents. Claude Bissell said Frank Stone is Eric Phillips's bulldog: if finances are difficult in the early years, do we want the man who owns the bulldog as part of the College?

To the Crest Theatre and see an Australian play, *The Shifting Heart* by Richard Beynon. Argument: an Italian family (Bianchi) have been eight years in a Melbourne suburb and are not "accepted"; the

6 Sirluck had returned to the University of Toronto from the University of Chicago at the urging of Claude Bissell to become the Graduate School's associate dean of humanities and social sciences, with the understanding he would succeed Andrew Gordon as dean. He was the first Jew appointed to a senior position at the university.
7 Theodore Heinrich, director of the Royal Ontario Museum, which at this time was part of the University of Toronto.

son, Gino, resentful of this, makes a scene at a dance hall where he is refused entry, and is killed; his sister, Maria, married to an Australian, bears a son and he is named Gino; thus "acceptance" is attained. Good theme and dramatically worked out, but I am offended by the mindlessness of everyone; two minutes' quiet reflection on anyone's part would have saved all the fuss. But so many of these proletarian tragedies (and noble ones, too) are rooted in a passionate stupidity.

TUESDAY, FEBRUARY 13, TORONTO: To Eaton's at 3:30 and met A. Russell of the Contracts Department, who took me to R. Howard, who is to do the College work—a wee Scot, professionally dubious but knows his job, I judge. We agree that some parts of the College have a 1910 Frank Lloyd Wright air, which can probably be mitigated by the furnishings. Encouraged by their competence and plain good sense.

FRIDAY, FEBRUARY 16: Busy day: Miss Whalon has cracked three ribs. Write *Star* column on *The Seven Deadly Sins* and read books for the *University of Toronto Quarterly* review.[8] In the evening help Miranda with notes on Sheridan. At bedtime attempt h.t.d.: no go; back too painful; all the humiliations and pain of February.

SUNDAY, FEBRUARY 18: Lie late; Jenny went to Toronto with friends last night and was not in till 2:45. In the afternoon the whole family walk at the zoo and in Lakefield. Miranda returns to university on the 7:45 train. Read Kenneth Tynan and chat with Brenda, who also has a form of 'flu. February is always a brutal month: Brenda says my depression and desire to give up the *Star* column is due to

8 "Letters in Canada: 1961: Drama and Music," *University of Toronto Quarterly* 31, no. 4 (July 1962); review of Gratien Gélinas, *Bousille and the Just.*

this. She is upheld by thoughts of going to Australia, another journey in search of herself, we both feel.

WEDNESDAY, FEBRUARY 21, TORONTO: To the O'Keefe to see *The Unsinkable Molly Brown* by Meredith Willson, which seemed to promise well in the first half but went to pieces in the second. As always in that vast warehouse, everybody screamed, and any nuance the thing might have had was lost. Tammy Grimes has an urchin charm but the rest of the cast was as obvious as cornflakes. Theme: a determined mountain girl gets rich, gets position, is loved for her naïveté, and at last returns to her first love. American twaddle. The music is unmemorable.

FRIDAY, FEBRUARY 23: Lionel Massey calls to say that the Queen has approved the augmentation for Vincent Massey "in principle" but its precise nature has now to be worked out and this will take time—as what does not, in the world of heraldry? Today also I received an acknowledgement of my letter of December 28 to the governor general from his secretary, Esmond Butler, who writes an oddly illiterate hand for a man in his place; fifty-seven days to answer a letter!

SATURDAY, FEBRUARY 24: Heavy snowfall. Walk to the office with snow almost to my knees. Mark some twenty student essays. In the afternoon shovel a lot of snow and enjoy the unwonted exercise. In the evening read Kenneth Tynan on the theatre. Brenda has 'flu and its characteristic waves of exhaustion.

SUNDAY, FEBRUARY 25: Bouts of sinus, headache, nausea, and cold sweats have left me unwell for the day. Brenda and I lay on sofas and read. Went for short walk. What a hateful winter! Every winter has its low point and I hope this is it: is it age or bodily rot that brings this appalling *tedium vitae*?

MONDAY, FEBRUARY 26: Vincent Massey calls—he thinks trumpets would be nice for May 25 so I pursue trumpets. An awful day: feel ill and do a good deal of work. In the evening labour with *Death of a Salesman* by Arthur Miller, which baffles me. Excellent h.t.d.

In the night I dream of the Miraculous Child,[9] very fine (he smelled of apple blossom).

MONDAY, MARCH 5: A great to-do about Mrs. Pedak, who has been growing more removed, unheeding, and miserly with the food for some months. Brenda was angry with her on Saturday—no, Friday—an almost unheard-of thing. Brenda says, "She is having a great affair with herself." This morning this proved literally to be true. Mrs. Pedak confides that she discusses everything with her "love"—a Russian soldier she loved before her marriage—and writes poems to him, and lives with him in imagination. She did this all through her marriage, it appears. Brenda has persuaded her to have some talks with Dr. Currier, as this is rather too much. Mrs. Pedak has no friends, no interests, and is growing away from the world—with her "love." An extraordinary woman, very strong in her egotism and a kind of early nineteenth-century romanticism that one would have sworn was dead.

WEDNESDAY, MARCH 7, TORONTO: To the refurbished Central Library Theatre[10] to see the Red Barn company do N.F. Simpson's *One Way Pendulum*. Well directed and acted and the second act theatrically effective, but the Theatre of the Absurd is too remorselessly absurd. *Non sequitur*, to be telling, must emerge from a rich setting of *sequitur*. This play is Lewis Carroll and Edward Lear pushed too far. Perhaps one must be very English to respond fully:

9 A Jungian archetype.
10 Now the Robert Gill Theatre at the University of Toronto.

to me all the jokes are variations of one joke and the whimsicality grows wearisome. Anarchic humour? No, for the self-conscious disorder all too quickly becomes tyrannous, and as there can be no real characters we are bored with it.

THURSDAY, MARCH 8, TORONTO: Meditation in Trinity College chapel. I would like to continue this during Lent. I give a good lecture and then to a meeting of the Massey Foundation at the office in the Shell Building at 2:30. Vincent Massey, Lionel, Hart, Ron Thom, Bill Broughall, and Russell and Howard (from Eaton's) there and look at silver and china and discuss furniture, narrowing the field of choice. VM favours what is traditional; Hart, a little cantankerously, wants what is contemporary. I dare say something workable will emerge, with a few errors here and there. At 4 p.m. the typographer, A.R. Fleming,[11] arrives and we discuss the cornerstone. Thom wanted it on the ground: I pointed out the impropriety of placing it where dogs could pee on it. We progress. The cement footings begin to take shape. Those at the southwest corner must be complete before the frost goes, or there is a danger that the St. Thomas Aquinas Chapel may subside into our excavation! Persuaded VM against putting a Hammond organ in the chapel, which looks as if it might be charming. All of this encourages me and I am confirmed in my faith that the College will *really* be built. My doubt is irrational, and springs from my own impatience and the slowness with which all goes forward. My present fear is that the College will emerge as a Tom Thumb's castle, the foundations look so small: Howard assures me that it will continue to look smaller and smaller until the walls are plastered, whereupon everything will appear in its proper, appropriate size.

11 Allan R. Fleming, influential graphic designer, later chief designer at University of Toronto Press.

WEDNESDAY, MARCH 14, TORONTO: At 10 a.m. meet Ron Thom at the Park Plaza and discuss a few College details. Allan Fleming joins us and shows us the lettering he means to use on the cornerstone. The letters are from Trajan's Column, but as shown in rubbings from the column itself, and not from the British Museum casts—much freer, and the serifs very decorative. I suggest we use upper- and lower-case letters of this sort for all the signs in the College, which will be many. The rediscoverer of this Roman form is one Edward M. Catich.[12] The university's carilloneur has written me about the foundation stone laying: he won't simply play some agreeable changes, but wants to do a "program" containing all the carillon clichés—sea-songs, patriotic airs, and whatnot. The army are being sticky about letting us have trumpeters.

To the Central Library Theatre to see Jean Genet's *The Balcony*. Idea good, but worked out in pseudo-philosophical style, not aided by the translation or the mispronunciations of the actors, e.g. no-MEN-clature, repeated several times. How short-winded these fellows are! Have been teaching Ibsen's *The Wild Duck* this week: it makes this look like a pretentious sketch. But then, revolution is never strong on organization. Toni Weinberg good as the Madam. Tiff Findley[13] castrated himself in a way that suggests either a very odd physique, or stylization gone mad.

TUESDAY, MARCH 20, TORONTO: To the Royal Alex to *Little Mary Sunshine* by Rick Besoyan, a spoof of musical comedy as it was in my very early youth. Well done and a relief after the *avant-garde* theatre-going of the past few weeks. Pat Galloway surprised us by being able to sing quite well and was funny with the kind of control and real wit Tammy Grimes lacks. Dominique Michel the best *soubrette*

12 American Roman Catholic priest, teacher, and calligrapher.
13 Timothy Findley, Canadian novelist and playwright. He began his career as an actor.

I have seen in years: she comes from La Comédie-Canadienne. The whole production from Montreal, and is dying on its feet, Ernest Rawley, the Royal Alex manager, says. A pity; it deserves better. But two women next to me were taking it perfectly straight! How extraordinarily variable the sophistication of Toronto audiences is.

WEDNESDAY, MARCH 21, TORONTO: To the Crest to the opening of *Roar like a Dove* by Lesley Storm, a vapid comedy but I laughed a good deal, and Herbert Whittaker was tart with me about it in the interval.[14] He grows dreadfully pompous and self-honouring, but writes no better; grammar rickety and vocabulary all reach-me-downs. Charmion King was too vehement as Lady Dungavel, but Drew Thompson has become a good character man. There was a party after at a hotel on University Avenue—one of those affairs where you buy tickets for drinks. I think it was designed to make the opening seem modish, but who was impressed?

THURSDAY, MARCH 22, TORONTO: See a graduate student working on Heavysege[15] and give a good lecture. We get Rosamond at BSS for her Easter break and are home by 5. Scott[16] and Judith Symons to dinner: he talks bitter Tory nonsense all evening and I have to swallow it from courtesy. A fatuous ass and an archaic, farcical Tory.

SUNDAY, MARCH 25: Do an hour's work on my Academy of Medicine speech in the morning. In the afternoon walk with Brenda, who has slight 'flu, and finish speech: Miranda returns to university at 7:45. Read and chat in the afternoon and evening, but we are nervous and unsettled. Brenda's imminent departure for Australia

14 Davies had a very distinctive, carrying laugh; actors always knew when he was in the audience.
15 Nineteenth-century Canadian poet. In *Leaven of Malice*, Solly Bridgetower was studying his work.
16 Novelist and art historian; brother of Tom Symons.

keeps us all rather on edge, though it is hard to say why. I welcome the cessation of lectures and make an attack on other work. I gave the *Star* notice Friday.

TUESDAY, MARCH 27: To Toronto with Rosamond at 7:30. A very busy day with graduate work and lectures. Dine at the Lord Simcoe with Brenda and Rosamond and to the O'Keefe Centre to *Irma la Douce*. Not so good as when I saw it in London in August 1959 with Elizabeth Seal and Clive Revill, but good nevertheless, because the foundation—the book and music—are so good. Taina Elg was Irma, and danced well, but there was a cold Baltic breath from the stage whenever she appeared. The O'Keefe is death to charm, and it speaks well for them that they got across as much as they did. Excellent h.t.d.

WEDNESDAY, MARCH 28, TORONTO: Took Miranda to the Central Library Theatre to Sheridan's *The Rivals*. It was a "theatre night" for library workers and they were a damned bad audience—worse even than teachers. We got turn-in seats and sat in the front row. A good production, and the wonderful old piece came through strongly in spite of some bad performances. Alan Nunn was loud and unvaried as Sir Anthony Absolute, nearly deafened us. Cosy Lee as Mrs. Malaprop had a bad cold and croaked and dried piteously at her first entrance—she could not even hear the prompter, who was bellowing. Glynne Morris played Sir Lucius O'Trigger with a dirty make-up. But Tiff Findley was a very good Captain Absolute and Lester Nixon an excellent Faulkland—really comic without once betraying the part. Al Kozlik a winning Acres—played him young and essentially serious. The girls Pauline Reynolds as Lydia Languish and Louise Nicol as Julia Melville, witty and charming. Enjoyed it greatly. And the language! What a feast of just, apt, and witty writing! I have seen this play butchered by amateurs. Also

saw it at the Old Vic in 1938 not very well directed by Esme Church, and remember only Anthony Quayle as Captain Absolute and beautiful Hermione Hannen as Lydia. Also the 1942 New York production: Mary Boland as Mrs. Malaprop, Walter Hampden admirable as Sir Anthony, and Bobby Clark wonderfully funny and strangely gentle as Acres.

THURSDAY, MARCH 29, TORONTO: Unwell from a poor night. I worked on graduate exams and lectured well. I was applauded at the end of both lectures this week. Very gratifying. Home by train for Rosamond's birthday dinner, held early so Brenda could be here. An uneasy evening of chat. Brenda wakes at 3 a.m. very apprehensive: should she postpone her journey? I comfort her.

Brenda was away in Australia from March 30 until May 6. Rob wrote to her a number of times while she was away (airmail took about six days). Some passages from these letters are included with the following entries.

FRIDAY, MARCH 30: We lunch early and Jenny, Rosamond, and I see Brenda away on the 1 o'clock train for first leg of her journey. In the evening began Allardyce Nicoll's *History of English Drama* and am absorbed, but what a prude he is!

SATURDAY, MARCH 31: Premier Robarts,[17] successor to Leslie Frost, in for a half hour's chat in the morning. He seems a nice man. Dinner with the Waddells at the steak place on the highway and then to *Spring Thaw*, at St. Peter's High School. This is the fifteenth year of this revue and it has grown from a somewhat amateur Toronto joke to a genuine national satire. Production was good,

17 John Robarts, premier of Ontario from 1961 to 1971.

humour savage. But their marks are too few: Canada Council, our theatre and ballet, and a rather narrow political range, and of course the National Film Board. But a good rozzling evening, and clear proof that Canadians *have* a sense of humour and that it is fiercely ironic. Afterward, the Jeanette Scott Chapter of the Imperial Order of Daughters of the Empire gave coffee and dainty bits to the cast and a few guests. These uneasy affairs are one of our pioneer hangovers: people from a distance must be fed. But oh! the genteel daintiness of it all, the eating with front teeth, the grisly *bonhomie*! Wrote a notice for the *Examiner* before bed at 1.

I have seen Lionel Massey on March 13th and 27th on foundation stone business, about which he fusses. Of course it must go smoothly, but why the agony?

I hope I am not getting Gordon Roper and myself into trouble but, following his suggestion that a really good librarian could add much to the College, I have been in correspondence with Pennington of McGill, who wants a change, and wants scholarly rather than administrative work. He is to see Roper in Toronto shortly. I would love to have a first-class librarian on the spot. But his salary would be considerable, and would the Masseys see the point? The Library has been achieved rather in their teeth. But Roper will find out, and report when next the Senior Fellows meet. Caesar Wright suggests we have a distinctive gown, Cambridge fashion. This would relieve Lionel, who pathetically has no gown and must be academically naked on occasions like May 25. Bill Broughall has his desire: the Massey Foundation may now legally invest in stocks and shares other than those approved for trusts, and he assures me that in a few years this will put the College out of any worries about money. Pray God this is true!

SUNDAY, APRIL 1: Woke at 8 and read. A quiet day. I hear some *St. Matthew Passion* and read *The Teachers* by G.W. Target. A walk in the

afternoon and a good chat with Jenny and Rosamond, and write Brenda. Read my 1945 diary, which shows me sour and testy and in revolt against Peterborough—not surprising. We all make a good job of Brenda being away and Jenny is most considerate.

MONDAY, APRIL 2: Miranda phoned at lunch: Stratford is taking her after all![18] I wire this news to Brenda. Rosamond away on the 4:45 train; a letter from Brenda. In the evening work on my speech and on Restoration drama.

TUESDAY, APRIL 3, LETTER TO BRENDA

I went to Toronto early on Tuesday, to be in good time for my meeting about the Southam Fellowships.[19] The elections committee was Dean Bladen,[20] Sword (Claude's chief assistant), Gil Purcell of Canadian Press, and Ross Munro, a very able journalist. I like the university atmosphere; we made the decisions quickly, and without gobbledegook, and off to lunch at the Faculty Club. No wasted motion. This gave me a chance to get a sleep in the p.m.—or would have done if I had not had five phone calls in one hour, which woke me up thoroughly. Prof. Woodhouse suddenly wanted an exam on Victorian drama—by this morning! He had forgotten it! A nice old josher but no administrator. Fortunately I was in a position (as we say in Pbro) to cough one up.

The Academy of Medicine affair was quite fun. Large dinner at the York Club before, and met a wheen of doctors, some nice and some rather silly. The president, Dr. Morley (brain surgeon), urged

18 Miranda had been waiting to hear if she would return to the Stratford Festival company for the 1962 season.
19 In September 1961 Davies was invited to serve on the selection committee for the new Southam Fellowships for journalists, established by St. Clair Balfour of the Southam Company Ltd. Since September 1963 the journalism Fellows have been based at Massey College.
20 Vincent Bladen, British-Canadian political economist, long-time leading figure at the University of Toronto.

me to take exercise. After forty-five it is necessary to open the tubes of the heart. An equally eminent colleague, Dr. Mumbledemum, warned me against it; it sets up a toxic reaction in the muscles which unfits one for intellectual work. Met Dr. Graham, the great gout man, who treats Walter Gordon; says gout rages on this continent, and goes unrecognized very often. At 9 p.m. to the Academy, where they have a wee hall, and after a too-long business meeting, I was let speak and it went very well.[21] Only trouble is my voice gives me trouble, and I croak; wanted a glass of water but there was none. A vote of thanks was moved by a chap who wanted to be funny, but was a green hand at such work, and said he guessed he had been asked to thank me because he was a birdwatcher, and was thus expected to be an expert on Queer Birds. Ha ha. As I had been received with warm applause, this went over (in Rosamond's phrase) like a truckload of dead babies.

The Academy has just inherited what is said to be the finest collection of medical objects on this continent and one of the best in the world—the Drake Collection. The ROM wanted it, and so did McGill, but were circumvented. Ten thousand objects, from elegant eighteenth-century pap-boats and vinaigrettes to tongue-scrapers and other horrid objects. An item which took my eye was an elegant female urinal in delicate porcelain, rather in the style of your Flight, Barr & Barr cups, painted with a pastoral scene of an Arcadian shepherdess (Phyllis) with her skirts coyly hoisted, peeing, while her swain (Corydon) lies at her feet peeping up toward the source of the stream. In the bottom of this object was a beautifully painted eye; real coarse eighteenth-century fun.

21 "Men and Books: Literature & Medicine," in *Canadian Medical Association Journal* 87, no. 13 (September 29, 1962).

THURSDAY, APRIL 5: Genest[22] comes today, a great thrill, and Britnell[23] phones to tell me the American history of drama is on the way: this is really collecting. I take Jenny to dine and to a film, *Majority of One*.

FRIDAY, APRIL 6: I begin work on my *Punch* play. It begins very slowly and I hate stirring myself but gradually something comes. In the evening read Genest and Montague Summers.[24] Miranda calls; she is coming home for the weekend.

SATURDAY, APRIL 7: Work on *Punch* unwillingly. The American drama books come and are very fine with Genest. Miranda comes on the midday train. In the evening work on the play, then chat with Miranda about her work and her friends. Jenny goes dancing. Rain.

SATURDAY, APRIL 7, LETTER TO BRENDA

Queen's University want to make me an LL.D. on May 19, and I am to make a speech. Will you come? Very kind of them, considering how I have roasted Queen's in my books. But I shall be very glad to have a degree from Queen's at last, for they were decent to me when my matriculation exams fell through.

SUNDAY, APRIL 8: Lie late. In the afternoon walk with Miranda, then hear Glenn Gould playing Bach on TV. Work on *Punch* to good effect. Jenny is out most of the day bowling. In the evening play duets and talk to Miranda about Swift and then about love and family relationships.

22 *John Genest: Some Account of the English Stage, from the Restoration in 1660 to 1830*, 10 volumes, 1832.
23 Roy Britnell of the Albert Britnell Book Shop, which is now a Starbucks.
24 English author, clergyman, and eccentric, known for scholarly works on seventeenth-century drama and idiosyncratic studies of witches, vampires, and werewolves. Davies saw him at Oxford and found him fascinating.

It is curious the physical unease, almost amounting to illness, that comes on me as soon as I begin to *write*—as opposed to journalistic production. *Punch* makes any rest impossible: I am distraught and uneasy, physically frowsy and under the weather.

WEDNESDAY, APRIL 11: To Toronto and met Vincent Massey, Lionel Massey, and Allan Fleming at the College site, where we gather at 4 p.m. to discuss the cornerstone with the builders. After some discussion we agree that it should face inward at the gate, and not to the street. Progress is being made: almost all the foundation is in. VM shares my opinion that the building looks very small and my hope that it will look bigger when finished. Then to Lionel's office in the ROM where we discuss lettering, the invitations, use of arms on letter paper, etc. VM is not pleased that heads of the Veterinary College, Household Science, etc. are to be asked to the foundation stone ceremony, but we cannot show ourselves sniffy. We agree to forget trumpeters, as the army is so disobliging, and to try to control the carilloneur. It is greatly encouraging to see the building progress, and to move nearer our first public act. Some objects are to be put in a copper box in the foundation stone: VM suggests a speech of mine and I think the October 18th one[25] would be suitable. Our arms still hang fire—some slip-up between the Palace and the College of Arms. We must have it soon. Ron Thom likes my suggestion of an ikon as the focal point of the chapel. Hope this comes off.

THURSDAY, APRIL 12, LETTER TO BRENDA
Am much oppressed in spirit because I have begun the *Punch* play for UCC. It goes well, but *such* hard work! Writing anything original just plain *is* hard work, and scribbling criticism is child's play to it. I cannot think coherently about anything else, and so all the

25 Osgoode Legal and Literary Society lunch, October 18, 1961.

university work has to be done by main strength. Also, for some reason, I am not sleeping well; woke this morning at 4:30 and could not get off again 'til 6. This sort of thing happens most nights and I don't know why. Maybe I am at the time of life when one just naps a lot and does not really sleep.

SUNDAY, APRIL 15: I miss Brenda all the time: there is no one to talk to about things that most press on my mind. She writes that she is meeting many old friends. It is three weeks until she returns. I want to complete a good deal of work before then.

SUNDAY, APRIL 15, LETTER TO BRENDA

I was at the university by 9 yesterday, and we sat for four hours, examining for Ph.D.s two young men who did not know their work. One was a Mute Inglorious Failure, who clawed the air and struggled for speech, whenever he was asked anything. His subject was modern lit. and he would gurgle something about what he called "the Eliot sort of thing" or "the Hemingway sort of thing" and then lapse into incomprehensibility. But the second one was worse—a young Englishman, who was very vocal but said nothing to the purpose. Poor wretch, he knew he was talking nonsense a lot of the time, but he hadn't the nerve to shut his cake-hole and stop the agony. When we had polished off these two no-hopers the five of us scampered over to the University College dining-room and ate and drank everything in sight and made unkind fun of the morning's work, by which we were all exhausted. But by 2 p.m. we had to be on the job again, for yet another victim. Thank God he was better, and did quite well.

These affairs are more trying than you might suppose. All the examiners feel for the candidate, and are torn inwardly with hooks when he makes a mug of himself. I questioned each man for twenty-five minutes on modern drama, and it was not easy work. But then I listened to all the rest, as each examiner is asked to give his

opinion on the answers given to all the other men. We sat on very hard chairs. Prof. Woodhouse, as chairman, was able to relieve his feelings by doing light housekeeping—opening and shutting windows, getting the candidate a glass of water (and for one of them even a cup of tea), and emptying ashtrays. Talk about lung cancer? I kept count during the third man's exam and here are the horrible statistics. Niggsies smoked: Prof. Woodhouse 10; Prof. Child 12; Prof. Wilson zero; the candidate 15; me, a cigar; and Prof. Buitenhuis burned a lot of goat's hair in a big hooked pipe. What we all needed was a big stiff drink, and I think I shall introduce this when I am chairman of an examination.

After the exams we were all so worn out none of us could add and got a terrible fit of the group giggles as one man seemed mysteriously to have got 472 out of 100—really he had got 47.2. Professors are strangely childish, which is rather nice.

MONDAY, APRIL 16: Cherrier of the *Star* tries to persuade me not to drop the *Star* column. I will continue it till June 1. I work on *Punch* and hope to finish the first draft this week. I talk with Jenny and watch TV with her.

WEDNESDAY, APRIL 18, LETTER TO BRENDA
Yesterday to Toronto by 'bus, and at once to another graduate *viva*. My afternoon was free so I went to get my hair cut; this time the barber called the manicurist to look at the snowy wonder of my wig. "You won't see one person in a hundred thousand with hair in that condition," said he. Do you think there are such things as hairosexuals? If so, he is certainly one, and God knows what will happen to me if he becomes too much aroused.

That evening I had a disagreeable task; a man had phoned, wanting to be considered as bursar for Massey College. I have known him since school days, and so has Lionel; he was Vincent's

secretary in London when he was high commissioner; he is a fraternity brother of Bill Broughall's. And we were all agreed he wouldn't do. He is rich, well-connected, well-educated, a gentleman, a lawyer by training, and knows everybody; speaks French well, and knows all about entertaining BUT is now fifty and has never stuck at any job for more than two or three years. Further, is a Big Jessie. I wish to Heaven he were just a bit more possible, for he has every quality we want, but also two or three that would make him a big headache for me and the Senior Fellows. So I had to give him dinner, take him seriously, and suffer the embarrassment of being courted by an old schoolfellow in slightly sticky terms, knowing all the time it would come to nothing. Tried not to lead him up the garden path, but could not prevent him from dashing up it himself. I think the ruin of him is that he is very rich; his papa was a big mines man in the days when mines were the thing. I did my stuff from 6:30 to 9 and then escaped and went to a Peter Sellers movie, *Only Two Can Play*—excellent, very funny, and captures the queer quality of Welsh provincial life (there is no other kind) and also all that wonderful old Welsh spite and bitchery.

Vincent Massey tells me in great confidence that there is nothing so economical as buying really good clothes, and showed me the label in his black overcoat, which shows it was made for him in 1928! Unfortunately, it looks it. Canada is to have a general election on June 18. Canada suffered national humiliation last night when the Maple Leafs were beaten 4 to 1 by the Chicago Black Hawks (this is *hockey*).

Jenny says to assure you that all is not lost; the hockey championships now stand two-two and the Leafs may yet win.

The professor of Chinese, Bill Dobson (who is going to be a Senior Fellow of the College),[26] has lent me a number of good

26 W.A.C.H. Dobson, head of the Department of East Asiatic Studies.

books about classical Chinese doings; you must look at them when you get back as you are our Chinese department. You will like Dobson: he is a charming Englishman, and full of jokes. A *real* scholar, not a toad.

SUNDAY, APRIL 22, EASTER: Up at 7 and with Rosamond to Communion. We had gifts from Brenda at breakfast. Then to bed with a hot pad for my back. In the afternoon chat with Miranda and Rosamond, then a walk and an excellent dinner. But Easter without Brenda is not the coming of spring.

MONDAY, APRIL 23: Rosamond returns to BSS at 4:45; I read fifteen exam papers, most of them written by Mrs. Malaprop when drunk. In the evening see a CBC *Macbeth* with Miranda—jejune. Lumbago has improved. Good chat with Miranda.

SATURDAY, APRIL 28: Lumbago is really bad. To Toronto on the 1 o'clock train and to the Club, where I doze and take aspirins till 6. Ron Thom dines with me and we discuss College matters. To the Harrises' for a chat, and drive home with Miranda by 2:30.

SUNDAY, APRIL 29: Lay late and loafed all day to my great benefit. A walk with Miranda in the afternoon. In the evening read and chat with Miranda and Jenny and drink cocoa: a real rest, first in a long time. Only one more week without Brenda. I need rest and think some respite in sight though perhaps not much. But hateful exams will soon be done and work better suited to me begins.

I have been marking a hundred papers in English and am astonished that these people admitted to first-year honours work cannot spell or compose grammatical sentences, e.g.: "humour wants (once) more enters the picture"; "Boyle is funny in that he has no shame in lying on the Bible"; "she was pregnant for a child";

"(Dogberry) believes in making a farce out of his studies"; and that *Oedipus* is by Aristotle, and that Lady Bracknell is very fond of pickles (cucumber sandwiches); at least five cannot distinguish between "no" and "know." I have to fail a great many, which may cause some trouble. But what else is there to do with someone who writes that "the Greek tragedy *Oedipus* has more unity of place . . . it all takes place on Othello's front steps," and thinks that comic elements are introduced into *Othello* by Beatrice and Benedick and Dogberry and says the Widow Quin "speaks only of the mundane things of life (e.g. dung)." It is the refinement coupled with ignorance that kills.

A number of notes on College matters from the past few days. The ikon for the chapel is now a certainty. Ron Thom told me last night that he wants to make the chapel congruous with the ikon— he conceives of this in terms of the film of *Ivan the Terrible*. Hope this works. As he describes the building to me, it sounds more and more interesting and romantic; his use of leather very much appeals to me. Ron says Vincent Massey had not understood the brick of the College was to be a leather colour, though I knew this. The army has at last promised us four trumpeters for May 25th.

WEDNESDAY, MAY 2: Rheumatism is no better: I am like a character part in a bad play. I finish the God-damned exam papers, all ninety-nine: twenty-three failures, however generous and undemanding I am. Donkeys! Illiterates! I doze all evening on the sofa. I am exhausted and really rather ill.

FRIDAY, MAY 4: Rheumatism abates slightly. I write a *Star* column on *A Pride of Terrys* by Margaret Steen and do some College business. Miranda arranges her belongings to go to Stratford. In the evening we fuss and dither and are excited about Brenda's return. Rosamond calls: she wants to go to airport to meet Brenda.

SUNDAY, MAY 6, TORONTO: At Hawthorn Gardens. Miranda comes to breakfast and leaves for Stratford at 12. Rosamond comes to lunch and I take her and Jenny to a film, *Only Two Can Play*. Tea and to the airport to meet Brenda at 9:50. Take Rosamond back to BSS, then drive home by 1. H.t.d. very delightful and chat 'til 3. Brenda looks thin and rather tired from the journey but is really very well and has obviously enjoyed her holiday, but her reports of her family are not very encouraging: they are so queer about money.

MONDAY, MAY 7: Back improved but still stiff. A lazy day. In the evening we heard Australian records, to bed early and h.t.d.—a wonderful rejoining of the human race. Then read Brenda's travel diary—revealing, full of artist's perceptions of colour and light.

FRIDAY, MAY 11, STRATFORD: Vincent Massey called at 8:30 p.m. with two pieces of very good news: (1) The "augmentation of honour" has been approved and after a few more civilities among the great ones we shall have, in dexter chief on the Massey arms, a crowned lion with a maple leaf between its forepaws, on a blue ground—very fine. (2) An unidentified friend has told VM he has remembered the College substantially in his will, and thus we break the difficult duck of benefactions even before we are open! I am greatly cheered. Things are looking up. Invitations for 25th come. H.t.d.—very good!

SATURDAY, MAY 12: In the morning busy at the *Examiner*. Brenda reads my *Punch* play and likes it very much and gives some good advice for revision.

SUNDAY, MAY 13: Lie late, then dye my beard and wash my hair. In the afternoon read, doze, and fuss about: idleness is very refreshing. In the evening Brenda shows slides of her journey, most

interesting, then we chat about the family situation in Australia. Brenda's return makes everything easier and brings plans for the next few weeks into focus.

TUESDAY, MAY 15: The vexed question for Massey College at present is: will the Chancellor bring his mace to the foundation stone laying? For two days this has engaged the attention of Robin Ross, the registrar, who seems very worried about it. I have been as diplomatic as I know how. The decision must, of course, rest with the *university* authorities, but I would like to see the mace[27] for the Prince, and also for Vincent. But Jeanneret,[28] the chancellor, Ross tells me on the q.t., is miffed because we have not invited *all* the Senate—more than a hundred extra. So no mace: the bedel will carry some sort of footman's staff. I call this petty toward Vincent Massey, who is, after all, a former chancellor, and toward the Massey Foundation, who are giving a college to the university. But the pettiness of academics surpasses that of eighteenth-century European princedoms.

Vincent Massey is agog to have some Honorary Fellows right away and names Harold Macmillan, Felix Frankfurter, and Père Lévesque. I oppose it. We shall look ridiculous with Honorary Fellows before we have any Junior Fellows.

Bill Broughall knew Ernest Sirluck, who is to be next dean of graduate studies, in the army and dislikes him—"a nasty little Hebe": but we shall see. He said Sirluck once boasted descent from a medieval knight called Sir Luck. Foolish, but understandable; not everyone is the great-grandson of Sir Something-or-Other Haggerty, once chief justice of Upper Canada, and author of a book of verse that Bill wants to give the College Library. These

27 The ornate silver and gilt staff that is the traditional symbol of the chancellor's authority.
28 François Charles Archile Jeanneret, 22nd chancellor.

Toronto Tories have damned stiff necks and I shall take Sirluck as I find him.

FRIDAY, MAY 18: A meeting at Devonshire House at 2:30 for final plans for the foundation stone laying. More people than I would have thought possible, from Ken Pringle, the site manager from Eastern Construction, through RCMP, city police, registrar's office, contractor, architect, and lieutenant governor's aide. Every detail is chewed over, every possibility canvassed (except rain). We all get our orders. The chancellor, it now appears, will have an "esquire bedel." Then look over the building with Ron Thom: the quad, now its shape appears, is very exciting, but what appears to be my study would be cramped quarters for a poodle. But patience, patience.

SATURDAY, MAY 19: To Kingston by car at 7 and to the Queen's University convocation at 3. I am made LL.D., which I prize, partly because of the Massey College appointment. I speak well, Brenda and Rosamond say.[29] At tea afterward see many old friends. Then to Arthur and Dorothy, who give us flowers. He is most kind. We dine in Belleville and are home by 10; h.t.d. A proud day.

SUNDAY, MAY 20: Lay late. A lazy day, sat in the garden and read and chatted with Brenda. I greatly enjoy a day of idleness and real irresponsibility. I have a sense of fulfillment at my doctorate from Queen's; a piece of unfinished business now very happily finished. My health is much better as the load of work lightens.

TUESDAY, MAY 22: Very busy: rewrite my speech for the 25th three times and am ashamed of being so nervous about it. In the evening

29 "The Deadliest of the Sins," in *One Half of Robertson Davies* (1977).

work on the seating plan of the luncheon on the 25th, which is troublesome. The *Galt Reporter* reports me dead!

THURSDAY, MAY 24: Nerves are troublesome: stage fright at my age! To the *Examiner* office in the morning, then rest and pack, and at 5 pick up Jenny. Drive to Toronto to Hawthorn Gardens and dine with the Harrises at 7:30 and spend a very pleasant evening with them.

FRIDAY, MAY 25, TORONTO: Laying of the cornerstone. At 11 a.m. to Hart House Reading Room with Brenda where the chancellor and Mrs. Jeanneret and the lieutenant governor and Mrs. MacKay join us. At 11:30 HRH Prince Philip appears with Vincent Massey and Claude Bissell, and we are presented. "This is an occasion when the men far outshine the women," says he, as Claude Bissell and the chancellor are in silver and gold, Keiller MacKay in a scarlet LL.D., and VM in an Oxford DCL, and I am in my new Queen's D.Litt. outfit, red and blue, with white tie and bands. HRH questions me about the College and I explain our organization. Then the ladies are off in the lieutenant governor's car and the rest of us walk in procession, as the streets have been closed. Procession thus:

Chief of University Police
2 RCMP Sergeants
Bedel
Chancellor
Claude Bissell and Robertson Davies
Lieutenant Governor
his aide-de-camp
Equerry and Secretary of HRH
VM and HRH

The much discussed mace appeared after all! Thus to the site, where I presented the Senior Fellows, who made the usual motley show, from Bill Broughall as a Dickensian barrister to Caesar Wright in purple. VM spoke very well to the 500-odd present (for all HRH's Commonwealth Study Conference came); then HRH laid the stone and our trumpeters played a rather poor fanfare very well. HRH spoke easily and cheerfully; his line, I judge, is the Jolly Tar and he does it so well that he must be a very clever man. I replied to him thus—and I may as well stick in the actual text from which I read:

Your Royal Highness, Your Honour, Mr. Chancellor,
Ladies and Gentlemen:

This is the first public act in the life of Massey College. It bears a name already honoured in our country and our University. We shall strive to bring new distinction to it here, by opening the path of honour to others. In this house the humanist and the scientist will live together as Fellows—that is to say, as companions and equals—thus to extend their curiosity and understanding beyond the bounds of any single discipline.

We have chosen as our College motto an admonition from Horace: *sapere aude*—have the courage to be wise. We have not done so, I assure you, sir, without a full understanding of how hard it is to get and maintain courage, and how much fool's gold offers itself to the prospector after wisdom. But we face our task with a good heart, and I dare to say a measure of gaiety, for what is the use of beginning a great task with a long face?

No one can say with certainty when the idea of this College first entered the minds of its founders. The ideal of education which it serves, however, is at least 2500 years old. That ideal is partly education by instruction, partly education by association,

and partly education by solitary labour; no single part, however fiercely pursued, can make up for the want of either of the others. The act of Legislature which brought us into being calls us "a community of scholars"; we shall strive to deserve that high compliment, and ever to be aware of the constant temptation of academic persons—which is to love, not the learning in ourselves, but ourselves in learning.

To you, Your Royal Highness, I offer our thanks for taking time from the demands of your work here to perform this important symbolic act. Nowhere is a symbol subjected to such subtle and complex interpretation as in a University. But we are happy in knowing that this symbolic stone can yield but one message: it will tell all who pass our door of your sympathy with the kind of work we mean to do here—the serious, rigorous and humble pursuit of all knowledge, all interpretation, and all fruitful intuition.

When our College is completed we hope that we may have the honour of showing you that scholars can be good company. Until then, I speak for the Founders and Senior Fellows of Massey College in declaring ourselves to be your grateful servants.

The whole thing took eleven minutes and went admirably, thanks to Pringle and a perfect May day. Then Brenda and I entertained the Senior Fellows and their wives at lunch at the York Club. My father arranged this for us. (*Later note*: My father refused to let me settle with him for this lunch, describing it as his contribution to an important day in the College's life. Characteristically generous!) A very pleasant affair and the first time we (i.e., the Senior Fellows) have met socially.

The lunch went very well, and did much to knit us into a unity. This is a side of our enterprise at which the Masseys are not very good. We toasted Robert Finch, our only absentee, and Claude

N.B: My father refused to let me settle with him for 37
this lunch, describing it as his contribution to an im-
portant day in the coll's life. Characteristically generous!

Then Brenda & I entertained the Snr. Sf. & their
wives at lunch at the York Club [WRD arranged this
for us] A very pleasant affair & the first time we have
met socially. Seating thus.

Ron Thom Esq.

W.H. Broughall Esq. — Mrs. Lionel Massey

Dr. C.T. Bissell — Dr. C.A. Wright

Brenda — Mrs. Eayrs

Raymond Massey Esq. — Hart Massey Esq.

Dean A.R. Gordon — Mrs. Roper

Mrs. Wright — Lionel Massey, Esq.

The R.t. Hon Vincent Massey — Mrs. Broughall

Prof. James Eayrs — R.D.

Mrs. Gordon — Mrs. Bissell

Geoffrey Massey Esq. — Dr. Gordon Roper

Miss Jennifer Davies

Bissell toasted the College. The menu was simple and very good, thus: cocktails, consommé with sherry, mayonnaise of Restigouche salmon, strawberries *praliné*, and wine: Neuchâtel.

In the afternoon the Massey Foundation meeting at the Shell Building began late as the Prince was thanking the conference staff. There was a crowd outside, and Ron Thom and I went in to applause which we acknowledged extravagantly. The crowd meant it humorously and we took it so. We agreed on the iconostasis[30] for the chapel. Then all of us to Eaton's where a mock-up of a Junior Fellow's room had been constructed, even to the brick walls. Larger than I had foreseen and very handsome. But we haver about designs, chairs, etc. for hours. Then to an office and look at Ron's chair for the dining-hall which looks to me as if Elbert Hubbard[31] had had a hand in it. Then an argument about dishes and silver. At 7 we all go to Lionel Massey's home: his children mix the drinks, and the smallest gave me a glass in which bourbon and Scotch had been poured on the remains of a gin and tonic. Lilias discovers this and is mortified. Raymond gets drunk and very sentimental about HRH. Dinner, with champagne, then more rather fruitless chatter about objects for the College, but great good will is shown and sympathy is established. The Masseys are muddled, but they *dream*. Leave at midnight.

SATURDAY, MAY 26, TORONTO: Meeting of Senior Fellows in the Senate Room at 12 and we do some very good work. Caesar Wright has untangled and regularized our statutes, and Gordon Roper gives an admirably concise and sensible report on the organization of the Library. Then our proposed new Senior Fellows go through without a hitch, Andy Gordon even speaking *for* Tuzo Wilson! All

30 A late seventeenth-century Russian work created for the devout to carry on their travels.
31 American author and publisher, and follower of William Morris.

done by 1 p.m. I am complimented on my chairmanship, which surprises me as I do not think much of myself in this role. I see Ron Thom in the afternoon at Hawthorn Gardens and he speaks enthusiastically about the College garden, which he makes sound very exciting, and we finally hammer out a plan for the Round Room. At 6:30 to Hart House to the dinner for HRH's study conference and find to my dismay that I am the only person present in dinner dress, as I was not told differently! Sit at the head table, between E.P. Taylor and Jones, the city planner—three down from HRH who talks rapidly and makes very good sense—strenuous, alert, driving man with the searching, disconcerting eye of a bird.

SUNDAY, MAY 27: Lay late; could not settle to anything; read a mystery story, listened to music, dozed, and enter my Massey College diary in full. A notable week and a great sense that the College has taken a great stride forward. Lionel Massey wants a special gown for Senior Fellows: I must ponder this and all protocol and ceremony. Jenny goes water-skiing and returns sunburned and tired.

THURSDAY, MAY 31: Again very busy: wrote *Star* column on Graham Greene, my last, *Deo gratias*! The announcement of Trent University[32] comes through and is first-rate. Read *The Bell* by Iris Murdoch with a new sense of release.

MONDAY, JUNE 4: Much busier than I foresaw: telephone about Trent University a great deal; worked on my *Shrew* and *Macbeth* public lectures. In the evening an impromptu h.t.d., then we abandoned ourselves to reading and were much refreshed.

32 Trent University opened in Peterborough in 1964. Several of the buildings were designed by Ron Thom.

TUESDAY, JUNE 5: All the new Senior Fellows now have accepted: no difficulty about Phillips, Wilson, or Dobson, whom I wired and wired back as soon as they could. But delay with Polanyi,[33] who then wrote declining—too busy. So today I got him on the phone and bullied him gently: all the Senior Fellows are busy men. Massey College is meant, among other things, to bring scientists and humanists together, but cannot do so if the scientists huddle in their stinks labs and won't join. I think scientists are a bit pretentious about their research—as if the rest of us had nothing important to do. He saw the point of this and was very decent and next day came his letter reversing his decision. I respect his desire not to take on anything he cannot do properly. But *busy*—*I* could tell him something about being busy!

A muddle again about the arms. The augmentation is the crest of Canada, and the Cabinet should be consulted before it is used! This in the middle of a general election! God, the neurotic pomposity of all this business!

In the afternoon we drive to Toronto, and at 8 I give my public lecture on *Macbeth*.[34] It was necessary to take a larger room for the unforeseen crowd. I did well. Afterward, drinks with the Harrises and home by 2.

THURSDAY, JUNE 7: In the afternoon to Toronto and to Hawthorn Gardens and rehearse, then give my lecture on *The Shrew* in Convocation Hall: 700 present! Good. To the Stewarts' for a chat. I am very pleased the lectures go so well.

33 John Polanyi, professor of chemistry; he won a Nobel Prize in 1986.
34 Davies was again giving public lectures on the plays in the Stratford season.

SATURDAY, JUNE 9: Work on *Tempest* lecture in the morning. Lunch with the Smiths at the Grove[35] and speak at the prize-giving about Massey College. Brenda gave the prizes. Home at 5 and rest and h.t.d. before dinner. In the evening work on *Tempest* lecture: these lectures demand much but are rewarding.

TUESDAY, JUNE 12: Worked in the morning on *Tempest*. In the afternoon to Toronto with Brenda, Jenny, and Rosamond and to the Club and rehearsed in the library. Lecture at 8 and it went well. Audience bigger than last week. Afterward to the Harrises' for a drink, home by 12:30.

THURSDAY, JUNE 14: To Toronto at 2. Jenny and Rosamond help me move books and pictures from my Trinity office to my University College office. My lecture on *Cyrano* at 8 goes very well—I am happy in the nineteenth century. Then to a party and meet Malcolm Ross[36] and like him.

FRIDAY, JUNE 15: To the *Examiner* office in the morning, then pack and to Toronto with Brenda and Rosamond. Dine at the York Club with George Harris, Helen Ignatieff, Liz Gordon, and Sir William Walton,[37] who is very charming and talks of the Sitwells. Then to the Harrises', and Norah gives me $500 for the College Library.

SATURDAY, JUNE 16, TORONTO: At 12:45 to the lieutenant governor's luncheon for the Queen Mother: she speaks very charmingly of the College. Away at 4. Jenny joins us and we dine at the Simcoe and go to an adventure film; restful simply to enjoy oneself. Already

35 Now known as Lakefield College School. The headmaster was G. Winder Smith, and Davies was on the board of trustees.
36 Literary critic and dean of arts at Trinity College, University of Toronto; founding general editor of the New Canadian Library series.
37 English composer.

feel the benefit of rest or, rather, a lightening of responsibilities: my imagination begins to stir: ideas for novel *5B* surge up.

On Sunday, June 17, Rob and Brenda drove to Stratford for the opening of the festival season. Miranda was in the company, and Davies as a governor was much concerned with the question of who should succeed the very effective Michael Langham as artistic director. He wrote reviews for the *Examiner*, and for himself in his theatre diary.

SUNDAY, JUNE 17, STRATFORD: To the dress rehearsal of *Macbeth*: director, Peter Coe. Macbeth, Chris Plummer, Lady M., Kate Reid. A misconceived production: Coe wanted to show a "classless society" with dog-eat-dog morals, and the Jacobean play cannot be bent to this, hack and rearrange as he will. This is as much "historical reconstruction" as anything of Charles Kean. Result: there was no tragedy, for Macbeth had no stature and gained nothing by his crime except, apparently, Malcolm's old clothes. Plummer's tricks were many: a high, singing delivery with big pauses between each word, e.g., "Come—seeling—night," all on a high F. Kate Reid was good in terms of the production, which stressed Macbeth's dependence on his lady—falling on his knees and gripping her loins, kneading her buttocks while butting her in the vulva. But in the sleepwalking scene she overacted, as has every Lady M. I have ever seen. Some accidents: in the fight with Macduff, Macbeth's sword flies into the well. Witches done as earth-creatures, almost mushrooms. All the "double double" stuff cut, and the King's Evil, and telescoping of battle scenes and the death of Young Siward. On the whole, a mud pie, and not good enough for Stratford. But let us see what tomorrow night will bring forth.

MONDAY, JUNE 18, STRATFORD: H.t.d. on waking. Breakfast, a walk, lunch at Miranda's flat, and a good sleep: dine, a picnic with the Harrises and Stewarts. The election returns the Progressive Conservatives with a scant majority.

First night of the tenth Festival. *Macbeth* seemed better than last night but some of this must be attributed to sitting in a governor's seat. Am struck with the uncoordinated air of the production, and silly tricks like rearranging the lines in the "England" scene; Plummer says "my *may* of life" instead of "way." Plummer ages Macbeth greatly in Act 5, but makes him a complacent, tooth-sucking dotard, rather than an old lion, and this gives an air of farce to his donning of his armour. He only shows his former spirit when he hears of the moving wood. Macduff kills him in a short-sword fight and when both are disarmed, disables him with wrestling tricks and at last stabs him and Macbeth falls headlong into the well. So—no severed head, and what happens to the prophecy. But though the production is "up" and the audience is better than last night's come-all-yez, it is not a thorough success. Evidence: the standing ovation usually granted after a tragedy was withheld; I met no one who really liked it. Curious that the excitement attending today's general election, which might have been harmful, was well controlled and could have worked *for* the play, but did not. It is extraordinary that Coe should have fumbled it so. If he succeeds Langham as artistic director we shall be in serious trouble.

TUESDAY, JUNE 19, STRATFORD: *The Taming of the Shrew* directed by Michael Langham. A different kettle of fish from last night— strong, clear line, firm character, and splendid detail subordinated to the main action. John Colicos as Petruchio, to my mind, is a better actor than Plummer—technically a master, and *warm*: an admirable voice and no tricks. A gentlemanly, swashbuckling, humorous performance. Kate Reid played Katherina in c major,

fortissimo. A bad actress; how does she get away with it? Fine minor roles: Eric Christmas a real clown as Grumio; Bill Needles a rare pantaloon as Gremio; Toby Robins a sweet bitch as Bianca; Hugh Webster a touching Sly. Michael Langham's passion for *clarifying* the text was very apparent, however, especially in the first scene of the induction, where they used scraps of the induction from *A Shrew*.[38] I do not like it. The induction scene was in eighteenth-century *commedia dell'arte* dress to some degree.

The Coe mess makes it imperative we do all we can to keep Michael; I will see him tomorrow to do what persuasion I can. Tonight a standing ovation, which must be bitter to Coe and Plummer.

WEDNESDAY, JUNE 20, STRATFORD: Saw Michael at 1:15. He says he is emotionally attached to Stratford but not intellectually persuaded it is good for him or the theatre that he should stay. I urge him to heed his emotions: the theatre is not built on intellect. Then Webster, Hemphill, and Polley[39] join us, and we almost convince him. I urge that he stay till 1967, to cover the Shakespeare four-hundredth anniversary and the Canadian centenary.

Tonight *The Tempest* magnificently mounted by Desmond Heeley, less well directed by George McCowan. The first twenty minutes were very slow going, Bill Hutt doling out Prospero's narrative as dully as may be; he was nervous, and it took him in stupid pauses. But after the interval it was much better. Prospero was never greatly magical but Bruno Gerussi as Ariel and John Colicos as Caliban almost made him seem so—two first-rate performances, especially Colicos. I wept at the end, for the reconciliation theme was finely brought out, the forgiveness was not easily achieved, and the release of Caliban and Ariel was splendidly touching.

38 An earlier version of the play, author unknown.
39 Hugh Webster, member of the company; Howard Hemphill, member of the board of governors; Victor Polley, administrative director.

The masque was exquisite; Miranda was one of the sea-nymphs and one of the dancers with the reapers. I have never seen anything that came so near the splendours of a Jacobean masque. At the cast party after I met George Hayes, my first Hamlet, now rather a sad old actor, fruity and "laddie-ish" in manner. Tanya told Brenda that Michael did not know what *commedia dell'arte* was or understand her costumes for *Shrew*; incredible what theatre people don't know about their own job. I said to McCowan, "A great night for the Jungians," which seemed to please him. That was how his production of *The Tempest* struck me—the integration of Prospero.

SATURDAY, JUNE 23: Busy morning. Sent letters,[40] reviews to several at Stratford. In the afternoon helped Brenda in the garden, very pleasant. In the evening read Edmund Wilson's *Patriotic Gore* with pleasure and chatted with Brenda. Webster wires from Stratford that Michael Langham is remaining. I am rejoicing in my freedom, but freedom from pressing tasks is confusing. Dr. Manette[41] misses his cobbler's bench: improvement in health and spirits already perceptible.

TUESDAY, JUNE 26: To Toronto and the College committee on fees: A.R. Gordon, Roper, and I lunch at the University Club and decide that $800 is not too much for Junior Fellows, and $125 for non-residents. Also that Senior Fellows' rooms should rent at prices comparable to bachelor apartments in Toronto. This raises College income a little above what I foresaw, but expenses are mounting as

40 Davies often sent appreciative notes to actors or others in a production. One of these letters was an elaborate spoof sent to Tanya Moiseiwitsch, purporting to offer her the ingredients of the witches' brew in *Macbeth* that was missing in the Stratford production. It was published in the collection *Happy Alchemy* (1997).

41 In *A Tale of Two Cities*.

well. Look at the College, which waxes, and at new Jags with Brenda and Rosamond; home by 6 and read and chat.

WEDNESDAY, JUNE 27: Lunch at the Golf Club with Arthur and Kit, and we have an *Examiner* directors' meeting where we discuss what action we should take if we have an International Typographical Union strike about hours.

FRIDAY, JUNE 29: The last two days made miserable because of College finances: Vincent Massey thinks Canada is headed for a depression and sticks his head in the sand. But the time has come for a firm commitment; I cannot, and will not, go on any hand-to-mouth gentleman's agreement. The Masseys are fantastic: I suppose they are unconscious of the fact that they want me to pledge fifteen years of my future to a venture which may turn out to be a nightmare of cheese-paring and begging. I shall have to face them with this, and soon. Fortunately, Bill Broughall understands my position. But both Bill and Lionel are at work on VM and want figures from me. So I work out a dummy budget, thus: income—$69,000; costs (catering, cleaning, staff and running expenses) at $144,800; leaving a deficit of $75,800 of which the university is obligated to pay no more than $25,000. And this includes not a penny of any of the luxuries they want, or books or even a bunch of flowers! Hope it knocks some sense into their stupid heads. I have pitched a note high, of course, because I do not trust my budgetary powers and have undoubtedly left a few things out. But if they leave things to a fiscal innocent like me they must expect bad figures; they need a bursar, right now. This is the shadow-side of the Masseys—their ostrich-like escape from definite discussion of money, their neurotic attitude toward it, their belief that gentlemen don't talk of such things. They know nothing of colleges, and obviously have no notion of the great land and property holdings

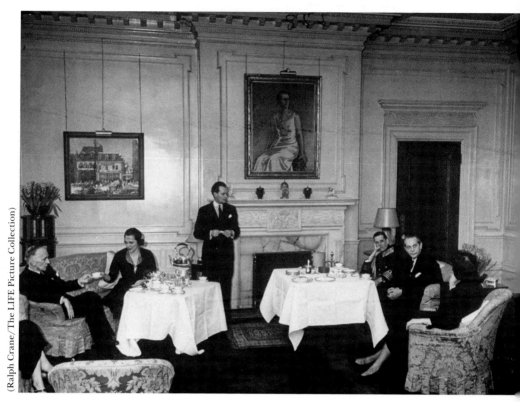

Vincent Massey as governor general, with his daughter-in-law, Lilias, his son
Lionel, chief aide, his brother, Raymond, and Raymond's wife, Dorothy.

Governor General Vincent Massey with Senator Davies (left)
and his business partner Roy Thomson, at the Canadian Press
dinner in 1956.

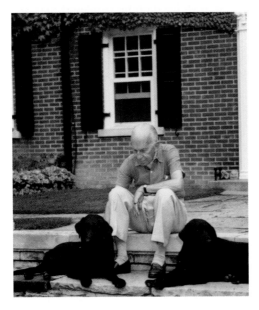

Vincent Massey at
Batterwood in 1962.

The young Wilmot Broughall, graduate of the Law Society of Upper Canada, who served as an officer of the National Trust Company, and a trustee of the Massey Foundation.

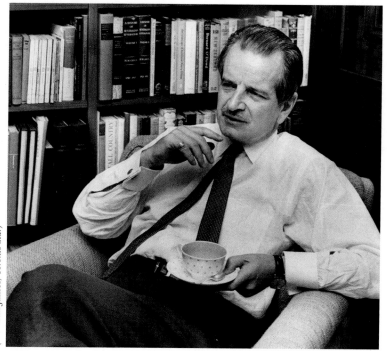

Claude Bissell, president of the University of Toronto from 1958 to 1971.

May 25, 1962: Prince Philip gives an address at the laying of the foundation stone at Massey College. From left to right: Chancellor Jeanneret, Claude Bissell, Lieutenant Governor John Keiller MacKay, aide-de-camp, unidentified man, Vincent Massey, Prince Philip, Robertson Davies, and Ron Thom.

Raymond, Lionel, Lilias, Hart, and Geoffrey Massey; Prince Philip,
Davies, and farther back Bill Broughall in legal formal dress.

Brenda and Rob inside the Master's Lodging, while it was being built, in January 1963.

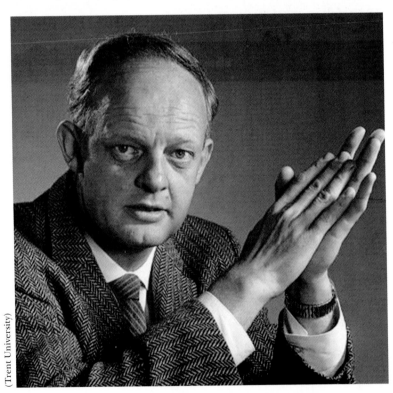

Ron Thom, the architect of Massey College.

Massey College under construction.

Outside the master bedroom at Massey College
in 1963, with Jennifer and Rosamond.

Miranda, Jennifer, Rob, and Brenda.

and the generations of legacies on which their beloved Oxford stands. But I won't despair: they have set this in motion and involved too many important people (including their friend HRH) in this thing to let it die. But apart from dying it mustn't have fiscal anemia. I'm not going there to worry about stamps and sugar in the maid's tea.

SUNDAY, JULY 1, DOMINION DAY: About twenty Philadelphia[42] readers have written to say nice things about the cessation of the "Diary"—and not one Canadian. That is why Canada has so little literature. A dull and unappreciative audience. (P.S. Some Canadian letters came later.)

TUESDAY, JULY 3: In the evening an impromptu h.t.d., then read Dryden's *Tempest*. I dream of my mother, mocking and harassing me.

WEDNESDAY, JULY 4: I dream Fred[43] lives again and is harassing me—a night of gloom and oppression with some hope in sight.

THURSDAY, JULY 5: Bill Broughall retails to me this morning in a thirty-five-minute phone call that he spent most of yesterday with Vincent Massey, working to persuade him that the College must have some firm money commitment from the Foundation to meet the deficit I foresee. VM was reluctant to commit himself; then says, "Why have you not brought this to my attention earlier, Bill?" (This, after eighteen months!) He complains he is unwell: has shingles, poor man. At last he agrees that something must be done.

42 "A Writer's Diary" was syndicated to the *Philadelphia Evening and Sunday Bulletin* and the *Providence Journal* as well as the Ottawa *Journal*, the *Winnipeg Tribune*, and other Canadian newspapers.

43 Davies's eldest brother, Fred, with whom he did not get on, had died in 1954.

VM calls about 6—can I go to Batterwood after dinner? Brenda drives me down. Hart is there, concerned about Thom's new plan for the lower library. He is right: Ron Thom's plan makes poor use of the space. We agree on a change. VM in good spirits and talks very interestingly about his book, to be called *What's Past Is Prologue.*[44] James Eayrs is doing some research for him in his seventeen filing cabinets: I want these eventually for the College. VM assures me *he* has taken steps to make the College secure!

FRIDAY, JULY 6: I dream of an obscene dwarf. A third "big" dream: my shadow? We drive to Toronto, to UCC and talk about my *Punch* play with Stephen, head of the Prep; Vernon Mould, art teacher doing the scenery; Michael Carver, director; and Henry Atack, composing the music. Drive to Stratford, dine at Miranda's flat and to the opening of Gilbert and Sullivan's *The Gondoliers.*

The director, Leon Major, knows nothing of G & S and has no English background, and his approach is thus different from that of Tony Guthrie, who knew very well what *Pirates* and *Pinafore* were about, even if he chose to disregard it. But Leon Major had missed the fact that *Gondoliers* spoofs opera and melodrama all through, so he produced it straight. Result, two plays which never meshed: a satire performed by actors—Jack Creley, Douglas Campbell, and Ann Casson—and a heavy muddle in which hook-nosed, liquid-eyed opera singers sang splendidly (though one couldn't tell the words) and acted after the vehement, vulgar Mittel-Europa style of their absurd kind. Realistic settings, à *la* Zeffirelli, with an occasional flash of good fantasy as at the end, when the Venetians leapt into a hastily constructed boat and set off for home. But *The Gondoliers* is English and Victorian: forget

44 Published by Macmillan of Canada in 1963.

this, and its intentional absurdities are lost, and a host of unin-
tentional ones arise to mock the actors. And the pronunciations!
"A-RIS-tocrat," sung in the very teeth of the music. John Cook
tried to persuade me it is thus in the score but I have checked
and it is not.

SATURDAY, JULY 7, STRATFORD: Board of governors' meeting at
10: a lively discussion about the dedication service this year (Rabbi
Abraham Feinberg had spoken too long). Lunch at the Country
Club, where I chat with Michael Langham who plans to reform the
speech of Stratford.

I saw Lionel Massey at the board meeting. He has urged his
father to make a pledge to the College and thus *he* has done the
deed! Frankly I don't care who has the credit so long as the College
does not make me a yearly beggar, whimpering to the Foundation
and Simcoe Hall for funds to keep the place going.

**On July 8, Rob and Brenda again drove to Arlington, Vermont, for a
week of Alexander Technique lessons with Lulie Westfeldt.**

SUNDAY, JULY 8: Leave at 11 and reach Saranac, New York, at 6:15.
At the motel, h.t.d., not very satisfactory, then a vivid Anima dream:
I am twenty, have pursued a girl of great charm, eighteen, and
never met her. In a house, suddenly she comes downstairs, sees me,
cries "There he is!" with great joy, and we embrace. Later, I am in
an old-fashioned hotel not unlike the one in Bussaco, Portugal, in
a lover's bed with her: pretty, as she was in youth, a fair, dark-eyed,
soft-mouthed beauty with long golden hair, but mature and a prac-
tised lover, for we kiss and coit and she responds excitingly. Later,
I am walking with hotel guests. We are an invited group. I see an
elderly woman in Edwardian dress and rather reluctantly walk with
her, giving my arm. But she is delightful, witty, and enchanting and

I am very glad I approached her. The Anima: Virgin, Bride, and Wise Woman, in one night's dream![45]

FRIDAY, JULY 13, ARLINGTON: A good lesson. We make progress: Lulie Westfeldt joins us for a picnic lunch above Sandgate, then we walk in the graveyard. The restorative power of the Alexander Technique is always a surprise. It acts this time remarkably, as we both were in a poor way. We have now had about sixty-six lessons and Lulie Westfeldt treats us as old hands.

MONDAY, JULY 16: Back to work and a host of nuisances assert themselves. Many letters. Bill Broughall calls to say he has sent Vincent Massey an eight-page memorandum on Foundation investments, showing it can easily assure the College of $65,000 p.a. and recommending it pay this to the Master in trust, so Simcoe Hall cannot discover the exact sum from the books. VM then calls and tells me we are still stuck over the College arms, for Governor General Vanier has had a fit of scruples and referred it to the secretary of state, who may take it to the Cabinet, who won't know beans about it but may well be obstructive to show how alert they are. If I had my way we'd go ahead, and then let anyone with enough heraldic nous to detect a discrepancy between our arms displayed and our grant from the heralds make what he could of it. I blame Esmond Butler, who seems a well-meaning, overgrown schoolboy, delighting in complication.

WEDNESDAY, JULY 18: Tom Symons[46] calls this evening to discuss buying this house and tells me a good deal from his experience as dean of Devonshire House, a tale of gloom. Graduate students are hard to get into residences, as they are always on the lookout for

45 Jungian dream analysis.
46 Symons was now the president designate of Trent University, but still dean of Devonshire House.

something free; he wonders if we shall be able to fill the College. Counsels against Frank Stone, the black pope of the U of T, an Eric Phillips appointee and responsible to Eric Phillips and not to Claude Bissell. Tom says Andy Gordon and Claude are both out of touch with the graduate students. He says there are many at the university who dislike the Massey College idea, regarding it as a citadel of tawny port. All this Job's comfort given with great good will and, I believe, considerable realism. But we shall see: I am grateful that he has pointed to the dark side, for I have been (except for Broughall) very much among the Pollyannas.

THURSDAY, JULY 19: Bill Broughall calls in the morning, almost distracted by Vincent Massey's attitude toward money. VM has vetoed his $65,000 and thinks $60,000 enough. Considering the time and expert knowledge Bill put into his memorandum, this is cavalier. Bill is very angry. He rails against all the Masseys. I understand him better now: he dotes on the College and is deeply involved. Brenda says it is a child to him. Bill says the Foundation could afford $75,000 p.a. He says Lionel pleads with him not to excite VM about money, as Lionel has an overdrawn account with National Trust he wants VM to cover. Who would believe people would set out to found a college with such a poor grasp of what is involved? I would, for one. Nobody with his head screwed on would involve himself in anything so hare-brained. I tell Bill of my talk with Tom Symons, and the upshot is I write VM saying the College may not be easy to fill to begin with and this makes financial independence doubly important. Hope this saves the day. Yesterday I sent him a sketch of a possible Senior Fellow's gown; the only person who really wants one is that poop Lionel, who has no gown and hankers piteously for one.

Where do I stand? I have been named as Master in an Act of the Legislature, and by the university, but so far I have not taken a

penny of money for my services: so I feel that if things become intolerable I could still back out without a breach of faith.

In the afternoon I get down to writing my Stratford seminar.[47] Hard work and I am tired in the evening and lie on the sofa and read Nabokov's *Pale Fire* and discuss the terrors of the College situation with Brenda.

FRIDAY, JULY 20: Vincent Massey calls this morning to say he appreciates what I said in my letter, and would be discussing finance with Bill Broughall next week. I take this as promising and call Bill to say so. He is pleased. He says Hart had said he wanted the Foundation to be in funds in twenty years or so to build something *he* was interested in: but this cannot be so if they support the College whole-souledly. Bill was indiscreet; says Lionel and Hart will not inherit half as much as they expect; they are so silly about money I think it very likely they have unrealistic notions of their father's fortune. Bill says if I want the College to be a success I must resign myself to fifteen years of kissing the Masseys' arses, as it was thus Griffith[48] made a success of Ridley (licking the Gooderhams'). He mistakes me: I will lick nobody's arse and I will make it a success without. He expresses himself foolishly, but I know what he means. Bill has the highest motives and methods and always attributes the basest to himself and everyone else: an idealist and ashamed of it. He called me twice in the afternoon: he is sending Vincent Massey what he calls "another rocket" to reach him tomorrow, as Brenda and I go to Batterwood for the weekend.

47 "Changing Fashions in Shakespearean Production." Published in B.W. Jackson (ed.), *Stratford Papers on Shakespeare* (1963).
48 Harry Griffith was the long-time headmaster of Ridley College in St. Catharines, Ontario. The Gooderhams were a wealthy family of distillers.

SATURDAY AND SUNDAY, JULY 21–22: To Batterwood by 5 p.m. and spent a pleasant evening during which Vincent Massey talked a great deal about his book, which obsesses him. He has a rash: I suggest it is from worry and work over the book and I think this flattered him, though that was not my intention. I learn that he *dictates* the book, which I think a mistake. He has been a lifelong diarist and note-taker, recording important conversations within a few hours of having them. On Sunday I join him on the terrace about 11 where he is exposing his rash to the sun: very angry all over his chest and into the armpits. (Old man's chest, sunken, and paps very low.) The talk leads to the College and I succeed in (1) killing the notion of a special gown, which he appears not to have liked; (2) suggesting special decoration of the chapel and its consecration as part of our opening ceremonies; (3) pressing home our need of independence even if we do not draw a full College for a few years. I hope these things are now settled for good.

VM's granddaughter Susan there, as Lionel and Lilias and their two elder daughters, Jane and Evva, are in New York. A nice child, but VM is caustic and sarcastic with her. I recall at Oxford, when he used to return Lionel's letters corrected and rephrased in red ink! He told us, as a "sweet" thing, that when she left, the child said, "I hope I wasn't too much of a nuisance to you, Gaudy." I think this sad. VM has great charm allied to great egotism and unconscious cruelty. On Sunday night we talked about pornography, in which he is interested and of which he has read a good deal. VM reads a lot of mystery stories and, like so many people who do, insists that "some of the best writing of our time" is done in them. He tells us of recurrent dreams of packing and being distressed that he won't get everything in. I suggest this arises from anxiety about the book and he accuses me of being a psychiatrist which, like a true Edwardian, he detests. So I tell him of my concern with Jung, which I don't think he liked, but he had better find out what is in my

intellectual luggage. Can the Edwardians really have lived so *externally*, so much on the surface, as he pretends? I suppose many of them were deeply religious, which gave depth to their lives.

VM told us he laid the cornerstone of Massey Hall when he was five or six. He tells us also of a movie he made at Batterwood with an Indian setting and Lionel the hero. Lionel found love-making difficult; however, VM urged him on! Poor wretch, I bet he did!

VM was intensely interesting and a fine host but unaccountably chilling to his grandchild Susan. His bodily use is very bad: head forward and down, back narrowed and abdomen thrust forward in tension.[49]

THURSDAY, JULY 26, TORONTO: Shop in the morning and visit the College, which grows apace. Lunch at L'Aiglon, then haircut and to Bill Broughall's office at 4 and chat for an hour and a half. All looks well. Vincent Massey and Lionel had spent the morning and lunched with him. An uphill battle but he has persuaded them the Foundation should pay the *whole* deficit for the first four years, to ensure independence, before asking the university for anything. This was against much reluctance, and a desire to make it three years, or two, and a desire to cut the guarantee after four years from $65,000 to $60,000. He is not sure he has won the fight, as they have now given him the task of persuading the other trustees *by mail*. But certainly we have come a long way in eighteen months, when VM did not see the College requiring anything but its fees and a handout from Simcoe Hall. Bill has worked wonders, and how true a friend of the College he is may never be known—the real guarantor of its independence, I devoutly trust. He says VM has been to a dermatologist and has eczema.

49 All contrary to principles of the Alexander Technique.

FRIDAY, JULY 27: Today Vincent Massey called me: Ron Thom is still reluctant to change the Library plan and the problem is to be dumped in my lap. About money, VM says: "I want you to know we have that problem very much in mind." If Bill has his way, the Foundation will become the College's endowment.

MONDAY, JULY 30: To Stratford with Brenda and Rosamond, a quick journey, and we rest on arrival from 3 to 4:30, then dine at Miranda's flat, and to the *Cyrano de Bergerac* opening. Great expectation in the house beforehand: applause after Lou Applebaum's seventeenth-century arrangement of "The Queen"; cheers after the first act. All this rather overheated enthusiasm is, I think, because many wanted Plummer to have a triumph after the *Macbeth* fiasco. And he had it: a standing ovation and five calls, mounting to a storm when he was left alone on the stage. A handsome setting: I would not have thought so many variations on brown and grey possible. The only colours were Roxane in deep red on the battle-field, and de Guiche in Prussian blue. A bang-up production: Langham at his best with the great crowds. But I found the play less moving than I had hoped: Plummer's style is dry and ironic and he cannot suggest *adoration*. In Act 1 Roxane gave him a white rose, which he later gave to the Orange Girl! What gallantry is that? Wished he might have some of the quality that Martin-Harvey[50] possessed—he treated women like camellias. And in Act 3 "Roxane's kiss" the bittersweet was lacking. But in all that was grotesque, humorous, and daring he was admirable. John Colicos was fine as de Guiche: he understands and believes in villainy. Douglas Rain a fine Ragueneau, a minor Cyrano. Toby Robins never suggested distinguished intellect as Roxane and was a bit Forest Hill, though

50 Sir John Martin-Harvey, actor-manager of the late nineteenth and early twentieth centuries, much admired by Davies and the model for Sir John Tresize in *World of Wonders*.

very pretty, as always. Miranda was a *précieuse* and a nun and did well what she had to do. But the play! They adored this bauble as they have never adored Shakespeare.

TUESDAY, JULY 31, STRATFORD: Miranda breakfasts with us, then we are away at 10:30 and home by 1:30. To the *Examiner* office, and a busy afternoon. Bill Garner meets the union again; a deadlock but he is very patient: not soft like Harold Garner, his father and general manager before him. In the evening unforeseen h.t.d., then pleasant reading and chatting.

SUNDAY, AUGUST 5: To the Shakespeare seminar at Stratford. Arrive at 1; lunch and to the Mendelssohn concert, very fine; then chat with Miranda at her flat. At dinner at the Country Club we meet Nevill Coghill, my tutor at Oxford, whom I have not seen since 1938. He is delightful and expresses regret he was not of more use to me with my boy actors book,[51] of which he speaks highly. He lectures in the theatre at 8 on "Listening to Shakespeare" and gives a fine example of Oxford wit, sensibility, and scholarship as a means, not an end, in appreciating literature. A party in someone's room at the Windsor Hotel: John Wain[52] was there, shows signs of being a drunk, with a sharp, disagreeable little Welsh wife. Reginald Foakes, a visiting English scholar, is patronizing to me about the line I mean to explore tomorrow. I sleep badly and am awake from 4 to 6. Coghill is a hard act to follow and I admire his style so much.

MONDAY, AUGUST 6, STRATFORD: I lecture at 10 in the rehearsal room on "Changing Fashions in Shakespeare Production." It goes

51 Davies's Oxford thesis, *Shakespeare's Boy Actors*, became his first published book in 1939.
52 English novelist associated with the Angry Young Men, writers of the 1950s.

very well and Brenda says I was good. To the matinée of *Macbeth,* which has not improved, though Plummer is better and Kate markedly worse. In the evening Foakes lectures on *Macbeth* at the Country Club, is tiresome about Coghill, and talks down in a very dull and obvious lecture. He must be extremely vain to think such stuff will do.

TUESDAY, AUGUST 7, STRATFORD: Gave my second lecture in the theatre and was complimented when Helen Langham said I "spoke out" so well and was very easily audible at the back. It went well and when I did the end of the tent scene from Cibber's *Richard III,* got a round. Two excellent rounds at the end—reward for a lot of hard work. In the afternoon John Wain lectured on *The Tempest.* A hotchpotch of conventional stuff, admirable personal judgment, and a moving plea for poetry in the theatre delivered in a fidgeting, throw-away, hung-over manner. Then Dama Bell talked on costume and props, incoherent in grammar but really communicating. Dined with Milly Hall and Jessup. Then to *Cyrano.* It is much improved, Christopher Plummer more touching and romantic and Toby Robins deeper, though it is a miserable part. Enjoyed it greatly. Nevill Coghill and Albert Trueman came back with us to Miranda's flat, where we drink whisky and chat about Oxford. Very jolly and a revelation to Miranda. Nevill Coghill delightful, simple, distinguished, and continually interesting: he never proses and never strains for effect. We part at 2.

In the night after the talk with Nevill Coghill I dream I am naked: I hold up my left arm and from my armpit spews yellow bile, very bitter and stinking. I am greatly pleased and relieved.

This meeting has had the oddest effect on me. I feel that at last, after so many years of feeling somewhat rejected by Oxford, I now have a friend there, and this comes to me like a benediction and is splendidly releasing. NC's views of literature are my own: that it is

an art, for the enjoyment of man in the deepest sense, and that one does not possess it but is possessed by it. Rich to find that the Oxford I loved still lives, and that what I remember is not invention. He tells me a strange tale of C.S. Lewis.[53] He loved a married woman, who at last divorced her husband. She then fell ill of cancer. C.S. Lewis overcame his scruple and married her and prayed that he might bear her illness; and developed symptoms and pain, while she had a remission. She died after two or three years, but had had a stay of execution and an extraordinary love. Would like to know more of this. Fully believe it could be: love is surely as strong as hate?

WEDNESDAY, AUGUST 8, STRATFORD: At 11:30 Dr. Rosemary Sprague lectured on the pseudo-Shakespeares and the Baconians; a pupil of Frances Robinson-Duff and speaks in the enriched, keep-a-smile-in-your-voice, "cultivated" tones of that woman. Her lecturing manner arch, and she quotes Gilbert & Sullivan with many a merry laugh. But she knew her stuff. In the afternoon to *The Tempest*, now greatly improved; Hutt is quicker and more at ease, and Colicos and Gerussi are now excellent. The conclusion is truly moving and the gawds of decoration did not trouble me so much as before. In the evening to *The Shrew*, now coarsened and with a lot of shouting, but Colicos had voice trouble and was forcing the pace. He *does* force, and has a great sway in his back, and I think he *does* too much, in the Alexander Technique sense.

THURSDAY, AUGUST 9, STRATFORD: In the morning there was an actors' panel, with Langham in the chair. Stupid affairs, for actors do not express themselves well extempore and come out as egotists

53 Lewis wrote *A Grief Observed* in response to the death of his wife, Joy Davidman, and first published it in 1961 under a pseudonym. The film *Shadowland* (1993) was based on this story.

straining for laughs. We took Madge Sadler and Maudie Whitmore from the Brae Manor theatre[54] to the Limelight restaurant where we had a reservation for 7; ordered at 8:10, were told the dishes we wanted were no longer available; grabbed something and ran at 8:25. Had a row with the headwaiter. Good gossip about Brae Manor days, and Christopher Plummer and John Colicos, whom they have both known from boyhood. Then to *The Gondoliers* and sat next to Coghill, who enjoyed it hugely. It is better. John Cook's conducting? He seems to accommodate the *tempi* to the words better than Lou. Delightful.

FRIDAY, AUGUST 10: To Toronto, leaving the Shakespeare seminar and the company of Nevill Coghill, which I much enjoyed, at the behest of Vincent Massey, who phoned yesterday. A meeting at 12:45 with Eaton's. The Foundation (Vincent, Lionel, and Hart Massey) and I lunched with Alec Russell and Bill Howard: VM uneasy and disgruntled. Then we havered over china, and chose some, and over silver, and phoned Eric Clements in London, and over glass and decided nothing. Hart is very negative and fusses that two sorts of silver might have different sheens that would not be congruous. Thank God I have no taste! What a burden it must be! VM angry and petulant and rude to Hart, who was patient and immovable; I have never seen VM so bloody-minded.

At 5 with Ron Thom to the building and saw more clearly than before what its character is likely to be. The Round Room is much smaller than I foresaw, and the chapel bigger. The quad is very handsome in dimension. Ron promises a fountain in our garden.

54 The Brae Manor Playhouse at Knowlton, Quebec, was an important summer theatre from 1935 to 1956. A number of leading Canadian actors including Christopher Plummer and John Colicos performed there before going on to Stratford. Both Rob and Brenda Davies were with the Brae Manor company as actors or directors in 1952 and 1953. The company was led by Madge Sadler and her husband, Filmore.

The lower library will be very interesting. Decided with VM to put the Founders' Stone on the stairs. To the Park Plaza hotel with Ron where Brenda joined us and we dined. Ron is a fine artist: truly original and deep. We called Tanya Moiseiwitsch, to ask her to consider the task of designing and decorating the chapel. She refused to believe we were serious and it was not easy to convince her. Home by 11:00.

SATURDAY, AUGUST 11: H.t.d. on waking. Wrote Tanya Moiseiwitsch to ask her to design chapel. Vincent Massey calls in a great dither about 10:30 p.m.: can Brenda and I go to Batterwood the Labour Day weekend with Lionel and Lilias to do some serious work on College furnishings? He fears time is fleeting and nothing is being done and won't be done in committee. It will be a nuisance as we are to go abroad on September 4 but perhaps we shall go to Batterwood on Sunday only. But this is surrender: he realizes the Foundation can't cope because it can't decide anything. And it can't decide anything because it is always quarrelling about matters of taste. I shall get some facts, and see if we can't make some progress.

MONDAY, AUGUST 13: Swam in blood: strike business, Vincent Massey calls, worry about College bursar, write an unforeseen article, a bushel of letters, Gordon Roper to lunch. Fall into bed too tired to sleep.

WEDNESDAY, AUGUST 15: Bill Garner meets the International Typographical Union for two hours and nothing gained. A strike is the next move. Very exhausting. Work on my report on College Hall furnishing and do academic work. In the evening worn out, read a mystery story.

THURSDAY, AUGUST 16: Bill Broughall called in the morning to say that his evening with the Masseys on the 10th was the most embarrassing in his experience. Vincent Massey and Lionel were very emotional and now want to put *all* resources of the Foundation at the disposal of the College; Hart demurred. Vincent said, "I have never been so angry with you since you were a little boy." Lionel accused Hart of trying to give Vincent a heart attack. Vincent asked what they would do if I threw up the College because it had no money. Hart said I would probably return to my profitable newspaper. Altogether a distressing scene. The real crisis would be if Vincent were to die before the College is launched, and Raymond were to head the Foundation! Apparently Mrs. Raymond, who is an American lawyer, is devilling National Trust because his money is in devalued Canadian dollars. What a comedy!

Bill says the Masseys sometimes use the threat that I will desert them and this would be a disgrace as I am "Canada's leading man of letters." Am I so? The distinction is roughly that of the best rose-grower at the North Pole, or the best architect of snow sculpture in Hell. Meanwhile I have an impending strike at the *Examiner* to keep me from growing dull. The ITU votes to strike—29 to 4! Histed the organizer double-crossed Bill Garner by getting a final offer, then telling the men he could get more. The air is now cleared. Spend the evening considering the problem.

FRIDAY, AUGUST 17: Spent all day planning a strike strategy, but I do not think it will happen: some of the men are now scared. I am very tired and wonder if I can stand the strain of a holiday after such a summer as this. What rest is there in continual movement?

SATURDAY, AUGUST 18: Many rumours about the strike, and Bill Garner, Ralph Hancox, Wilson Craw, and I sow a few more to cause dismay among the ITU types. Talk strategy with Bill.

MONDAY, AUGUST 20: This afternoon an interesting experience of labour negotiation: the *Examiner* branch of the International Typographical Union had voted 29 to 4 to strike, after contract discussions since last December. We met in Bill Garner's office: he, Mac Macauley, head of the composing room, and I for the management; for the ITU, Dormer and the Appleton brothers with Allan Histed, their organizer. He is a soapy blowhard of base mind: he told us as a great joke he did not suspect us of having a concealed microphone in the room to which they retired; left his briefcase with us, as he was sure we wouldn't rifle it, etc. The men were quiet and rather shamefaced; felt they had gone too far in taking their vote. We discussed and bargained from 2:30 to 6, and at last agreed. We gave more money than we wanted to, but gave no reduction in hours, and got a contract for three years instead of two, and a competency clause which will enable us to get rid of inefficient men. Wearisome, exhausting, and tending to make me cynical of union protestations of "brotherhood," as proposals had been made to us unofficially which were cut-throat in tendency. But the time taken by this—not this afternoon but for weeks past—has so disorganized my work that Brenda and I have had to cancel our trip abroad, to Chichester, Coventry, Amsterdam, and my beloved Wales, where I had hoped to be with WRD on his birthday.

FRIDAY, AUGUST 24: Bill Broughall calls at 11, very angry. Raymond and Geoffrey have written Vincent Massey saying they do *not* agree to foot the bills for the first four years, and VM has sent the letters to Bill to cope with! As Raymond's letter is very nasty about Bill and National Trust and altogether emotional and stupid, this is tactless. Bill is being treated like a troublesome servant. I advise him to tell VM he will not be used thus. So he calls VM and calls me immediately after. He has threatened to resign from the Foundation and all VM can think of to say is "But Bill, we need a lawyer!"—not "We

need a friend who understands what none of us do." Bill has worked on the Foundation for over five years for nothing—no glory, no fun, no money. But VM is shaken, and I gather Bill was rough. He calls again this afternoon to read me a letter he has written VM; a stinker, but well-argued and just. Now the ball is with VM.

But if Bill were to leave the Foundation I think I should have to throw in the towel; he is the only one who makes any sense. I cannot take on the College if I am to have to worry all the time about money; that would be the finish of me. The Masseys do not understand what they ask of other people. Their treatment of Broughall is cold and foolish, and if he left them who else would toil for them? Certainly I cannot make myself a care-laden drudge for the next fifteen years to satisfy their whims. Sometimes I wish I were out of all this, free and able to write another novel. Damned stupid, spoiled, cold-hearted, penny-pinching, ignorant rich people!

SUNDAY, AUGUST 26: Breakfast in the garden and talk with Brenda and Rosamond. Lunch in the garden. They go to the Waddells' to swim; I do odd jobs and think, to good purpose, and am much refreshed. My need for contemplation (if it may be so dignified) grows and without it I am adust and uneasy, and I do not find it abroad but at home. Would my diaries, edited, eventually make an autobiography?

TUESDAY, AUGUST 28: To Toronto, buy Purcell records, and in the afternoon to the CNE from 2:30 to 5. Dine at Lord Simcoe, Brenda's treat—shrimps, Caesar salad, filet mignon, and crêpes Suzette and cheese, and to Harold Lloyd's *World of Comedy*. I am forty-nine: delightful birthday and charming gifts. How lucky I am in Brenda and the girls!

WEDNESDAY, AUGUST 29, TORONTO: Brenda and I spend two hours in the morning with Young and Gwillim of Commercial Caterers and see the cafeterias at British American Oil, the Board of Education Building (which has a vulgar special dining-room for the trustees, replete with glassware "cut" within an inch of its life, and costly, nasty china), and the Board of Trade Building. Again was impressed by their good sense and thoroughness: both men are master chefs (a seven-year apprenticeship). I brought away some glass to show VM.

In the afternoon to Simcoe Hall to Ken Edey's office: I like him, and his worn, kind, witty face like a French man of letters. We discuss the College brochure with Allan Fleming and the man from University Press whose name I forget. We decide to use no pictures, and rely on fine type, heraldry, and paper. Return to Peterborough.

THURSDAY, AUGUST 30: Bill calls twice: he thinks matters may go well about money. VM has written six pages of, he says, eloquent good sense to Raymond, putting all the points very cogently. Bill advises me to be cautious when VM speaks of money, and not seem happy about talk of $65,000. I must persuade VM that this autumn the Senior Fellows must be told the facts about the College finance.

SUNDAY, SEPTEMBER 2: Brenda and I to Batterwood at 11:30 and at once with Vincent Massey, Lionel, and Lilias to the pool, where we sit in very hot sun and discuss College matters. First Vincent tells me of the Foundation's intention to guarantee $65,000 in early years. I am not enthusiastic, and point out that this sum probably will not cover the deficit. He assures me it is "just a beginning" and that he has it in writing from the trustees (even Geoff, I wonder) that the College is the last work of the Foundation, which will exist in future to nurture it. Then we discuss china and silver and agree the latter should be of good eighteenth-century design.

I have sinus from dust, and the sun gives me a tiresome headache. Lunch, and after, Brenda and Lilias go to bathe with the girls and VM and Lionel and I go into a session about glass. I show them the pieces we brought away from Commercial Caterers and they like them, which is a triumph for practicality. One way or another we spend all afternoon on College work, and get many things settled preliminary to the meetings of September 11 and 12, which promise to be bloody.

Lionel discusses Frank Harris's *My Life and Loves,* which he and VM have been reading with goggle eyes; they are both amateurs of pornography in a modest way. Lionel lends the book to me. For the first time he speaks of his wartime prison camp experience: I gather he read a good deal there, and thought poorly of those who never thought of anything but escape, which, he said, made them neurotic. Dinner, after which pleasant conversation, and VM tells of Victor Rothschild, the scientist and magnate, and Lionel recalls Michael Erleigh,[55] and VM reads Kipling. Home about 11 very weary and headachy, but pleased with the day's work. Dr. Dobson says I have low blood-pressure and I certainly felt a want of energy today. Brenda and I have put off our journey abroad as the College and the threatened strike at the *Examiner* have made me too tired for the exertion of a holiday. But if we can get the College well launched it will be worth many sacrifices.

MONDAY, SEPTEMBER 3, LABOUR DAY: H.t.d. on waking. Take lunch to Bryn Camlas. The girls go swimming and Brenda and I read and doze on the hill. Read a lot of Dr. Johnson. A pleasant evening and good talk. Read Frank Harris's *Life and Loves* and am amazed at his tireless lust.

55 Likely Michael Alfred Rufus Isaacs, Viscount Erleigh.

TUESDAY, SEPTEMBER 4: Delightful letters from my father in Wales and Nevill Coghill. To Toronto: shop, and lunch at Eaton's. In the afternoon put Miranda on the 'bus for Stratford. Take Brenda, Jenny, and Rosamond to see the Moscow Circus at Maple Leaf Gardens. The best circus I ever saw: European style—one ring and the emphasis on skill rather than spectacle. The only animals were dogs and some wonderful bears. Superb acrobats of all kinds. What gave it a great air was an artistic concept of a circus, which pervaded everything and expressed itself in ease, good humour, a grave courtesy to the audience and the other performers, and a "throw-away" style. The direct contrary of the feverish strenuosity of Ringling's, as I saw it in Madison Square Garden; no vulgarity of costume. Of course some vulgarity of conception: it began with a foolish "astronaut" tableau, followed by some trapeze people who were to perform on a "sputnik" which fouled its cable and would not work. But how astonishing to be given a form of catharsis, and left well contented, by a circus!

WEDNESDAY, SEPTEMBER 5: Lionel Massey has lent me Frank Harris's *My Life and Loves*. Why does he say *loves*? He has lain with many women, but nothing he says suggests that he loved any of them. He sought variety and sensation, and found them. His masterpiece seems to have been buggering a Japanese girl as she rubbed another Japanese girl's clitoris with her own, and they all achieved orgasm together. This when Frank Harris was about forty-five. But I cannot call that love. I have never desired or sought physical intimacy with a woman I did not love and do not think I could have borne it if I had. Now, I am sure I could not perform. Have never been given to lust, and copulation without love is no more.

FRIDAY, SEPTEMBER 7: I think I have a librarian. Douglas Lochhead,[56] whom I met last night at the Trent University dinner, is now librarian at York and, like so many at that ill-starred institution, wants to get away. Tom Symons wants him for Trent and will pay $12,500 (so he says), but Lochhead does not want the imperial pomps of a university library, in which he would be primarily an administrator, but a place he can do scholarly work; he is a bibliographer. Massey College excites him and he would accept $10,000. More than I had foreseen, but we cannot afford to have less than a first-rate man and he could save us money by expertise. The librarian at Cornell thinks Douglas Lochhead one of the two or three best men he ever had. He came at 10:15, stayed to lunch: I think he is the man. I called Gordon Roper, who will take a look at him next week.

Tanya Moiseiwitsch writes from Ireland: she will do the chapel if she can. That was September 1; she is now in Stratford. I called her at 6 p.m. and tentatively arranged a meeting for next week. Tyrone Guthrie is urging her to do it. Vincent Massey has sought her out in Stratford and, she says, was very stern in demanding that she do it, but this is her fun: he is too smooth to bully her yet.

Brenda and I have read VM's Frank Harris book and agree that it is flatly and cheaply written. VM thinks the style good but perhaps he expects pornography to be full of dirty words. There is a vein of simplicity in us all: if VM objects to women near his College, perhaps it is to be expected that he should be taken in by a book by a ruffian who uses women as things, and not fellow-creatures, which I think detestable. Brenda and I agree that one of the signs of true cultivation is an ability to talk and write of sexual and scatological things with some grace (e.g., *Fanny Hill*) and not with vulgar gloating or tumescent solemnity. The Masseys lack this.

56 Douglas Lochhead, Canadian poet, founding librarian at Massey College, 1963–75, and Senior Fellow. Later he became the Davidson Professor of Canadian Studies at Mount Allison University, Sackville, New Brunswick.

TUESDAY, SEPTEMBER 11: To Toronto. Meet with the Foundation in Eaton's fifth-floor board room at 11:30. Everybody late but me and VM, and he begins in a bad humour. Hart and Geoffrey are obstructive, and our arms are still delayed and decisions are havered over for hours, it seems. The battle of the silver is fought again. We adjourn for lunch to the University Club and do ourselves well, but I already have a headache. At it again the whole afternoon—chairs and rugs. At 6 to Lionel Massey's house on Dunvegan Road. Brenda joins us and we dine. Get away about 9:30. A dreadful day.

WEDNESDAY, SEPTEMBER 12, TORONTO: We meet at Eaton's 10:30. I walk from Hawthorn Gardens and so arrive refreshed and exercised. But everyone else was in bad temper and quarrelling begins at once. Hart and Geoffrey accuse Eaton's of stealing Scandinavian chair designs and righteously refuse to be party to such doings. Russell says Eaton's pay royalties to all designers and is understandably tough. Hart and Geoffrey want to reverse yesterday's decision to have low-priced glass: they want Orrefors at $2 each. I say I cannot go to Simcoe Hall with a budget and deficit caused by breakage of such things and warn them that the College will be a white elephant if it costs too much to maintain. This is gleefully supported by VM and Lionel and received with sour faces by Hart and Geoffrey. I also become crusty when VM is petulant about the carrels: "I'm not even slightly interested!" Marie Antoinette!

Lunch at the York Club. Great excitement! The plates there are crested in gold and green and we have been told cresting cannot be fired on china in gold and a colour! I get away and have my hair cut as they want to talk family secrets. Rejoin them at 4 at Dunvegan Road.

Bill tells me the family meeting was a knock-down-drag-out. Geoffrey does not want "family money" put at the disposal of

professors who may use it in ways the Masseys might not like. Bill is brutal, and tells them the Massey Foundation is the smallest of the many that National Trust administers. A bloodbath. We discuss typographical matters with Allan Fleming. Hart does not like "A merry heart doth good like a medicine but a broken spirit drieth the bones" (Proverbs 17:22 KJB) for the Hall. He thinks it frivolous, that we should have something with more "weight," i.e., gloom. I lecture him on the text. Then stamp on Bill for anti-Semitism. We are all edgy and I am glad to get away and dine with Brenda at the Club and go to the movie *Lolita*, which I thought very moving in places.

THURSDAY, SEPTEMBER 13, TORONTO: I had C.E. Friesen to lunch at the University Club—a possible bursar, now working in Peterborough for the Bank of Commerce. Liked him: a dedicated, conscience-ridden man who was the accountant at the bank when the manager committed suicide. I hope he may come to us. At 5 with Ron Thom and Lorimer[57] to the College and go over it thoroughly. It looks dreadful but full of promise. Nothing can ever change the fact that the sun will never shine in my study, which is a cave. At 6:30 Brenda and Tanya Moiseiwitsch join us, and Tanya sees the cement box where the chapel will be. Then to the University Club to dine (trailing the burr-like Lorimer, who is dog-like toward TM) and talk about the chapel, not very successfully, as Ron Thom will not throw out ideas and encouragement, which is what the very feminine Tanya needs. I try to do this, but I am no architect so it is not very helpful. At 10 Brenda and I leave them at the Park Plaza and drive home. A tornado hit Toronto at 8:30 and our conversation went on to sounds of thunder and torrential rainfall.

57 Alan Lorimer, representative of the local supervising architects, Hancock, Little, Calvert Associates.

FRIDAY, SEPTEMBER 14: Bill calls at 4:30: at last the skies clear and the Masseys are—not perhaps willing, but agreed—to support the College *in toto* for five years. God be praised! Bill explains that he feels unhappy about betraying so many confidences, but does it from enthusiasm for the College, and I believe him, though Irish fondness for gossip and intrigue enters into it too. But without his breaches of confidence I would have resigned or gone mad months ago. Bill is as much the architect of the College as Ron Thom, and I hope some day to be able to tell him so in some fitting manner. He says I will be summoned to Batterwood this weekend for the great *dénouement* of the money drama. Sure enough, at about 7:30 this evening the summons came. I think we now see daylight at the end of the tunnel.

Gordon Roper is much impressed with Lochhead and thinks we should do all we can to get him. I suggest Claude Bissell might use him in the Graduate School, thus helping with his salary.

Bill says he and Zoe were guests at Batterwood late last year and VM showed them his Christmas cards: very grand for royalty and such, a good one for the quality, and a cheap one for *hoi polloi*. When the Broughalls got theirs at Christmas it was—no. 3. How can anyone be so tactless? Yet I wrote to him some weeks ago, asking him to support my nomination for the Athenaeum[58]: he has never referred to it. Is Bill right when he calls him "a selfish little bugger"? This has been a week in Cloud-Cuckoo-Land.

One must admire Hart Massey; if ever a man was short-changed by Nature or Fate, it is he. Not so pitiful as to provoke easy compassion, but handsomely formed—and nearly a midget. A bad head wound in the war—to which he would go. He has striven to play a man's part and succeeded. But he is cold, minatory, and suspicious. And all his store of wisdom and philosophy is of the naysaying kind.

58 Davies was elected to the Athenaeum Club in London in 1964.

He brings chill with him in the dog-days, and because of the exaggerated attention that we all pay to what he says, he has much more than one man's influence. Lionel responds to Vincent's egotism by knuckling under, Hart by a firm, calm intransigence.

SUNDAY, SEPTEMBER 16: To Batterwood. After lunch Brenda persuades VM to have a nap, and we walk in the gardens. Then a long talk with VM, who tells me plainly that *the Foundation will guarantee (1) that the College will be its main concern from now on, and (2) that it will pay the deficit for five years.* This is splendid, and I say so in what I hope are adequate terms. Now we can go ahead free of university supervision, and establish our way of work before we ask them for a cent. We talk about the Eaton's estimate, much of which looks like guesswork, for $205,597.60 to furnish the College. We also talk about Ron Thom's desire for a Japanese garden in the Quadrangle and damned ferns and palms in the building. VM is a fine host and a delightful companion and we had a splendid day, quite apart from the good news. He hopes to finish his book in two months. We agreed to ask Vincent Bladen to be a Senior Fellow.

VM told us that he had been entertaining American guests, enemies of the present administration, who assured him solemnly that President Kennedy is unappeasably lustful and has to have a new girl *every morning,* and does not care if they are the most degraded prostitutes, and Mrs. Kennedy is inured to this. What mythomaniacs Americans are!

Davies took a holiday from work at the *Examiner* from September 17 to September 30.

MONDAY, SEPTEMBER 17: I take a holiday. In the morning go with Brenda to Buckhorn and walk. Afternoon sleep, chuck wood into the basement, and mess about. In the evening, to the film *Bird Man*

of Alcatraz directed by John Frankenheimer, very good. We took Jenny, who is more friendly to us now, and I hope this will grow. Rest does wonders for me!

WEDNESDAY, SEPTEMBER 19: Lionel calls me to offer advice, viz.: that I see that the College is very well equipped *now*, with all it may need, so that these things will not appear during the next few years as expenses. He has seen Tuzo Wilson and Bill Dobson, who express great enthusiasm for the College and are determined to take their Senior Fellowships very seriously. God keep them long in that mind!

SATURDAY, SEPTEMBER 22: To Toronto and get Rosamond, who is very jolly. We shop, buy wine for winter, lunch at the Club, get new specs, go to film *Phantom of the Opera*, hammy but restful. Chat at Hawthorn Gardens, dine at the Lord Simcoe. Home by 10:40, a very pleasant day.

SUNDAY, SEPTEMBER 23: Dismal misunderstandings are inevitable with daughters. One so wants them to have all that is happy and delightful, which is in fact to be inhuman. For whose life is all good, all free of pain?

THURSDAY, SEPTEMBER 27: Get away to Toronto at 2 and to BSS sports day. Rain and disorganization. Chat with Miss Nicks, the headmistress. Rest at Hawthorn Gardens. Dine at the Lord Simcoe and to the O'Keefe Centre for the sophisticated London revue *Beyond the Fringe*. It was undoubtedly clever but not so deeply satirical as I had been led to believe. Jokes about God, the royal family, and Jews do not cut very deep; a skit on the sentimentality of war recollections was partly good satire, partly "bad taste" of an adolescent kind. The best things were the nonsense—"Groves of

Academe," "Little Miss Britten," "Sitting on the Bench." A good
evening, not fire from Heaven but very lively and restoring. Return
to Hawthorn Gardens. H.t.d. in library.

FRIDAY, SEPTEMBER 28, TORONTO: To an appointment with
Claude Bissell at 11 and am with him until 12:30. I tell him of the
Foundation's financial plan and he is very pleased. I ask him for an
academic appointment for Lochhead and he promises to do what
he can, and I think it is safe. As always when I see him, my confi-
dence is strengthened. He asks me to serve on a committee to in-
vestigate the museum, if it should be necessary.[59]

In the afternoon to Eaton's with Brenda and we choose some
mundane things—mattresses, pillows and the like—that the
Foundation will not trouble with, helped by Sedgwick and Howard.
They are worried about Ron Thom's domination of the furnishing.
So I tell them Vincent Massey thinks they are not doing enough,
and they are startled. I urge them to write to VM and suggest more,
and they are going to do so. I think this is necessary and my indis-
cretion justified, both with them and with Claude Bissell. Indeed,
where would this College be without indiscretion?

SATURDAY, SEPTEMBER 29: To Stratford for a governors' meeting
and closing performances of the season. Lionel Massey corners me
and pours into my ear the tale of his troubles at the museum. They
are grievous and real. I ask him, will he continue at the ROM when
his father is dead? Yes. His Masseydom stands in the way of his

59 The director of the museum, Theodore Heinrich, was a flamboyant figure
but erratic financially. The museum board, concerned with the situation,
had appointed Lionel Massey as administrator and then established a
special committee to look into the question of Heinrich's successor. Davies
had a conflict of interest on this committee as it concerned the position of
Lionel Massey, who was both Davies's friend and his patron as a member of
the Massey Foundation.

being appointed director, which is hard lines. During the day I discussed the College with Erwin Schuller, who is a wise fellow. He was astonished that we are *charging* fees and cannot *give* fellowships, like All Souls. He suggests the Ford or Gulbenkian Foundations or Sydney Hermant, the owner of Imperial Optical, might help. He says I must develop "controlled irresponsibility" in ruling the College or I will get no fun out of it, and will do it less good than I could. Wise counsel.

Cyrano: Christopher Plummer better but still far from chivalry. Toby Robins poorer, thinner, and more artificial. The production has grown and ripened. A standing ovation, which I fear has become a mannerism of this production. A party afterward: the governors give it, but nobody seems to know this. All the excitement and sentiment of the close of a successful season. At lunch Michael Langham tells us about Sir Laurence Olivier visiting Stratford and his interest only in technical things: "Where do you put your hands when you climb down those pillars?" etc. Also about the new Chichester theatre Langham says, "Toilet accommodation awful. Men queue and enter by fives; women queue, five go in and never come out!" The buzz is that ML is taken up with Pat Galloway, but cannot get any real confirmation. Last year it was Bill Needles, who brought her fresh eggs from his farm. She is a beauty, but has a very English lack of taste in dress.

SUNDAY, SEPTEMBER 30, STRATFORD: Breakfast at 10 with Miranda and Karen Austen, her flat-sharer, and to Toronto very heavy-laden. Lunch at Hawthorn Gardens with Rosamond. Brenda, Jenny, and I home by 6:30 and spend an inert evening. My bowels sour from sweet things eaten last night.

Thus ends my holiday, which I enjoyed but it is not enough. Must practise Schuller's suggestion of "controlled irresponsibility" or I shall fall ill this winter. Oh! for a light heart!

TUESDAY, OCTOBER 9: We progress: both Friesen and Lochhead have made formal application for the appointments, and have expressed enthusiasm for the College idea. I will be glad to have Friesen take over all money matters, as will Bill, for they are not my line and I want someone to do some close figuring.

This afternoon about 4:30 Vincent Massey called: at last the matter of our augmentation of heraldic arms has been broached by the governor general to Diefenbaker, who has summarily vetoed it! Political rancour, I suppose. It would have been more glorious to accede, and show oneself magnanimous, but who could expect a prairie Baptist to see it that way? So now we must begin again. The "crest of Canada" has been denied us because Garter[60] and Sir Michael Adeane, the Queen's private secretary, *would* be so pernickety; let us hope the next suggestion is nothing the Prince Albert Messiah has any control over. The joke is that Alan Beddoe, the heraldist in Ottawa, has been put to work to unearth the Diefenbaker family arms!

WEDNESDAY, OCTOBER 10: To Toronto 8:30; meet Herbert Irvine[61] at 10:30, work and lunch with him. At 4 p.m. meet Thom and Irvine at the College and discuss details of our house and get things arranged of which I had not dreamed, e.g., where light switches are to be. The illuminated ceiling in my study about which we had grave misgiving sounds much better as Ron explains it. Not a room in the house gets light from more than one side. Herbert Irvine has excellent, practical ideas and Ron Thom is most obliging.

I gave my first graduate lecture 2 to 4 in Room 109 in University College—a cellar box. But I like the work. Nobody seems to know

60 The Garter King of Arms is the senior heraldic authority for England.
61 Irvine, the Toronto interior decorator who had worked on Rob and Brenda's house in Peterborough in 1960, was advising on the interior of the Master's Lodgings at Massey College.

that I am trying to learn the trade of a professor amid the College hubbub.

Bill Broughall saw Friesen today and thinks well of him. I am glad to have my opinion confirmed.

SATURDAY, OCTOBER 13: Work on my lecture and enjoy the drudgery. In the afternoon I help Brenda plant bulbs and devise exam questions. In the evening read Dostoyevsky's *The Idiot*, a grossly over-written book, and why is a Christ figure necessarily without wit or gumption? Excellent h.t.d.

SUNDAY, OCTOBER 14: Enjoy preparing graduate work as I never did undergraduate lectures. I feel much better than in August. College matters are now advanced so that I am more at peace. Hope for a jolly winter.

TUESDAY, OCTOBER 16: To Toronto, and Ron Thom lunches with us at the University Club. Lilias Massey and Miss Leavings, the secretary of the Massey Foundation, were there, and I beg Lilias to use any influence she has to dissuade Vincent Massey from having sterling silver flatware in Hall. Ron Thom is very spent, but has College details at his fingers' ends and makes good sense about the Upper Library. To the College with him and Brenda, and meet Herbert Irvine and Ken Pringle and work out some details of our house, which looks as though it would be really handsome. Go over the rest of the College with Ron, and everything is much better than I dared hope: Senior Fellows' Dining Room will have a very fine outlook; Round Room promises fairly. In the evening dine with A.S.P. Woodhouse and University College English professors at the Faculty Club. Fair conversation, dismal food. Chat with Norman Endicott. I am tactful and modest about the College with Ernest Sirluck.

WEDNESDAY, OCTOBER 17, TORONTO: See Ron Thom at 10 about College details and with him at 10:30 to Lionel Massey's house: the Masseys (Vincent, Hart, and Lionel) try to catch him on details left unattended to, but can find none. So to Eaton's for another choosing meeting, and it goes very well and we get a lot done: plate ordered for the Hall, and sterling for the Senior Fellows' Dining Room. It appears that Diefenbaker has vetoed not simply our use of the crest of Canada, but *any* augmentation. What spite! Yet I hope still. VM and Hart have ordered the crest on the china smaller, so as not to be vulgar! Why not have *no* crest and set a new standard of genteelism—the absent heraldry?

FRIDAY, OCTOBER 19, TORONTO: Gordon and Helen Roper dine with us at the University Club. He has talked with Lochhead about money and they arrive at a figure of $25,000 to make a start on the Library, which is wonderful, as we already have that. Bill Broughall says much library expenditure can go on the books as "furnishing": "Don't let 'em know it's for books and you can take 'em for a grand," he says.

Lochhead has a hand press and may move it into the College—this would be magnificent for bibliography classes! I have met Sirluck and see what it is Bill dislikes about him. But he seems to yearn for acceptance and status—chatters about his wine, etc. I think he can be got to understand if not the College idea, at least that it is wise for him to feign comprehension.

Lionel Massey's museum problems are still great.

After dinner with Brenda to film *Waltz of the Toreadors,* amusing.

I dream I am lying in bed having an emission. I lie on my back looking down at my member, which is enormous, and sprouts seed in firework-like bursts of beautiful pattern. This gives me a special ecstatic pleasure.

SUNDAY, OCTOBER 21: Things are going so well about the College that I am almost worried, which is silly: why does one fear good fortune? This savagery and superstition is part of the dark side of my life.

WEDNESDAY, OCTOBER 31, TORONTO: The Master and Fellows meet at 4:10 in Simcoe Hall, the Senate Room: Dobson, Bladen, Polanyi, and Eric Phillips are present and formally elected. I felt I handled the meeting badly for I was very tired and somewhat confused, and because I am too vain to wear bifocals I got mixed up in reading one or two things, but not very badly. Phillips is a strong, aggressive man and I was astonished that the Masseys did not resent him; but he has befriended Lionel in the museum fight and this pleases them. He proposed that the formal appointment of Friesen be postponed until Frank Stone has a look at him; must warn Friesen against becoming Stone's creature. The appointment of Douglas Lochhead went smoothly, Claude Bissell seconding Gordon Roper's motion to appoint, and speaking of a cross-appointment for Lochhead.

I am tired of the detail work which is laid on me: *why* do I have to discuss the teapots? I cannot work on the total concept of the College if I am kept to that sort of thing. The Masseys are getting very sharp with Ron Thom, who *will not* heed directions, whether from stubbornness or inadvertence I cannot tell.

Today at lunch Norman Endicott said to me that it was a pity the university had no people like Anthony à Wood or John Aubrey recording the minutiae of university life. I said nothing about this diary: its secrecy is its value. Who will read it? Will it indeed survive? Will anyone know of the weariness I feel today, which dulls the whole prospect of this College in which I so strongly believe?

Eric Phillips is going to see what he can do to fix things so the College can have a club licence for liquor: this will be his value—great influence, practicality, and drive. Vincent Massey announced

the Foundation's intention of supporting the College alone for five years, and Claude Bissell and Phillips spoke generously of this, indicating that the university would be handsome in its behaviour when the five years was up.

SUNDAY, NOVEMBER 4: Lie late, reading and chatting. In the afternoon walk near Douro in wonderful autumn light. Work on Dryden and read about Horace Walpole. Watch TV and chat with Brenda. A delightful day. I sense a lightening of spirit, which may be permanent, a deliverance from the underdoggery which mars my work in so many spheres. Leaving Peterborough is undoubtedly a part of it: to a world where the mind is valued for itself.

TUESDAY, NOVEMBER 6: To Toronto, and look at antiques with Brenda. Club lunch, then meet with Vincent Massey, Lionel, Hart, Ron Thom, and Sedgwick, Russell, and Howard at Eaton's from 2:30 to 6, a meeting too much prolonged and VM became weary and peevish—but he will not admit to his weariness and pretends everyone is being unreasonable. Several difficult choices: Ron Thom's chair for the Round Room is once again a curiosity; VM vetoes it and we are to have a version of the Hall chair, but in black. Ron Thom's occasional table is also an Oriental monster, and is vetoed. They are in so far with Eric Clements that they feel they must bring him to Canada—God knows why!—to design a "Founders' Cup";[62] this is to some degree a placebo, as they have so little else for him. The Upper Library is to be reconsidered.

At 8:30 to Lionel Massey's house, and VM, Bill, Roper, Eayrs, Wilson, and Bladen come and we discuss the College till midnight, very fruitfully and encouragingly to me, for Bladen and Wilson

62 Vincent Massey presented this cup to the College at the opening ceremonies and it has been used every year since 1964 at the Founders' Gaudy.

think we can get our men, and also that we can keep going with pretty much a full house all summer. I am much cheered by their practicality and good sense.

THURSDAY, NOVEMBER 8: Ron Thom comes to Peterborough to dine and stay the night. We discuss the Upper Library and work out a plan for it which would greatly extend the facilities of the College. Talk of many details and I am again impressed by Thom's stature and individuality as an artist.

(P.S.: Ron Thom came to us about 6 p.m. and went to bed at 12:30 without once retiring to the w.c. A man of iron—or perhaps he is like those lizards of the Australian desert who absorb all their moisture and very occasionally void a few crystals.)

FRIDAY, NOVEMBER 9: I go to Toronto for the first meeting of the president's committee on the museum, which promises to be interesting and important.

SATURDAY, NOVEMBER 10: A busy morning and revise the Conservatory speech again: thought it finished but no. Brenda says it is a major advance in my ability to say true and intimate things to audiences—to really do a good job and not waffle like a Personality or a Professor.

MONDAY, NOVEMBER 12: Frank Stone has seen Friesen, so that is all right. Vincent Bladen can offer Friesen an office—good. But apparently I must make a formal application to Simcoe Hall for "fringe benefits" for everybody. Lochhead wants a secretary and will need one. I must appease, or soothe, the Basilian Fathers[63] because Ron

63 The Roman Catholic Basilian Fathers owned the Chapel of St. Thomas Aquinas, adjoining the Massey College property.

Thom has made it impossible to get to our back gate without going on their land. The brochures must be sent off to draw applicants. All of this is just the kind of detail I hate and do clumsily, and thought I had left behind. But it must all be done, or we shall have no College. Today I got very cold feet about the budget, which is but a frailty of the mind, prepared by me, by guesswork. Must be sure the Finance Committee—Bill, Lionel Massey, and myself—are always aware how we are getting on, so that I do not have to shock or astonish the Foundation with unexpected figures at a year-end.

WEDNESDAY, NOVEMBER 14: To Toronto and lunch with Sirluck, very interesting and helpful. Give a good lecture and look at the College. We dine with Boyd Neel[64] and the Bissells at the York Club and then to the Royal Conservatory of Music convocation. My speech goes well.[65] Bad coffee after. Return to the Park Plaza and exciting h.t.d.

SATURDAY, NOVEMBER 17: The brochures came, and Miss Whalon and I have now sent them to all graduate schools in the U.S. and Canada, to the Senior Fellows (twenty each with a personal note asking them to send the things to friends), to the governors of the university, and to the administrative staff; we shall send them to all department heads. It is a handsome piece of work but I think I have grossly over-ordered. Still, we shall get rid of them in time. Vincent Massey wants the revised Upper Library called the Combination Room and is rather testy about it.

Lochhead writes that Blackburn, the university librarian, had assumed our library would be a "departmental" library of the main

64 English and later Canadian physician, conductor, and academic; dean of the Royal Conservatory of Music.
65 An excerpt from this speech was published January 19, 1963, in the *Toronto Star*, titled "The Artist Looks into Himself."

university establishment. He certainly did not say anything of the kind when we met on October 15, 1961. This is utterly unacceptable to Lochhead, to me, and to Gordon Roper, so we are going ahead independently.

On November 21, Rob and Brenda left for a week-long visit to New York for Alexander lessons with Lulie Westfeldt, a session with Davies's astrologer, Hugh MacCraig, and lunches with his agent Willis Wing and others.

FRIDAY, NOVEMBER 23, NEW YORK: Jackie Davie exerted herself very kindly to get us seats for *How to Succeed in Business without Really Trying*, as she said it was very special. I was somewhat sad not to find it so: not a good tune in it, and the theme the sour one of the young man who gets on by shameless flattery, throat-cutting, and charm. Robert Morse brought great sweetness to this hateful role and Rudy Vallee was technically brilliant—wonderful command of the stage and no wasted effort. But so loud! And so thin!

SUNDAY, NOVEMBER 25, NEW YORK: To the Village South Theatre to *The Coach with the Six Insides*, adapted from *Finnegans Wake* by Jean Erdman for herself and four actors. Jean Erdman is wife to Joseph Campbell, the scholar of myth. She danced, rather too much, and they mimed and acted. In parts it was poetically moving, and always interesting: a wonderful *veiled* music in much of the dialogue—the true dream effect of hearing and almost comprehending but never fully. Poor devils, the papers smote them unkindly; I think imperceptively. Has New York not even a tiny theatre for such a piece as this?

I am delighted with the big city, and the freedom: a release from the Masseys and the insistent needs of the College and teaching. We are not shopping much. I do not want *things* but sensations and impressions.

MONDAY, NOVEMBER 26, NEW YORK: Visit Hugh MacCraig, the astrologer. He says I am in the new phase of my life which began at the end of August this year and will continue for seven years. Am now "clearing the decks," reconsidering and revising my ideas and pursuits. My *forte* is reshaping the old, the historic, to modern uses. From 1969 to 1972 will be the "peak period" of my life. Am now in a "training period" and must "listen, learn, and take orders." I am not to worry about age: I shall look young and be so in spirit. My "re-learning" may be associated with the world of entertainment, and this will emerge in the autumn of 1964 and a money aspect of it in 1966: I need a framework, a routine, for my activity. Massey College appears as a training-ground for later work. My activities during 1954, 1955, and 1957 hold the key to the pattern of my life. (Wrote *Leaven of Malice* and *A Mixture of Frailties*.) Thinks I should do a book in 1963 or by the end of 1964 at latest. Conditions after midsummer 1964 would be good. Says I must watch diet and back—and indeed, lumbago!

He says Brenda and I are "like two kings on one carpet." She too is clearing her decks and maturing: whole inner attitude to life changing: must not be short-tempered with stupid people as a consequence. For the first time since she was seventeen is making a new beginning. A wonderful worker with people and will be able to do this more than ever.

All this Ben Jonsonian interview in a tiny dark room. He told *me* all he had to say before I told him how right he had been last time. Very sure of himself and does not suggest the charlatan.

In the evening to the much discussed *Who's Afraid of Virginia Woolf?*, Albee's first long play, and long indeed it is, 8 p.m. to 11:15. Theme: a professor and his wife bring two young guests home from a faculty party and go into a prolonged intellectual strip-tease—abuse, sadism, smut, and Billingsgate. Young wife vomits: young husband lies with middle-aged wife. Everybody proves to be

a failure and a cheat, but the older two are artists in abuse. Fair enough, though sustained sadism taxes Uta Hagen and Arthur Hill to the limit, ingenious players though they are. But in the last ten minutes we learn the reason for all this viciousness and brutality—the older couple cannot have children! The old American sentimentality, and not good enough to carry such a piece. But the audience is enchanted by the rasp and horror of the dialogue. Every time the wife shouts "Screw you!" they guffaw; when the husband says the wife is her father's "right ball" they are in ecstasy. Easily pleased.

THURSDAY, NOVEMBER 29: At home a wad of letters to be answered, chiefly about the College. In the evening enter my theatre diary and MacCraig's predictions in my "big diary." What a man I am for diaries and records of all sorts!

SATURDAY, DECEMBER 1: Brenda is ill. With Jenny to Toronto and to UCC Prep at 6:15 for a good dinner, and see the boys do my *A Masque of Mr. Punch,* which I wrote for them. An excellent evening. They cannot plan or sustain any effects and their voices are small, but they bring a zest to it which is delightful. The music by Henry Atack was not as spirited as I hoped and he repeated Queen Judy's song three times, which was too much; also he has a passion for "symphony" introductions, and the actors had nothing to do while he played these. But it was very good fun and both boys who played Punch had charm and attack. The best actor was the lad who played Samuel Bucket. Toby was charming. Scenery excellent: costumes as good as one has a right to expect, short of very costly work. The Adjudicator was made up rather like me. But it was *real* theatre: people really gave themselves to it, which was heartwarming. I made a speech at the end. A very happy event and I am glad to have done *A Masque of Aesop* and *Punch* for them. Drinks afterward at the

Stephens', then to the Harrises' and to the train, which is one and a half hours late: fog.

SUNDAY, DECEMBER 2: Well pleased with *Punch* and the news that *A Mixture of Frailties* has appeared in Dutch. They combine to assure me that I am still primarily an author and not a bad one.

TUESDAY, DECEMBER 4, TORONTO: I entertain Broughall, Roper, and Lochhead to dinner at the University Club to discuss the Library. Do them well: two Scotches before, a bottle of Fleurie with dinner (lobster, filet mignon, and *pêche Melba*), brandy, and another Scotch. Bill is enthusiastic about the Library and thinks we can go the $70,000 or so. Lochhead says we need to do the job properly. He has persuaded Lionel Massey of this, he says. They all got on well and I felt something important had been done.

THURSDAY, DECEMBER 6: Vincent Massey phones, very angry with Ron Thom, who has given him no information about the Combination Room. I broach the cocktail party idea and he is enthusiastic about it. I received an application from a man born in Bountiful, Utah, who writes enthusiastically that he has had "intimate relations with men in many fields." *Sancta simplicitas*!

WEDNESDAY, DECEMBER 12, TORONTO: Much crippled with lumbago. I meet Lochhead and Eric Clements, the English silversmith, at the College at 11 a.m. and show them through the cold, resounding, cheerless place for an hour. Then take Clements to lunch. He is an English sensualist—fine, rosy skin, a moist eye and red, pouting lips. Good at his job, but rather a bore otherwise. Talks about silver as if he personally discovered it.

THURSDAY, DECEMBER 13, TORONTO: At 3 to Eaton's and meet Vincent, Hart, and Lionel Massey and the three Eatonians and Clements. He persuades them to buy a lot of silver I don't think they need, by pouting and looking superior when quizzed; the Masseys are very open to this sort of bullying from Englishmen. So now we have some "contemporary tableware" (i.e., squared off) and a Founders' Cup, which will be very handsome, and is the sort of thing Clements does, I suppose, as well as anybody in the world.

This morning met Young and Irwin from Commercial Caterers and took them over the College. Young has a dicky heart and the cold got him; he with his heart and I with my lame legs were a queer pair. They have things well in hand.

Lionel Massey's Christmas card is of his daughters being presented to Prince Philip at the airport. Bill says Lionel sent one to the man at National Trust who looks after his affairs, who said, "Next year I must try to send out a picture of my kids with the Holy Family!" Vincent Massey's card is of himself with Prince Philip, Lionel, and Lilias at Batterwood. Innocent snobbery, but it will not make it easier to establish the College as a place where intellect is the chief desideratum.

To *Oliver* at the O'Keefe. A fine production by Peter Coe of a very mixed musical. The boys sang distressingly—choirboys shouting. The notion of Dickens's London was Olde Englyshe. But much of the atmosphere of menace, of desolation, of innocence at the mercy of vice and squalor that makes the book great was conveyed by brilliant designing and good ensemble work. Two revolves, the inner fairly solid and the outer a rim of scaffolding, and these served for everything except one book-flat for Brownlow's house, and a platform for London Bridge. Clive Revill a fine *comic* Fagin— the movements of a rheumatic rat, and a feverish rapacity when counting his treasure. The horror was not stressed: Sikes's murder of Nancy *not* very dreadful, and Fagin thinks he will "go straight"

at the end. But they did it with great gusto and charm. Now—what
will New York make of it? Too intellectual? Not enough sex? (Not
a leg seen above the knee.) No catchy tunes?

FRIDAY, DECEMBER 14, TORONTO: H.t.d. on waking: like rejoining
the human race. Home by 12. In the afternoon work on letters and
on museum committee reports. In the evening work with Brenda
on Christmas packages and hear the *Christmas Carol* record by
Ralph Richardson and Paul Scofield.

SATURDAY, DECEMBER 15: Busy at the office with memos to Ralph
Hancox and Wilson Craw about salaries and positions next year.

SUNDAY, DECEMBER 16: Gradually disentangling from *Examiner*
work and feel a deep sense of release. But university work? I am *not*
a scholar nor an administrator: will I survive? What am I?

WEDNESDAY, DECEMBER 19, TORONTO: Minor bothers: car goes
crook; parcels get mislaid, etc. Rosamond is out of school at 12.
Give a good lecture at 2. We call on the Edinboroughs and have
mince pies and rum punch. In the evening to *Kind Hearts and
Coronets,* my favourite film.

THURSDAY, DECEMBER 20, TORONTO: At 9:30 meet Vincent, Hart,
and Lionel Massey and Clements at Eaton's. Clements has every-
thing well organized and about $30,000 in silver is accepted with
no demur. Then to the College and look over it thoroughly. Ron
Thom is there, somewhat weary and bleary from the wrangle he
had with the Masseys last night, when, I gather, blood flowed about
his tardiness and his extras and his unbusinesslike methods. VM
was bullying him badly today about the position of the Foundation
plaque. The College looks better but our house is still a mess. The

Masseys have vetoed Ron's plan for a quad full of shrubbery. Lunch at the York Club, and I suggest we eliminate the pool, and Hart says, wisely I think, that any further major changes now might trouble Ron Thom too much and harm the building. I like the idea of a pool, but don't want the place to look like a motel.

In the afternoon we are back to choosing furniture, and there is all the usual haggle and bad temper. VM is angry because each carrel will cost about $925 for cabinetwork—he wants the cost cut. So much for silver, so mean about whatever pertains to scholarship! I shall fight this parsimony quietly. What annoys me is not their desire to keep expense down, but VM's petulant references to the Library as if it were a tiresome whim of mine and Bill Broughall's. A gruelling, maddening day. Glad the holiday season brings me some respite from all this nonsense.

Home by train and Tom Symons in at 9:30 for a chat. Very tired and sleep poorly.

FRIDAY, DECEMBER 21: Work on *Examiner* affairs and arrange that Wilson Craw be executive editor and Ralph Hancox editor. Both are well pleased.

I have a vivid dream that I am a helper and server of some sort to two young English people, a boy and a girl, of noble blood, somehow related to Churchill; I too am young, about twenty-one. The girl is very attractive, dark, with a beautiful voice. At last I help them into a barouche on the drive of UCC. I move toward the girl, who puts forward her cheek to be kissed, but in a way that displeases me—as if I were not a man. "I won't kiss you while you're eating," I say. "Damn you!" she says, but I know she recognizes me as a man and is attracted.

MONDAY, DECEMBER 24: In the morning do public relations and give out gifts at the *Examiner*. In the afternoon rest and wrap

presents and to the Thompsons' for drinks before dinner. In the evening, music and bustle and we put out the gifts after the girls are in bed. An odd feeling Christmas has stolen on us unawares.

TUESDAY, DECEMBER 25: Up at 9:30. The tree is a great success; WRD gives us a superb wine cellarette. Afternoon, sledding in Jackson Park. A fine dinner (goose) and Tokay.

THURSDAY, DECEMBER 27: Back to work and I get everybody's troubles at once. In the afternoon Tom Symons in with a tale of woe. In the evening read WRD's privately published *Far-Off Fields*: it is well done and a charming nature emerges, but what a lot of misery, despair, and discouragement he has left out!

SUNDAY, DECEMBER 30: This week a delightful respite in the bustle and worry of the present time. Will I be able to stand the unremitting quality of life at the College?

H.t.d. 56 in 1962; Brenda absent five weeks.

1963

—

AS HE CHANGED CAREERS, Davies maintained all his diaries: his daily personal diary with cryptic entries; his "big diary" with occasional, more contemplative entries; the Massey College diary, in which he wrote extended daily entries as he began to devote himself full-time to the College; a travel diary covering the European trip he and Brenda took in July and August; and his theatre diary, with entries for many but not all of the plays and operas he attended. Altogether he and Brenda saw about three dozen productions during the year, as well as over two dozen films. Selections here are drawn from all the diaries, with the Massey College diary increasingly carrying the main narrative. The family moved into the Master's Lodgings in mid-June.

TUESDAY, JANUARY 1: I begin this year with considerable misgiving, having given up the editorship of the *Examiner*,[1] which I knew,

1 Davies remained publisher until March 31, 1968, when the *Examiner* was sold to Roy Thomson. Until then, he continued to have a share in the ownership, attend meetings, and write occasional editorials.

for headship of a college where I have no defined duties and must therefore *make* the job myself—this in the academic world, for which I am by no means well qualified. I can easily become an ornamental hermit, or a lodging-house keeper, or an inferior pedant. Or I can make my work, and especially I can write my books. I am gaining some practice as a diplomat, dealing with the whims of the Massey Foundation. I begin to get something of the feel of the university and its division into able men who would have commanded respect anywhere, and the men swamped in detail, or muddled in some branch of pedantry, who are not scholars but who cumber the preserve of scholarship. I do not regret leaving the *Examiner,* only its security. I have outgrown it. As for the future, I am not quite a fool, and some men who are in no way fools think I can do the job, so I shall.

In the home, peace, and Brenda changes in anticipation of the move: we squabble about unimportant things, which I take to be a sign of greater freedom of spirit. We have quite a bit of money now—security if not wealth, and if we sell this house to T.H.B. Symons we should be well set.

Obedient to the words of the soothsayer,[2] I read my diaries for '54, '55, and '57, and what emerges is this: I am not successful as a playwright and I do rather well as a novelist, critic, and speaker—a good lecturer in a formal, rather carefully considered style. This chimes with my falling out of love with the theatre since *Love and Libel.* And two novels persist in getting notes made about themselves. Must think carefully about this.

WEDNESDAY, JANUARY 2: To Toronto at 8:45 a.m. To the O'Keefe to see the D'Oyly Carte company in *Iolanthe* and enjoyed it; many of the chorus movements precisely as they were when Daddy

2 The astrologer Hugh MacCraig.

Stewart[3] taught them to us at UCC in—was it 1932? He had them
from the Company, of which he was stage director for years. But
the effect of being a charming fossil was weakened by a permanent
set upon which very good extra pieces were mounted. How much
was my enjoyment a re-creation of past devotion? And am I wrong
in thinking that Henry Lytton, Bertha Lewis, and Darrell Fancourt
had greater impact than these moderns? One can never know, of
course, but I hate to think that at forty-nine I am a fogey, hoicking
up the past to rebuke the present. Conducting was Isidore Godfrey;
has he really been with them over thirty years? Can a man do that
and keep any sort of artistic conscience? Apparently he can, for he
conducted with great charm and sensitivity, and by and large the
piece was better played than sung. The entry of the Peers in Act 1
had all the charm, satire on chivalry, and theatrical power that
Camelot aimed at and missed.

FRIDAY, JANUARY 4: Very pleasant drive to Toronto and to the
Park Plaza: dress (full fig), and at 6 to the Stewarts' and thence
to the Royal York to the Crest Theatre Ball to celebrate ten years
of the Crest, as guests of the Harrises. We sat at a table with them,
the Stewarts, Bill and June Maclean, and the John Edisons. A very
Canadian affair: head table guests brought in by a piper, the lieu-
tenant governor and party by another piper. Nobody thinks this
strange, but suppose I were a lieutenant governor and wanted to
be preceded by a harper in green robes for Wales? What an outcry
there would be! The usual Royal York bad dinner: tinned fruit
salad, tinned consommé, chicken and veg, a common dollop of
ice cream mounted in cherry jam, coffee in big thick cups. George
Harris gave us good Pol Roger. Arnold Edinborough spoke

3 George Stewart directed the production of *Iolanthe* for the UCC Music Club.
 Davies played the Lord Chancellor.

tactlessly: the Crest "strangely begotten by a sister and two broth-
ers"; then heavy play on the names of plays performed and on crit-
ics' names—"the *Star* is not *Cohen* our way," etc.; then a stupid
attack on the O'Keefe, with Hugh Walker[4] present. A strangely *un-
related* performance. I was asked to thank him and did so very brief-
ly, and a lot of people thought I scored off him but such was cer-
tainly not my intention. There was a cabaret from 11 to midnight:
Barbara Hamilton sang a witty song about the Crest, and suggested
a new art-form. This proved to be a stripper, a pretty girl named
Toasty Towne, who got down to a fringed bra and G-string and
shook her bosom and her bum very fetchingly. But the orchestra
went on too long, and when she had shaken her breasts, waggled
her bum, and done a few grinds and bumps very well, she had ex-
hausted all her arts of pleasing that the organizers would permit,
and did it all over and over again, signalling vainly for them to stop.
This should have been better managed. Also, the four nice girls
(Dinah Christie was one) should not have been put in quite such
shaming costumes to sell drinks; net tights and tiny drawers which
showed them above the overhang of the buttock. Not a bad party
but it notably lacked grace and ease or any feeling of good breed-
ing. And *very* expensive for what it was.

TUESDAY, JANUARY 8: To Toronto by 3:30. Met Ron Thom at the
College; he tells me it will not be finished till mid-May or June. I
had suspected this, but did not like having it confirmed. He and
Tanya Moiseiwitsch are agreed about the chapel, which can now go
ahead; he will design and she do colour and decoration. See the
Combination Room for the first time without the scaffolding in it,
and it is at once apparent, as I had feared, that it is too small and
low for any sort of assembly. We agree on what I have always

4 Hugh Walker was the founding general manager of the O'Keefe Centre.

wanted—a tall, pulpit-like lectern in the northeast corner of the Hall, for grace, speeches, and announcements. Ron is enthusiastic; wants it to be very tall, with a canopy, and what he calls "a big, decorative piece of junk." He has succeeded in cutting the price of the carrels by $2,200.

WEDNESDAY, JANUARY 9, TORONTO: To the Frontenac and Kawartha radio and TV stations meetings with WRD and Arthur, then lunch at the University Club. Lecture from 2 to 4; then to the ROM committee from 4 to 6. In the evening to the Trinity College Dramatic Society play, *Trumpets and Drums* by Brecht after Farquhar's *The Recruiting Officer*. Miranda sings well in a jolly if rough production. She comes back to chat with us at the Park Plaza.

THURSDAY, JANUARY 10, TORONTO: Bill Broughall and Ian Montagnes of University of Toronto Press lunch with me to talk about Burgon Bickersteth's[5] memoirs, of which Ian Montagnes has a partial transcript; they think the very revealing complete manuscript should be in the Massey College library. I am depressed by their tales of Burgon Bickersteth—so deft, tactful, and so wonderful with young men, and so "in" with the great ones of the earth. In 1939, after George VI and Queen Elizabeth had toured here, Bickersteth was summoned to tea with Queen Mary: "How did the children behave themselves in Canada, Mr. Bickersteth?" she asked. No—I am not in that class. What class am I in? More and more I wonder if I am in any at all.

SUNDAY, JANUARY 13: The pressure of College work increases, and the nuisance of having to wait two more months to get into

5 Bickersteth was a well-connected Oxford graduate who had come to Canada on an Anglican Church mission in 1919 and became the very influential warden of Hart House from 1921 to 1947.

the building is particularly vexatious. Freud was right: artists hate to finish things.

MONDAY, JANUARY 14: Vincent Massey calls. He likes the notion of the Hall as our chief assembly-room. Says he does not insist on "Combination Room" as the name for the Upper Library. He is still angry with Ron and disturbed we have had no more applications as yet. This afternoon I wrote a piece about the College for *Faculty Notes,* which I hope may do some good, and Vincent Bladen has set February 8 as the date for his dinner, at which I shall be able to talk to some people who can be helpful. But I am nervous, and wish I had some assurance we would get a full house, or near it.

TUESDAY, JANUARY 15: Bill Broughall called with encouraging words about getting applications for the College: they will be attracted by *me,* he thinks! I wish I agreed, or even thought it likely. He says Burgon Bickersteth has written to him, asking that I should write to him. Bickersteth says he had great problems with Vincent and Alice Massey during the first five years at Hart House, as they *would* keep "bumming around"—an odd phrase to use of them. I wrote Bickersteth at length, unbosoming myself, and hope this was not wildly indiscreet. Also wrote VM saying I think it a great mistake to have the chapel Anglican. It should be non-denominational, but not greasily and United Churchily so. He won't like it and will probably balk.

WEDNESDAY, JANUARY 16: On January 10 we went to see John Gielgud's touring production of *The School for Scandal* at the O'Keefe and again on January 16 because we were so impressed. We both remember his 1938 production as a high spot and his Joseph Surface as the finest high comedy playing I have ever seen. This was better, gentler, more *easily* elegant and with more due attention to

the sentimental side of the piece. Also more *human*: none of Tony Guthrie's restlessness, and less of John Gielgud's frigid elegance. Delightful details: Sir Oliver's costume very much in the Eastern taste, and old-fashioned; Moses not *too* Jewy but given to fur collars and earrings and side curls; the wine bottles the *right* shape; the closet where Sir Peter hides so small that he emerges doubled up; the screen placed so that we can see Lady Teazle's response to the scene. One useful transposition: Act 5, Scene 1 played before 4.3; otherwise trivial cuts.

On our second view we sat in the second row and saw everyone very well from the knees up. The subtleties of the acting very clear, and also rather too much of the art of the sets to be seen. Contrast Gielgud's very simple makeup with Ralph Richardson's elaborate and not very effective one. Gielgud again plays Joseph in the finest high comedy manner—no obvious hypocrisy, the lightest possible touch, and now and then an artistic appreciation of his own villainy. Richardson plays Sir Peter broadly but never too much so—a good dash of eighteenth-century eccentricity, but never inhuman. Afterward to Gielgud's room (he wrote to the university inviting us), and he talked most interestingly about the easy beauty of Sheridan's dialogue—only one or two words in a sentence that need emphasis, and always perfectly placed—so that the writing dictates pace, and character. Showed us an intaglio a fan gave him, which he wears in place of one he had which belonged to Keats, and which he gave to a friend. Apparently he took it to Cartier's to be cleaned, and they scorned it because it was glass! What is Keats to Cartier's! Gielgud says they had a beastly time in Detroit— perhaps everyone does.

The productions I have seen which have most impressed me and formed my standards are the Habima *Dybbuk*, the Olivier-Richardson *Uncle Vanya*, the Evans-Gordon *Country Wife*, the Margaret Leighton *Lady from the Sea*, the Metropolitan Opera *Eugene Onegin*, the Paris

Opera *Oberon*, and Gielgud's *Richard II*, *Three Sisters*, *School for Scandal*, *Love for Love*, *Importance of Being Earnest*, *Lady's Not for Burning*, and *Winter's Tale*. Quite as powerful an influence on me as Tony Guthrie indeed!

THURSDAY, JANUARY 17, TORONTO: James Gow, the College solicitor, lunches with me and for a seemingly taciturn man talks a great deal. He is what Brenda calls a typical Canadian— concealing unusual abilities and shrewdness under a rustic guise. As I go on with this job I find more and more that all I need to do is listen. Everybody wants to talk: let them have the run of their tongues and they will do much for you. We go at 2:30 to the Liquor Licensing Board of Ontario offices to talk to Judge Robb[6] about a licence. The judge is a tiny, silvery old man, genial and delicately courteous. Gow plays naïve and asks advice; the judge gives it, frankly and freely. Upshot, we must form a club within the College and it must have been in existence, though not incorporated, for more than a year. This piece of legal contortion apparently smoothes the way. Was surprised by the judge, so gentle and seemingly simple but obviously full of crinkum-crankum. And why not, in a job which demands knowledge of so many irrational and contradictory laws? Gow will get to work at once.

SATURDAY, JANUARY 19: Colin Friesen comes at 10 and we spend three hours on College business. As I hoped, so much that puzzles me is easy for him and the kind of work he must do is the kind he understands and likes. He lunches with us and Brenda likes him, which I set store by for she is very intuitive about people. Rest and walk in the afternoon. Miranda home for the weekend and we sing and rejoice.

6 W.T. Robb was chair of the Liquor Licensing Board of Ontario.

SUNDAY, JANUARY 20: To Batterwood through the snow for lunch. Beforehand Lionel tells of being taken last week to John Gielgud's dressing-room, and he "never saw anything so evil" as Gielgud, his dressing-gown open, a cross on his naked breast; his daughters "shrank" from the sight. What tosh! I recall Lionel at Balliol, roaring drunk at a party, leaping on a table shouting, "Let's all worship the Great God Bugger!"

We discussed the chapel matter and reached a compromise—a quiet consecration, Church of England, at Christmas. Suits me well; non-denominationalism is foolish. We hope to have at least a monthly celebration. Vexation with Ron Thom grows; there will probably be another bloodbath on February 5.

Vincent Massey was in excellent form: his book is finished and he wants me to read it (I have also to read a thousand pages of Montagnes's transcription of Bickersteth's conversations!) and to look over his contract. Home by 5, as it was snowing heavily. Before we left Lionel drew me into the drawing-room to tell me that he was revising his will to leave his pictures to the College and also that he meant to leave Batterwood to the College. He is forty-five to my forty-nine, so I am unlikely to have to make any decisions arising out of such bequests.

The gossip from Vancouver (from Mrs. Pedak through her daughter Senta) is that Ron Thom got drunk and was lured by a designing woman and carnally enjoyed, and his wife is divorcing him. Sounds silly but may be true.

T.H.B. Symons offers $27,500 cash for our house: $1,000 less than we asked, $1,500 above his first offer. The tiresome fellow objects to our having Ross Thompson as agent, but it would be foolish not to have an agent.

MONDAY, JANUARY 21: Ross Thompson in at 5:30 and we sign to sell the house to Symons; Brenda feels this, but I do not very much as I am never deeply attached to houses.

FRIDAY, JANUARY 25: In the morning worked on Montagnes-Bickersteth transcription; afternoon to Toronto and to the College, which progresses and offers shocks and charms. At 4 to the Graduate Studies meeting, as ill-run as usual. Home by 8:20 and early to bed. Joyous unforeseen h.t.d.

MONDAY, JANUARY 28: Have finished reading Montagnes's conversations with Bickersteth with some dismay: he had every quality I lack. I have made some notes from the manuscript which may be helpful. Now—what sort of man emerges? Generous, kind, courageous; artistic side developed along visual lines, pictures and sculpture. No snob but not indifferent to the great. A wee bit of an old woman and dainty: i.e., candles in grapefruit and such tea-roomery. A genius with young men, drawing them out and encouraging all that was individual and distinguished. Does not seem to have liked women at all, though Ian Montagnes says this is unjust. None of any satiric, misanthropic vein but also, if I may say a word for myself, none of my literary cast of mind and high standards in that realm. In no way an original or unconventional thinker but a very good mind of the best, educated, liberal English stamp. I am a very poor specimen beside him, but I have a flash or two he lacked. I am grateful to have been given the benefit of his experience in this extraordinary fashion.

SUNDAY, FEBRUARY 3: Odd how many decisions I have to make now, but I am getting better at it; the secret is not to say too much and Jowett's "Never regret, never explain, never apologize" has great merit, in principle.

MONDAY, FEBRUARY 4: To Toronto with Miranda by train. At 8:30 p.m. to Hart House to meet the '49 Club, who are graduate geophysicists, and talk to them till 11. They are intelligently interested in the College and ask good questions. The matter of a chapel comes up: about even pro and con, and the general feeling seems to be that a college does not serve the whole man without a chapel and that it should be *something*—not non-denominational.

TUESDAY, FEBRUARY 5, TORONTO: At Eaton's from 11 to 4 with no lunch, only sandwiches and coffee. Vincent, Lionel, Hart, Bill Broughall, Ron Thom, and the Eaton's trio. They savage Ron rudely; VM began in this mood. Hart as negative as ever. I found it wearisome and destructive and was glad to get away.

WEDNESDAY, FEBRUARY 6, TORONTO: Meet in Lionel Massey's office at the Royal Ontario Museum with a representative of the contractor. We make an attempt to pin Ron Thom down and at last got May 30 named as probable date of completion. Lionel was very distressed, as a girl had committed suicide in the washroom of the ROM yesterday. Then to the College, and Vincent Massey and Hart compel Thom to restore the stone baluster to the main stairway: he wanted wood, and they said they had never heard of the change, though I remember it. But Ron Thom's muddle lets him in for such things. Then Hart killed the notion of having cork on the walls of the Senior Fellows' Dining Room, dear to Lionel's heart. Hart sourly protested that in the Club Room (new name of the Upper Library) there would be no place a man could take down a "current novel" and "browse." I bit his head off: we have no budget for necessary books, let alone novels for browsers. Got away from them at lunch. At 4 meet Brenda and Ron Thom at the College and discuss

our house[7] and the plan of our garden, which could be exciting and delightful.

SATURDAY, FEBRUARY 9: The McInneses[8] stay with us, and we talk all day and greatly enjoy fresh company and fresh subjects. Joan and Graham are calmer and more self-knowledgeable. Success becomes Graham, but Joan cannot shake her need to justify herself at the cost of others and to run down Colin and Lance for the aggrandizement of herself and Graham.

SUNDAY, FEBRUARY 10: More talk with the McInneses. We walk in Burnham Wood in the morning and in the afternoon put them on the train at Port Hope and collapse after a stimulating but exhausting weekend.

MONDAY, FEBRUARY 11: I meet the Guthries in Toronto to show them Massey College, which impressed them. They bring a somewhat farcical figure, Joe Martin, their jam man from Newbliss.[9] Meet them with Miranda for dinner later at the Simcoe and find them well away, downing double Irishes in the bar with two jam

7 The house, known initially as the Master's Lodgings, is at the southeast corner of the College; it has its own entrance on Devonshire Place as well as access to the main building. When the Davies family lived there, it had five bedrooms with four bathrooms, plus a guest suite of two bedrooms and a bathroom. Outside the main-floor sitting room and dining-room are a patio and garden. The Master's study is up a few stairs from the entrance. A large basement area, known as the Green Room, was used for choir rehearsals and later for Davies's teaching.

8 Graham McInnes, writer, film producer, and diplomat, met Davies in the 1940s, and their families became lifelong friends. He and his wife, Joan, had grown up in Australia. Graham was the son of Campbell McInnes, the singer, and Angela Thirkell, a prolific popular novelist. Graham's brother was the writer Colin MacInnes, and Lance Thirkell was his half-brother. Graham had just been appointed the first Canadian high commissioner to Jamaica.

9 The Guthries had begun a jam business using the fruit picked from their garden, as described by Davies during his 1959 visit, to provide some local employment.

prospects. Tony sets upon Miranda, warning her that a singer's life is not all glory, etc.—he is not good with young people, and never credits them with any intelligence. We had a merry time with them; both look much better than when last seen, which was in New York on Dec. 8, 1960. Tony tells me that was the day that the British consul sent for him to ask if he would accept a knighthood; also that Philip Langner and Don Herbert gave him a cigarette case inscribed "To a great human being" or some such bosh. But he was vexed with them for putting up the notice cancelling the production without telling me, and also for trying to get money out of me on Dec. 6. Tony says he knows I exerted myself over his knighthood; he affects to care nothing for it but I know he likes it. He says the Minneapolis theatre is "a bugger" outside but good inside. I have written a piece about Tony for the April issue of *Drama Survey*[10] and have tried to be sensible about his contribution to Stratford. It is never easy to write *justly* about him—so dear a friend.

TUESDAY, FEBRUARY 12, TORONTO: Lunch with Basil Coleman. He is doing very well and looks happy. At 4 p.m. go carefully over the College building with Brenda and Lionel Massey and make notes. Detached from the Foundation, Lionel is the most practically and realistically intelligent of the lot. At 7 dine with Tuzo Wilson and his wife, Isabel, the first of the Senior Fellows (barring the Ropers, who are old friends) we meet in this way. He commands great respect and is enthusiastic for the College.

WEDNESDAY, FEBRUARY 13, TORONTO: With Ron Thom at 9:30. He is more cheerful and exuberant than I have seen him and talks of *warm colour* in the College! I suspect a woman. I fear that the

10 "Tyrone Power and Dr. Thomas Guthrie in Canada," *Drama Survey* 3, no. 1 (May 1963). Reprinted in Judith Grant (ed.), *The Well-Tempered Critic* (1981).

decoration and colour scheme of the College has suffered dreadfully from Vincent Massey's old age, Hart Massey's affliction, and Ron Thom's divorce—all life-diminishing.

THURSDAY, FEBRUARY 14: Flowers to Brenda and also a card index, which she wanted. Fifteen letters on College affairs, and worked on John Gay. Feel ill and wretched and wonder if it is low blood pressure; as always when unwell, worry a great deal; bad dreams.

FRIDAY, FEBRUARY 15: Feel somewhat better: work on eighteenth-century playwrights all day. Rosamond home for the long weekend. It is now decided Jenny goes to Rome for three months in March and I hope this enlarges her world. Relax in home atmosphere.

THURSDAY, FEBRUARY 21, TORONTO: Visited the College, which progresses—plaster, chimney in Hall almost done, ceiling in Senior Fellows' Dining Room, crockets on lantern, bell up—and then to see Friesen, who has been pegging conscientiously away, and is beginning to make sense of the budget, is interviewing possible porters, has repelled a man who wants to put a coin laundromat in the basement, etc. He worries that he is not doing enough *work*: I urge him to sit still and *think*. Ron Thom lunches with Brenda and me; he is confused and disorganized. There *is* a woman, Molly Golby, whom we met last night at Allan Fleming's— not a little lady to whom I warmed, though Brenda was inclined to like her. Ron Thom got drunk and passed out, when the rest of us were in an ordinary two-drink evening. They are engaged. I do not think it can work well: Ron is one of Nature's *victims*, and I suspect women are Nature's means of bamboozling him. A man of genius, without self-knowledge or self-protection, naked, bruised, and wondering.

FRIDAY, FEBRUARY 22, TORONTO: Meet in Lionel Massey's room at the ROM at 9:30. Lionel, Vincent, Ron Thom, Lorimer, and the man from the contractor's firm. Hart Massey, *Deo gratias*, could not come, so some decisions were possible. He means well, but he creates an atmosphere in which indecision is the norm. All details of the building now pretty well settled, though I suspect we shall have a row about the lectern in the Hall. VM now wants the Club Room called the Upper Library again. Fuss, fuss, fuss! To Eaton's about 11 and attack the chair for the Senior Fellows' Dining Room—literally, for Howard gets a saw and hacks arms and spikes off it until a goodish, chair-like thing is left, and not Ron Thom's Roycroft rubbish. This small dining-room is to be cedar panelled and (my suggestion) have red velvet curtains! Also Lionel and I are empowered to choose a *red* curtain stuff for the Common Room. All this red because Vincent is off to Barbados and thus cock-a-hoop, and Hart is far away in Ottawa. So the forces of Life and Joy get a chance!

Take Lionel to lunch at University Club and talk ROM business. He says frankly he will be very disappointed if he does not get the directorship, which he says Eric Phillips, Bissell, and Bladen have more than once assured him should be his. And why not? He can run a show and has imagination. But he has not even a B.A. to bless himself with.

Thirteen new applications for the College. Brenda and I to Eaton's about lamps and drive home by 5:30. Jolly h.t.d.

I have read the first two binders of Vincent Massey's book, *What's Past Is Prologue*: full of meat, especially the political stuff, and I think I have persuaded him *not* to chop bits out for fear of offending somebody, or using Cabinet material. Can't be an author and a gent. Very spicy about William Lyon Mackenzie King. But it has the air of a *dictated* book. He depends on speech rhythms to make points, and of course they don't do and the effect is often dry and curt. Regret this especially in his description of nineteenth-century

Toronto: he knows the milieu, he has the literary skill to fix it for-
ever, poetically, but he has muffed it. A pity.

WEDNESDAY, FEBRUARY 27, TORONTO: To our lawyers' and see
their Mr. Hamill, a precise Scot with some sort of nervous, scruffy
ailment of the scalp. He is handling our liquor licence and seems
to think we should get it, as Leslie Frost[11] has given the word.
Hamill says we "have pierced the corporate veil," which I take to
be a Scotch joke for having whistled through the regulations. I
sign the application to the attorney general to incorporate the
"Common Room Club," for Leslie Frost says the name of Massey
College must never be mentioned.

SUNDAY, MARCH 3: Basil Coleman comes on the 12:10 train. In the
afternoon, Miranda sings for him and we go to Burleigh Falls to
walk. Talk with Basil about families till 11:45. Jenny is much excited
about going to Rome and it is good to see; she is somewhat fearful
of the journey but I am sure she will manage admirably and have a
glorious spring.

MONDAY, MARCH 4: At the *Examiner* office in the morning. To
Toronto at 1 and to the University Press. ROM committee meeting
at 4. Suspect Claude Bissell will not recommend Lionel Massey as
director, as professional pressure against him is too strong. Home
and chat with Brenda, Jenny, and Basil Coleman until midnight.

WEDNESDAY, MARCH 6, TORONTO: Last night a long talk with
Lionel Massey about College details: he tells me Raymond can never
be chairman of the Foundation as he is an American citizen. This

11 Frost, former premier of Ontario, was still serving in the Legislature. His wife
was an ardent temperance supporter.

afternoon to see Friesen after my lecture, and he tells me there are only sixty-seven Junior Fellows' rooms: he and Gord[12] have counted twice! So Ron has lost three sets of rooms somewhere. We get some applications every week and now have thirty-nine. We have altered the final date for applications to April 30, and the University Press is mailing 1,600 brochures, with this additional information, next week, so we move.

Hart is against cedar for the Senior Fellows' Dining Room: says it is not a first-rate wood. Also he and Ron have had a great row about the skylight in the Round Room, which *still* lets in water. Bad design, says Hart, and Ron must pay for putting it right. But a man who can lose three sets of rooms might do anything.

SATURDAY, MARCH 9: Wrote many letters in the morning. In the afternoon a long rest in bed, sleeping and reading, then a drive in fine weather. In the evening read Wilde's *Letters,* especially "De Profundis," then to the Thompsons' for chat with the Curriers. Brenda scolds me: says I am rude to her. She is right: I have grown more self-assertive and probably rude. It is part of the price of my new freedom, and it will pass: but to be free of so many things which have burdened me for twenty years—who would not lose balance a little?

TUESDAY, MARCH 12, TORONTO: For two weeks we have been considering a possible porter, one Captain C., of the Royal Canadian Horse Artillery. Good references, good appearance. The former commandant of Royal Military College says of him, "Not the smartest fellow in the world . . . ," but nothing against him. But Friesen arranges that Captain C. and *Mrs.* C. meet Lionel Massey in the College today, as though by chance. The wife is crucial. Mrs. C. does

12 With Eastern Construction.

not pass the test: smokes at Lionel and fusses about the quarters. Friesen calls me and says he thinks it won't do. So does Lionel. So we next see a regimental sergeant major of the Queen's Own Rifles. The porter *must* be right or we shall have endless trouble.

WEDNESDAY, MARCH 20, TORONTO: Lunch at Eaton's with Herbert Irvine, lecture on Sheridan at 2, meet Lionel at the College at 4:25. We have twenty-five more applications; Brenda makes great progress with the house. Our new porter is one RSM McCracken, who seems to me the right sort—vast waxed moustache, intelligent, and gives out a good feeling. The past fortnight has been a welter of detail and I am spent. Our applications now stand at seventy-one residents and fifteen non-residents, and there are more to come as 1,950 brochures have been sent to Graduate School men and fourth-year men. Have also composed a report to the Senior Fellows. Trouble with Commercial Caterers: Sedgwick and Vincent Massey have talked so much about "quality" that they have grandiose and foolish plans—a "hostess" in the dining hall, God forbid! And very elaborate food. Must crush this, without undercutting VM, who has brought it on his own head: special silver and china, so why not special food? Strangely, I seem to be the only person connected with this venture who recognizes that 10 cents more per man per day can mean close to $4,000 a year to the College. The woodwork is going into the College and looks handsome, and the bronze fire-doors are splendid. It is all exciting and I wish I had more time and spirit to enjoy it and was not so absorbed in details. Must conquer this (and the details too, of course) or I shall never be properly useful to the place.

SUNDAY, MARCH 24: Brenda and I talk with Miranda from breakfast to noon; in the afternoon walk at Omemee. In the evening, read and chat about T.S. Eliot and Jung. A spring day and I have

my annual spring headache. But a sense of achievement as the College goes into final stages of preparation. Lionel relays to me some handsome compliments about the work I am doing, which cheers and refreshes me. Who can live *sans* appreciation? Not I.

TUESDAY, MARCH 26, TORONTO: Lionel Massey, Bill Broughall, and Friesen lunch with me at the University Club to discuss catering and budget. Friesen cannot get it into his head that the object is *not* to get the budget as low as possible but to keep it from going higher than the Foundation can pay—so that the cushion may be used for the Library, which the Masseys still think of as a needless, if not frivolous, expense. Poor Lionel, as usual, has to face the consequences of family pride and stupidity, and I instruct Friesen to contradict Vincent Massey and tell the caterers to get their price down.

THURSDAY, MARCH 28, TORONTO: To Harcourt's[13] again about College gowns. Hit on an Oxford doctor's undress gown stripped of its braid and with a red-brown rosette on the collar at the back. Miranda and Brenda with me: they find Harcourt's fascinating.

FRIDAY, MARCH 29, TORONTO: To Lionel Massey's office at the ROM at 9:30: Hart, Ron Thom, and that dummy Lorimer present. We work till 12 on plans and details. Ron wants to add ironwork to the tower and gate to enrich the stone. Whence this new yearning for ornament? The influence of Molly Golby, perhaps? Anyway, I am for it, and strangely, so is Hart. Ron has designed a fine lectern, but has not got it quite right yet. Then we all go to the site and Hart makes some excellent suggestions, including filling in those holes in our garden wall. But oh! the doors in our cellar are stained

13 Makers of academic, legal, and other specialty robes.

a hideous diarrhea yellow; must talk to Ron. Home, and in the evening prepared a plan for Vincent Massey for the opening ceremonies in October—a workmen's party, a garden party for officialdom, and a formal ceremony to acknowledge the transfer of the College from the Masseys to the Master and Fellows and at which I suggest the intrusion of a *terrae filius*[14] to enliven the affair and bring the Junior Fellows into the scene. Hope VM likes it, as it would lift our opening right out of the ruck of muddled, self-conscious, hick university ceremonies.

SATURDAY, MARCH 30: A device is needed to go on the north wall of the chapel, in relief, so tonight I paint a phoenix to show Ron, whose *forte* is not Christian symbolism. What a lot of odd jobs I am let in for! Design a gown, symbolism for the chapel, shall we have "French" or "semi-French" service in Hall, what uniform shall the porter wear? I am the Inigo Jones, the Capability Brown, of the place. Am sometimes led to mild deception or pious fraud. What should be inscribed on the bell? Nothing old is really right, so I fudge up this:

S. CATHARINA
Vivos voco: mortuos plango
Excito lentos: paco cruentos[15]

and it is accepted as genuinely traditional stuff. It is rooted in tradition, but it is rather boldly adapted. Anyhow it is now on our large bell and our Hall bell too. Enjoy this sort of thing hugely, but if I did not do it, who would? Endless committees, I suppose, with

14 "Son of the earth": traditionally someone appointed to perform a satirical Latin poem at public events at Oxford.
15 Davies's translation: "I summon the living: I mourn the dead / I rouse the sluggards: I calm the turbulent." Saint Catherine of Alexandria is the patron saint of scholars and of Balliol College.

the usual committee results. One must be both bold and discreet when trying to set something going which may become traditional. I enjoy the really creative College work, which now is in full swing, and also the sense that the drudgery draws to a close. But I become overwrought during these taxing mid-weeks.

WEDNESDAY, APRIL 3, TORONTO: The Southam Fellowships are awarded today, and the committee is anxious to get the new Fellows into the College. Claude Bissell gives a lunch for us and the outgoing group of Southam Fellows, and if we get such a good lot next year they should be an asset to the College.

MONDAY, APRIL 8: Election Day and Brenda, Miranda, Mrs. Pedak, and I vote at 9. Work all day on my last lecture of term. In the evening back to the *Examiner* and enjoy the excitement of the election returns, but result so far is indecisive and a Tory is returned here, as predicted: Tory Peterborough!

TUESDAY, APRIL 9: To Toronto and to a ROM committee meeting: Bladen and Stone speak very well of Lionel but I fear he cannot be director, as he is not academically qualified. We dine at the flat, and with Brenda to film of *Long Day's Journey* directed by Sidney Lumet, very good but long indeed!

WEDNESDAY, APRIL 10, TORONTO: Haircut in the morning. I give my last lecture at 2 and am applauded at the end! Work on graduate exams, then to Park Plaza at 5:30 and spend an hour with Ron Thom; dine at Lichee Garden with Brenda and Rosamond and complete exams by 11.

THURSDAY, APRIL 11, TORONTO, MAUNDY THURSDAY: Met Lionel by chance at the University Club and we lunched together. He

asks me about my salary and I tell him I have drawn none so far, and he is astonished: I am glad to have established this, for while I do not in the least grudge giving my work, I am not quite willing that it should be unknown. We go to the College and meet Vincent Massey, Hart, Allan Fleming, Ron Thom, the foolish Lorimer, and Norah Leavings (as secretary) in Hall—the first meeting of any sort in our building. We agree on the Founders' Plaque, which Allan has done in a fine humanistic script, and decide on door numbers. Ron outlines what he wants to do to the building and gets approval *if* the prices are satisfactory. Then Ron works through a long, dismal list of accounts, some of them very high prices—chapel $10,000—and the staggering sum of $7,500 for the two book presses in the Upper Library! This is refused. Then the Quadrangle and south garden plan: full of trees and silly plants which would require expert, constant attention. So VM vetoes all but *one* tree in the quad, and wants the south garden replanned. Some costs relate to our house—$1,500 for book-shelves in TV room, and $450 for a wine cupboard! I was embarrassed. Finally choose curtains for the Common Room. All this done to screams from a power-saw, and the yelling and crashing without which nothing can be built. But VM was good-tempered and philosophical about it all and looked well, though Lionel is worried about his health. Our anxiety about admissions is now over but there is a new and difficult problem. We have lost five rooms! Ron refuses to admit that he ever said seventy but we all know he did. But VM, who is a realist at heart, agrees that we rent five of the non-resident Senior Fellows' rooms to make it up, and thus our budget is protected. It is now firm that all work inside the College must be finished by June 1, and all outside work by August 15. So Brenda and I decide to move in on June 10 if we can possibly manage it.

WEDNESDAY, APRIL 17, TORONTO: Dean Roland McLaughlin of Applied Science and Engineering gives a lunch for me at the York Club, introducing his departmental heads; Claude Bissell was the only other non-engineer. They are very friendly and all goes well. Breckenridge, who is also an associate dean of graduate studies, tells me the rumour now goes around that to get into Massey College you must have gone to a private school. He teases me about the rejection of women from the College. Then Friesen and I go to the College and meet Ron Thom and discuss creating a suite for Robert Finch and also converting a non-resident Senior Fellows' room into a room for Friesen. Ron immediately wants to "build in" a desk: he has a passion for these immobile rooms, frozen forever as he creates them.

FRIDAY, APRIL 19, TORONTO: At 2:30 meet the Massey Foundation in the College and find that Ron has told them I want a built-in desk for Friesen! Not a lie: he cannot understand that anyone disagrees with him unless they are vehement. A *very* obtuse mind. Vincent Massey looking old and stiff and unwell, and playing the distinguished proconsul troubled by nit-wits. Poor old man! I am sorry for him but he *will* act a role, and that rather puts us all in the position of supporting characters with very minor business—which holds things up.

After they had gone I roamed the building and tried to get some message from it—for I must breathe life into the place and I must know what it says to me before I can do that: the newborn, sleeping building must speak something, or murmur, before I can make it speak aloud. Am very tired, nervous, and worried: expenses for the Library are nearing the $25,000 mark and I must talk to Bill Broughall or we shall have a flaming row with the Foundation. Am planning a vacation in July, but before that a multitude of decisions must be made, and some difficult corners must be rounded, of

which the Library is probably the most troublesome. I am fed up
with College matters, but I cannot think of anything else. Friesen
reports McCracken is having all his teeth drawn and a false set
made, to look handsome for his new job.

In the evening with Brenda and Miranda to *Cat on a Hot Tin
Roof* at the Crest, much better done, to my mind, than when I saw
it new in New York. Toby Robins excellent as Maggie—great vari-
ety and real tenderness and strength when she had a chance to
use them. But the real performance was Bruno Gerussi as Brick—
a fine study of the calm of despair. How the classical work helps
in these modern pieces! The whole cast good and the nuance
better marked and more telling than in New York. Do not like the
play; it rubs me raw to no purpose, but it permits virtuoso acting,
and got it.

SUNDAY, APRIL 21: Brenda speaks of spiritual dryness, the trouble
of middle age: if one succumbs to it I am sure one gives in to ail-
ments and bitterness. We are both conscious of this danger and
work against it.

TUESDAY, APRIL 23: Now that a Liberal government is in, and the
prime minister is Lester B. Pearson, a former assistant to Vincent
Massey,[16] we may yet get our augmentation of honour. I mentioned
it to Lionel Massey in a phone conversation this evening and he
says Esmond Butler is already going ahead with it, and had not VM
told me? No, VM has not. Indeed I wonder if VM is not rather tired
of me. Bill Broughall says the Masseys always turn on those who
serve them. We shall see. I have never conceived of a college head
as "serving" anybody. Have finished VM's book. It ends well. It is the

16 Pearson had been first secretary at the Canadian High Commission in
London from 1935 to 1941, while Massey was high commissioner.

middle part that is weak. But, in the cant of the day, it "projects Vincent Massey's image" successfully. The shame is that his "image" is not the best part of him.

Felt low, discouraged, and bleak all day, nerves jangling and unable to concentrate, but got a lot of routine stuff done. In the evening a misery of self-doubt and despair. Sleep badly.

WEDNESDAY, APRIL 24: Still heavy in spirit: Friesen calls—caterers' estimate still extreme and he is worried and so am I. In the evening I write a long unwise letter to Vincent Massey but shall not send it. Hear an early Mozart opera, *Bastien et Bastienne*.

THURSDAY, APRIL 25: Weary but do a good day's work on College affairs. Trouble about the caterers; they will *not* get their price down. Colin Friesen phoned me yesterday, discouraged, and flops all his troubles on me. So this morning I phone the caterers' man, and tell him, firmly, that we can't pay the $90,000-odd he asks. He whines. These people look like men of business, but they have a servant mentality. As I have long suspected, that wretched man Clements and Sedgwick visited the caterers and filled them full of nonsense about fine china and silver, and the class of service that would be required. What impertinence! Write Vincent Massey and mention this; in the end it comes back to his lack of realism and his passion for rather stuffy grandeur. I am very tired and worn down, and sick to death of all this lodging-house detail. Why do I worry and sleep badly because the Masseys are stupid with their money? Perhaps I have a servant mentality too—Old Rob, the good grey steward to Milord Massey. Christ have mercy!

In the evening work on my lecture on *Timon*[17] and hear the Schubert Quintet. An admirable h.t.d. but cannot get to sleep and moither for, it seems, hours, worrying about the College.

FRIDAY, APRIL 26, TORONTO: Bill Broughall lunches with me and is worried about the Foundation: Raymond is being silly, so Vincent Massey wants not to have an annual meeting, oblivious of the fact that the law requires it. Also, VM draws $7,500 *per annum* as chairman and this is illegal, and Lionel counts on it when his turn comes. How can Bill break it to them? I suggest it be paid to VM through the College as an honorarium to the Visitor: this nails the Foundation to the College and makes it, in effect, the College's endowment. Bill says, "A stroke of bloody genius!" and I think it is not too bad for a non-financial man like myself. Bill tells me that, when VM was governor general, Bill was summoned mysteriously to Ottawa for *very* important instructions: VM wanted a clause in his will that when he died the embalmers should not get him till a doctor had done all that could be done to ascertain that he was indeed dead! Of course Bill had to advise him that he could not tinker with VM's will and that such promises should be exacted from his near and dear, and not his executors. Embarrassing and pitiable. We agree to pay for the Library partly out of running expenses and partly out of furnishings.

Bill has let me see the letter he wrote VM on August 1, 1962, about the Foundation's ability to support the College. Significant figures: College expected to cost $1,750,000 for the building and $250,000 to furnish; $60,000 has been granted the College for working capital plus $100,000 common stock endowment fund, and $25,000 library fund. All this leaves the Foundation with about

17 For the Stratford season. The plays were *Timon of Athens*, *Troilus and Cressida*, and *The Comedy of Errors*.

two millions, money which should yield it annually about $100,000. I do not want to be a schemer, but if the Visitor, i.e. VM, got his money through the College, it would be a good thing.

THURSDAY, MAY 2, TORONTO: I give the College Admissions Committee lunch at the University Club: A.R. Gordon, Tuzo Wilson, Bill Dobson, and Gordon Roper. Despite predictions that had reached me that Andy Gordon would be intransigent about the admission of anyone not registered in the Graduate School, he was not so, insisting only that they be not called Junior Fellows. He drives us to his office, cursing the man at the parking lot—"Hurry up, you old bugger!"—and students on the road—"Out of the way, you bastards!"—and we make up a final list quite quickly. But none of them can count, so although they say a few places are vacant, there are no resident places open, and only one non-resident, and this may prove a nuisance. I then show them over the College, and Andy, who has not seen it before, is deeply impressed. And indeed it is impressive, but the details! That idiot Ron tells us one thing about our house and then leaves orders for something else—so that today we found the painter staining all the woodwork in the kitchen (which is *all* woodwork) the darkest oak brown! Am happy at last to have chosen some men for the College; they are quite a star-spangled group. It means that the place today took a huge stride into life, and away from mere architecture and furnishing. We have a balanced group, arrived at quite naturally—mostly Canadians, but U.K., U.S., Nigerian, Indian—the lot, and happily a couple of French Canadians. I am greatly restored by this, and a cloud lifts. As I sat in my poky office at University College making up the list to send to Miss Whalon in Peterborough, I positively sang!

WEDNESDAY, MAY 8, TORONTO: Attended a Ph.D. *viva* this morning in a desperately overheated room painted green in the Graduate

School building. How badly they need our Round Room. In the afternoon I interviewed Duncan Fishwick, a classics don from St. Michael's College, who will superintend Hall for us and do a Latin grace for a small reduction in his rent. T.H.B. Symons dines with Brenda, Miranda, and me at the University Club to discuss 361 Park Street. A useful day and bed early.

THURSDAY, MAY 9, TORONTO: I go to the College alone and for two hours visit every room and clear my mind about it. Then to a Graduate School meeting, an eternity of muddle, 4 to 6:30. We dine at the flat and go to *That Hamilton Woman* at the Crest, Barbara Hamilton's revue, supported by Tom Kneebone and Bill Walker. Several good numbers but somehow amateurish in total effect. Barbara wears some flashy, ill-made gowns. She has learned a lot, but is not confident of herself and so falls back on her stock jokes—that she is ugly and has a fat bum. Neither is true, and would not be funny if it were. She is a curious, lost creature, convinced she is a clown; she might be an actress but I fear it is too late now to find out.

FRIDAY, MAY 10, TORONTO: Moffat St. A. Woodside, university vice-president (academic), very kindly has me to lunch at the York Club to meet his department heads and talk about the College. I know most of them and it goes well. Fulton Anderson, professor of philosophy, says to me at parting, "You're the only one in Canada that could do it—manage the university, manage the College, and manage Vincent Massey—and he's a son-of-a-bitch to manage!" Kind, and from Anderson I appreciated it greatly.

SATURDAY, MAY 11: Help Brenda clear the attic, a tiresome job. In the evening the girls clear out the children's books. I play Handel and Mendelssohn duets with Miranda. We are all working

at clearing the accumulation of twelve years living in this capacious house.

SUNDAY, MAY 12: Seized with rheumatism while washing my face, severe all day. Rosamond returns to school in the afternoon. Make notes for my *Comedy of Errors* lecture and glad to be at it. Beautiful day, but oh! the twinges! lumbago, right arm affected. Have been working up to rheumatism for weeks: felt it coming: too much wine? too fat? fatigue? Do not want to become its steady prey.

TUESDAY, MAY 14, TORONTO: At 3 to the College and found Vincent Massey in a bad temper about the light in Hall. Eaton's, suspecting it would not do, had one made and hung before going ahead with the other nine. It is really dreadful, made of raw silk and plastic of a deep amber colour which would kill all other colour in the room. VM vents his ill-humour on Lorimer, who has not provided any chairs. I have never seen VM so cruel or so angry. Of course Lorimer is an ass, but I was sorry for him; he is so stupid he never knows *why* he is being savaged, and like many stupid people he underestimates the intelligence of others. VM hastily designs a lamp himself, which at least is inoffensive, if dull. Hart condemns it as "feminine" because it is round! (Lionel not present: has had virus pneumonia. I visited him at his house this morning. He pretended he wanted to talk College but really was worrying about his situation at the ROM, which I think is what brought on his illness.)

Meeting of Master and Fellows in the board room at 4:10. Elect Sirluck a Senior Fellow. All goes well except that VM fusses because one man is identified as a French Canadian; if it got into the "wrong hands" it might give a "wrong impression." So that page of the report must be done again. Our liquor licence draws nearer, but I shall not be at rest till we have it secured. I learned this morning that one of our Junior Fellows, Nikola Stanacev, has had a

laboratory accident and may lose his sight. Must visit him in hospi-
tal—first of many such duties on the pastoral side of my work.

WEDNESDAY, MAY 15: A busy day at the *Examiner* and worked on
notes for *Comedy of Errors*. T.H.B. Symons visits the house, eats six
scones with jam, and is worried about its size but likes it greatly.

THURSDAY, MAY 16: To Dr. Dobson for a checkup. Painful, squeez-
es testicles and ravages anus, but gives me a very good report.

THURSDAY, MAY 23: On Wednesday to hospital and saw Stanacev
and liked him—courageous, intelligent, and what a learned man
should be under adversity: the College must do for him what it can.
Home and immediately learned of an important meeting today—
Vincent Massey is breathing fire, Ron is said to be ready to throw
up the job, etc.—so reluctantly go back to Toronto again this morn-
ing, to be a make-peace if necessary. The Foundation present in
the bodies of VM, Hart, Bill, and Miss Leavings; Lionel is in hospital
with virus pneumonia, pleurisy, and blood clot, poor soul! After all
the nonsense nothing untoward happened. VM's lamp was made
and hanging and looked like a wind-sock at an airfield; compro-
mise—Ron is to try again, as he says his last, very bad, lamp was
ill-made and he wanted opal plastic instead of the dreadful amber
that appeared. My guess is that his orders were verbal, muddled,
and muttered—and so useless. The lamp done with, we go over a
list of other things to be done: the Masseys make Ron pay $280 for
an error (which incurred work to this sum but saved over twice as
much in materials!) and were in high glee, having apparently made
some money. Copper on the veranda of our house and metalwork
over the gate discussed, and though VM fusses I think we shall have
them at last. VM is away to England for the summer, Bill Broughall
says, to renew his assault upon the heart of the relict of Fruity

Metcalfe (i.e., Lady Alexandra "Baba" Metcalfe, née Curzon), though I find this suggestion grotesque—but one never knows.

I get some time with Ron to discuss the lectern in Hall and we work out a possible notion. The College looks more exciting every day now, and the Lodgings very fine, if somewhat austere.

Lunch at L'Aiglon with Brenda; we work on wallpapers and buy a Pembroke table. Drive home by 6, Miranda has passed with a II: i[18] and is fifth in English in the university. Very good, and we are all delighted.

SUNDAY, MAY 26: H.t.d. on rising. Bask in sun all day and read Jung's memoirs, deeply interesting and evocative. Vincent Massey calls—augmentation approved by Pearson—victory at last!

We have enjoyed the last of ease at Park Street—henceforth packing and dismantling must have sway: excitement tinged with regret—a delightful old house.

FRIDAY, MAY 31, TORONTO: Spent the morning at the College with Ron and went over a host of details—including a fidget from Armstrong, bursar of Trinity, about the drainage of St. Hilda's garden directly to the north of us—as suspicious and pennymite as his master the provost. Will our house be done by June 10? I doubt it; Eaton's are as slow and stupid as they accuse Ron and the contractors of being. Brenda and I entertain Helen and Alison Ignatieff[19] at lunch at the University Club and Alison talks wonderfully about the Masseys: Hart "the most inflexible man I've ever known; Uncle Vincent is afraid of him"; "the Masseys have sentiment in plenty but no compassion." I ask about Bill Broughall's

18 Second-class honours, upper division.
19 Alison Ignatieff, wife of George Ignatieff and a niece of Vincent Massey. Her father was W.L. Grant, headmaster of Upper Canada College while Davies was there.

repeated warning about the fate of those who serve the Masseys. "Not true and it won't happen to you; remember, they need you and your reputation more than you need them; they were dreadful to Daddy but he won, because he was strong and they respect that." She was amusing about "Baba" Metcalfe, who is very beautiful, and says Vincent Massey is considered still a very desirable *parti* among grand old ladies in London. I'm very fond of Alison, the first girl I ever took to a dance and my headmaster's daughter. Alison tells this of her grandfather, Principal Grant of Queen's: Sir John A. Macdonald dined with him one evening at the Principal's Residence, and Dr. Grant settled down for what he expected would be an evening of interesting talk. But Sir John rose to go: "I must call on the coloured barber," said he. "But Sir John," said Grant, "can you mean that you would rather talk to the coloured barber than to me?" "Indeed I would," said Sir John, "for you must realize that the coloured barber controls seven votes, whereas you—you'll always vote at the dictates of your conscience!" We go on to Convocation, where J. Burgon Bickersteth is given his honorary LL.D.

SUNDAY, JUNE 2: Preparatory to moving I make another assault on the papers of John Pearson.[20] I cannot keep them—remorselessly full diaries kept from age fifteen onward; a record of adolescent self-doubt, of unresolved love-affairs with girls, of homosexual affairs, of the dreary attendance on his dying parents, of the gay days on Capri, of the *katzenjammer* that led him to a monastery, of the flight thence (with my help), of a squalid life in Hollywood, of his experience in a home for alcoholics, of his journey to B.C. and trying to "go straight," of adultery with Earle Birney's wife, of flight east and the awful "group therapy" for

20 John Pearson was a friend of Davies from their school days at UCC. He was gifted but led an unhappy and unaccomplished life and committed suicide on October 31, 1958. Davies was his de facto literary executor.

alcoholics in Toronto; and all rendered somehow farcical by his childish inability to spell and his strange lack of humour. Wit, fantasy, yes. Humour, especially about anything associated with himself—absolutely none.

I have kept his thesis, what he had done of his novel "Bottle in the Smoke," and his verses, and a few letters. The diaries it is kinder to destroy, and I have done so; they show him small, vindictive, and uncharacteristic. But I have been wrong about him: he was learned but not wise. He thought philosophy could resolve his troubles, but it was love he needed and love must be paid for with love, and he could not give in that coin. Poor John—you were the most learned of us, and I have had to destroy your literary legacy because it was worthless! N.B.: Interesting that when I was twenty and Pearson eighteen, he complained in his diary about what an unsatisfactory creature I was in an argument because I was always changing ground and did not seem to take anything seriously. Meaning himself, and the metaphysical whimwhams with which he delighted to torture himself and everybody else. But this frivolity in me has always given offence: not for nothing was I born when Mercury was powerfully in the ascendant.

MONDAY, JUNE 3, TORONTO: Brenda and I have a small dinner at the University Club for Burgon Bickersteth. Our party is Helen Ignatieff and Bill and Zoe Broughall. It goes well and as Helen says, we are an interesting group. J. Burgon Bickersteth, the warden of Hart House in its early years; herself, as the widow of Bickersteth's successor, Nicholas Ignatieff, in the middle of its history; and Brenda and I the beginning of a new Massey venture. We take them to Hawthorn Gardens afterward and discover there is nothing to drink, but nobody cares.[21]

21 Rupert Davies was away for the summer at his house in Wales.

TUESDAY, JUNE 4, TORONTO: I meet Burgon Bickersteth at the College at 11 and show him over it for an hour; he is tirelessly curious and enthusiastic, and likes it very much. What energy these old men have! I greatly like him; a gentleman but not caught in the *persona* of a gentleman—very easy, interested and delightful. No wonder he did so well and meant so much to generations of men!

But at the College there is confusion, and architect, contractor, and Eaton's are at odds. One problem: our stairs are cement, and Ron says they were never meant to be finished in wood. But we would like wood. However, our wishes are as nothing in the vendetta between the Foundation and the architect: the Masseys keep saying, "We must teach Ron a lesson," and considerations of College and of us are nothing to that. Bill Broughall has intervened, and as always, I don't know how much he tells me he has said to the Masseys is truth and how much Irish phantasia. But I am worn down and rather frightened, and for the first time wish I had never been involved in this mess. But the only path is forward. Bill Broughall warns me that Lionel has a notion that if he inherits Batterwood he will give it to the College right away, in trust, to ease his tax situation. Will resist this; it would sink us.

In the evening I lecture on *The Comedy of Errors* in the Edward Johnson Building to a good audience, over 300. Home by 12.

THURSDAY, JUNE 6: In the afternoon to Toronto and to the College, where confusion reigns, as Lionel Massey told me in a morning call. We rest at Hawthorn Gardens, dine at the club, and I lecture on *Timon* to a much bigger audience. To the Stewarts', and home by 12:30.

SATURDAY, JUNE 8: Work all morning at the *Examiner* on sorting and throwing out. To the Curriers' for a pleasant dinner and evening of talk. This is a strange suspended time. We are grateful to

the old house but not regretful at leaving it. We have been happy here but hope to be happy in the new life and cannot indulge in luxurious, meaningless regret.

SATURDAY, JUNE 15: <u>We move into the College.</u> At last I sit in my study at the College to enter this diary, after a week of hard physical work and some spiritual strain—breaking with the *Examiner* and leaving the Peterborough house which we all liked so much, and in which we had known so much family unity and happiness. It took Tippet-Richardson two days to pack our traps—Friday and Saturday, the 7th and 8th. Sunday we hung in suspense in an echoing house; Monday they loaded the van and almost did not get everything in, as they had underestimated my 150-odd cases of books—we drove to Toronto and dined with Helen Ignatieff and the Goldschmidts and slept at Hawthorn Gardens. On Tuesday from 8 a.m. to 5:30 p.m. they unloaded here, and at 7 p.m. I gave the third of my pre-Stratford lectures, on *Troilus and Cressida*, to a crowded house. On Wednesday the men unpacked and chaos descended. Thursday and Friday we settled things about, dealt with new things that were delivered, dealt with tradesmen and painters and men with noisy floor-polishers, and people who wandered in off the street (including six army padres from Trinity) who "wanted to see the new building" and were huffy that they could not trudge through our house. Coped with the fire inspector, who insisted that we should have a hose on the wall on each floor. In the midst of this I tried to do something about our liquor licence, which it seems we may not get until late autumn, as Eric Phillips, the great "fixer," has not fixed it, so I have asked the aid of Leslie Frost.

Claude Bissell sends me a draft of the ROM committee report, which appoints Dr. William Swinton as director for two years; this galls Lionel as Swinton is now set above him, and I think Lionel has been ill-used. Phillips and Bissell, he says, promised him the

directorship: Bissell denies this. But Claude Bissell is a man in a great hurry and I do not think Phillips a man to depend on, so the truth is probably somewhere in the middle. I can see Bissell's predicament: obviously he is worried, for he called me on Friday morning for advice about what to do with Lionel, and I suggested that some face-saving device be found. Thus I discover myself in the middle of the *mêlée*. The plain fact is Lionel could *not* decently be appointed: he is not qualified, and it would be taken as a naked *quid pro quo* for this College. His trouble is at least half imaginary. He is well paid and has a job well suited to his capabilities: he could make himself indispensable. But he yearns to be top dog. He visited me this morning in my study and almost wept as he went over the story several times. So already this room has been a scene of passion and a measure of intrigue. This place already demands a degree of hospitality strange to me but I must learn to do the polite.

Our first visitors, Wednesday night, were Hart and Ron Thom, and for the first time I truly liked Hart: his level-headedness in dealing with what his father and Lionel confuse with emotion, and his charm and courtesy as a guest, are winning. We shall be friends yet. Ron tells me a carpenter rushed to him, saying, "You know that nice room we fitted with all those nice clean shelves? That fella's put a dirty old brown bookcase in it!" My fine 1800 bookcase! My study is indeed a fine room and the whole house is beautiful, though plagued by the ills of new houses—doors that bang or won't open—doors that won't shut—no space for food in the kitchen—the stairs still naked concrete. But we are here and College life has begun.

Bickersteth has written most kindly, asking a blessing on Brenda and me, and our work here. I take this seriously, for without God we shall do nothing—"Except the Lord build the house, they labour in vain that build it."[22]

22 Psalms 127:1.

MONDAY, JUNE 17: I called Claude Bissell and visited him at 12, and for half an hour we discussed Lionel Massey's *crise nerveuse*. He is sympathetic but annoyed that Lionel called Vincent Massey and made a to-do, and indeed it is rather shrieking for Daddy. Claude is willing to help Lionel save face and shows me the letter he is sending; together we tinker it, offering Lionel the title of associate director of the museum, which he will love, and a good leave of absence. I think this generous of CB.

To Stratford with Brenda. We picnic in the motel. The eleventh Stratford Festival opens with *Troilus and Cressida*. A good production by Michael Langham but perhaps not enough emphasis on Troilus's disillusion, which may have had something to do with Peter Donat, who is not really a romantic actor—just a handsome man. He thinks a man in love shows it by clumsy tumbling about and being tongue-tied. He fumbled and left out some of his great Act 1, scene 2 speech: "O Pandarus, I tell thee, Pandarus, etc." He was often out in his lines, and missed "heel the high lavolt," a favourite phrase of mine. He was coltish, rather than a young prince. Martha Henry as Cressida worthy of a better partner: delicate, wanton, fresh, and enough to rouse the desire of every man in the house. But Diana Maddox as Helen was a Welsh tub and James Douglas as Paris laughable—insignificant, petulant, and meanly colloquial. As Nestor, Bill Needles was just as he was last year as Gremio: presume this was Michael Langham who seems to have Tony Guthrie's obsession with youth—old age always contemptible; but there is more in Nestor than this. Max Helpmann a good Agamemnon, Leo Ciceri an excellent Achilles, and Douglas Rain brilliant as Ulysses—spoke the "degree" speech and "Time had, my lord, a wallet . . ." superbly. What a good actor but how unsympathetic! Hutt a very good Pandarus—epicene, wincing, but coarse as hemp underneath. Had shaved his arms; some of the others very woolly for Greeks, especially Garrick Hagon as Patroclus—a

masculine whore should not be so goatish about the legs. Tony van Bridge played Ajax rather like Bottom. Eric Christmas admirable as Thersites—a man consumed with spleen but a sort of left-handed moralist. Beautifully dressed, and good music by Lou Applebaum. On balance very good. The audience were not greatly pleased, but they must learn to know a great play that is not an obvious favourite. They accept disillusion in modern drama: let them savour it in a great classic.

WEDNESDAY, JUNE 19, STRATFORD: *The Comedy of Errors* produced by Jean Gascon. Play begins: *zanni* enter to pleasant music; one gestures us to our feet as "The Queen" begins in seventeenth-century manner—but stops just before "Long to reign over us": audience sits, puzzled, then the orchestra plays last seven bars of "O Canada." A good joke though some took it in bad part. Play done *commedia dell'arte* style and perhaps a little too much so: a great deal of shouting, falling about, and precious capering, but no moment of poetry, no lull in the storm. Eric House and I agreed afterward that it was a mistake to be as funny as one can at all times. They created in me, at least, a sense of wearisome strain. Kate Reid good as Adriana; Martha Henry, as Luciana, was so tidied and primped that she looked commonplace; her beauty is of the now fashionable just-out-of-bed kind. Donat stylish as Antipholus of Syracuse, and Christmas a good clown as Dromio of Ephesus. As Pinch, Hugh Webster had a wig that caught fire, a good device. After to the cast party and had a pleasant talk with Michael Learned, Donat's wife, who is truly beautiful and charming, and she flattered me so that I quite lost my heart to her for half an hour. She is a natural blonde, with an exquisite skin and easy, endearing manners.

FRIDAY, JUNE 21: There are mice in this college, and very impudent mice, too. We must get a College cat. Intruders still frequent, though

not as bad as a week ago. But signs of Private and No Admittance mean nothing to the university community. There is water at the base of the dumbwaiter shaft. Colin Friesen has made peace with Commercial Caterers, so *that* is settled. Finch is having some work done in his rooms and his carpenter—a German—says the College work is very shabby. How ready people are to complain and sow dissent! Received today H.W.C. Davis's revision of *A History of Balliol College* and read with amusement about its founding and the period before 1283 when money was always in doubt. History repeats herself, though never word for word. Bill Broughall still worries that the Masseys might desert the College but I have more confidence: for their family name they dare not do so. But if they do I shall not hesitate to make public comment, and the university could not let us down. It may be rough, but I think we shall manage somehow.

WEDNESDAY, JUNE 26: We see Miranda off to Jamaica.[23] Then to Peterborough for an *Examiner* directors' meeting and to close 361 Park Street. Feared we might be deeply depressed, but as soon as we entered the old house we knew it had gathered itself together and knew us no more: it had that indescribably Victorian smell, of damp chimneys and old plaster, not disagreeable, but old and private. It did not remember us, and was back in some dream of the earlier owners, the Dennes and the Gilmours. When we returned to our brand-new, unfamiliar, and untamed house, we knew that we were home, or in the place we must make home.

SATURDAY, JUNE 29: Yesterday Swinton was announced as director of Royal Ontario Museum and Lionel Massey as associate director. I saw Lionel last night at the Balliol College dinner at the York Club and he seemed very pleased, but did not want to discuss it and even

23 She was going to stay with Graham and Joan McInnes.

brushed aside a man who congratulated him, as though modestly dismissing any thought of honour. Ha ha! Trouble with cheeky visitors continues. At 5 this afternoon I challenged a young man who was taking pictures in the quad. Yes, he had climbed the barrier, disregarding the sign: he was an architecture student and such notices were not for them. Said he knew Thom and a building belonged to the architect in a truer sense than it could ever belong to anyone else. And more, in the same vaunting vein. Had to be stern with him.

I blush to record that since coming to this building I keep seeing, from time to time, little black figures running from my approach— about eighteen inches high, with goat hindquarters and tails— heads are horned. I glimpse them out of the corner of my eye. Devils, plainly. I know there are rats here, but these are not rats. What does it mean? Am I visited with Luther's capacity to see devils, or is my sight amiss, or is this exhaustion?

THURSDAY, JULY 4: Tonight Brenda and I go for a holiday; got none last year so we look forward to it eagerly. We leave things here in pretty good condition—gates going up, water going into the pool, etc. Glad to get away. I need time to think of what the College really means, and how it can be made to do its best work.

Now that Rob and Brenda were installed at Massey College, and with the College opening scheduled for September, they departed for an extended European holiday, travelling by sea on the outward journey.

FRIDAY, JULY 5, MONTREAL: To the *Franconia* and find our cabin, M29, more like a hotel room than quite becomes a ship. Breakfast heavily, as we are very hungry, and establish ourselves as senior inhabitants of the ship. We are put at the captain's table, a dubious

distinction, with Mr. and Mrs. Higgs of Worcester—steel-rolling machinery, and Mr. and Mrs. Blake of St. Louis—administrator of a music school. Mrs. Blake a compulsive talker and boasts about her only daughter, who is twenty-three and has a Ph.D.—all but dissertation. In the afternoon to film, *Some Like It Hot* and were refreshed by Marilyn Monroe's soft beauty, so unlike the metallic lustre of many screen idols. We eat, fashionably, at the second sitting, and finish dinner in time to stagger to bed. Brenda looks better already and I think I do so, as well.

WEDNESDAY, JULY 10, LETTER TO MOIRA WHALON
Dear Miss Whalon,[24]

. . . I see the carpenters' strike is on; I hope it is not holding up our carrels or the finishing work. Did Gord and Fred complete the list of minor jobs in the Lodgings? Staining the floor inside the heating case in my study, for instance, and making the windows work properly. Their intentions were excellent, I am sure; but their execution was sometimes weak.

We are having a calm voyage: just enough movement to be pleasant, though a few people have been ill. Mrs. Davies and I have slept day and night, recovering from rather a lot of worry and dashing to and fro, of which you know the details. Did the Porter tell you we have a raccoon in the College? The sooner you get that cat the better, and it should be a BIG cat, or a kitten with unusual promise, and we should give it a fine College name, such as Diogenes, Socrates, or Hodge—Dr. Johnson's cat was called Hodge and it was a very learned cat. Of course, if it is female it will need to be called Saint Catherine—Kitty for short. If a eunuch, call it Nathan Cohen.

Enough of this frivolity. When you send the mail to Leighton,

24 Davies and Moira Whalon, who had moved to Toronto to become his secretary at Massey College, remained on formal terms for most of the thirty-nine years she worked with him.

would you include a line to say how things are going? I hope all goes well with you.

RD

WEDNESDAY, JULY 10: Land fever begins to possess the ship. Cocktails with Captain R.J.N. Nicholas, who has been invisible because of two cracked ribs. He is a roundabout, nervous man with no social sense, and seems to have memorized every conversational cliché, which he yelps in a high, cheerful voice. Why do big steamship companies make their expert navigators double as salesmen and greeters? Our mysterious table steward, who looks like a bargain basement Laurence Olivier and has a soft, palavering voice, proves to be an Irishman named Kennedy.

THURSDAY, JULY 11: Wake when we anchor at Cobh, Ireland, and the wonderful "otherness" of Europe hits me again, and strongly. It is a sensation of a world I long for, and love, and partake of in part, but which is never mine. Where am I at rest? Not here and certainly not at home.

SATURDAY, JULY 13: Dock at Rotterdam in heavy rain and debark with the minimum of trouble about 12; the taxi to the station tries to cheat me but I am getting better at this sort of thing and circumvent him. To Amsterdam by train and gape at the rapidity with which we dash through virtually all the principal cities of Holland on our way. To Hotel de l'Europe, an old-fashioned, nice place, and are put in 213, which one enters oddly through the bathroom. Late lunch in their excellent restaurant, a little daunted by mail from home. Four airmail letters from Miranda in Jamaica about *la vie diplomatique chez* McInneses, which make up, I think, the best-written letter I have ever received in my life. She has great gifts of observation and expression.

This was a holiday, but both Rob and Brenda were serious tourists, and Rob again maintained a detailed travel diary of their holiday trip to Holland, Denmark, and Scotland, including Shetland, and then to Wales, where they stayed with Rupert and Margaret Davies at Leighton Hall. Jennifer joined them there, and then she and Brenda visited Brenda's aunt in Cornwall while Rob went on his own to Oxford for a few days of contemplation and practical research for running Massey College.

TUESDAY, AUGUST 6: We leave Leighton, and I am saddened to say goodbye to WRD on the platform at Welshpool, for these partings in Wales cannot be many more, and I have come to associate him with that country more than with my childhood. At Shrewsbury I wait—it seems for hours—for my Oxford train. Once aboard I settle down to my task for this part of the journey: an examination of my life and an attempt to clear the decks for the next developments. I have some success, but so intimately does this sort of thing affect me that I become rather ill, and arrive at Oxford with a headache and some sensations of a cold.

Oxford station is bleak as ever, and had some trouble getting a cab. To the Mitre and I am taken back to my first visit to this hotel, when I "came up." What a place it is! Leaning heavily on its 500 years as an inn, quaint, uncomfortable, and smelly, the only modern thing being the offhand slovenliness of the staff. Set out to walk the High and looked in at the Examination Schools and revisited the Schola Magna Borealis, where I used to hear Tolkien, and the room where I had my *viva* from Chambers and Simpson.[25] I visited All Souls, and the University Church and Jesus College. Did it all with thoroughness and was footsore by dinner. Afterward

25 E.K. Chambers and Percy Simpson were among the leading Shakespearean scholars of the time.

walked Beaumont Street, which I greatly admire, then to Nuffield College, the quad of which has ornamental water like ours, and down to Folly Bridge. Back to the Mitre very tired; hot bath and asleep by 11. Why do I feel ill and apprehensive here? The town is somewhat disappointing: dirty and squalid and noisy: the noble buildings seem to sit in a trash heap. And such crowds! Also the shops do not seem to be so good as in my day. I wander like a ghost—or no, I do not wander, I pelt doggedly along, like the Wandering Jew—seeking not only my past, but my present and my future—indeed myself.

WEDNESDAY, AUGUST 7, OXFORD: Woke feeling heavy and depressed. But after breakfast my day takes a sharp upward turn. I phone Peter Swan,[26] and his wife tells me he is expecting me at the Ashmolean: go there, pausing at St. Giles for a moment, and find him very agreeable. We talk of the Royal Ontario Museum and I tell him he is talked of to follow Swinton as director: we discuss matters very frankly and openly for an hour. Then to Balliol and have a thorough look at the chapel and hall, and look again at No. 8, Staircase 22, my old room: new furniture, which is not surprising after twenty-seven years. Thoroughly enjoy my visit.

Swan picks me up at the Mitre at 12:45 and we go to St. Edmund Hall, of which he is a professorial fellow: sherry in the Senior Common Room and lunch with the dons in an upper room. VERY pleasant and I am amused at the combination of squalor and splendour: two dusty Anglepoise lamps and some paper parcels in the Senior Common Room—over-driven boy in a dirty white coat serves a poorish lunch. But who cares? The spirit and the conversation are good. Swan is a good example of the Oxford type I like—learned, merry, and easy. Tells of a remark of Sparrow,

26 Peter Swan, then an assistant keeper of the Ashmolean Museum.

warden of All Souls, deploring the marriage of some of his Fellows: "Imagine"—looking around Hall—"imagine giving up all *this*, for a single body!" Swan is married to a very good 'cellist and has three daughters, the eldest nine. Says Lionel Massey is a very good fellow "but a dreadful snob." Yes.

Swan walks me up to St. Antony's, in a former Anglican nunnery, to meet its bursar, an agreeable man who tells me how they cope with Junior Fellows' wives and advises against too many rules, with which I wholly agree. Gives me their statutes. By cab to Nuffield and meet B. Keith-Lucas, who gives an excellent account of how they manage small conferences there, usually Friday to Sunday and get first-rate people to sit in with their students. All of this very encouraging and crystallizes things I had dimly apprehended. He shows us the college and I think it not so fine as ours. See Piper's[27] chapel and do not much like it. His bulbous candlesticks quarrel with the scrap-iron cross and reredos: good stained windows, the Damned and the Blessed, but who can say which is which?

At 7:15 to the New Theatre to see *Wildest Dreams*, Julian Slade's new musical comedy, and advertised as successor to his *Salad Days* and to *The Boy Friend*: indeed it is so—an innocent charade, amateurish in production, unsophisticated in humour, literate but not adventurous in its music—and savouring very much of a rather better-than-average university show. But the English love this sort of thing, and not all the *West Side Story*s and *Pal Joey*s to come across the sea can shake them. And have they not much right on their side? This was a jolly, agreeable evening, putting no strain on the ear or the intellect, and the well-to-do innocents around me were loving it. But one felt that one was too old for such artless nonsense. Back to the Mitre and had fish and hock and Stilton, and so to bed.

27 John Piper (see May 13, 1961).

THURSDAY, AUGUST 8, OXFORD: Stirring with the lark, and buy ties, handkerchiefs, and whatnot, and at 10:30 to the pen-maker, R.C. Phillips in Oriel Street, who listens patiently to my difficulties and says he will make a pen to suit my needs. Then to Blackwell's and buy some nineteenth-century stuff, including sets of Barrie and Wilde. Then to Balliol and looked at the new and good arrangement of the library, then to visit Corpus and Merton, got my tailor-made pen from Phillips, and to Evensong at Christ Church Cathedral, in the chapel in which I was confirmed.[28] Found all of this peaceful, restorative, and productive of ideas useful to Massey College. I have an opportunity to reconsider what Oxford *is*, and to see its grubby and commonplace side, as well as to recapture its charm and richness. And I wonder if, after all, we cannot, with diligence and luck, get some of what is best to flourish in Toronto. It would never be Vincent's dream Oxford, but that does not exist here, now, and perhaps never did. But the attitude toward learning, and toward life, may be transplantable in the special circumstances that confront me.

This evening again to *Wildest Dreams* because there is nothing else to do, and because popular entertainment is now my line. It stood up to a second viewing better than I would have expected, and some of the songs are really very good. So back to the Mitre for another ghastly supper, and to bed happy that my visit to Oxford has fulfilled my hopes of it so well. Impressed that at the bottom of the Balliol war memorial appear the names of five Germans; one, von Bohlen und Halbach, was up with me. That is the proper spirit—the feeling of "all my sons" proper to a great house of learning.

28 After leaving the Presbyterian Church, Davies was confirmed as an Anglican on March 1, 1937, by the bishop of Oxford.

FRIDAY, AUGUST 9: To London and meet Brenda and Jenny and take the train to Canterbury, where Burgon Bickersteth[29] is waiting for us, and at once to the Chaucer and lunch with him. He is very pre-1914, says "menoo" (menu) and snaps his fingers at waiters. Then to the cathedral, and from 2:30 till 5 he keeps up a fascinating, learned and dramatic lecture on history and art and shows us what I presume are the highlights—noble glass, fine tombs, the library, the Chapter House, site of Becket's shrine, and the noble Romanesque crypt, and the St. Nicholas chapel which he and his brother decorated as a memorial to their parents. See also the Dark Entry and Meister Omers, his former home and now part of the school. Then tea with him at his flat, which overlooks the cathedral. We rest till dinner (but not JBB, who at seventy-six is indefatigable) and rejoin him for the meal and for most of the evening. He talks of his work as prison visitor, and talks of cracksmen who won't touch a job under £10,000, of Billy Hill the king of the underworld, of murderers, etc. Tells of a Toronto marriage in which two homosexuals were "married" with ring and nuptial sermon by a homosexual priest. Tells of the fate of those who "scream" on another criminal. Fascinating. Tells me he has altered his will and his letters now come to Massey College. We leave about 11, and look at the great cathedral in the moonlight before resigning ourselves to the austerities of the Chaucer. A great day at the heart of Anglican Christendom, with a wonderfully knowledgeable and devoted guide.

Burgon, like many old men, tells surprising details in conversation. Telling us how one of his prison friends stole his repeating watch: "I went into the w.c. to relieve myself; of course I've had the prostate operation and can relieve myself instantaneously; so I

29 Bickersteth had retired to Canterbury, where he grew up. His father had been a canon of Canterbury Cathedral.

wasn't more than thirty seconds and when I came out he was hurrying back down the hall." Interesting, but odd in his charming Edwardian speech before Brenda and Jenny. But one of his charms is an assumption that everyone is as well-bred as himself and that among well-bred people anything is permissible for conversation. I heartily agree.

FRIDAY, AUGUST 16: We fly at 12:30 to Prestwick, then on and arrive in Toronto 10:30 English time, or 4:30 Canadian. The flight the usual dull business: I read *Brideshead Revisited*. No trouble with Customs, but no sign of Miranda and Rosamond! They are at last discovered in the parking lot, having waited a long time, wondering if they had missed us! So home to great talks and a good meal, and cleanliness and comfort, and Jenny's first sight of the new house. And how good, and familiar and home-like it looks! Thus ends our holiday and it has achieved, for me, all that I had hoped. I am rested and refreshed; I have dredged up some good ideas for the College and—more important—have achieved a concept of the College and an attitude toward it which are coherent and firm without being inflexible. Could not have done this by brooding on the spot. My time in Oxford was invaluable, personally and in the inquiries I was able to make about work at St. Antony's and Nuffield. So it has been a huge success, and I hope that from now on we shall be able to travel regularly. And that, so far as this journey is concerned, is that.

SUNDAY, AUGUST 18: At once we are engulfed in College considerations: Ron Thom's parents were in a dreadful accident, his mother killed, his father badly hurt, and grievously distraught. Vincent Massey is on the warpath about the building, which is still a long way from finished. In the house there is no sign of stair carpet and spare beds, and idiots have fastened the TV aerial to the chimney,

very prominently, just as we did *not* want it. But furniture is in and the Library shows progress. Saturday morning I wade through the accumulation of correspondence; in the afternoon Tanya Moiseiwitsch comes at 2:30 and we have a good chance to discuss the chapel seriously. Sunday, at 11, VM, Hart, Sedgwick, Friesen, Tanya, and I meet and discuss the chapel and decide to defer decision on the phoenix until all else is done. VM is pleased with the altar furnishings we turned up in London.[30] He tried the bell, and was as pleased as a schoolboy: it gives forth a clear, respectable, but undistinguished note. On Wednesday the Archbishop of Canterbury[31] is coming to view, and he will formally ring it for its first official or acknowledged time, but I mistrust unrehearsed effects and wanted VM to test it. We also have our Visitors' Book, a handsome piece of work by Liselotte Stern, and although it is not supposed to be ours till October 4, the archbishop will sign it. Would we miss the one hundredth Archbishop of Canterbury, and lead off with Professor Ezekiel Gump of Dogpatch U? Not bloody likely!

MONDAY, AUGUST 19: Colin Friesen shows me the piece in *Maclean's* (August 24 edition). Its tone is nasty and some of the things it says are downright lies—such as that seven men run the College and five of them are Masseys. He tells me also he was asked to a cocktail party where they tried to pump him, and he learned that a girl in the corner, to whom he was not introduced until he insisted, was a *Maclean's* writer. We agreed that to say nothing was best; when we show what we can do, much of this sort of criticism will be disarmed.

In the afternoon, Tanya Moiseiwitsch, Vincent Massey, Ron, Lorimer, Sedgwick, Howard, and I meet in the chapel and quickly

30 Rob and Brenda had brought photos of a chalice and candlesticks they had seen at S.W. Wolsey in London.
31 Arthur Michael Ramsey was the one hundredth Archbishop of Canterbury.

decide what is wanted. Why quickly? Because Tanya has prepared an excellent water-colour sketch showing what she suggests, and VM bought it with enthusiasm. Ron could learn from this: they *see*, they do not *hear*. Then to the Round Room and Hart tries to persuade us that the Master's chair should be six feet tall in the back and upholstered in red velvet! Why? To give an "accent" of colour against the white wall! No thought that the poor brute who sat in it might look rather ridiculous. I argued against it and won. Then to the Senior Fellows' Dining Room—a long haver. Then the fountains, which look like fire hydrants and gush in an ugly, blubbering fashion. VM wants the heads and pipes submerged, and a thinner jet. All this takes from 3:15 to 6:30, and I am almost dropping with fatigue. But they return at 8:30 and we play Lights-in-the-Quad, and Unwrap-the-Founders'-Cup (which is a beauty), then choose the colour for the lampshades in the Hall. Then comes the lectern, and the ill-fated Ron has forgotten his plan: so he goes for it, while we wait. VM and Hart veto the canopy: without it the thing looks like a Baptist pulpit, but Hart, who wanted six feet of red velvet in the Round Room for an "accent," thinks the canopy (which is light and pretty) is too ornate. They have their way, of course, and VM says that if it proves that the canopy is necessary it will be added later. Says jocularly, "The Master will keep after us till we do." But I say, "If you decide against it you will never hear it mentioned again by me"—I am too proud to tease for canopies. But I think they are wrong and so does Ron. Then we adjourn to the Lodgings and sit in the drawing-room and chat and show them the house. Hart's wife, Melodie, has joined us. It went well but VM does not like anyone to talk but himself, and in a large group—there were nine of us—this means some silences. If a by-conversation begins, he stops short and glares until the offenders shut up. A busy day and much done. I regret the canopy, but one cannot win all battles, and I have had my way in much.

TUESDAY, AUGUST 20: Spying Ernest Sirluck in the quad, I hail him in. We talk for an hour about the relation of the College and the Graduate School, and I think we understand one another and can work together. I am encouraged. Lochhead has excellent ideas about the Library, bibliographical exhibitions all through term, and pictures in the Common Room on loan. Then talk to Colin Friesen about keys, and maintenance. Felt that the *work* of the College became more real today.

WEDNESDAY, AUGUST 21: Visit from the Archbishop of Canterbury. The Ramseys arrive with Vincent Massey at 4:15 and have tea with us. We offer an English tea—thin bread and butter, light cake, and fruit cake. They are charming and easy, the archbishop very quiet, which surprised me for his pictures suggest a thunderer. Then we tour the College and to my delight he spends most time in the lower library, which should impress VM, as other scholarly visitors will do the same. When we have done the tour, the archbishop rings the bell at five o'clock, and away they go. Our first grandee dealt with pretty well but not so well as we shall learn to do.

THURSDAY, AUGUST 22: Ron Thom comes to the College in the afternoon and we go to Hall and discuss the lectern; he is going to try again. Meeting in my study of Vincent Massey, Miss Leavings, Friesen, and myself at 5:30 to discuss the opening parties; we make good progress. But VM inveighs constantly against Ron, and I fear for Ron. He is dreadfully incompetent, dilatory and ill-organized, but he is an artist of capacity and should not be bullyragged. He is at fault in many things and I am as vexed with him as anyone, but he is not to blame for everything. If what I hear is true, Hart is very slow about approving and returning plans—but of course VM will hear no word against Hart. Now VM

has made Friesen his agent to push the building through to completion, which pleases me, and I hope it will save time and hurry things up.

This morning I tried to get some sense out of Gow about our licence, but who ever got satisfaction from a lawyer? He assures me our application is in and complete, but the secretary of the licensing board says November is the earliest we can hope for a hearing. Discouraging. Leslie Frost and Eric Phillips, the great "fixers," have fixed nothing for us. One of the problems here is keeping one's courage and optimism in repair. And keeping the wood in mind as one stumbles from tree to tree.

FRIDAY, AUGUST 23: Call from Colonel Phillips, very affable: says he had been on the phone to "our friend" and had been given an assurance we should have our licence in October and could have a banquet licence to tide us over from September 20. This is splendid, but I wish I knew who "our friend" was: Premier Robarts? Leslie Frost? Judge Robb? Called Gow and asked him to go ahead. He is somewhat hesitant and I understand why: these fixes are delicate matters and he may put his foot in it. But I feel better about it. Junior Fellows come in to bring their traps; they look a decent lot on the whole and I am less worried about budget than before. Painful lumbago all day and much incapacitated.

SUNDAY, AUGUST 25: The weekend makes work—*real* work, and what I call work—possible. I have written 300 words for an architectural magazine and 1,200 words for the *Times Literary Supplement* about the College. Vincent Massey called Saturday morning to say that Eaton's had asked that a sign be shown at the openings, saying they had done the furnishing! He dealt tactfully with this. Gave him Friesen's quite good news about progress here, but he does not want to hear anything that might lessen his anger against Ron.

I persuaded him to omit the usual approval from Ottawa (i.e., Hart) in the case of the lectern.

MONDAY, AUGUST 26: Eric Rump, a Junior Fellow in English, has moved into his room— our first man in residence; wish he were not quite so early. Lionel Massey calls this evening: sounds weary, but better, and his enthusiasm for the College is unfailing. Ron comes in to make a sketch for the lectern, and discusses Tanya's fee with me—a matter she brought up herself as she had no notion what it should be; he suggests $2,500, which I think steep, but who can say what an artist's work is worth?

TUESDAY, AUGUST 27: A day of varied crisis, beginning with the discovery this morning that we have no hot water; this proves to be because the superintendent's department has failed to inform us that they shut down on the 23rd for their annual overhaul and inspection and will not resume operation till September 3. They also failed to speak of this when they examined our plans and saw we had no auxiliary heating system. So after much discussion they admit themselves at fault and will assume most or all of the cost of whatever electrical installation we need. But this is not achieved without much brouhaha. Meanwhile a storm brews about a mechanic's lien against the College by a steel company amounting to about $1,000, which is unpaid; but the Foundation are withholding $200,000 from Eastern Construction, to be paid when all deficiencies are made good. Eastern want their money; the Foundation will not meet them or their lawyers to discuss the matter, this being Hart's stand—"It would be too embarrassing." Consequence, a possible row in which Eastern might take all men off the job for thirty-seven days, with resulting liens of all sorts from subcontractors, and the Foundation in court. The law and reason of all this evade my understanding, but Bill Broughall and

Ron are very exercised about it, and of course it makes completion of the building difficult, and creates ill-will where none need be. What suspicious people the Masseys are and how high-stomached! I shall get hold of Lionel tomorrow and see if I can make peace, and Friesen is trying to untangle the rights and wrongs of the matter.

WEDNESDAY, AUGUST 28: My fiftieth birthday; Brenda gives me a beautiful loving-cup, Irish, by Matthew West, 1780, Dublin, which makes a fine figure on my study mantel. I feel a little unwell, for it is thundery weather and my sinus bothers me; I hope for a quiet day. Books come from Blackwell's and I get them on the shelves, and in the afternoon settle down and read *Auld Licht Idylls* for an hour to my great content. But at 5 Lionel Massey comes (looking much better than when last I saw him) and gives me the other side of the fuss about the contractor; then Friesen comes in and substantially supports him. In the middle of this, Vincent Massey calls, fidgeting about invitations for the various parties. At 6:30 Ron Thom arrives and puts his case to Lionel; nobody's stories quite jibe. But by 7:10 they have all gone, and McCracken at Brenda's bidding attempts to ring the bell fifty times. But something goes wrong and after forty-seven strokes it will ring no more, and we go out for dinner at the Lord Simcoe, and to a film, *Sparrows Can't Sing.*

THURSDAY, AUGUST 29: Make some progress planning my graduate course on nineteenth-century theatre, and collect an ominous mass of manuscripts which must be read for the Epstein Award.[32] Vincent Massey calls and fusses about parties; what a man for

32 The Norma Epstein Foundation Award for Creative Writing is a national contest open to students registered in an undergraduate or graduate program.

detail! Bill Broughall calls, still very cross with the Masseys; but I begin to know Bill for an emotional Irish blatherer; a good fellow but says far more than he means and loves crisis, so I soothe, but do not heed him. Ernest Sirluck comes to lunch and is an excellent guest. Afterward we discuss the College *vis-à-vis* the Graduate School and he advises (1) seeking some contact with the Graduate Students' Union; (2) circularizing the heads of graduate departments; (3) inviting graduate clubs to use our Upper Library; (4) putting up visiting lecturers gratis; (5) seeking the good will of the Canadian Association of Graduate Deans; (6) giving an affair for the Canadian Association for Graduate Studies on 21 and 22 October; (7) having continuous bibliographical activity and exhibitions; (8) trying to have some presentations of recondite drama or music; (9) trying to establish an annual gala – *son et lumière*, poetry, or whatever; (10) seeing that lots of non-College men come in for dinner; (11) seeking the good will of the *Varsity*;[33] (12) advising Junior Fellows not to regard themselves as an elite. All good, and some of it in train already. Says also, if we truly establish our Library as a Canadiana centre, he will try to persuade Claude Bissell and Robert Blackburn, the chief librarian of the university, to make over *all* Canadian material to us. We part on excellent terms.

Lionel Massey comes in to say all is well with the contractors. Colin Friesen comes to say the work on deficiencies is going ahead. Then George and Norah Harris come to see the College, and Norah is pleased that part of her $500 donation should go on a first edition of *The History of Emily Montague*.[34] They are surprised and delighted with the College. Books from Rota in London come,

33 The University of Toronto student newspaper.
34 Frances Brooke, *The History of Emily Montague* (1769), generally considered the first Canadian novel.

including the three Kelmscott[35] volumes I am giving to the Library for an opening gift; they look even better here than in London. Douglas Lochhead also tells me he has bought Carl Dair's hand press for $200, a great addition. So things progress and the *reality* of the College begins to assert itself.

FRIDAY, AUGUST 30: Lionel Massey is in crisis again for Bill Swinton has had some form of collapse near Edmonton, where he was on a dinosaur hunt. Claude Bissell appears unexpectedly about 3:30: I show him what has been done and he is impressed and repeats what Sirluck said yesterday about transferring the Canadiana from the central library to ours. Coincidence, or have they been talking? Prepared a draft of a statute defining Visitor and Master: Brenda says it is like writing one's obit to lay the plans for retirement before one begins. But I must keep the Senior Fellows busy and interested, and statutes are impressive. I used Nuffield and St. Antony's as models, but changed and I think improved some of their wording.

SATURDAY, AUGUST 31: With Brenda to St. Lawrence Market for a change of atmosphere. A feast of autumn colour and bought a lot of asters, which I love. The cries very good—"Fresh, fresh, fresh from the sea! Alive, alive, alive!"—as he holds up a small octopus, chilled to inertia. And "You can't live on love; you gotta have meat! Here! here! here!"

Have completed my draft statutes and written Vincent Massey about the October 4 ceremony transferring the College from the Masseys to the Master and Fellows. Talked to the porter, who has a good ceremonial sense and thinks we could seat 160 in the Hall and have people standing.

35 The Kelmscott Press, established by William Morris in 1891.

This evening heard records of *La Bohème* as preparation for my lecture on September 17;[36] am also reading Murger's book,[37] which is a far better work of art than Puccini. Disturbed that my study will be noisy; footsteps and talk in the Common Room very plainly heard.

MONDAY, SEPTEMBER 2, LABOUR DAY: As we mess about with kettles and cans of water heated on the stove, I am annoyed to find in the minutes of our Foundation meeting of September 16, 1961, that a note was sent to the architect about Item 48, an auxiliary water heating plant. I suppose he forgot it, as he has forgotten so much else. Vincent Massey and Hart are right—a brilliant designer but a damned poor architect.

Tuesday, September 3, was the first day the College was officially open, but Davies did not see it as a day of celebration.

TUESDAY, SEPTEMBER 3: Reached a low ebb, and wondered seriously whether I had not made the mistake of my life in coming here. Processions of people, many of them on the most trivial pretexts, occupied my time; I shook hands till I was distracted. Chatter, chatter! Had much business to do; Miss Whalon got no lunch; I do not think I had ten uninterrupted minutes from 9:30 to 6. By nightfall I was too broken to read or recreate myself in any way, and told Brenda of my despair. We are both suffering from the public character of our life. I think with awe of the master of Balliol, whom we so rarely saw when I was there, and of Dr. Homes Dudden of Pembroke College, who sat in his study editing Fielding,

36 Davies was to lecture for the university's Department of Extension (today called the School of Continuing Studies) on the Canadian Opera Company's season.
37 Henri Murger, *Scenes of Bohemian Life* (1847–49), on which the libretto of *La Bohème* was based.

and appeared like Jove, from time to time. But I am always on call, and if I do not do what is wanted, who will? I must find a way out of this labyrinth of tiresome detail, or it will kill me. Was I a fool to give up the dullness, with retirement, of Peterborough, for this frantic place?

WEDNESDAY, SEPTEMBER 4: Remarkable contrast: a day in which all goes well and much is achieved. An architect, Professor Acland, comes to see the College and write a piece. How brash, possessive, and patronizing architects tend to be toward another man's work! I got a walk in the afternoon and went to Britnell's, where Roy Britnell entertained me with tales of the vanity and impudence of the late Perkins Bull.[38] Returned and shortly Vincent and Lionel Massey appeared. VM ages apace; dodders slightly, but rallies quickly; forgetful in an old man's way; tells you something twice in five minutes. Also: "Everyone is astonished at our fees; we must raise them." And: "Rob, are we going to have to call all these young puppies of Junior Fellows 'Doctor'? What nonsense, when the president of Princeton is always called 'Mister.'" I hope VM is not going to become a pest about such things. But he approved the lectern *with* canopy! And was philosophical and sensible about the likelihood of thieving of silver and china. Old men are extraordinary; they go soft in patches and are admirable in other realms.

A cat joined us today, a gift of Bette Hooper of Peterborough, grey with pretty white markings. I name it Hodge, after Dr. Johnson's great cat, and Miss Pat Kennedy,[39] of the Library, has taken it to her heart. It slept on the shelf beside the *Oxford English Dictionary*, a good omen.

38 Prominent lawyer and politician; grandfather of Tom Symons and Scott Symons.
39 Pat Kennedy came from York University, where she had been secretary to the chief librarian, to serve as the Massey librarian's assistant and later as assistant to the bursar until she retired in 2009.

THURSDAY, SEPTEMBER 5: Colin Friesen and Douglas Lochhead give me their introductory letters to the Junior Fellows: DL's is good, but CEF no stylist, so I do a lot of work on it and remove the business clichés. Spent some time with him allotting rooms to the Senior men; how good they are! Lionel appears with Lilias and his daughters to look at the building and come in for tea; I tell him what Claude Bissell and Ernest Sirluck said might come of the Library and he was delighted—truly enthusiastic. Says also that a man who has left his all to the College is sick of a cerebral hemorrhage. God, what vultures we become in such cases! I do not even know the man—I think his name is Hudd[40]— and wish no harm to him but—how much has he? Lionel says "a small estate" but however small, it is more than we have now. These are vile thoughts.

FRIDAY, SEPTEMBER 6: Sinus headache. Morning on College affairs. Ron Thom sets the lectern in train at last. Then to Stratford to see *Cyrano*[41] with John Colicos in the lead: better than Plummer— more chivalry and high breeding, as with the Orange Girl in Act 1, and he can do *adoration* as Plummer could not. Also he was more repellent in appearance—grotesque sausage of a nose and huge eyebrows, creating a fox's mask. Diana Maddox very good as Roxane, for she makes sense of her words and is not so trivial and selfish in impression as Toby Robins. Eric Christmas played Ragueneau and had blunted his naturally sharp nose, so that he looked like all the really *French* actors.

SATURDAY, SEPTEMBER 7, STRATFORD: H.t.d. Visit Dama Bell. Matinée of *Timon of Athens*: a triumph in modern dress. Langham

40 Frederick Hudd, a friend of Vincent Massey's, died in 1968 but it was many years before the estate was settled. The Hudd Fellowships to offset Junior Fellows' fees began in 1978.
41 The Stratford production of *Cyrano de Bergerac* had been revived for a second season.

has created a corrupt timeless society of opportunists, among whom Timon is a rather vulgar tycoon. Some minor liberties, not so much with the text as with interpretation, but justified. Imaginative business, as when Lucius is importuned for a loan in a Turkish bath; Lucullus (in a hairnet) as he admires a fine bronze in a crate marked "Sotheby's" which has just come. Alcibiades's revolt cast in the uniforms and mould of Castro's. Apemantus played by Douglas Rain as a newspaper correspondent, with fine compassion. Do not know why Duke Ellington had to be got for the music, which sounded exactly like what Lou Applebaum has been writing for every tragedy for the past ten years. Fred Euringer played Cupid rather as Dr. Stephen Ward,[42] but had not the art to project it sufficiently, and his clumsy step was out of character. Colicos splendid as Timon: magnanimous, brainless, proud, and at the end, a disintegrated wreck. Admirable variety of voice; it is here he so far outshines Plummer.

Rest at the motel and h.t.d. To the evening performance of *Troilus and Cressida* again. Now much firmer—William Hutt and Martha Henry and Douglas Rain all much improved, as was Garrick Hagon. Peter Donat not. The pathos of the play more marked. Both *Timon* and *Troilus* productions are very modern in spirit, but on the same day such a dose of cynicism and misanthropy is strong.

Afterward to the Bells. I hear *Comedy of Errors* is all to bits, and very coarse and disordered now. It was headed that way. Alf Bell says Peter Hall[43] ill and Michael Langham may be offered Stratford England and what will Stratford Ontario do then, poor thing?[44] Helen Langham dislikes Stratford Ontario (very provincial, she says, with some reason) and will be strong to change.

42 Ward's role as the facilitator in the Profumo scandal in the U.K. had been much publicized.
43 Sir Peter Hall was then artistic director of the Royal Shakespeare Company.
44 "What will poor robin do then, poor thing?" From "The Robin," a traditional nursery rhyme.

SUNDAY, SEPTEMBER 8: All my married life I have suffered occasional brief periods of impotence, always associated with stress. I can never convince myself that they will pass. From August 21 to September 6, I was powerless and this was distressing both for Brenda and me. Night of September 6—no go; then in the night an emission; lay with Brenda on waking and again later in the day, very powerfully. The holiday at Stratford did it.

The weekend was splendidly restorative. We must find a way of coping with this place so that we are not exhausted and maddened by it.

MONDAY, SEPTEMBER 9: I was amused this morning by Ron, who appeared in the quad at 9, fussing and making a show of efficiency. "Nobody returns my phone calls: nobody keeps appointments: nobody does what they promise," etc. The pot calls the kettle black. The ineffable Lorimer fusses most of the morning because his firm has not had enough garden party invitations and think themselves slighted. Lionel Massey comes at 10:30 to discuss parties: he looks better. Peter Swan comes to lunch. I hope he may succeed Swinton at the ROM. Doug Ambridge wants to be shown the College just when I have settled for a rest. Colin Friesen discusses his problems of maintenance staff: I insist that we need weekend porterage. Colin Friesen creates confidence: a very good man.

I call in Robert Dinsmore, a Junior Fellow in English, and discuss with him the *terrae filius* wheeze for our October 4 ceremony. A pleasant young man and I think he will do it and do it well.

In the evening to the opening of the refurbished Royal Alexandra Theatre, which has been rescued from demolition by "Honest Ed" Mirvish, the discount-store man. A handsome restoration by Herbert Irvine in deep reds, white, and gold. Makes it look bigger, and the foyers also, as a lot of partitioning has been taken down and original fine proportions restored. The ushers wear tawdry

livery: velvet coats, silk breeches and slippers—but badly cut and poor in finish—and the doorman looks like something from an ice carnival topper. These stupidities are not Herbert Irvine's but the inspiration of a friend of Mirvish. There is even a foyer for the second balcony, decorated with pictures of those who have played at the Royal Alex—only one of Martin-Harvey, and that bad, in *The King's Messenger.*

But the play! *Never Too Late* by S.A. Long, a vulgar trifle about a couple in late middle age who are about to have a child. Produced by George Abbott in his run-about, shouting style of the '20s: a bathtub and toilet on stage, a drunk scene, a dully lecherous young woman—nothing spared us. So truly *vulgar*—and everybody belting out comedy lines facing over the footlights. Brenda and I were almost dropping with *ennui* by the first interval and would have left if we had not been invited guests. Champagne afterward and many professed themselves delighted with this trashy thing. There are a lot of rich rubes in Toronto.

TUESDAY, SEPTEMBER 10: In the midst of the hubbub began writing my lecture on *La Bohème.* At 3 p.m. Vincent Massey brought in his friends the Airds and Mme. Roy to shake hands. The Masseys met in the Senior Fellows' Dining Room at 4, with Friesen and Ron and Miss Whalon as secretary. I was not present. Miss Turpin, Vincent Massey's secretary, phoned at 4:30 to know if VM had taken his 4 o'clock pill! They appeared in my study at 6:30 greatly exhausted, having harried Ron to their satisfaction. Gave them a drink and they lingered till after 7, by which time the Architectural Conservancy people were assembling, almost a hundred strong. Let them in, gave them a talk about the building, and let them wander. Got some dinner about 8. Got the Conservancy people out by 9:30, by blowing a whistle in the quad and turning out the lights. Then with Brenda to the Faculty Club to a party given by

D.C. Williams[45] for Boyd Neel, Geiger-Torel,[46] Mavor Moore (who could not be there), and me. Very agreeable.

WEDNESDAY, SEPTEMBER 11: Took an hour to get my hair cut. One cannot be consumed by this place. Howard has very skilfully accentuated the coats of arms in the Round Room. The Masseys come to my study to discuss the ceremony of October 4, and of course Hart, that Friend of the Minimum, is against a *terrae filius*. So I argue, and it appears he is afraid it might fail! Of course it *might*, but I shall take care it *doesn't*. Poor wee man, failure is so much bigger to him than to the others. But Vincent Massey is on my side, and it is to be, though they don't like the notion of the bull's head: how they fear mockery! But I shall contrive something.

In the afternoon a meeting of the ROM committee, which at last begins to look as though it might wind up. When Peter Swan lunched with us he confided to me that on this continent he tends to eat too much and becomes constipated—the English preoccupation. But he ate a lot of our home-made bread, and three peaches, casually, after downing a lunch that was sufficient for me.

Lionel called after dinner about College details: the stonework is going up over the gate and the Founders' Plaque has been redone. Tells me not to worry about Hart, who has quarrelled with Ron and with his father.

In the evening visited Rosamond in hospital, who had her tonsils out earlier in the day.

THURSDAY, SEPTEMBER 12: In the Round Room this morning find a red velvet chair for the Master; Howard tells me it was ordered some weeks ago; only yesterday Vincent Massey asked me what I

45 Carl Williams, psychologist, director of the Department of Extension.
46 Herman Geiger-Torel, general director of the Canadian Opera Company.

thought about such a chair and I said I was against it. How arbitrary the Masseys are, and I think quite unconsciously. Well, I shall have to accept it, I suppose, as I beat them about the lectern, and Lochhead needs another display case in the Upper Library. Ron's is too small and, as it only opens underneath, ridiculously inefficient. VM has sent in what he called "quite a short list" for October 4. With the Senior Fellows and Junior Fellows it would be about 250, and the Hall will not hold so many. He has all sorts of Port Hope neighbours and such nincompoops as Esmond Butler on it. How do I cope with the growing tendency of the Masseys to domineer in this place and intrude their silly social pals into it? Must find a way. Tanya Moiseiwitsch arrived at 10:30 and is organizing work on the chapel. Delightful person: she stays with us, and she and I play duets after dinner.[47]

FRIDAY, SEPTEMBER 13: Most of the morning in chapel with Tanya and Howard, then Coughey, the picture framer, who is framing the cross, then a man from Strand Electric about lights. I surreptitiously coloured the pool a blue-green with ink, to its great improvement and Friesen's delight. At 4 a meeting in the chapel, where a wall has been painted. Vincent Massey: "Well, Hart, what do *you* think?" (Pause, longer than Olivier in *Henry V* film when the French ambassadors bring the tennis balls), then, "Well, I think I preferred it without the paint on the pebbles." (This in the grinding, icy voice of a hanging judge.) He continued to be negative throughout, saying at one point that he thought the whole chapel fake and theatrical in concept and design. Ron was shot down about his design for a light fixture. Fool, he had no model, only a mechanical drawing, and tried to show what it was like with his hands. Of course it failed, and of course they ate him. I am now heartily sick

47 She was the daughter of the great pianist Benno Moiseiwitsch.

of these nervously exhausting meetings about architecture; they disgust me, as shows of wilfulness and caprice, and ill-understood personal animosity disguised as taste and principle.

In the evening we had the party for the workmen: I think they all came and it was a considerable success. Only one or two embarrassments, as when the Masseys had forgotten to provide cigarettes and Jenny had to rush out for a carton, and when Kendall the metal man cornered Vincent Massey and lectured him on Ron's shortcomings and why he, Kendall, was late with the ironwork. I was very pleased that of our Senior Fellows, Gordon Roper, John Polanyi, Tuzo Wilson, Bill Dobson, Caesar Wright, and Robert Finch all came. The College is quite a different place with people in it—the Hall truly beautiful and the quad at night splendid. Made a blunder in supposing vm sufficiently softened by success to be persuaded to leave the fountains alone; but no—he went off like a bunch of Chinese crackers. True, they are not the best, but what he proposes will be vastly worse.

To bed very tired. It is not the work, it is the expenditure of tact, the holding of the tongue, that makes this a job that would be a challenge for Sisyphus. vm asked me what I thought of the Round Room with all Ron's huge square pottery ashtrays on the table. "It looks as though someone had laid covers for the Last Supper," said I. A joke softens him a little, but not for long.

SATURDAY, SEPTEMBER 14: The Masseys on one of their tours in the morning, and after came to my study to discuss the list for our October 4 ceremony. Vincent Massey very understanding and cut his list heavily. The Harrises are to be asked because of Norah's gift, which pleases me.

Our garden party from 4 to 6 for all the university and civic officials who had been involved in settting up the College was a great success: splendid autumn day and the College looked as if it had

been here for a century. Guests wandered at will, and had a very bad tea and chatted, and seemed to enjoy themselves: compliments about the building on all hands and the Masseys so far reconciled to Ron that I hope the fountain matter may be resolved. Afterward vm and Lionel, Lilias, and Evva, their daughter, and John Polanyi's wife, Sue, with us and Tanya Moiseiwitsch into the Lodgings and had well-earned drinks, and vm gave his impression of the action of a drum majorette, lying on his back on the sofa, to amuse Tanya. She has made a conquest of Bill Broughall, who wants to know where she has been all these years! He knows nothing of the theatre. He had to tear himself away as one of the Pekes is due to whelp and he must cut the cord as it seems these undershot-jawed creatures cannot do it for themselves.[48]

SUNDAY, SEPTEMBER 15: Michael Langham calls at lunchtime in a swither because Jack Winter of York University attacked him in the *Star* last night. The usual nastily worded stuff; says some things I have said—Donat a cloddish Troilus, Kate Reid a gorbellied roarer—but in hurtful terms and Michael is stung. He talks of libel and urges me to reply on behalf of Stratford! As if any libel of a creative or performing artist were recognized by the courts, and as if I were a mastiff to be released against enemies. Just like Alec Guinness during the first year of Stratford, whom I was called in to advise when he got so hot about a spiteful article in *Maclean's*. Have written a letter to Michael advising masterly inaction. He is oddly unworldly: was it his long term as a prisoner of war that made him so?

WEDNESDAY, SEPTEMBER 18: Enjoyed this morning for it was the kind of work I can do for the College better, I think, than anyone. Talked to Robin Green, a Southam Fellow, about his work—he

48 Bill and Zoe Broughall bred Pekinese dogs.

wants to be a drama critic; talked to Jack Best, a Southam Fellow who thinks his journalism degree (Western, under George McCracken) was wasted time and is going to do political economy here. Talked to Duncan Fishwick, who is to be don of Hall and is composing our Latin graces. At 12:15 to Hall and ate lunch—an invited group including Lilias, Misses Leavings and Whalon, Brenda, Jennifer and Rosamond, et al. Very good: juice, soup, steak and kidney pie, two vegetables, salad, and choice of pastry, pudding, or fruit—all excellent quality. A great success. After lunch Lionel comes in. He wants to persuade his father the chapel should be non-denominational: Sirluck has put a bug in his ear. I encourage this and it may come off. But Lionel says he and Hart are concerned at the change in VM during the past six months—intransigent, forgetful, capricious, in fact an old man. This could make great difficulties in the years to come.

THURSDAY, SEPTEMBER 19: Junior Fellows come in all day, in drenching rain. Talk to Robert Abra, one of the Southam men, a good chap but nervous as he is not a university man. First dinner, and I go up with Fishwick, who gives them Hall rules and reads the anteprandium.[49] He is nervous and speaks of "Massey Hall." A good sight to see them at table in their gowns, and all very decently dressed. Take the family to dinner at the University Club.

FRIDAY, SEPTEMBER 20: At last some information about our licence: Judge Robb well disposed, and says I can dispense liquor from my house, and is there no way by which I could sell it there! A typical civil service notion—turn my house into a blind pig on the q.t. because the regulations are so stupid! But the word is still the same: a licence late October or early November. At 5:15

49 A Latin grace said before dinner at the College.

assemble most of the Junior Fellows in the Common Room and talk to them about the College and the hospitality in our house, and the College Conversation,[50] which I began today. It seemed to go well, though everything is a bit sticky—all new men, no friends re-met after vacation or any of what greases the wheels in such places. But a beginning has been made and one must work slowly. Speed will only bring mistakes.

SATURDAY, SEPTEMBER 21: Our first strictly College lunch in the Lodgings. Robert Finch, Duncan Fishwick, Blake, John Rigby, and Smith. Give them sherry, trout, salad, a Bavarian cheese, fruit, and coffee. None of them smoke: it goes more and more out of favour. All goes well, except that Smith had not acknowledged his invitation and had to have his intentions inquired after by the porter. Offered cheese, he said, "Aye, this is the cheapest kind you can get in France." A Methodist, from Blackpool, and a mathematician, he has spent all his spare time working in settlements. Fishwick socially skilled, Rigby a jolly parson's son and deft, and Blake a medieval-English man. Finch, of course, a great help.

To University College to talk to freshmen: tried to say something about the pursuit of knowledge as a path to wisdom and thence salvation, or integration, or maturity. Did not do it as well as I should, and I think the theme was too strange for many of them. Gordon Skilling, of Slavic Studies, who spoke after me, was much better. Afterward, a boy of eighteen with a creditable beard and moustache tackled me: wants to write, but how can he give all to his art and at the same time acquire the rich experience from which to write? A girl next: adores the theatre and wants to work with me. The third, a boy, very precise: what must he do to get into

50 Davies posted quotations to encourage dinner conversation among the Junior Fellows.

Massey College? He can act—"I'm English-born, you see, so I'm pretty good at it, and of course I can put on the accent"—but is going to protect himself from entangling alliances, to see how to get the most out of the university. All freshmen. Better the first two, innocent and silly, than the third, calculating and self-seeking.

SUNDAY, SEPTEMBER 22: Lionel phones about 7 p.m.: Vincent agrees entirely about the non-denominational character of the chapel. He has entirely forgotten his conversations of January 20. This suits me well enough: an Anglican chapel would be little used and might affront some people who associate that church with Toryism and the English ascendancy. Personally I would like to have an Anglican chapel, but I know my desire is unwise from the point of view of the College's future. Once again Lionel emphasizes—get everything you need before Christmas.

Tonight some ladies in Hall as guests: we progress and I am purposely making haste slowly.

WEDNESDAY, SEPTEMBER 25: The problem this diary now proposes is—what to record? *Minutiae* or only the big things? But who can say what trifle may swell into something of significance? Consider the farcical scene of February 22 when the chair for the Fellows' dining-room was so hacked about: would we had hacked the dining-room chair for the Hall as well, for the spikes on the back make self-service and maid service devilish hard and things are spilled. And the little banners on the table lamps drag in the food. Friesen is worried already about the heavy catering costs. But I refuse to be depressed: he and the Masseys must worry about money, and if I do so in detail I become a lodging-house keeper and an impossible head of a college.

This is the week of university freshman initiations, and last night we had several girls invading us at different times because they had

been told they must get one of our crested forks in a scavenger hunt. Some crept through the gate when a Junior Fellow was going out: six got through my garden gate and were trapped: three were darting up to Hall when I nabbed them, just as McCracken took them in the rear. Nice children, except for one spectacled piece (a school principal in embryo, obviously), who wanted to argue that she should be given a fork in the interests of women's rights, or freshman encouragement, or some such nonsense. Was firm.

This morning at 9 a.m. our first Ph.D. exam in the Round Room. The candidate, a chemist, arrived betimes: a real scientist, a gowk with an ugly voice who described the College as "pretty." Ten examiners were listed for him, but to get a quorum distress calls had to be sent out. One of their number says he may get his degree with some protest as there is serious doubt about his conclusions. But he got it, and departed as self-satisfied as he came.

What wears the spirit in this job is the continual necessity to praise people for doing apparently simple things in which one is not really interested—the man who puts on the locks, the man who advises on whether or not the Hall chairs should have nylon slides on their feet, etc. If one has a beard, and is called "Dr.," one must be a fount of praise and reassurance, and what a bore it is!

THURSDAY SEPTEMBER 26: A long day, during which I did not set foot outside the College and rarely out-of-doors, which simply will not do. Began the day by venturing into the quad and struck up a talk with John Ower of Alberta, a raw youth who wants to do his thesis on Edith Sitwell, whom he considers "a worthwhile poet, but limited." The impudent self-assurance of the prairies; he is a child, but full of green learning. At noon Vincent Massey came, and savaged Jowett, the photographer, who, it appears, is working for Ron, though Ron denies him and abuses him: Ron is devious. Jowett, though a nuisance, is following orders. Lunched in Hall: a bad

lunch, after which VM came to my study and we settled on a non-denominational chapel, and discussed his book, which appears October 4! What a glory-day for him! Then Robert Dinsmore, the *terrae filius* for October 4, comes in and VM reads him his verses[51] for October 4, and I suggest to Dinsmore that he read VM his notes, which he had given me: this was mean of me, for Dinsmore's notes were careless, undergraduate, and rather offensive, and spoke of VM as a "has-been governor general." I wanted Dinsmore to realize that the humour of insult was a more complex mechanism than he knew. Kept him in somewhat horrified suspense for a moment, then let him off the hook. An afternoon of furious business—when do I do my scholarly work?—and at 6 Lionel comes in and we go to Hall. Fishwick had brought Father Shook and Father Sheridan of the Pontifical Institute of Mediaeval Studies, both good talkers and witty. Excellent conversation at table and after in the Common Room. Then Lionel to my study and we talk of College affairs till 10:30. He tells me a significant thing: the accident which wrecked Hart's life was caused by Lionel throwing him downstairs: pituitary injury, a choice of blindness or no growth; then a serum found to encourage growth and it does; then Hart's wound in the Battle of the Bulge and the back of his head horribly injured and the serum can no longer be used. Result: Hart as he is, and Lionel with a sense of guilt and obligation. Poor, poor Lionel! How life has pummelled him! Poor Hart; who can, at last, blame him, chilly, negative mani-kin as he is?

TUESDAY, OCTOBER 1: As the 4th draws near, excitement mounts, and work increases. The Junior Fellows, having found their feet, now want all sorts of things—billiard tables, ping-pong; the Upper

51 Davies's plan was that the *terrae filius* should read a satirical verse on the establishment of the College, to which Massey would reply, also in verse.

Library for personal cocktail parties, a laundromat, a coffee-vend-
ing machine—and all this must be handled with tact. In the *Star*
on Saturday, September 28, Arnold Rockman published an ugly
piece, ostensibly about the building but blaming us for neglecting
women and New Canadians and leaning toward WASPs, and also
finding fault with the Senior Fellows as coming from within "the
contact network of the Massey family and the U. of T." Why are gifts
and benefactions treated to this sort of cankered criticism? This
article, I fear, means that any further writing for the *Star* would be
out of the question for me. Yet when I tell them so they will un-
doubtedly say I have been forbidden by the Masseys or am afraid
of them. I resigned from the editorial board of *Saturday Night* be-
cause of its vicious attack on Vincent Massey, and Jack Kent Cooke,
the owner, never spoke to me afterward. One of the Southam men
tells me the *Telegram*'s attack on the College was set off by a memo
from John Bassett, the publisher. For years I have been defending
the newspapers against their detractors, but how true it is that the
Toronto evening newspapers, hugely rich, are controlled by little,
vulgar minds.

Yesterday I was so over-driven I had to go to bed at 8 p.m., after
a day which culminated in tasting claret with Lionel to choose
one for the 4th. Chose a South African Roodeberg at $1.40 per
bottle, which was what I wanted anyhow. At 6 Vincent Massey
called in a swither: Bill Broughall and Zoe were not asked to our
dinner party beforehand on the 4th and would they not be of-
fended? Of course they would, but we have not been fortunate in
our social relations with them. So Brenda calls, and Bill says they
would be delighted. Meanwhile a letter arrived from Geoffrey
Massey: he and his wife accept for 4th: so Jenny has to be dis-
missed from table.

In the evening with Brenda to the Canadian Opera Company's
Aida and enjoyed it thoroughly, as a distraction from all this.

Excellent and most refreshing. Ella Lee sang Aida sensitively but strongly; the costume designer had put her in a straight orange sack and with her short neck, big bosom, and thin Negro legs she looked oddly triangular. By contrast Cecilia Ward as Amneris looked beautiful but sang and acted weakly. Victor Braun, last seen by me in *The Gondoliers,* was an admirable, direct, convincing Amonasro—really a savage with the single-mindedness of a primitive.

WEDNESDAY, OCTOBER 2: Telegraph Geoffrey inviting him and his wife to lie with us, as decency rather than inclination dictates. Brenda phones Zoe Broughall, who called last night when we were out: Bill has accepted without thinking, as another Peke bitch is due to whelp and they must be at its side. Bill calls me and blames himself for having left Zoe alone in the critical hour on September 14, and the puppies died! God, these childless people! Then a telegram comes from Geoff. He is coming alone. So Jenny is back at table and a real Massey crisis has been provoked about somebody else's dinner party.

Claude Bissell calls: he doesn't want the Master's stipend specified in the statutes, as a non-professional person might get it, and also "someone of substantial private means." What fussers they all are! Sometimes I wonder very seriously if I have not made a grave mistake in accepting this maddening job. My heart misgives me. These academics are so capricious and waspish.

THURSDAY, OCTOBER 3: This morning I had a chat with Bill Dobson in his rooms and tell him how harassed I feel; he comforts me by saying that when he was setting up the East Asiatic Department he thought the university as a whole was in league to denigrate, thwart, and humiliate him, and there were dark days when he thought he would shoot himself; sleep was a stranger. Found all this comforting. In the afternoon, a meeting of the College Corporation in the

Round Room for the first time, and all were present but Phillips, Bissell, Gordon Roper, and Raymond Massey.

VISITOR

The Right Honourable Vincent Massey

MASTER

Robertson Davies

SENIOR FELLOWS

C.T. Bissell, President of the University of Toronto

V.W. Bladen, Dean of the Faculty of Arts and Science

W.H. Broughall, Barrister-at-Law

W.A.C.H. Dobson, Professor of Chinese

J.C. Eayrs, Associate Professor of Political Economy

R.D.C. Finch, Professor of French

A.R. Gordon, Professor of Chemistry, Dean of Graduate Studies

Geoffrey Massey

Hart P.V. Massey

Lionel C.V. Massey

Raymond H. Massey

Lieut. Col. W.E. Phillips

J.C. Polanyi, Professor of Chemistry

G.H. Roper, Professor of English

J.T. Wilson, Professor of Geophysics

C.A. Wright, Dean of Law

I had previously had a long talk with Vincent in what are to be his rooms in the NE corner of the quad. He greatly likes this notion as he is understandably loath to be cut off from the College, which is so much his creation, and it is a small thing to do for him. We understand one another very well about this venture and I have

not seen him looking so well and alert in many months. The meeting went well—several men wore gowns and resolved they would wear College gowns at future meetings. Visitor's statute passed with one change, but we decided to hold over the Master's statute until Claude Bissell explains his objections. Was pleased by this show of independence, for though I understand Bissell's points, I thought him somewhat cavalier in his manner of stating them; I suppose Laddie Cassels or Frank Stone objected and Bissell simply passed it on.

Vincent Massey, Hart, Lionel, and Geoffrey all dine in Hall and are impressed by the young men they talked with. I sat next to a young Jesuit, a guest of Scott Dunbar, who evinced the subtlety and suavity of his order in such remarks as, "You certainly got a lovely plant here, Professor."

After Hall and conversation, Vincent, Hart, and Lionel came in for a drink, and we get on good terms and Hart is positively genial. I see VM to his rooms about 11 and returning find Scott Dunbar gazing into the pool. This grotesquely shy man became quite friendly, said how beautiful the College was physically and he hoped in spirit. We talked of religion: he grew up a Quaker and has sought what the Church of England has to give and cannot like it. Odd talk in the splendours of a fine autumn moonlight night. But this building encourages good and direct talk. VM and I rehearsed tomorrow night's ceremonial.

FRIDAY, OCTOBER 4: The morning goes in organization and being photographed with Vincent Massey in full academicals for his Christmas card. In the afternoon I have my first meeting with my graduate students about nineteenth-century theatre, eighteen of them. At 6:30 all the Masseys, Helen Ignatieff, and the Bissells assemble in our drawing-room and at 7 proceed to the Senior Fellows' Dining Room, where we had a meal carefully ordered and planned

by Brenda and clownishly served in the style of a bad restaurant by the College caterers—baskets of bread offered, "How d'you like yer steak?" hissed in each guest's ear, wine jellies as hard as Pharaoh's heart, and the wine (a good Moulin à Vent) poured out in brimming glasses, and no chance for me to try it. All bad and vulgar. But everyone knew it was the first try of the arrangements and the talk was good; Raymond Massey a splendid guest; we toasted VM's book. Returned to the Lodgings for coffee and brandy, then to the Upper Library to robe.

The subsequent affair[52] may reasonably be called a triumph: forty minutes and not one of them dull. The *terrae filius* surprise was splendidly effective and Dinsmore was excellent; the business with ringing Saint Catherine admirably timed; the party afterward rode on the crest of this and was really merry. I was very well received and especially by the Junior Fellows, which delighted me, and my speech went to laughter and clapping. I felt truly that in this hour I became Master—not chief administrator or landlord but *Master*— of this college and that its future lay in my power.

SATURDAY, OCTOBER 5: I woke with a feeling of peace and accomplishment. Chat with Vincent Massey in his rooms before he leaves. He tells me Bill Broughall broached his plan that the Foundation set up a separate trust with $1,500,000 for the College, with the Master a trustee, at the Foundation meeting on Friday, and it was shelved and Broughall was cross. But the seed has been sown and VM assures me the Foundation has no thought of deserting the College after five years. Nor do I see how it well can when the Massey name is on it, and I told VM so and he entirely agreed. I am not worrying about money. Hart, Geoffrey, and Raymond have all

52 This was the final handover ceremony in the Hall. There were a hundred guests including the Junior and Senior Fellows. Davies described this as "the birthday of the College."

been impressed and pleased by what they see here and it must have time to work with them. We must make the place live and live splendidly before we ask for money either from the Foundation or the university.

SUNDAY, OCTOBER 6: H.t.d. on waking. A wonderful autumn day: we go to Tuzo Wilson's cottage at Kleinburg. In the evening Green, Dick, and Levene come for coffee. This week marks the end of the very long haul to get the College built and going, and the beginning of the varied task of making it work properly.

SATURDAY, OCTOBER 12: A peaceful week compared with what has gone before but not without event. Lionel tells me Hart has written to Vincent definitely stating his opposition to endowing the College. Lionel and vm, however, want this and it might come to a vote. Too early to fuss, as Lionel sees that the death of vm or himself, or of Claude Bissell, could gravely endanger the College. They will move as fast as they can and need no prodding from me. Tanya was here Monday to Wednesday and the chapel begins to take shape; Ron's lighting fixture is complex and rather ugly but gives a good light; Norbert's[53] alternative looks well but may be too dim.

The *Star* is after me again to resume the "Writer's Diary"; Philadelphia offers $50 a column and *Montreal Star* $30, which is flattering and I am tempted. I reread some of the stuff and it is good. If only I thought I had true worth as a novelist! I know I am a good journalist. Should I do what I do well, or continue with what I want to do well? Malcolm Ross wants *Leaven of Malice* for the New Canadian Library, and I approach Clarke, Irwin, the publisher, but with small hope. But Ross thinks my novels important.

On Thursday Melvyn Pelt, a Junior Fellow, visits me, aggrieved

53 Norbert Iwanski, later the College's master cabinetmaker.

because Colin Friesen and Miss Whalon have been chipping him about feeding College news to the *Varsity* and Rosemary Speirs, whose March on Massey organization threatens to picket us. Pelt has no sense of humour and a poor grasp of grammar, but I try not to dislike him; how *do* these grammarless oafs get high marks in history? He greatly dislikes College Conversation and thinks it should be abandoned: how pompous! But apart from him the Junior Fellows seem to like it here.

On Saturday and Sunday of the Thanksgiving weekend, the quad was used really properly—several men lay on the grass in the sun, reading, and though there were some visitors, they were few. On Saturday Robert Finch in to see me about College music; he is getting a harpsichord and clavichord himself, and suggests the Masseys might consider putting in a baroque organ, and making this a home of baroque music. As Gordon Wry[54] has approached me about a small choir here for madrigals and kindred music, this makes good sense and I shall write to VM about it.

With Brenda and the three girls to Canadian Opera *Don Giovanni* at the O'Keefe Centre as part of our Thanksgiving celebrations. Orchestrally good under Walter Susskind, and Beverly Bower as Donna Anna and Frank Porretta as Don Ottavio sang splendidly. The best acting—good singing, too—from Jan Rubeš as Leporello. As Don Giovanni, Don Garrard fell into some common faults—a too domineering manner which made him severe rather than attractive, and a lack of humorous ease, or relish of his bad reputation. The demands of the role, of course, are phenomenal, and the notion of a philosophical libertinism hard to understand and convey. The sets, by Rudi Dorn, were well conceived and reminded me strongly of Portugal, but were crudely painted—and of course

54 Tenor and conductor. Wry and Giles Bryant began the Massey College Singers.

that stage is a killer. It killed Mavor Moore, whose direction was sometimes merely frantic and his use of the chorus inspired by despair. The use of Dent's translation, flat as it sometimes is, keeps one in mind that the piece is a comedy. In one way Mavor scored heavily: he walked the Commendatore before our eyes from the grave yard to Don Giovanni's hall, and it was thrilling—here the vast stage was employed with real imagination.

TUESDAY, OCTOBER 15: The much-touted March on Massey took place, 9:30 to 10 a.m. About twelve or fifteen girls, and one or two male sympathizers, shuffled back and forth outside the gate with signs. I accosted them and they came in and paraded around the quad, and I walked with Rosemary Speirs. Decent girls, and their complaint seems to be that they have to pay a lot for lodgings, and want a college. At least, that is what they told *me*. But they made it clear they have no hatred for Massey College as such. As a demonstration, a feeble thing, but they got lots of publicity. At lunch the Southam men, Jack Sword, and St. Clair Balfour were here and we ate in Hall. This is a part of my work here to which I bring no relish. The food is well enough but I am pernickety. But it went well and the men like the College, and Robin Green says the College Conversation is indeed discussed.

WEDNESDAY, OCTOBER 16: Jenny is twenty-one: we give her money and sundry gifts. She is to have an evening party on Friday.

SATURDAY, OCTOBER 19: The *Varsity* continues its weak harrying: the danger in this lies not in anything it can do to the College but in the impression these amateur journalists get that manufactured incident and one-sided reporting is news. The *Star* makes me a flattering offer to resume "A Writer's Diary"; they offer at least $110 weekly as my share—which means the income tax would not leave

me more than $55. But I have looked over the column for the thirty months or so I wrote it, and though well done it is thin stuff; if I take it on again, in fairness I ought to do it for at least five years, and the hack nature of the work, the mass of reading entailed, and the association with a paper I scorn all persuade me to refuse.

Bill Broughall returns to the attack on an endowment for the College and this time he may succeed, for he has convinced Lionel of its necessity, and has also discovered that Hart virtually cannot resign as a trustee, so his threat to do so is empty. Thinks $1,250,000 might be the figure.

Some Junior Fellows agitate for a coin-wash machine. What penny-pinchers they are! And there are thirty-seven private phones in College! How dare they bleat of poverty? Our Russian Junior Fellow, Vitaly Korsun, arrives Friday night about 10 with a camera and a paper suitcase and is astonished by the size of his quarters: "So many metres for one person?" he said. I have been asked to write for the *Varsity* and suppose I must, but only once.

MONDAY, OCTOBER 21: Last night I put it to my father—should I write for the *Star*? Immediately came the answer: "Certainly not; it would be *belittling*"—and a lot more about money never being the best reason for doing anything. So I shan't, and today as I sat in some Ph.D. orals, ideas began to occur to me for my novel, as though released by this decision.

Tonight Junior Fellows Bob Alden and Stewart Goodings came to me to discuss College affairs and talk about calling a meeting to work out some things with the Junior Fellows. Welcomed them warmly; this was what I wanted—for some proposals to arise from the College rather than being imposed from the top. They say that all but a few are very well pleased and now is the time to pull things together before the notion of the place as a convenient hotel gains ground. I am greatly pleased by this development.

TUESDAY, OCTOBER 22: Talked with Bill Dobson this morning about the establishment of the College character. We shall have to educate the Junior Fellows, he says, as they do not understand Common Room life. He says Toronto's notion of an academic is pompous and aloof—non-Oxonian. Interesting.

My Casanova play returned by CBC: Basil Coleman tried to interest them in it. But it is not their thing, and it seems to be an unlucky play. I should heed the finger of fate and abandon the writing of plays. Mine are not quite good enough, and much too good to be despised by the boobs of the CBC.

SUNDAY, OCTOBER 27: Week goes well and Alden and Goodings's circular has caused great discussion. Thursday Saint Catherine was rung for Jock (Tuzo) Wilson's birthday. Vincent Massey in on Thursday afternoon and is very well pleased with the way things are going. We discuss the baroque organ and decide to move slowly, which pleases me, for an organ is a solemn and somewhat limiting instrument for such a place as this: but we agreed to cherish the choir. No word of the endowment, but Lionel tells me it is much in mind and it is not a thing to be rushed; Colin Friesen has given Lionel budget figures to work on. Friday I spoke at Prize Day at Upper Canada College and thus missed a Foundation meeting here, but Friesen tells me Ron Thom is now bored with this place, and vexed because his light fixture in the chapel was rejected in favour of Norbert's development of Vincent Massey's original idea. Ron also made a scene in the Round Room, which was arranged for an exam and was, he said "a travesty of itself." Sad that he should leave this fine building in so sour a mood, but he is not a man to yield on anything and has a desire to freeze into forms of his making types of activity he does not comprehend.

Saturday a very long talk with Bill Dobson: met him in the quad at 11—he stayed to lunch and left at 4:30. Learned, sensitive, witty,

and far more fastidious in character than I. Saturday evening we dine with the Sirlucks: other guests, the Bissells, Bora Laskins,[55] and Robin Rosses.[56] Very good wine. Their children undisciplined and rude, and Sirluck plays that silly game of telling them they are nuisances without either sending them away or including them in the conversation. Sirluck much coarser at home than elsewhere: one sees what Dobson means. Claude Bissell talks very freely: he wants to get the stadium moved out of town and use that land more profitably. He grows more hawk-like, drives and pounces. I talk to him of an endowment for the College and he is keenly interested, as why would he not be?

Today (Sunday) my father and Margaret and my uncle Percy lunched with us to see the College, though the two old men did not go up to Hall as the stairs are many. My father offers to give some type for use with our Albion press. He stumbled on the steps leading from the quad to the Round Room, and I recognized for the first time that he is really an old man.

TUESDAY, OCTOBER 29: To Hamill in the afternoon to fill out *new* applications for a liquor licence, which have been required on the grounds that our first one was filed too long ago. I do not like this: is someone playing with us? Bill Broughall thinks so but he is professionally pessimistic. I am to appear on November 21 to represent the College. Hope this is a formality as we want as little publicity as possible.

Dine at the York Club with the Stewarts and to Grant Macdonald's exhibition of pictures, then home with the Stewarts. Excellent h.t.d.

55 Bora Laskin, later Chief Justice of Canada, was a professor of law, University of Toronto.
56 Robin Ross, registrar and secretary of the Senate, University of Toronto.

THURSDAY, OCTOBER 31, HALLOWE'EN: This morning there are bearded pumpkin-heads and one with McCracken's moustache on the tower and on each staircase; also a beard on the bull and a carp in the pool. Good! We have a sense of community here, it seems.

To a dull lunch given by Oxford University Press to mark the publication of *A Masque of Mr. Punch*: kindly meant but Ivon Owen, the editor-in-chief, has no talent for merry-making. Vincent Massey was here when I returned: his delight in the College grows; he talks very freely of an endowment, is sure it will come, and bids me not to worry. Meanwhile I must devise an order of service for opening our chapel. At 5:15 we have five men in for drinks and for the first time it was a bit sticky. Three talked well, but one, a surly mathematician, was rude and uneasy and another, poor fellow, who came wearing a sweater, never opened his mouth for shyness. We refreshed ourselves by going to the Pro Musica concert afterward.

SATURDAY, NOVEMBER 2: This morning Goodings, Beer, and Pross came to see me to report that their Junior Fellows' meeting on Thursday was a failure: nobody wants organization. But I already had heard this earlier as I had been in the Common Room talking to Rump, Levene, and Horn, who say the men are contented and do not like the Conversation, and I think I shall give it up, but perhaps not till Christmas. They are content with their association as they have it. Well and good—but I still want to pull the College a little closer together and will find ways to do so.

Must be careful not to take the College's rejection of an organization as a rejection of me personally: must make my influence felt by subtle means; the trump card is always in my hand.

TUESDAY, NOVEMBER 5: Curious and somewhat embarrassing incidents arise from the visit of Professor Richard Sterling, who

professes "government" (of all things) at Dartmouth, a very American type, ruggedly handsome and noisy, who is the guest of Jim Eayrs. Invades my study on Monday and makes a fuss about Quebec secession, which he declares to be imminent; he has been in Canada three days, "fallen in love with it," and had visited a nightclub in Hull where "Le Grand Tex" sang "God Save the Queen" and other subversive songs. On Tuesday he gave a seminar in the Upper Library: about seven attended because the lecture was a failure. Sterling attempts to discredit any contrary opinion by alluding to the racial background of the speaker—thus Gregor is a Czech, and a Jamaican is anti-U.S., and I am Ontario and thus a United Empire Loyalist Tory. Talks maudlin trash about "Mr. Lincoln"; declares politics, poetry, and religion are one, then regrets the U.S. did not arrange the assassination of Batista ten years ago. When I ask him to reconcile this with his loudly trumpeted Christianity, he says, "I distinguish between murder and tyrannicide!" Made a fool of himself in College: hugged Oragwu, that shy Nigerian, and urged him to make Lincoln his hero. When crossed by Silcox and asked to give facts to support his extreme views, he became huffy and said, "I have a B.A., an M.A., a Ph.D., I am a full professor at forty-two, etc."—quite discrediting himself. Discuss it after dinner with men in the Common Room and they are wickedly amused: Adler says, "We don't have to read about the Ugly American—we've seen him." Could hardly have believed this man if I had not seen and heard him. Later, Eayrs told me he had been warned Sterling had become very odd, but had not heeded because he owed Dartmouth a debt of gratitude for hospitality it had shown him.

MONDAY, NOVEMBER 11: Claude Bissell tells me he has had a letter from the secretary of the Ontario Temperance Federation, one Royal F. Moulton, warning him that the College is applying for a

licence, thereby bringing liquor to the campus, and advising Claude that they might make a protest. I do not like this, naïve though it is, and hope it does not create some difficulty on November 21.

SATURDAY, NOVEMBER 16: Robin Green goes on optimistically with his plans for a Christmas dance, and I gently warn him that the College must have a hand in it.

I have some conflict with Campbell Russell, the university Anglican chaplain, who does not like my "Prayer for the College" and wants to substitute some very conventional tosh of his own; my prayer may be Gnostic, but his is the old "It takes no brains to be a Christian and knowledge is dross" stuff.

Friday night Abra, a Southam Fellow, had a woman in the Common Room, though two notices call attention to the rule forbidding it. Was very angry but determined to sleep on it. This is my problem here: I have to control my irascibility and try to see reason. Probably he did not see the notices; he is a decent man and would not, I think, try to encourage anyone to break a rule. As the soothsayer told me, I must listen and learn— the hardest things for me to do, with my irritable, morose temperament. And so it proves: the woman was his wife, and she and their two children are here for the weekend and are enchanted with the College. How unjust it would have been to trample him. I wrote him a decent note, for a rule is a rule. But I am always at war with my urge to humiliate, dogmatize, thunder, and bash at people. My lifelong fault, a tempestuous, suspicious, resentful nature, and at fifty I am worse than I was at twenty.

WEDNESDAY, NOVEMBER 20: On Friday engineers raid the College, as they have found that the lock on the East Gate is useless—can be opened with a pen-knife; they play tricks with Brenda's potted tree. But what is serious is that they—or someone at the same time, for we have no evidence—stole the barometer from our hallway, a

handsome $75 one of which I was fond. Hateful to have to cope with such things but I phone Dean Lennox of Devonshire House, who is very decent and promises to investigate. John Ower, a gowk from Alberta, on Saturday lent his keys to some girls and threw McCracken into a fit. He has a suspicious mind about girls anyhow, and in justice, it is his job to maintain security. Had Ower in and scolded him, but not too much. Monday evening to Hart House to talk about the College to their graduate association—middle-aged men who play games there. They were intelligently interested. Then a chat with Joe McCulley, who is somewhat patronizing, but I can cope with Joe; he is not so bad a warden as Vincent Massey thinks, but he is a coarse bounder.

Tuesday, Sir Basil Spence, architect of Coventry Cathedral, visits the College and is extremely complimentary about it. I should note that on Monday, November 18, the long-awaited Polanyi child was born, to be named Michael, and at 1:30 p.m. we rang Saint Catherine nine times for him—the first child to be born to a Senior Fellow.

THURSDAY, NOVEMBER 21: At 9:20 pick up our lawyers Gow and Hamill at the Bank of Commerce Building, and by 9:30 to LLBO offices on Front Street and to a room with about 125 people in it, all prosperous and well-dressed but of greatly varied type. Judge Robb and his train ten minutes late. He enters; we rise with the abject courtesy of suitors; he gestures that this is needless, but not until we are on our feet. Hearings very rapid and conducted in an undertone as each group is called forward. We are the third called. He says, "There have been no objections made to your application. Is there anything you wish to add to it?" There is not, so we are smilingly dismissed, and I presume we are now a "licensed outlet" though this was not said, and I suppose we must await official confirmation. A reporter from the *Telegram* present,

especially because of our hearing. Hope they do not make a great thing of it.

FRIDAY, NOVEMBER 22: John F. Kennedy assassinated and everyone stricken in their characteristic mode; very depressed and chilled; dine with Grant Macdonald and the Stewarts at the Westbury. Grant stays with us.

SUNDAY, NOVEMBER 24: This has been a strange week strangely shadowed by death: the mayor of Toronto, Summerville, died playing hockey on Tuesday; on Friday President Kennedy was assassinated; on Saturday Aldous Huxley died of cancer. C.S. Lewis also died at this time. The mayor came to our garden party—a decent fellow. The news of JFK's awful death came just as I was about to begin my graduate lecture, and we had our work cut out to go on about mid-nineteenth-century drama in the face of such a brutal blow to the whole concept of civilization and order. Huxley's death affects me deeply. He was my favourite among living writers: reading *Antic Hay* when I was sixteen or seventeen changed my attitude to life, and I have read all his work since. His combination of a strongly religious feeling with a great and astringent wit appealed to me without wearying, and his last thing, *Literature and Science*, was in his best vein. Such a death makes one feel lonely, though I never saw him save once on the street in New York beside the garden wall of the Museum of Modern Art.

MONDAY, NOVEMBER 25: The university sobered, as the world is, by the assassination and the savage shooting of Oswald by Ruby; this is our civilization! The Kennedy funeral on TV, a vulgar affair in which Cardinal Cushing snarled the Mass in a voice like a Yankee auctioneer, while a tenor sobbed out the Schubert "Ave Maria": how do Catholics of taste stand it?

TUESDAY, NOVEMBER 26: Gow phones: Judge Robb has called and says some of his men may call to make some inspections and perhaps recommend some structural changes! Colin Friesen tells me that not a month has passed since February in which some inspector from the licensing board has not been here. A fortnight ago a fire department man and an RCMP man were here. I think we are being given the runaround by bureaucrats (1) to spite the Masseys or (2) to show Frost and Phillips that they will not be dictated to. I loathe the whole affair; it disgusts me to be "inspected" by these boobs who have no notion what a College is, and refer to it as "an outlet."

This evening to a reception at Derwyn Owen's for Miss Melinda Seaman, now principal of St. Hilda's and previously an English teacher at BSS. Owen tells Brenda "nobody lives on campus now"— one of his characteristic remarks, the wonder of which is that one cannot decide whether they are calculated affronts or inadvertent stupidities. I was cornered by George Edison, who vapoured about the Kennedy business, about which Canada had not shown enough national concern to please him: we are ruled by little men, Churchill would have done better, blah, blah, blah. He keeps shop as a philosopher at Trinity but I fear he is just an Irish rhetorician. Last night Professor K.E. Bullen of Sydney, one of the world's great seismologists, lay here: a quiet wee man with a wise monkey face and a hearing-aid, very pleasant.

SATURDAY, NOVEMBER 30: On Wednesday to a buffet dinner at the president's; about fifty guests. Such affairs, with ill-assorted guests, are not much fun. Poor Brett, head of textiles at the ROM, there in his wheelchair looking ghastly—a skeleton at the feast: how fortunate one is to have health! How dismal the women! One is not surprised if a man is a dowdy bore but somehow one always has hopes of women.

The College of Heralds writes to Vincent: we may *not* have the augmentation on the College arms; it is personal to him. But we have it, in stone, over the East Gate. VM thinks they have seen it in the *Illustrated London News* and are teaching us a lesson. I suggest we simply say the arms over the gate are the Founder's arms, and grind the hart off the chevron. Vincent thinks this an ingenious solution.

Brenda and the girls are helping Robin Green and his group with the floor show for the dance on December 13. I have written the girls some words for Mendelssohn's "Lift Thine Eyes," as a College song.

In the evening to Congreve's *The Double-Dealer*, done by the University Alumnae in the Coach House Theatre, which I believe used to be a synagogue, seats about 120, and has a good atmosphere, and one of those three-quarters round stages. Intelligently directed and well understood, but suffered from acting which was quite inadequate, though pain was taken to speak it as well as they could. Costumes dreadful and wigs seventy-five years out of period, and horrible on top of that. Restoration comedy is for the finest of professionals only. But in justice I must say this production gave us a good evening, not embarrassing or angering: what good amateurs could do, they did, and that is vastly better than not seeing the play at all.

SUNDAY, DECEMBER 1: Lay late while we decided on overseas Christmas gifts. Brenda finds constant hospitality a strain, but is doing a splendid job. As Christmas approaches I think the College is moving in right direction and a Christmas gaudy[57] would work well.

57 Davies was planning a gaudy, an evening of music and entertainment like those he had experienced at Oxford.

TUESDAY, DECEMBER 3: Put up the notice about the gaudy to be held on December 17 yesterday; today someone has scrawled over "The Master and Fellows invite . . ." "How can we invite ourselves?" Such bad manners, and I am angry. So many Junior Fellows have no manners, only the arrogance of the clever boy in a common-place family. But one of my jobs is to teach 'em manners, and to do that I must first of all be faultless in courtesy.

THURSDAY, DECEMBER 5: A catalogue of Canadiana from Joseph Patrick lists *Twice Have the Trumpets Sounded* as by "Tyrone Guthrie et al."[58] Just call me Al.

Rigby tells me a few men in College are exercised because the choir is called "Massey College Singers," as *they* were not consulted. What egotists they are! Told him to tell them that as they have no organization, no consultation of the College body is possible.

FRIDAY, DECEMBER 6: Chapel dedication at 5:15 to 5:40 and a handsome reward for all the work it has been to prepare it. Senior Fellows present: Bissell, Bladen, Dobson, Wilson, Broughall, Roper, Polanyi, Lionel and Lilias Massey, quite a few Junior Fellows, and the chapel full. Ecumenical service truly moving, and a good spirit was to be felt in the place. Ian Montagnes was much moved; Norbert was there, who did so much good work on it; also McCracken and his wife. Jock Wilson said, "It's like having a family chapel." And so it is.

I was really pleased when Lilias said, "Well, Master, you've brought it off again," which gave me warm satisfaction, for it is not easy to combine dignity with the warmly familial quality this service had. And I welcome the chapel: I would not have sacrificed a library to it,

58 Guthrie, Davies, and Grant Macdonald published *Twice Have the Trumpets Sounded* in 1954.

but that was not necessary. And religion? "People will accept certain theological statements about life and the world, will elect to perform certain rites and follow certain rules of conduct, not because they imagine the statements to be true or the rules and rites to be divinely dictated, but simply because they have discovered experimentally that to live in a certain ritual rhythm, under certain ethical restraints, and as if certain metaphysical doctrines were true, is to live nobly, with style. Every art has its conventions which every artist must accept"—thus Aldous Huxley. But there is more. I cannot get beyond the beauty and the solace of the belief, but I sense that there is more, and I want to be directed toward that—whatever it may be or however athwart the accepted notions of God or religion.

SATURDAY, DECEMBER 7: H.t.d. on waking. Shop with Jenny for Christmas. In the afternoon write a College ghost story which Brenda thinks will be good for the gaudy on December 17. Miranda's birthday party in evening; we lurk in gate room.[59]

SUNDAY, DECEMBER 8: Lay late. Work on story, Christmas cards, then walk an hour with Brenda in Forest Hill; in the evening, the Singers rehearse in Hall. We have entertained sixty-eight people here since Sunday last.

Little by little the mists clear and I see my way to what the College is and how it will work: I have over-estimated the maturity of some of the men and undervalued my great ally—time.

MONDAY, DECEMBER 9: Appointment with the president at 10 to discuss the statute about the Master, the possible endowment, the visiting-professor plan, and an appointment for Lochhead to teach

59 A room on the second floor of the Lodgings, over the gate, was used as a sitting room by Rob and Brenda. It was more private than the main-floor sitting room.

bibliography. All went very well, and we see eye to eye on the knitting of the College to the university. He gave me comforting counsel: one cannot reach all the students in a group, and one can but do one's best with those who will listen; rules, especially those relating to morality, must be made and kept and nothing is so salutary as an expulsion or two. I should think of getting a junior academic to take some of the disciplinary problems off my hands so that I may, he flatteringly said, not be impeded in my literary work.

WEDNESDAY, DECEMBER 11: From 10 to 11 with Jack Sword, who offers me the chair of drama that the university hopes to establish in place of the Edgar Stone lectures. Everything about it is good—the stress on scholarship rather than foolish pretense of training actors and directors, the independence linked with University College, and the seriousness with which the English Department regards it. I am to meet him again next week for further talk.

Ian Montagnes came to see me this morning about his book on the history of Hart House. When leaving he asked me how Melvyn Pelt was getting on and asked me to be patient with him as these young Jews have special difficulties. Montagnes himself is a Sephardic Jew and a very fine man.

SATURDAY, DECEMBER 14: Last night the College dance, an undoubted success; good band, good supper, and good floor show arranged by Robin Green, directed by Brenda and with Stuart Niermeier, Dinsmore, Bill Dick, Garry Clarke, and our girls. The girls' College song "O Community of Scholars" sung to Mendelssohn's "Lift Thine Eyes" the best and best-received. Claude Bissell and Vincent Massey both delighted. Quite a resplendent evening, and again much was done to knit the College into a community. We went to Robin Green's rooms for a party after and got to bed at 3 a.m.

TUESDAY, DECEMBER 17: Maygames early. Busy, worrisome day preparing for the Christmas gaudy, depressed and with stage fright. Would it be possible to bring off yet another successful function? But it goes like a charm, mulled claret and all, and my ghost story a great success. The dinner went splendidly: Vincent and I had decided against the loving-cup ceremonial as too elaborate, but one of the maids inadvertently filled the cup, so we did it at High Table, and then were delighted when the Junior Fellows filled water jugs at their tables and did it too! Royal toast and College toast only, and Fishwick gave us the long graces in fine style. Could not have wished it better, and to crown it, Colin Friesen announced to High Table that the LLBO man had been to see him about 5, and we shall have our licence by Christmas!

Chat in the Common Room and again to Hall at 9: 175 people, I judge. Choir sings a selection of traditional carols, after which mulled claret was served, and very good it was. Then Lochhead reads—not a good reader. More wine, then my ghost story,[60] which I think I read well and which went to great laughter and applause. Then "Blow, Blow, Thou Winter Wind" (the Stevens glee[61]) and "The First Nowell." Everything went splendidly and I felt truly that the College was knitting, and good standards of taste and feeling were being established. Very happy and grateful for having been able to manage it. Endicott, a keen Max Beerbohm man, said the story was good enough for Max—a great compliment from him. The singing of the carols by the full Hall not good, but hearty. I think—I dare to think—that Massey College can do something for this university.

WEDNESDAY, DECEMBER 18: Meeting of Master and Fellows at 4:10 and serious debate about the statute defining the office of Master:

60 "Revelation from a Smoky Fire," in *High Spirits* (1982).
61 A type of unaccompanied English part-song.

Claude Bissell tactful but firm, and Vincent sticky but not intractable, so at last all is worked out, though Sirluck and Eayrs intervened unexpectedly and unhelpfully. Many compliments on the gaudy.

THURSDAY, DECEMBER 19: Vincent in College and comes to see me. Delighted with the progress of the College. Bill Dobson comes, delighted with the gaudy, and pays me a compliment: "You'll be a very hard act to follow," said he.

FRIDAY, DECEMBER 20: Following Bickersteth's example, I want to give a Christmas gift to every man who is in the College over the holidays, and have bought forty copies of Huxley's *Literature and Science* and written a personal letter to go with each one. But now I am worried: will those touchy, suspicious young men think once again that I am trying to "influence" them in some horrible way? We shall see; they are unlike anything I have ever encountered.

The liquor licence, so long looked for, arrived today: another worry dismissed. Now—a curious thing: at the dance, standing by the fireplace during the cabaret, and again at the gaudy just as I was about to begin my story, in the doors on the southeast of Hall, a strange figure has been seen. A man, very neatly dressed, but with long white hair, and a face variously described as no face, or like a skull. Brenda has seen it and several of the men. Some think I planned it, but I have not seen it and know nothing of it. A College joker? An intruder?

SATURDAY, DECEMBER 21: An agreeable vacation peace settles on the College. Tonight to the Toronto Symphony Orchestra Christmas concert; Sir Ernest MacMillan[62] conducts and I am sorry to see how old and moonlit he now looks. A formative figure in my boyhood,

62 Eminent Canadian conductor, organist, and composer.

and as I watch him bow courteously to a bad house, saying, "Doubt-less many people have been detained by Christmas shopping," I am irresistibly reminded of Sir John Martin-Harvey, thanking a few folk years ago at the Royal Alexandra. After to a literary party at the John Grays' of Macmillan of Canada. Jack McClelland, owner of McClelland and Stewart, tells me he wants to buy out Clarke, Irwin; I should like that. I am set upon by one William Kilbourn of York University who wants to come here to see how we have made the College "go." They want twelve colleges with 1,000 undergrads in each. I say these are far too big for colleges and he admits it. Jim Eayrs, who was present, says they are under-standably jealous of Massey College and want its secret, a kind of "instant tradition."

SATURDAY, DECEMBER 28: My fears about the Huxley book ground-less: I have had ten letters of warm thanks; that is about one in four, which is not bad. On Christmas Day we gave the seven men in College cocktails in the Lodgings, then special dinner in the Senior Fellows' Dining Room, with two bottles of Beaune among them. Not bad commons!

To the Royal Alex to see the Obratsov Puppets, taking Jenny, Rosamond, Sharon Hooper, and Mrs. Pedak with us. A very fine, unusual concert: the uttermost, surely, that glove puppets can do— funny 'cellist, pianist and singers, dancers, a baby in a pram who played a Hungarian rhapsody, gypsy dancers, trick poodles, a magician who made things disappear (baby chicks, wine in glass-es), tap dancers, a brilliantly observed American jazz singer and her "combo," and magnificent trained lions. All of this presented by a delightful *conférencier*, reminiscent of Baliev.[63] Great charm of

63 The Russian impresario Nikita Baliev founded Le Théâtre de la Chauve-Souris, which combined serious drama with cabaret, in 1908.

detail: when the curtain rose, a puppet stagehand was arranging spotlights. Afterward to Helen Ignatieff's and met Obratsov and his party, vegetarian ex-actress wife; other guests were Marion Walker, Herby Whittaker, the Goldschmidts, and some more Russians. Ate a Russian dinner—herring in sour cream, "little doves," and sweets, with vodka and wines. Obratsov replies to a toast by Nicholas Goldschmidt with a moving, because true and sensible, plea for peace and understanding between us and the U.S.S.R. He also shows us, with a puppet supplied by Herby, how the Chinese pup-peteers can make a glove puppet fold its arms behind its back— they spin it rapidly and imperceptibly. Also that the great fault of most puppets—German especially—is that their heads are too big and heavy. A delightful evening, with real artists, which is always refreshing after social nonsense and emptiness.

SUNDAY, DECEMBER 29: In the evening read and hear music: I am dull and out of sorts and feel a failure. Too much celebration? I feel my writing trivial and my life a mess. This could be indigestion or just the inevitable weary self-recognition of middle age, but damned disagreeable. But admirable h.t.d.

TUESDAY, DECEMBER 31: In the morning work, in the afternoon read and walk. Herbert Whittaker comes and I discuss the drama professorship with him. In the evening we go to the Hoopers' from 9 to 11, then to Helen Ignatieff till 2. H.t.d 67 in 1963.

WEDNESDAY, JANUARY 1, 1964: Well, I have so far avoided being an ornamental hermit, a lodging-house keeper, and I hope an in-ferior pedant. Adventures with the College I record in detail in the College diary, and my theatre-going in the theatre diary: I am in a fair way to being a neurotic diarist and hoarder of experience, but I do not really want to break the habit—a harmless hobby. I begin

to see a little more clearly what I should do here. The chapel is a great friend to me; I go there and think and pray and am quieted and strengthened; as I grow older I know more and more that I cannot live without this awareness and invocation of the Other. I do not think it has much to do with Christianity: it is Man and God and in my case I want to pray in the language of a man of my education and temperament, addressing that which has made him.

We all like the College and the life here, and without being ungrateful for Peterborough we praise God that we are not to spend another twenty years there. Brenda has her friends in Peterborough and sees them when they come to Toronto, but for a long time her closest friends have been here. I am glad to be in a society where I need not always talk below my weight, and watch my vocabulary lest some unfamiliar word offend or exclude my hearer. Domestically, Brenda and I are somewhat astonished by having all our three girls at home for the first time in several years, and it makes for uneasiness, as they are now two adults and one large-spirited adolescent. And love and marriage are in the air, though nothing serious yet impends. But we are as happy as it is in our natures to be—which is very happy indeed, consciously so, though somewhat ironic— and what blessing is greater? The prospect of a professorship of drama pleases me but I am anxious that I should not cease to be a writer, and in this I have almost too much encouragement. Clarke, Irwin want a superior book on writing English for high schools; Jack McClelland and Alfred Knopf want an anthology of humour, which I might do on the plan of Aldous Huxley's *Texts and Pretexts*; and I want to write my Thamesville novel and also my servant's memoir. How to choose?

But this morning the papers carry the news that Roy Thomson has been given a barony, and this surely is a tribute to persistence and utterly unreasonable ambition. Why should a Toronto barber's son, a radio and TV entrepreneur, a collector of newspapers, be "my

lord"? Because he wanted it and would not give up. Now, admitting that the arts do not yield to thrust as does the world of business, cannot I do more than I am doing to make a reputation as a writer? I think my Thamesville novel the most serious thing I have yet projected, and technically interesting. So I must get on with it.

SOURCES AND
ACKNOWLEDGEMENTS

Bissell, Claude. *The Imperial Canadian: Vincent Massey in Office*. Toronto: University of Toronto Press, 1986.

————. *The Young Vincent Massey*. Toronto: University of Toronto Press, 1981.

The Canadian Encyclopedia, http://www.thecanadianencyclopedia.ca.

Davies, Brenda, and Jennifer Surridge. *Beads in a String*. Toronto: Pendragon Ink, 2001.

Davies, Robertson. Selected works.

Davies, W. Rupert. *Far-Off Fields*. Privately published, 1962.

Dickson, Lovat. *The Museum Makers: The Story of the Royal Ontario Museum*. Toronto: Royal Ontario Museum, 1986.

Forsyth, James. *Tyrone Guthrie*. London: Hamish Hamilton Ltd., 1976.

Friedland, Martin L. *The University of Toronto: A History*. Toronto: University of Toronto Press, 2002.

Grant, Judith Skelton. *A Meeting of Minds: The Massey College Story*. Toronto: University of Toronto Press, 2015.

————. *Robertson Davies: Man of Myth*. Toronto: Viking, 1994.

The Internet Movie Database, http://www.imdb.com.

Pettigrew, John, and Jamie Portman. *Stratford: The First Thirty Years*. Toronto: Macmillan of Canada, 1985.

Spadoni, Carl, and Judith Skelton Grant. *A Bibliography of Robertson Davies*. Toronto: University of Toronto Press, 2014.

Wikipedia, The Free Encyclopedia, http://en.wikipedia.org.

[SOURCES AND ACKNOWLEDGEMENTS]

We are grateful for the advice and help we received from John Fraser, Master Emeritus, Massey College; Catherine Hobbs, Literary Archivist and Senior Archivist, Library and Archives Canada; Jill Spellman, Archivist, the Upper Canada College Archives; and from our agent, Dean Cooke. We would like to thank our readers, Miranda Davies, Rosamond Bailey, James Neufeld, Judith Skelton Grant and John Grant, and to acknowledge the support and enthusiasm from our publisher, Doug Pepper, and our editor, Jenny Bradshaw, at McClelland & Stewart, and the exceptional attention of our copy-editor, Barbara Czarnecki.

Readers may be interested in the projected publication of Robertson Davies's complete diaries in digital format, to be edited by James Neufeld, professor emeritus at Trent University. This online edition is affiliated with the Editing Modernism in Canada project. The digital edition of the diaries will allow readers to browse at will, or to search through the diaries, focusing on passages of interest to them and choosing from among a variety of formats and presentations that will include digitized images of the original, verbatim transcripts, corrected transcripts, and annotated texts. The diaries will be enhanced with hyperlinks to visual, audio, and textual materials from various archives and collections, to provide background and colour for the events Davies describes. The digital edition of the Davies Diaries will begin with the theatre diaries, with a target date of 2017 for release.

INDEX

In order to accommodate more entries, page ranges may indicate non-continuous references.

Gilbert and Sullivan, 71n19, 77,
224–25, 235, 267–68
Glass Menagerie, The (T. Williams),
77
Globe and Mail, 60, 78, 116, 139, 162
Godfrey, Isidore, 268
Goff, Lewin, 100
Golby, Molly, 279, 284
Goldschmidt, Nicholas, 300, 361
Goldschmidt, Shelagh, 300, 361
Goldsmith, Oliver, 63n
Gondoliers, The (Gilbert and
Sullivan), 224–25, 235
Gone with the Wind (film), 164
Goodings, Stewart, 345, 346, 348
Gordon, Andrew Robertson, 141,
167, 188n6, 214, 221, 227, 292,
339
Gordon, Liz, 63, 112, 217
Gordon, Ruth, 272
Gordon, Walter, 63, 112, 199
Gould, Glenn, 78, 200
Goulet, Robert, 84
Governor General's Literary
Awards, 16, 58, 64, 66–67,
75–76, 135
Gow, James, 162, 273, 317, 351, 353
Graduate (U. of Toronto), 154
Graham (Toronto doctor), 199
Grant, Charity, 165
Grant, Duncan, 67
Grant, George Munro, 297
Grant, George, 10n
Grant, W.L., 296n19, 297
Gray, Dulcie, 46
Gray, John, 360
Great Expectations (film), 145
Green, Robin, 331, 342, 344, 350,
354, 357
Greene, Graham, 47, 147, 215
Gregory, Wilf, 17, 155
Grief Observed, A (C.S. Lewis), 234
Griffith, Harry, 228
Grimes, Tammy, 190, 193
Guinness, Alec, 72, 146, 331
Gurian, Manning, 74
Guthrie, Judy, 19, 20, 22, 23, 25, 29,
31, 32, 36, 37, 54, 61, 82, 98, 102,
105–6, 113, 115, 144, 155, 277
Guthrie, Tyrone (Tony), xi, 1–4,
6n3, 15–39, 49, 53–58, 61, 65,

68, 69, 71–73, 76, 78, 80, 82–83,
85–99, 101–13, 115, 117–18, 120,
144, 149, 150, 224, 243, 272,
273, 277–78, 302, 355
Gwillim (caterer), 158, 240
Gwynn, Michael, 150

Hagen, Uta, 260
Hagon, Garrick, 302, 325
Haines (biologist), 168, 172
Hall, Amelia (Milly), 71, 81, 233
Hall, Beth, 155
Hall, Peter, 325
Hamill, Frank, 281, 347, 351
Hamilton, Barbara, 81, 85, 114, 269,
293
Hamlet (Shakespeare), 23, 34, 221
Hampden, Walter, 196
Hancox, Ralph, 10, 53, 67, 76, 77,
78, 156, 161, 237, 263, 264
Handel, G.F., 67, 156, 293
Hannen, Hermione, 196
Hansberry, Lorraine, 15; (film) 168
Happy Alchemy (RD), 221n40
Harding, Esther, 12, 13, 15, 49, 187
Hardy, Laurence, 81, 85, 87, 90, 92,
109
Harris, Adrienne, 112
Harris, Frank, 241, 242, 243
Harris, George, 59, 63, 65, 74, 75,
92, 112, 115, 130, 155, 173, 185,
205, 210, 216, 217, 219, 261, 268,
320, 330
Harris, Julie, 74
Harris, Norah, 59, 63, 65, 74, 75,
92, 112, 115, 130, 155, 173, 205,
210, 216, 217, 219, 261, 268, 320,
330
Hart, George, 46, 47
Hart, Moss, 83, 84
Hasso, Signe, 73
Haste to the Wedding (Gilbert), 42
Hawker, James, 187
Hawtrey, Kay, 81
Hayes, George, 221
Hayes, John, 74
Hayman, Joseph, 69
Hays, David, 78, 81, 96
Headmistress, The (A. Thirkell), 187
Heart of Jade, The (de Madariaga), 67
Heartbreak House (Shaw), 55